A SWORD FOR THE IMMERLAND KING

A Sword For The Immerland King

F.W.FALLER

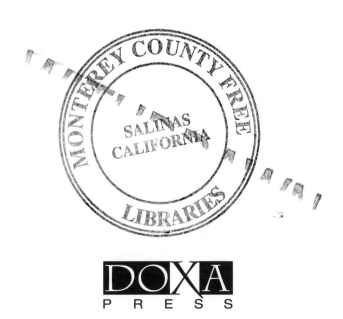

DOXA
PRESS

A Sword For The Immerland King

Book One of the *Portals of Tessalindria* series
© 2002 by F. W. Faller

Published by DOXA Press, an imprint of
Discipleship Publications International
2 Sterling Road
Billerica, Massachusetts 01862

Printed in the United States of America

ISBN: 1-57782-175-0

Cover design and illustration: Scott and Farley Vigneault
Interior design: Thais Faller Gloor
Interior illustrations: F. W. Faller

To every man, woman and child
who has lain on the grass,
stared into the grand infinity
of the night sky and wondered,
If everything could be different,
what might have to remain unchanged?

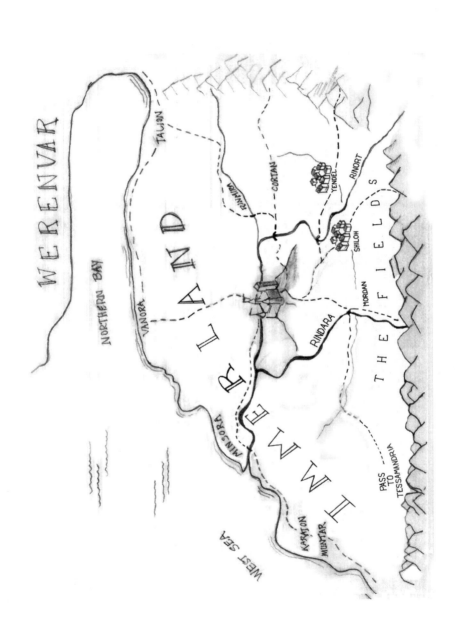

Pronunciation Guide

Carnados	car · 'næ · dos
Chronista	kro · 'nis · tå
Eladra	æ · 'lå · drå
Eladrim	æ · 'lå · drim
Erengnira	'e · reng · 'neer · å
Galar	'ga · lar
Haniah	ha · 'nī · ah
Kor Alura	kor å · 'lur · å
Lutaka	lu · 'tå · kå
Mah'Eladra	'måh æ · 'lå · drå
MahMoralda	'måh · mor · 'al · då
Mankar	'man · kar
Meekar	'mee · kar
Mirradach	'meer · rå · dåk
Morahura	'mor · a · 'hur · a
Mordara	mor · 'da · rå
Narahu	na · 'rå · hu
Omberon	'om · ber · on
Paca	'på · cå
Patira	på · 'teer · å
Phartang	'far · tang
Psadeq	'pså · dek
Rapahoogin	'rap · å · 'hoo · gin
Sandihar	'san · di · har
Sessasha	se · 'så · sha
Timmanaeus	'tim · ma · 'næ · us
Verclan	'ver · cln
Vishtava	vish · 'tå · vå
Vishtorath	'vish · tor · ath
Vrengnia	'vreng · niå
Windarad	'win · då · rad

NOTE: -a … as in cat, hat
       -å … as in Bach, father
       -æ … as in hate, day

When the spring of life is polluted and senseless, you must look deeper. There in the depths, at the source of the fount, you will find a purity of sense that is more profound than your most vivid imaginations.

The Tessarandin, Book 13

NARAHU KNEW THAT IT WAS NOT COLD ENOUGH THAT HE SHOULD BE SHIV-ering. He was also breathing hard, his lungs burning for air, but he knew the reason for that. The two hundred yards he had run to where he lay gasping on the damp earth under the bridge was faster than he had ever run before, but the terror of the scene behind him had driven him recklessly onward in the semidarkness of the young night. Tal, the smaller of the twin Tessalindrian moons, paled orange as she hung low above the mountains far to the east, offering little light. She had drawn him like a magnet away from the inferno in the smithy behind him to the shelter of the bridge.

He knew they would come after him. He knew *why* in the same instant. The clarity of what had happened swept over him in his brief moment of refuge. Images of the events leading to this moment flooded through his mind for what seemed like hours; he knew it was a mere few minutes.

His father was—no, had been—a bladesmith for the great King Lutaka of Tessamandria. Although he had worked exclusively for the king, he had had no use for the busy-ness and distraction of the fortress and had preferred to have his smithy a fair distance from it. He had often remarked, "Too many people, too many comings and goings. It is good for a king, but not for a smith." The smithy was about a mile from the fortress, outside the city that surrounded it. Here on the outside, separated from the outermost city houses by a stand of trees, it was quiet at night. He could see the stars and the mountains and hear the river wending its way north to places Narahu never expected to see.

His father's work for the king was unusual for a smith. Lutaka had an entire smithy in the fortress where his smiths made all the weapons of war: the swords, javelins, daggers, spears and other things that were necessary for his campaigns to unite Tessamandria. All the work of making other blades he had given to Narahu's father: the knives and choppers for the kitchens, the sickles and scythes for the harvests, the axes, froes, adzes, threshing bars and tailors' shears that were needed in sundry places throughout the fortress and his kingdom.

One month ago, late in the evening, they had had a surprise visit from Mankar, the commanding officer in Lutaka's army. Mankar knew his father, but such a visit was unusual. He had come alone, secretly. His father was finishing an experimental blade for cutting thatch used in roofing houses in the town when Mankar entered.

Mankar's request was unusual. He wanted his father to make thirteen swords, one for King Lutaka and the other twelve for himself and his generals. It was to be a surprise for Lutaka, a special favor for his king. His father had resisted, insisting that it was not his place to make swords, but Mankar pressed him and offered larger and larger sums of money until he relented and agreed to make them.

The king's sword was to be a little bigger, and if he were to put a special effort into any one sword, that would be the one to favor. "Only the best for the king, you know," Mankar had said, smiling.

Narahu sat up slowly, his head spinning as he lowered it between his knees. He remembered feeling a vague apprehension when the final sum was determined. Perhaps it was Mankar's smile that had made him uneasy. It was more of a sneer, really. His father had looked directly at Mankar's face when they shook hands. Had he not seen it?

His father had started work on the swords immediately, working late into the evenings after spending long days at his commissioned work for the fortress. Narahu had worked the bellows, watching and listening as his father sang the forge poetry, metering each hammer blow and heat by the rhythm of the words as they poured forth from his father's mind and mouth. The forge poetry for the swords was different from the poetry for the other blades his father made. Narahu remembered understanding all the words, but it seemed darker and tangled somehow, as if its origins were from another world entirely. He had not liked the sound of it. It was not like the poetry of the knives and the hatchets, which was warm and strong.

They had finished the swords two days ago and laid them out on the bench in the center of the smithy, awaiting Mankar's arrival. Narahu studied his father's work carefully. He had grown accustomed to the masterful craftsmanship for which his father was renowned. Even so, he had been stunned by the surpassing excellence of the swords. They were beautifully made in every detail, flawless. Narahu had doubted that he could discern one from any of the others except that the king's sword, though identical in form and detail, was a bit larger. Narahu shuddered involuntarily as he pictured the swords laid out on that table.

His father had sent a message to Mankar at the fortress. Word came back through a page that he would be arriving tonight, shortly after nightfall. Narahu had sensed that his father was tense, as he had been since he started the swords. He had snapped often at Narahu, which was not his way, and had exhausted himself in perfecting the swords. Now he seemed eager to get them out of his possession, and he moved nervously about the shop fidgeting with tools and placing and replacing everything he touched.

Narahu had helped tidy up the smithy for the arrival of the great commander. He had set tong racks in order and swept the floor, cleared the vise bench and refilled the slack tub with clean water. At his father's request he had retrieved extra lanterns from the storeroom and lit them and hung them about the bench to illuminate the swords on the table. The swords glowed in the lantern light, casting muted reflections across the beams and walls of the smithy.

Mankar had arrived as expected, but not alone; several of his generals accompanied him. Narahu could see only four of them, but he was sure several others were waiting outside. Those who had come inside remained by the door in the shadows. Narahu was not able to see their faces, but there was a certain darkness surrounding them, like a shadow; a darkness that should have been dispelled by the abundant lantern light. As they entered the shop, Narahu sensed that something was wrong. How he knew this, he was not sure, but his suspicion about Mankar was confirmed when the commander saw the swords and smiled at his father; there was evil in it, pure and cruel.

Mankar stepped forward to the bench and picked up the king's sword. As he swung it slowly back and forth, it hummed softly. His father spoke: "They are the finest—"

"Quiet, little man," Mankar growled as he continued to wave the sword. "These are fine swords. Only the best for Mankar, don't you think?" There was that sneer again, reinforced by the ugliness of the voice issuing from the commander's mouth. Narahu tasted revulsion in the back of his throat, but there was no time to identify it.

What happened next was to be burned forever in Narahu's memory: His father said something about the sword being for the king. He must have sensed the same wrongness that Narahu felt because when the sword flashed the first time—*haarrrraannggg!*—his father ducked and the blade struck the post vise where it was anchored to the bench. With a blue flash the sword clove the solid iron as if it were a melon.

His father leapt behind the forge bed and yelled, "Run, Narahu, run!" He remembered the quick movement of the fire shovel. A shower of glowing coal from the dying fire bathed the commander who howled in pain as the fury of that evil being was unleashed on his father. "Run, Narahu! Now!" The other generals leapt to the table to claim their swords. *Haarrrraannggg!* Mankar's sword slashed through the edge of the forge bed with a blinding flash, followed by billowing, hissing steam as his father dumped a bucket of quench water into the fire. Mankar cursed as the searing steam blasted up from the firepot. The generals behind him began yelling obscenities.

Narahu remembered hearing the crash of glass and tin as one of the lanterns near the forge yielded to a blow from his father's forge rake. Paraffin from the lamp rained down onto the fire, and with an eerie *whoosh*, an orange fireball leapt toward the ceiling. More cursing followed, more crashing. Two generals started toward him. *Crack!* The lantern on the wall between them exploded. "Run, Narahu!"

"Father!"

"Run—now!"

Harrraaannngg! the king's sword sang again. There was another blue flash followed by the splintering of wood. The whole building lurched down as Mankar severed the support beam in the middle of the smithy.

Two generals crashed through the fire from the second lantern. The one in front tripped over something, and the other fell over the top of him cursing and growling.

"Run—ru—"

Narahu felt the blow that cut down his father, as if it had cut his own heart out of him. How could he have felt it? He knew what it meant. Mankar laughed. That hideous, cruel laugh fairly erupted in his ears. It shook the smithy. It shook his vorn, the core of his being. It shook the foundation from under his feet, and he turned and ran toward the back door.

Having dodged the stack of anvils and the ring mandrel, he rolled under the rack of iron bars and spare tongs. The thrashing, swearing and growling was right behind him, like a nightmare against the backdrop of Mankar's snarling laughter.

Through the back door he ran—into the night—into the freedom of the open endlessness of the outside world. He knew it well, even in the dark—every turn, every jog and dip of the trail to the river. The angry shouts of Mankar's generals made his body light and his feet swift, giving him strength he did not know he had. They were not far behind. Something flashed so brightly that for an instant the entire landscape was illuminated as if by the sun. The generals burst into another string of profanity. Swords clashed and their guttural curses mingled with other voices, shouting. There were more flashes. Narahu could not risk looking back; he dared not, lest his winged feet fail to carry him as fast and as far as possible from the holocaust behind him.

His heart was still pounding like a drum in his chest as he gasped in the cool clean air. His hands were shaking. His head swam in a numbness he hardly had time to notice. They would be coming. He knew it with a certainty that transcended everything else at that moment. He must keep going, but where? There was no going back. The fiery glow in the night sky behind him told him that there was nothing to go back to but death. He knew his father was being cremated in his own smithy. He choked back the tears as his body heaved. He threw up between his legs.

"Narahu!"

A new wave of terror swept over him as viselike hands gripped his upper arms. He tried to scream but an icy palm was clamped over his mouth, choking his cry. "You must not run, Narahu. Listen carefully. There is little time." It was a language he had never heard before, but he understood it perfectly. He tried to break free, but the beings on either side clamped his arms tighter. "Are you afraid of the water?"

He tried to shake his head. "Take a deep breath." The hand came off his mouth and he drew in deeply. He knew what was about to happen. Horses' hooves clattered toward them on the road, rapidly approaching the bridge. In the next instant he was in the river, still in the grip of his captors as they pulled him deep into the dark water.

"No!" he wanted to shout. He knew he couldn't.

"Stay calm, Narahu. Save your strength and breath." Voices? Underwater? He felt the powerful stroke and kick as they swam downstream in the watery darkness. He was face up between them, watching the faint glimmer of the surface, surreal and quiet, about ten feet above him. "Stay calm, Narahu…your strength…your breath."

His lungs began to burn again. He needed air…had to break free! He started to struggle. Suddenly, the shadow of one of his captors' faces pressed down upon him. His breath was sucked out of him and then returned to him before he understood what had happened. The new air was strong and vitalizing, and the burning in his lungs stopped abruptly. Cold water rushed past him as his captors swam on powerfully, deep in the middle of the river.

Without warning, they turned in perfect unison, like flocking birds that dive and turn in formation. Narahu guessed that they were headed to the riverbank. He was cold now, and shivering, though he did not seem to need air. Something about the man's breath—

They broke the surface quietly under a tall overhang of bushar reeds. As they came up the hand clamped over his mouth again. He did not need to breathe, but guessed it was to prevent his crying out. He was right. "You must remain quiet." The hand fell away and Narahu exhaled softly. "Listen."

He had already heard the cursing and shouting from the bridge, now about a hundred yards upriver. The welter of angry voices carried over the water, yelling at each other, threatening, swearing. Mankar's men had lost their quarry and were blaming one another for it.

The warriors still held Narahu firmly. For several minutes they waited silently under the reeds with only their heads above water. Not until the confusion on the bridge abated did his captors move.

"You must head north to the mountains. Travel only at night." It was the being on the right. He released Narahu's arm.

"Do not light a fire. Stay off the main roads. There is great danger," warned the other as he released his grip also.

"Who are you?"

"Servants of Mah'Eladra, Guardians of Psadeq. I am Vishtava," said the one on his right.

"And I am Vor," said the other.

"Eladra?"

Vor nodded. "Your life is in grave danger. Your father is dead. They have killed your mother also. You cannot go back." Narahu shivered. He already knew that.

"When you get to the mountains, hide in the caves you find there. Keep moving. There is no safe place for you in Tessamandria. We will be watching," Vishtava said with a smile.

They ducked beneath the surface of the river simultaneously and vanished as quickly as they had appeared under the bridge. Narahu shivered again. This time he was not sure if it was from fear or the chill of the water.

Pulling himself along the bank, he found an opening in the reeds where he could climb out of the water. He crouched low and listened. No sound came from the direction of the bridge or the smithy. Still, he needed to be cautious. He had lost his shoes in the river, but he did not need them now. They were heavy shoes anyway, for protecting his feet in the smithy. Outdoors, he preferred bare feet. Keeping himself well down in the tall reeds of the riverbank, he removed his tunic and shirt and wrung them as dry as he could, then his pants and socks. He must travel tonight. He would hide and let his clothes dry in the sun the next day.

When he stood up, his knees were shaking. He felt weak. He tried to think back, but his mind mercifully blanketed the ordeal with numbness. He headed north cautiously. The mountains lay low and barely discernable in Tal's low-slung glow. Somehow, he had to reach them. That was all he knew.

SEVEN CENTURIES
LATER...

Youth has no anticipation of failure.
It watches, not to see if it will succeed,
but when.

Karendo Marha
Journey to the Infinite

PACA WATCHED HIS FATHER'S HAMMER FALL ON THE HOT STEEL LAID ACROSS the anvil. It fell as it had a hundred thousand times before, striking square and flat with a near perfect precision, honed by his fifty-some years working the forge. It bounced on the anvil with a ping and floated up to fall again and again as the scythe blade took shape under its impact.

The blows stopped as the blade lost its orange glow and with a swift, knowing stroke from his father, found itself back in the fire. Paca pulled on the bellows toggle, and the fire growled as the air forced its way up to the surface of the glowing pile of coal.

"You are no ordinary young man," his father said quietly in the brief moment before he laid his gloved right hand on another blade in the fire. "Though we live a very ordinary life, in a very ordinary little town, you must never settle into the ordinary yourself."

The glowing blade swept over to the anvil. The hammer fell, *pinged*, floated and fell again. Paca watched his father's face. He had to look up slightly, even when the older man bent to bring the hammer to bear. His was a wise and impassive face; it was thin with a neatly trimmed graying red beard, and a full head of fiery copper hair cropped short so errant sparks could not catch in it. From under thick eyebrows, his gray eyes sparkled in the forge's orange glow with a concentration that heightened the intensity of his countenance.

Paca waited patiently. He knew that as soon as the blade was back in the fire, the conversation would resume. For now, he was content to watch the older smith.

Shiloh was indeed a very ordinary town. Paca had thought so all his life and still wondered why his father had chosen to live there. It was filled with the ordinary people who are needed to make a town. There were ordinary bakers and butchers, candle makers and bricklayers, carpenters and roof thatchers, merchants, a mayor, a woman who made pies, a couple of tailors and many other assorted ordinary men, women and children. Paca knew them all well, and being the son of the smith, was well known about the town himself.

The knife blade slipped back into the fire and Paca tugged. His father's gray eyes rested on him gently. "You have served me well, but soon that will change." His glove came to rest on the third blade in the fire, another scythe for the upcoming barley harvest. Paca watched him pull it from the fire and take the single step to the anvil.

Paca loved his father and respected him as well. From the age of seven, it had been Paca's task to clean the tuyere, chip the clinker out of yesterday's fire, set the tinder and coked coal in the firepot, and heap the green coal around it. He would soak the coal and light the fire, and by the time his father was ready, a bright smokeless fire was burning evenly in the forge bed. Then he would tend the bellows and watch intently as his father fashioned the bars of gray steel into prized tools for the Immerland people.

His mother had died in the Timeron Plague two years after he was born, so his father had engaged him at the smithy as soon as Paca could manage it. It was all he could remember of his life. His father had made the smithy into a school of sorts, teaching him about life during the heats and letting the short lessons sink in during the hammering.

"What will change?" Paca queried as the third blade slid back into the coal.

A hint of a smile appeared at the corners of the smith's mouth and vanished as quickly as it had appeared. "Remember Lesson One," he said as the first blade came to rest on the anvil again.

The smith had several other men who worked for him at his forge along with Paca. These other smiths did most of the routine ironwork required for a modest and ordinary town. They fashioned the latches, hinges and knockers for doors, coat hooks, hat hooks, boot scrapers and window latches, gate hooks, horse shoes, hasps and clasps of various sorts that one might find about, but his father reserved all the tools with sharp edges for his own work. These pieces of welded iron and steel were extraordinary. He had a way with steel and an understanding of the fire and forge that surpassed all the other smiths, and he had become known throughout Immerland for the keenness of his edges and the grace and usefulness of his tools.

None of the other smiths in his employment were allowed to make edged tools. This was part of their agreement when they came to work for him, and none of them were taught his trade, except for Paca himself, into whom he continually poured his knowledge and the wisdom of his craft.

Over his own forge fire, he had a peculiar sign that read:

Imagine any blade you can,
But never a blade to hurt a man.

He called this "Lesson One."

"How could I ever forget Lesson One?" Paca frowned at the blade switch.

His father eyed him keenly. His lips uttered nothing but his eyes asked, "Really?" just before the hammer fell for the first time on the last heat.

With "Lesson One," his father absolutely refused to produce a blade of any kind for a person in whom he perceived any evil intent. Never in his life, as far as Paca knew, had he forged a blade which had as its design the harm of another person. Each tool he made was designed and fashioned with a specific person and use in mind, and every stroke and movement of his father was focused into that person and that use. When the blade was finally finished, the smith would summon the new owner and place the tool in his hand, then laying his own powerful hand on top of the tool, and locking his gray eyes into the eyes of the recipient, he would say:

"Bless this tool to this worker's hand.
Bless it to function at his command.
Bless him to use it as he should.
Bless its edge for a common good."

Paca had seen this exchange many times, but was not sure he understood it fully. It seemed so important to his father, yet only a ritual to him. What was more, he knew that his father knew that he did not understand. Paca could see it in his eyes, though the older smith had never said anything about it to him.

Paca remembered the time he had asked his father, "Father, why do you bless the tool so? These simple words cannot protect this blade against an evil use. You pour your vorn into the blade, and it is keen and hard, to be sure, but now it is beyond your hand and subject to use and abuse as desired by someone quite beyond your control. Do you really believe this blessing does anything?"

Shaking his head gently, his father had smiled and responded, "Has even one of my blades ever been used to injure another person?"

"Why, no, not that I have heard anyway. But that may be just coincidence or luck or—"

His father's eyes had cut him short. "Someday you will understand that there is no such thing as coincidence or luck. Until then, there is still much for you to learn about the making of edged tools."

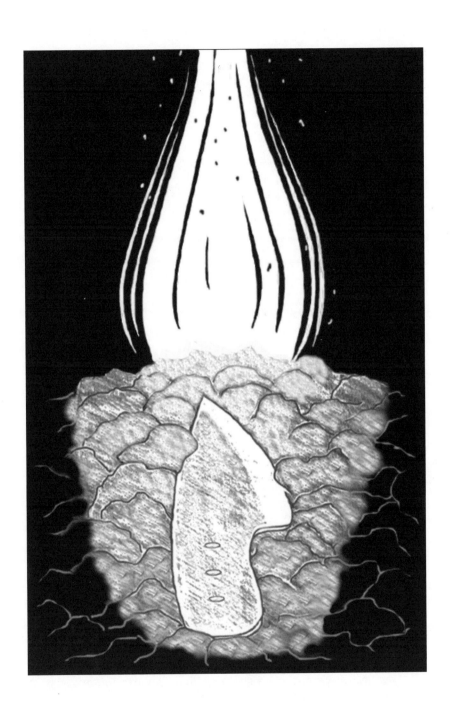

The royalty of a being cannot be measured by position, physical strength or its collection of wealth. Royalty is a state of mind that belongs to those who know who they are.

Mindar Colloden
The Great Fathers

V RENGNIA WALKED SLOWLY BEHIND HER FATHER AS HE AMBLED ALONG THE parapet overlooking the great courtyard of the Immerland Castle. His stride was easy and his three advisors walked easily beside him. He was the king: King Sandihar of Immerland. He took his time when he wanted to and hurried whenever he felt like it. Today he was in no hurry. The kingdom was at peace and had been for several years, except for the continual skirmishes with the mountain people along the southern border.

"And what do you think, my dear?" he asked, stopping suddenly and turning toward her, his eyes flickering with mild amusement.

"I…well, I need to think on it a bit more, I…" Vrengnia paused, looking her father in the eye as it twinkled merrily. "I haven't the faintest idea what you are talking about!"

The king guffawed uproariously. All three of the advisors showed their personal amusement by snorting and smiling. "My birthday!" said the king. "It's going to be my fiftieth, don't you know!"

"Surely it isn't, Father!"

"But it is! It is. We must have a grand celebration—a genuine party—for everyone. What do you think?"

Vrengnia smiled. "I need to think on it a bit more," she repeated tactfully.

"Yes, yes…hmmmmm…a bit more. Well, when you have had your thoughts, I surely would like to hear them." He turned and resumed his walk.

Vrengnia could have been embarrassed, but she was not. She loved her father and respected him as well. Her mother had died giving birth to her. She was not sure about the details, except that she knew her father had loved her mother dearly and had poured that love into her own life in response to the queen's untimely death. Since the age of six, she had been following her father around with his advisors, with the dors and with the mayors of the towns surrounding the castle while he talked with the merchants or gave orders to the captain of the guard. He had never sent her away.

She knew he was teaching her, but she always thought it must be a bit boring to be king. There were so many details, most of them mundane and trivial. It was almost as if the simplest of decisions had to be made by her father, as if everyone feared making decisions in his presence. She had become very accustomed to not listening unless there was something very serious at hand.

She had known that her father's birthday was approaching. She remembered his fortieth. It was quite a party, so she was not sure how much bigger this one could be. Besides, it was such a beautiful day. Plans like these should be discussed at night after it was dark.

She looked over the parapet as she followed along behind the royal quartet. Today she could see for miles, and the soft, late summer breeze bore a potpourri of the stables and the hayfields with hints of lavender and ripening apples. The early afternoon sun bathed the towns that surrounded the castle, allowing her to see the busy-ness of all the people about their daily tasks. These were the last days of summer, and preparations were being made for harvesting the fields that stretched into the distance outside the towns. They were like a patchwork carpet of gold, green, yellow and amber, rolled out to the foot of the blue mountains to the south and east. Perhaps this afternoon she could escape on her horse, ride through the towns, and visit this busy-ness herself. It would be a welcome change from the controlled ambiance of the castle.

"Should it be in the banquet hall—or the courtyard?" Her father was looking at her intently.

"What?"

The king roared again. "You are hopeless sometimes. I think you need to get that horse of yours and get out of here for the afternoon."

She blinked. "If you don't mind—I was thinking that myself."

"Well, you're no good to me in this daydream of yours." He stepped forward and hugged her. "Go! I'll see you at dinner."

Vrengnia bowed and turned to leave. She thought she heard Carnados, her father's most trusted advisor, murmur something about her being very much like her grandmother. Carnados was a kindly man who had always treated her with dignity and respect. He was a good deal older than her father, in fact old enough to be her grandfather, which is the way she thought of him. He had known her grandmother, the Great Queen, and thereby was the only one in the company of her father with the authority to say such a thing.

The Great Queen Vorania had ruled Immerland for forty years before her death. It was during that time that the castle had been built and the townships surrounding it unified. As she was dearly loved by those who knew her and well respected by those who didn't, Vrengnia reasoned that there were few others to whom comparison would flatter her as much. Today she would ride, as her grandmother had often done, out among the people, and away from the stultifying formality of the castle and its synthesis of grandeur. She bolted down the stairs from the parapet and ran across the courtyard to the stables. Mahala, her horse, would be waiting, eager to run as he always was.

The guard at the castle gate straightened and saluted as she cantered Mahala under the portcullis and onto the drawbridge. She wasn't sure if it was the sudden change in the light or perhaps the freshening breeze; maybe it was the wide openness of the fields rolling down the hill on which the castle stood, or her sense of escape, but she caught herself in a deep sigh as the clip-clop of the horseshoes on the drawbridge changed to the muted thumping on the softer, more solid ground. She pulled to the left and lightly urged Mahala into an easy gallop.

The castle seemed to slip away, to melt off her heart, as she left its confines behind her, Mahala's powerful gait carrying her like the wind away from...from what? The castle was her home and always had been. It probably always would be. Recently it had begun to feel more like a prison, a place to be escaped at every chance. Something was not right. Her father was changing. No, perhaps it was *she* who was changing. The lifelong ambition to be the Queen of Immerland had changed from the bright fantasy of youthful eagerness to a dark dream from which there seemed to be only one escape. It grew darker with each passing month, and her singular relief was the bright otherworld outside the castle. There was nothing particular that she could grasp, nothing to ask about, nothing specific to change. It was vague, like shadow dancers in a dream, ominous but untouchable.

She looked back as Mahala carried her into the wall of trees at the bottom of the hill. The castle gleamed in the brilliant sun for a moment; then she lost sight of it, as the rich, green foliage streaming past her occluded her view. She sighed again as she emerged from the other side of the barrier wood and set her face forward into the warm wind. For now, she was free. For now, she did not have to think about being a queen. For now, the wind and the sun washed her vorn and she shed the vague haunting of the castle, its effects dropping off her with each rippling wave of Mahala's strong shoulders.

As to this day or that, who can tell what will make any one of them important. Are they not but convenient containers in which we categorize the passage into the Infinite?

Oratanga
Passages

"THE IMAGE OF HER GRANDMOTHER, THE QUEEN," WAS WHAT CARNADOS had said.

"Yes," sighed the king as he watched his daughter disappear down the steps, "never missing a chance to get out of the castle for a ride." He turned back to his advisors. He was actually tired of talking about his birthday celebration, and the moment seemed right to change the subject. "She will be eighteen four days after my birthday, Carnados—on the equinox, don't you know."

"Yes, I do."

"I keep waiting for her to show signs of growing up."

"There will be plenty of time for that." Carnados smiled knowingly.

"Yes, I suppose so, but even the smallest sign—a tiny change— would be nice."

"Like what, Your Majesty?"

"That hat! It's got to go." The king laughed as he pictured his daughter. She was not what most of the people of Immerland had expected in a princess. Her garb was more manlike than many believed it should be. He could not remember a time when she was interested in any clothing made for women, and her usual selection was bright and varicolored, giving rise to the affectionate title "the Pied Princess." She was often about in loose pantaloons and a long-sleeved flowing blouse, cut more for a fanciful soldier than a would-be queen. She kept most of her hair tucked up under a comical purple and green leather cap, which was commonly thought to accentuate her green eyes. She always wore a gray sleeveless tunic that bore her grandmother's crest on both the front and the back. The crest was three diagonal slashes of cobalt blue, one above the other, with a brilliant yellow sunburst just to the right of them. In the end, though considered a bit odd by many, the king knew she was loved and admired for her frankness and simple innocence.

"By your leave, Sire, she will lose it someday." Carnados was smiling. King Sandihar knew it was a genuine smile. Carnados was the wisest of his advisors, whom he had charged with the routine running of the castle and the kingdom. Carnados in turn delegated the mundane functions at the castle to other advisors and managers of the domestic servants and housekeeping staff—the laundry, the kitchens and gardens, the stables and kennels, the library, the treasury, as well as responsibilities extending beyond the castle walls, such as getting information to and from the towns via heralds and pages, and arranging the feasts. He oversaw almost everything with the exception of training and leading the king's army and managing Immerland's retinue of spies.

"She is a lot more like you than you might think," Carnados continued. "She is an apt pupil and all that you have been teaching her over the years will rise up in her at the necessary time."

The king studied him thoughtfully for a moment, weighing the fullness of his statement. Carnados often seemed to cloak his wisdom in riddles. The king was never sure if he should be puzzling out some profound meaning, and Carnados, always genuine and sober, never let on one way or the other. He had served and loved Sandihar's mother, the Great Queen, and Sandihar often felt small by her measure in Carnados's eyes. If not for Carnados's unswerving loyalty and support, Sandihar knew he could easily be suspicious of his motives. Even so, Sandihar was never fully assured that Carnados might not be secretly mocking him.

As Sandihar watched Vrengnia bound across the courtyard and disappear through the archway leading to the stables, he changed the subject. "Call Galar," he said, turning back to Carnados.

"Galar?"

"Yes!" The king smiled. He had been pondering something for a while and it had just occurred to him how it might work. "I have a special errand for him."

Carnados waved and Mindar, the youngest of the king's advisors, swept away from his elders toward the staircase off the parapet.

Galar was the leader of the dors. He could be trusted with this errand. The dors were the warriors of the kingdom, valiant men, proven in battle and unmatched in loyalty to the king. In times of peace, he had made it their job to keep it that way. They traveled about his kingdom, serving as judges and arbiters, intervening as necessary to see that justice was done and disputes were settled.

He had personally selected each of his dors. Whenever he would appoint another dor to his service, he would place both hands on the man's head, lock his coal black eyes into the eyes of the dor and say:

"Bless this man to this king's own hand.
Bless him to function at my command.
Bless him to follow as he should.
Bless him now for a common good."

Often when he blessed a dor into his service, he could see the dullness in his daughter's eyes that betrayed her ignorance of what this blessing meant. He remembered the time she asked, "Father, why do you bless the dors so? These simple words cannot protect this man against his doing evil. You have poured your vorn into them, and they are wise and true, to be sure, but now they are beyond your hand, and subject to influences quite beyond your control. Do you really believe this blessing does anything?"

He wanted to help his daughter understand, but he was not sure he understood it himself. He was sure it touched some deep truth, but it eluded him, and he repeated the blessing simply because it was something his mother had always done. "Has any of my dors ever done evil to injure another person?" he asked his daughter as his mother had always asked him.

"Why no, not that I have heard anyway, but that is just coincidence or luck or—"

"Someday you will believe in neither coincidence nor luck. Until then, there is still much for you to learn about the making of a great and wise queen." Sandihar winced inside when he thought about this answer. It was the answer his mother had always given him, and he was sure that she had understood and believed it, just as he was sure that he did not actually understand it enough to believe it himself. What bothered him most was that he was equally sure that Vrengnia was skeptical and he had nothing further to offer her. His only consolation was that she seemed content not to press the issue. He dreaded the day she would.

"Dor Galar, Sire." Carnados's voice shook him from his reflections.

He smiled to himself as Galar approached along the walkway. Galar was a tall man with an easy, long stride that conveyed royalty to anyone who saw him. It was royalty that went beyond his service to the king, a royalty of character, a man who knew who he was and what his business was. Mindar was forced to trot to keep up.

"My good Dor," said the king as Galar bowed slightly in deference to his sovereign, "I have a special errand for you in preparation for my birthday...." He let his voice trail off as he looked out over the fields to the south. Galar remained motionless. The king could feel him watching.

"Do you know the town of Shiloh?" He waved his hand toward the tiny hamlet to the southwest, barely visible beyond the small hill to the south.

"Yes, Sire, I have been there many times." Galar's succinctness pleased Sandihar.

"Do you know the blacksmith who forges there?"

"I know his reputation, but I would not say I know him."

"Yes, yes—well, I have been thinking. My birthday is coming up, my fiftieth, you know, and…" The king paused, eyeing the dor thoughtfully. Galar stood unmoving. "Well, I thought that we might ask the good smith if he would make a sword for my fiftieth birthday celebration!"

"And my role, Sire?"

"Well…you…you would ask him—for me, of course."

Galar was cautious and respectful. "Sire, this man is the finest bladesmith in the kingdom—"

"I know." The king smiled as he interrupted the dor. He knew the smith's reputation well.

"He refuses to make swords, Sire…blades of any kind that are designed as weapons. You know this also, Sire."

"He is older now; and wiser. Surely he will not defy me a second time."

"I do not know for sure."

"But you will ask for me?!" He purposely posed the question somewhere just this side of a command. Galar shifted slightly without breaking eye contact with him.

"I will engage the smith for you this very afternoon."

"So soon?"

Galar bowed to the king. "There is no reason to delay." His answer was resolute. Without a glance back, Galar turned and strode off to his new task. The king watched him go silently; he always liked a man who knew his purpose.

The advisors remained still. When the last sound of Galar's descending steps faded in the tower stairway, the king breathed heavily. "He certainly has a way of confirming his appointment to leadership of the dors."

"Yes, Sire," murmured Carnados, "he does indeed." Sandihar felt a double-edged twinge in the way Carnados said it. He hated it, but loved the man who said it.

The depths of Moraven deep, the heights of the Crown of Tessalindria—these are but floor and ceiling to the infinite expanse of possibilities for our short lives and our small world.

Pratoraman
The Middle Way

THERE WAS NO HURRY, NO MORE URGENT TASK REQUIRING HIS SERVICES, AND Galar loved riding at this time of the year. Everything was in slow motion, so Galar took his time, allowing his horse the privilege of an easy walk. Above him, riding the warm eddies from the sun-drenched fields, a hawk was drawing lazy circles on the infinite ceiling of the sky. It was the only thing that was moving as far as he could see, and its effortless turns set his mind drifting slowly to the circles surrounding the king's request.

He knew that the blades of the smith at Shiloh Forge were known throughout Immerland. It seemed to him that all the best working blades in the kingdom were made there. He had heard rumors that these blades could actually cut chains, nails and bolts without becoming dull or chipped. Such a blade would be a perfect accouterment for the king. He also knew that the smith at Shiloh Forge had refused in the past to make weapons for him or any of the dors, and he knew that the king knew this as well.

He was curious about the king's request. It was not his position to disdain the king for thinking that perhaps for this special occasion, he might convince the smith to do him a favor. The timing was somewhat abrupt and out of character for the king, whose habit was usually thorough and cautious, bordering on banal. Might it be linked to the unsettling reports about the mountain clans that had begun filtering in from the scouts stationed along the southern edges of Immerland? Yet, it was not the king's style to obscure his purpose in that way. Besides, this was not the first time they had had such reports.

There had been a subtle change in the king lately, occurring gradually over the past two years. Until then, he had been profoundly predictable, ruling as Galar remembered joking with Dor Windarad, "by the book." Though they knew there was no such volume, Galar smiled to himself at their image of the king and his secret book, given to him by his mother and containing every wise thing a king could say or do. He envisioned the king hiding away late at night to pore over its pages, searching out how to run the kingdom as she had.

Recently, it had been different. Galar had spent many an idle moment trying to correlate the change to something he could put his finger on. He was not sure, but its beginning seemed to coincide with the appointment of Omberon as the captain of the King's Guard. On the other hand, he was not sure that this suspicion did not simply arise from his personal distaste for Omberon. Windarad had voiced the same suspicion, but could not substantiate it. The sudden request to open an old wound by asking the smith to make him a sword was more curious than all the rest. The attempt to understand this odd direction left Galar chasing the tails of vague forebodings through his mind, and the approach of Shiloh was a welcome diversion. *In any case,* he thought, *right now I am on an errand for the king.* He had a job to do and he did want to meet this smith personally.

The smithy was on the southern edge of Shiloh, at the end of a lane leading out into the barley fields. The smell of the air altered as he entered Shiloh, and polite hellos and quiet smiles surrounded him as he wended his way through the village, ever closer to the metallic ring of multiple hammers on their anvils.

The doors and windows of the smithy were wide open, and Galar could see the faint spirals of smoke curling upward from the five chimneys poking through the roof. He approached the long, low building and dismounted to the left of the door. As he tied his horse to the dragon's head hitching post, he was aware of the smell of coal and hot iron drifting from the dark doorway. Taking a deep breath, he paused and listened thoughtfully to the diverse sounds, anticipating what each might be before entering. Above them all, clear and strong, the voice of a man singing captured his attention:

> *"Layer the steel and iron pure.*
> *Heat and hammer the weld secure.*
> *Draw it long and fold it then*
> *Weld, draw, fold—again, again."*

The singing stopped abruptly as he entered the shop. Galar saw one of the smiths lay down his tongs and hammer and wipe his hands on his dirty leather apron. He signaled his assistant to lay off the bellows, bowed briefly and waved the other smiths to stop hammering so he could be heard. "What is your business here, good Dor?"

"I am Galar, Head Dor to the King of Immerland. I have been sent by the king to request your hand in making a sword for the king's upcoming birthday."

The man looked up and pointed to the small, carefully carved sign above his forge fire. Galar's eyes flicked to the sign, absorbing it quickly, then back to the face of the man before him who offered politely, "I do not make swords," as he turned back to his forge.

Galar knew this was the smith. Even if they had met elsewhere, he would have recognized him. The gray eyes, deep-set and clear, said without words that here was the man of legend. He also knew he had to finish his errand for the king, notwithstanding that he already knew what the outcome would be; some long-held, well-thought-out conviction already stood at odds with the king's request. "This is for the king—for a very significant occasion."

"—And I do not make any tool for anyone who does not come to me personally," continued the smith as if Galar hadn't spoken.

"Why?"

"Because I will know the character of the one into whose hands I commend any tool I make."

"So if the king were to visit here personally, you might make his sword?"

"I would not," said the smith gently. Pointing again to the sign above his fire, he turned back to his forge and waved the other smiths back to work. The conversation was over. Galar had encountered such men before, though they were rare: a confident, well-respected master of his domain. There was nothing left to say; his business was finished. He turned and walked out into the sunlit yard of the smithy, leaving the king's desire unfulfilled.

When we speak in riddles, Tessalindria is confused. When we jest, she is amused. When we speak in anger, she retaliates. When we speak simple truth, we shake her foundations and she trembles.

Sessasha
It Is Said

P ACA WAS INCREDULOUS. HE HAD TRIED TO MAKE A HABIT OF UNDERSTAND-
ing his father before he questioned him, but the abrupt treatment of the king's emissary was far outside the boundary he had drawn for himself. "Father, this was a request from the king, a good and wise king—surely you can make an exception for the king?"

The elder smith looked at him thoughtfully, measuring his words carefully as he responded. "Goodness and wisdom are only percep-tions. He *is* the king, but when he comes here, he will be *just* a man, possibly good, possibly wise, but wanting a sword. I will not do that to any man."

"Do *what* to any man?"

"Inflict upon him the burden of bearing a tool that was designed to injure another person."

"I'm not sure I understand," said Paca

"When I make a blade, the intent of the blade is forged into it from the first stroke of the hammer. You know this. If this is not done, then the blade has no specific use; it will be a blade much like those made by other smiths of Immerland. My blades *live* their intent into the hands of their owners. This is the last and greatest secret of blade-smithing. To make a sword for a man is to inflict on that man the bur-den of the intent of a sword: to kill other men. I will not do this."

Paca stared unblinking at his father. He knew his father well, and he knew there was more coming.

The elder continued, "When you understand this, you will pass from technical brilliance to greatness in your craft." Paca's insides were churning. He watched his father pick up the steel blade again and turn his attention back to the process of its creation. He had heard this many different times, in various ways, but was not sure he believed it. It was at the core of Rule Number One. His father obviously believed it with a conviction that had often made Paca uncomfortable. Now he felt more than uncomfortable. It made him angry.

He held his tongue as his father raked out the fire and laid the blade flat on it to begin heating it for the next step. Paca felt his father's gaze engage his own as the song began to flow again. Paca knew it well:

> *"Pack the edge and pack it tight,*
> *Pack the edge while the blade is bright.*
> *One-two-three, one-two-three, heel to tip.*
> *Tappity, tappity, lickity split.*
> *Bury the blade in the ashes deep;*
> *Overnight, its softness keep."*

The discussion ended there. Paca tried to argue with his anger, but that just made it worse. There was no specific thing to be angry about; nothing specific he would say to his father, even if he had the chance. He concentrated on the bellows and giving the fire its breath for his father's work.

✠

The next day started out like any other day at the smithy. Paca's chores had been done except for the fire. Today it would be unnecessary. The blades had been pulled from the ash bin, cold and gray after cooling overnight, and the task for the day was filing and shaping the edges. As he dusted the ashes off the steel, he could feel the words welling up and rolling off his tongue:

> *"Cut to shape and dress and file.*
> *Apply the lines of grace and style.*
> *Flatten the faces, a gentle wedge.*
> *Smooth the tang, but leave the edge.*
> *Sharpen the—"*

The door to the smithy opened abruptly, interrupting Paca in mid-sentence. King Sandihar was standing in the doorway, scanning the shop for the man in charge. Paca had seen him many times before but never this close. The king was a head shorter than Paca's father, with light brown hair that was graying around the temples. His eyes were as black as the forge coal; small crow's feet extended from their outer corners to his temples. Here was a man who was content in general, Paca reasoned, but he did not look content now.

He wore no crown. Paca guessed that he had hoped to make the visit less formal, but his gold forearm bands and his tunic, with its tasseled epaulets and the Immerland crest emblazoned across the chest, left no doubt about who he was. The princess stood just behind his left shoulder. She was almost as tall as her father, but much less royal in appearance. Paca smiled to himself: the Pied Princess herself. Three other men hovered behind her whom Paca could only guess were the king's advisors. Behind them, just outside the door, stood several guards partially obscured by the doorframe and the bright mid-morning sunlight.

Paca saw the king recognize his father and walk rapidly toward him. The princess followed one step behind. When she stopped, she was not more than an arm's length from where Paca stood with his hand still on the post vise where he had clamped the chopper blade. He could have touched her. She brought with her a fresh scent of the outdoors that hung about her. It was not a perfume as one might expect royalty to wear, and it was subtle, but noticeable. Her clothing spoke of gaiety, simplicity and function all at the same time, a rare combination for a young woman. He guessed she was little older than sixteen.

"I have come to request that you make a sword for your king." The king was looking up into his father's steel gray eyes.

"No," said the smith softly, as he turned and pointed to his simple sign. Paca saw the king's eyes darken as his father bent to the task of positioning a blade into his filing vise.

Paca guessed that the king was not used to being told "no" with such authority. "I am the king—," he began, his voice trembling on the verge of rage.

His father interrupted him without looking up from his vise, "You are a *man* who wants *me* to make him a sword. The answer is no!"

Uneasiness filled the smithy as the king glanced over his shoulder at his advisors. Paca looked quickly at the princess who was staring at him intently. Her eyes spoke of surprise, fear and pleading, as if Paca might intervene in the sudden affront to her father. He knew he could not and would not. The advisors looked away, unnerved, leaving the king on his own to face his father who, having tightened the vise, straightened and faced the king.

"Your Highness," said the smith softly, "we have been through this before. There is no man in the world, not even the king, who would be safe carrying a sword I had made for him. If it is your pleasure to have a new sword, I beg of you to request this of one of the other smiths in the kingdom. The smith at Yendel is a fine—"

"No!" interrupted the king. "I will have a blade of *yours* at my side. You have until tomorrow at this time to consider my offer. I will pay you handsomely. But if you still refuse, you will be imprisoned until you do as I ask."

The smith opened his mouth to speak, but the king had turned his back and headed out the door. His advisors kept their eyes on the floor, not wishing to look at the smith or the king. The princess hesitated. Paca felt her penetrating gaze for an instant before she broke it off and followed the entourage out of the smithy. He felt as if she had reached inside him through his eyes and taken something...no, maybe she had left something; what it was he was not sure, but now she was gone.

As he looked back and met his father's quiet eyes, the smith smiled reassuringly and bent to his task, adjusting the knife blade in his vise. Paca waited, sensing a great sadness welling up in his father. When he did not speak, Paca busied himself with the work before him, trying to focus on what he had been doing before the interruption by the king.

⊞

The next day was bright and clear, breaking upon Shiloh with warmth and exuberance belonging only to the quiet days of the late summer, but Paca could sense the darkness over his father as he continued working on the chef's new knife. While his father finished his filing, Paca swept the floor around the forge, arranged the tongs and the fire tools, topped off the slack tub, and set the forge fire. Today they would harden and temper the knife, making the edge of the steel hard and keen, leaving the back of the blade flexible and springy.

The words of the forge poetry sprang from his father's lips as the blade lay in the fire. Paca could feel his father's gray eyes fix onto his own, imparting a strength of wisdom that could be had no other way:

> *"Heat the blade to lodestone red,*
> *Even and bright in Timmanaeus's bed.*
> *Slice it fast in the tepid wave.*
> *Slice it straight, its fairness save.*
> *Temper it slowly, temper it true,*
> *The edge to straw, the back to blue."*

Paca knew the words by rote, but there was something in the intensity of his elder's voice that made them new and alive each time they were sung.

The steel squealed as his father plunged it into the quenching brine—an agonizing but momentary ordeal the blade must endure, a rite of passage on its way to its ultimate purpose. Back and forth the blade went as the cry of the steel subsided into steam. He had barely pulled the blade from the tub, still steaming lightly in the cool morning air, when the door opened. The king strode in with the princess and four soldiers close on his heels. His father gently laid the blade on the edge of the forge and dropped the steaming tongs onto the packed clay floor. He stood up straight behind the forge as the king made his way toward him. There was a pause as the two men faced each other and locked eyes.

"Have you considered my proposal?" the king spoke with all the authority he could bring forth before the smith.

"I have not."

"You would defy your king a second time?!" The king was incredulous and outraged.

"Your Highness," his father said as he bowed slightly in deference to the man before him, "it is a privilege to live under your leadership. You have brought peace and prosperity to this land where we live in abundance and freedom under your wisdom and grace. All your people love and respect you and you walk freely among us without fear. You have accomplished all this without the use of a single blade from me—"

"Rubbish," interrupted the king. "Your blades slice my food and most of the food in the kingdom. Your blades chop our wood, they harvest our fields, they shape the wood and cut the stone for our houses and the castle, and in all this, never has one of these blades injured its owner or another. Most certainly, my kingdom is in debt to your workmanship for our prosperity and success. Is it such a large thing to ask you now to make a sword for your king's fiftieth birthday?"

Paca saw his father's gray eyes light suddenly as if they had caught the fire of Timmanaeus himself. The smith straightened to his full height, his face taking the appearance of chiseled iron.

"I am a man of peace. Each tool I make is forged—from the first hammer strike to the last stroke of my strop—to be used for peaceful purposes. It is this intent that lives in the blade, that protects its owner and others. If you consider this to contribute so significantly to your success as king, I am doubly honored and indebted to you to be allowed to continue with my work in your service. But I cannot impart such life into the blade that has as its purpose to take another man's life—"

The king interrupted again. "This will be a blade of peace—"

"There is no sword that is a blade of peace," said the smith sternly, his eyes dancing brighter. He seemed to grow taller as he said it. "The life of my blades springs from their intent. There can be no intent in a sword other than harm to others. If that intent is *not* forged into the sword, it will be no different than any other sword. If it *is*, then surely there will be no peace. It has been said that you cannot prepare for and prevent war at the same time."

Paca could feel the darkness fall on King Sandihar's handsome face, and for the first time he noticed the face of the leader of the King's

Guard. He could not be sure if it was a smile or a sneer that lurked behind the crooked nose of that dark face. Something was not right. He knew it in the depths of his being. He glanced quickly to the other guards. They looked calm and alert, honest men paying attention to the details of their job. He looked back to his father, imposing and solid.

"So you are saying you will not make a sword for me?"

"I will not."

The king whirled around, raised his hand, and said firmly, "Captain, take him away!"

Paca felt frozen in time and space as everything slowly revolved around him. He saw the princess hesitate. Her eyes looked directly into his father's, and he held her gaze briefly until she turned suddenly and followed her father out of the smithy. Paca was sure that much had been said in that brief moment.

As the king and the princess disappeared through the doorway, Paca saw the captain and two soldiers step forward. The shackles rattled as they prepared to manacle his father who moved forward to meet them. "I am a man of peace. There is no need for chains. I will go with you willingly, but I need to talk to my son first—in private."

The captain sneered and opened his mouth to speak. Paca was sure that if anything came out, it would be ugly, but the mouth shut deliberately without a sound. The captain signaled the other guards to step back and wait. Paca saw his father motion and followed him to the corner of the smithy for a hurried conversation. "Father, you cannot let them do this—"

The elder smith ignored his plea and spoke urgently and firmly: "You must now take over the duties as the head smith until I return. You know the poetry of the forge, and you are capable of managing the other smiths. There is enough steel in the storeroom and coal in the bin to last several months. By that time, I will be out of prison and back here to manage. All this I am confident of. But you must promise me one thing—"

Paca looked up into his eyes inquiringly.

"You must promise me that you will not forge any blade that has as its design and intent the injury of another human being."

Paca dropped his eyes. He felt his father's hand reach over and firmly lift his chin, forcing him to make eye contact again. "Promise me!" he commanded.

"I promise."

"Promise what?"

Paca knew what he had to do. The nature of psadeq demanded it of him. He was being made to feel like a child, but he understood the urgency of the situation. His father was being taken away, and Paca knew he would have no peace without Paca's promise. He looked squarely into his father's eyes and spoke firmly. "I promise not to forge any blade that has as its design or intent the injury of another human being." Even as he spoke, he felt his own doubt sweep over him like brine enveloping a hot blade.

His father clapped him smartly on the shoulder. "Good." He looked at Paca thoughtfully. For a moment, Paca wondered if his father could read his mind and see his doubt; he willed his vorn to be stout for his father's sake. His father gripped his shoulder and said, "The princess is your friend. I see it in her eyes. Let her be your friend, but nothing more." He turned and followed the soldiers out of the smithy.

Great is the being who, seeing two paths
of truth, is able to reconcile them into a
single greater truth.

Hispattea
The Essences of Corritanean Wisdom

KING SANDIHAR WAS ALONE IN THE TOWER ROOM. HE HAD BEEN THERE FOR nearly an hour, anticipating the arrival of the smith with the soldiers. He had ridden ahead with his daughter and his advisors, leaving Omberon and his guards to escort the captive. They were taking longer than he expected, and the uneasiness creeping through him was a feeling that he hated.

He created a distraction for himself by looking around the room for the fiftieth time, rechecking each detail. It was a large room about halfway up the South Tower of the castle, perhaps twenty feet in diameter and furnished at his command to be spare but comfortable. Even with the windows open to the warm, midday breeze, the faint fragrance of mint and pine oil lingered from the thorough washing it had needed after years of disuse. The three windows, set into the thick eastern, southern and western walls, had been cleaned. Their hardware had been checked for soundness, brushed off, and oiled so that its black patina shone against the freshly oiled wood. The furniture included a firm clean bed, a small desk with a chair and a leather couch to sit on. A wardrobe for clothing stood against the wall between southern and western windows and beside the bed was a nightstand shadowing a pitcher of water and the chamber pot. Although he had made the room livable, he could not imagine a man staying here by choice.

Looking between heavy bars out the southern window, Sandihar tried in vain to smile to himself; a gnawing doubt that the smith would ever give up and grant his request plagued him. The thought of imprisoning a man who had done nothing wrong—unless personal conviction should be considered insulting to the king—further fueled his frustration. How or why would a man be so stubborn? He made blades for a living. Why would he draw such a distinction? This thought had kept him awake most of the previous night. He sensed the answer floating just beyond his mind's grasp, making him feel like a child again, trying to understand something he was not sure he ever would. He hated this feeling most of all.

The sound of the approaching party of soldiers and his prisoner was a welcome relief. He had never liked being alone. When he was alone, there was little to do but think in small circles that usually went nowhere. He was a man of action, and action to him was being surrounded by people. This is how he ran his life, his castle, his country and his world. Without them, alone with himself, he felt small and insignificant.

He leaned back against the window, waiting expectantly. A small gloat was rising in his throat as the smith ducked slightly to step through the door from the semidarkness of the corridor. Omberon should have been in the lead.

The smith stood to his full height and scanned the room quickly. Sandihar met his eyes and watched as the smith walked to the middle of the room. With a quick, civil bow, he acknowledged his king. "May I sit down?"

Sandihar nodded.

The smith sat down on the small couch and leaned back staring comfortably into the king's eyes. His expression was completely unreadable: not angry, not frustrated, not sullen. There was no visible passion in any emotional direction. "Thank you for your hospitality. How long do you expect that I will be here?"

Relief unleashed the king into activity. "That depends—"

"On whether and when I make your sword?"

"Precisely."

The king waited for a response. Realizing that none would be forthcoming and seeking an excuse to break eye contact with the smith, he looked up at his guards. All four of them had entered silently behind the prisoner. Omberon was smirking; the others stood behind him. "Was there any trouble getting here?" He directed the question to Omberon, hoping to discover the meaning of that twisted smile. He liked Omberon; he had always felt drawn to him, but the captain's face seldom seemed to be appropriately set to the occasion. He had come to accept this quirk, but it always left him wondering what thought lay behind those expressions.

"None, Sire. We stopped to get a few things from his house, is all." The captain tossed a small burlap sack onto the couch beside the smith. Sandihar glanced at the sack and found his eyes drawn immediately back to the smith, who was still looking at him impassively.

"May I be left alone, Sire?"

"Uh…of course. Is there anything else you need?"

"Nothing." There was still no emotion, not even the slightest hint of resentment, fear or anger.

"If you decide that there is, you can knock on the door and the guards will see to it that your needs are met." Sandihar had that feeling again: the child, left wondering what all others seemed to know. He bowed suddenly and stiffly. He didn't know why. It made his ears hot. He whirled and headed for the door, expecting that the smith might say something. Omberon saluted. That crooked smile—was the captain laughing on the inside? "Follow me…lock the door."

8

Pride is the consummate nemesis of
clarity of mind.

Hispattea
The Essences of Corritanean Wisdom

COME, VRENGNIA, WOULD YOU LIKE TO VISIT THE SMITH? I AM VERY CURI-ous to see whether he has made any effort to use the forge I set up for him." Dinner had just been cleared from the table in the banquet hall, and Vrengnia lingered over a glass of after-dinner sherry with her father.

Vrengnia set down her glass and stood up. "I should like to see the smith...."

"You seem hesitant—is there more?"

"Yes...and no. It just seems a bit harsh to lock up a man who has done nothing."

"Nothing? He defied me to my face. This is the second time." A storm gathered in her father's eyes.

"The second time?"

"Yes, years ago. I should have dealt with him then."

"What happened?" Vrengnia could not recall her father ever mentioning this.

"I will tell you about it some other time. It is not important."

Vrengnia was not so sure, but she realized he was not going to explain it now. "He refused to make a sword for you, but what has he done, really?" she continued.

The king rose to face her, setting down his glass in a dramatic flourish of care. "Come along. We shall see if he has *done* anything."

Vrengnia followed him out of the banquet hall. He did not say anything. She knew that he was angry or sullen or some mixture of the two. He was always quiet when he was sullen. She could also tell by the hunch in his back. She had spent many hours walking behind her father and could tell what he was feeling by the shape of his shoulders. Right now they mostly said, "Sullen."

"I am not angry with you, Father, but I do not understand. That is all."

"Ummmhh." It was an acknowledgment that he did not like what he was thinking, but didn't know what to say about it yet. She let it go and followed in silence.

Two guards stood stiffly at the door to the room below the smith's prison. She saw them stiffen further as the king came into view. "Anything happening in there?" he asked softly.

"Not a sound, Sire." The tall soldier on the left with the wart on his nose spoke with a guttural growl characteristic of the guards. "There has been no sound since you left this morning."

"Was he served lunch and dinner?"

"Yes...both."

"Did he eat?"

"I don't know, Sire."

"Hmmmmmm...open the door!"

There was no lock on the door, but the heavy bolt was inaccessible from the inside. Vrengnia watched the shorter guard pull it back effortlessly and the door swung into the room. The soldier stepped in first. A moment later the king followed him. The tall guard waved Vrengnia in behind her father. She obeyed, and with a quick step stood behind her father's shoulder. She had always stood there. It was her place, but recently she had begun to resent being there. At the moment, in the presence of the smith it seemed a little silly as well, but she made no effort to move, out of respect for her father.

The room was identical to the one above it in the tower, but her father had transformed it into a crude smithy. It was comical, after seeing both the intensity and the detailed organization of the smithy at Shiloh. A small forge had been set up against the southern wall beside the window. A neat but forlorn looking bench with a small vise stood near the forge with a few tongs and other tools scattered about on it. She guessed that the large burlap bag that stood open by the forge was full of coal. The anvil, on its stump to the left, seemed whimsical compared to the great anvil that the smith owned in Shiloh, and the half-barrel of water on the floor beside the forge was leaking. None of it seemed to have been touched. The bulk of the room was empty and echoed with the slightest movement. She could not imagine anyone actually hitting an anvil in this stone chamber.

The king glanced quickly about and his eyes came to rest on the smith. He was standing by the western window gazing out at the twilit fields.

"Good smith, I would have thought you had begun my blade by this time. I am disappointed." There was an air of sarcasm in his voice, but his face was stern. "Is something wrong?"

The smith turned, but remained leaning against the window casement; Vrengnia sensed that he was relaxed, thoughtful. He waited before he spoke and measured his words carefully. "Yes, there is something wrong. The coal is bad, the anvil is saddled, there is no flue for the forge, the steel you left me is inferior, the bellows are not sufficient for the kind of work you require, and I am imprisoned against my will—"

"Details, details," her father interrupted with an impatient hand gesture. "Instead of telling me what is wrong with my provisions, why don't you tell me what you need, so I can get it for you?"

"What I need…" mused the smith. "What do I need? I need to be in my smithy with my son, earning my keep making blades for your kingdom and—"

"Stop!" commanded the king angrily. Vrengnia did not often see her father angered so quickly.

The smith paused. "By your leave," he began again more cautiously, "I do not mean to be trivial with my king. I consider you a wise and kind man and a good king. You have protected us, and our land is safe and prosperous. However, the wisdom of imprisoning me seems faulty. It seems out of character for you to hold me hostage simply because I wouldn't make the birthday present you wanted, particularly when I have served your kingdom and your person faithfully."

Vrengnia saw her father softening as the smith continued speaking. His shoulders dropped ever so slightly.

"I cannot help but think that there is something bigger at stake, something you fear that you did not fear before. You must see that if this is true, a better sword is not the remedy for fear. And now, I request, as a faithful servant, that you release me to my service to you at my smithy."

The two men stood staring at one another thoughtfully. Vrengnia shifted her weight from one foot to the other. Silence made her uneasy. Her father once told her about the necessity of silence at certain times, but she was not sure she understood what he meant exactly. She was not even sure that he did.

The king sighed. "You are indeed a good man, with a great wisdom, and perhaps I have made a mistake in imprisoning you. But I will have a blade from your forge ere I set you free to my service. I will supply anything you need, and you will be well taken care of in my service here, but there will be no release until this task is complete."

He hesitated. The smith turned back to the window.

"When you are ready with a list of what you need, I will spare no expense to get it for you. Until then, you will spend the days here and the nights upstairs."

Again he waited, but the smith remained silent and still, silhouetted in the window against the western sky.

"Take him to his chambers upstairs." He said to the guards. He strode out of the room. Vrengnia followed. His shoulders said, "I'm frustrated." Vrengnia felt embarrassed.

9

A short sword for the soldier boy,
A long sword for the king.
A wrong sword in an idle hand
Is quite a fearsome thing.

                             Ancient Mooriman Rhyme

S ANDIHAR SMILED AT CARNADOS'S QUESTION ABOUT HIS TIME WITH THE smith. "I have spent a good part of two hours with him every day since he came to the castle. Why do you ask?"

"I was curious what you might talk about for such a long time. Surely not convincing him to make your sword—"

"No—no, nothing like that. He won't let me." Carnados raised one eyebrow. "Well, it seems that every time we get anywhere near that subject, there is always a compelling diversion that brings us to something else entirely…I usually don't even realize it until after it has happened."

"He is a clever man."

"Clever is too mild, I would think. He is knowledgeable beyond his own natural intelligence, but I cannot figure out how…or why…or where, or even when he could have gotten such knowledge."

"What do you mean?"

"Remember all the history you used to insist that I learn—or at least should have some familiarity with?"

Carnados shifted in the armchair, straightening slightly and smiling. "I seem to remember it ending up mostly the latter."

"Well…uh…yes…well, he seems to know all about all of it!"

"All of them?"

"Umhumn…and the strangest thing is that I don't think he can read."

"Impossible. No one could know the ancient literature without being able to read, and the ancient linguals at that!"

"Well, he does. Moreover, he knows the glyphs and runes. I have caught him several times writing on the floor with a chunk of coal. It's always in glyphs. He quotes from Hispattea and Mortag of Horrinaine.

Remember when I called Mortag an old windbag? In the smith's mouth his words are a refreshing breeze."

Sandihar saw Carnados shift again and lean forward, his fingers on his temples, his eyes concentrating intently on one of the floor tiles. "It goes on and on. He knows every detail of Vortang's *Theory of War*; he draws diagrams that would shame Marhaigan and his best pupils. Several times, he has referenced Karamanta's elucidation on the Eladra and spatial infinity. He converses fluidly about the Kirrinath, and he quotes liberally from the *Tessarandin*—"

"How old is he? Do you know?"

"I don't. I have asked, but my questions never are answered. He will not speak of himself."

"Hmmmmm…" Carnados looked up briefly and then back at his tile. "Do you suppose he could be Sessashian?"

"It crossed my mind. He did not say, though it is unlikely that he would. He is a natural teacher, without being 'teachy.' When I leave, I feel like a child that has been listened to—that has been, in fact, heard—and I feel like I have been taught; not taught things, but life itself. Have you ever had that feeling?"

"Your mother made me feel that way sometimes."

"My mother…hmmm…yes, except I never felt like I understood very much when my mother taught me."

"Really?! Do you understand the smith?"

"Yes—and no." Sandihar coughed to relieve the tightness he felt in his throat. "I mean, it all seems so clear when he is teaching, but when I leave, I feel as though the most vital ingredient of the thoughts is left behind, as if he is unlocking them to me, but holding on to the key. I have not had a decent night's sleep in a week, trying to put together the pieces of some infinite fabric he is weaving."

"Has he spoken to you about his imprisonment? Has he asked for release? Has he asked for *anything*?"

"He seems perfectly content to stay where he is led. He's been no trouble to the guards whatsoever."

"Strange—"

"Worse than strange, he seems to enjoy it. Sometimes I get a vague feeling that he is actually in charge, that somehow, from within his cells, he is changing the world around him. Whenever I visit him, he acts as if he expected me. It's frightening, frankly. I have only felt that kind of fear one time before."

"Verclan?"

"Yes, but don't remind me—"

"I don't think I need to." There was no disrespect in Carnados's tone.

"You are right, but perhaps you can help resolve—" He looked up suddenly to see Vrengnia in the doorway to the throne room.

"May I come in?" She seemed troubled. Her face was drawn and tired. "Am I interrupting something?"

"No...no, come in, sit down." Sandihar had cultivated the habit of never refusing his daughter. It had served him well, particularly in the last few years when their relationship had been strained heavily by her becoming a young woman.

"Father, I have been troubled since you arrested the smith. Particularly after the discussion he had with you about there being something greater behind all this." She had circled in front of him and was looking directly into his eyes. "What he said that day...well, I have been unable to get it out of my mind...as if it were true. There is something bigger here, isn't there?"

He sighed, "There is." He paused. He could feel Carnados watching him. He wondered whether it was wise to continue. Vrengnia stared into his eyes expectantly. She seemed to be saying there was no turning back now. "What I tell you today you must utter to no other. Do you promise me this?"

"I will tell no other," she affirmed.

He did not want to continue, but he knew he must. He was not sure he could even trust his daughter. "We have had several reports that"— he found himself struggling to say the next word—"that Verclan is amassing an army, near the southern border, and that he intends to attack Immerland again."

"Verclan! Can we not just repel him as we always have?"

"There is more," he continued darkly. Vrengnia lowered her eyes. "There are rumors that he may have a smith working for him who is fashioning weapons that can cut steel like clay and pierce mail like linen. We will not be able to stand against such weapons in an assault."

His daughter was still looking at the floor. "Where did the rumors come from? Where did you hear them?"

Sandihar did not want to answer her question so he ignored it altogether. She looked up as he continued. "Our hope is in the jailed smith, whose blades are fabled to do the same. My hope is that if we can convince him to make one blade, then he will relent and make many—the key is to get him to break down and make the one, first." He was not sure that she noticed his evasion, but she seemed to accept it.

"Can you not tell him of the threat to our land? Would he not be more willing to help us then?"

"No, this would only make him more stubborn, I fear. After all, the reports are not substantiated. We have no proof and we do not even know the true source of the rumors. But we must be prepared, and the key is this smith." The king paused. His eyes narrowed as he continued, looking squarely into his daughter's eyes. "You must not tell this to anyone. Fear in our people is a greater enemy than Verclan and all his army. There must be no word of this until the truth is known clearly. The only ones in the kingdom who know of these things are the scouts, my advisors and you. Promise me again that you will tell no one!"

"I promise to tell no one," proclaimed the princess solemnly.

Sandihar eyed his daughter thoughtfully for a moment, but said nothing more. Something told him she was not sure. It was a feeling he knew well. He had said such things to his mother many times.

10

*Each must understand, without hesita-
tion or pause, that within the first
Cymbic Sphere, complete acceptance
and understanding do not have to be
sought; they simply are.*

The Tessarandin, Book 4

W HAT IS IT LIKE TO BE IN CHARGE HERE?" VORDAR SMILED AS HE SAT ATOP
the anvil watching Paca clamp his work in the vise.

Paca shrugged. "It's not the being in charge that is different. What is different is not having my father here. It just seems quiet." He bent over the vise to see the fairness of the thatch knife before he started the finish grinding.

"Yes, quiet is the right word, though your father does not do a whole lot of talking." Vordar was a young man, like Paca himself, and a good smith for his years. Paca had appointed him to work his bellows until he could find a suitable apprentice. He could have tended the bellows himself, along with the fire, but he knew from watching his father how much more he could get done with a good helper.

"Hmmm…yes. But it wasn't that kind of quiet I was talking about."

There was a pause as Vordar uncrossed his arms. He was idling for a few minutes before lighting his own forge fire, since Paca had no need for a fire this morning.

"Are you going to the castle again? It's been three days now since you last went."

"I think not…what would be different? If nothing else is different, why would the outcome be different? I have been there thrice. I don't even know for sure that he is there."

"You need to find that princess."

"That's enough, Vordar."

"But we all saw her look at you. Didn't you see it? And then those other visits, I mean—" Vordar was smiling. Paca was smiling to himself, trying not to let it leak out onto his face.

"There is work to be done," he muttered as he stepped toward the huge sandstone grinder by the window. "You should get to yours." He was not trying to be rude. He really appreciated Vordar's friendship and ease, but he did not want to follow the path of this conversation, at least not right then. Vordar shrugged and spun around on the anvil, slipping easily off the other side on the way to his forge.

The poetry sprang from Paca's mouth. He was never sure exactly how this happened:

"Grind it rough on the sandstone round,
Work with care 'til the hollow's ground.
Pitch in the bevel, constant the length,
Bevel the point, but watch its strength.
Stone it by hand to platinum sheen,
Strop it on leather to make it keen."

He said it through several times, tumbling the pictures associated with each word over and over until he could visualize every nuance of each blade before he started.

In the middle of the fourth time through, on the second blade, a movement at the front gate interrupted his concentration. He looked up through the window to see the princess fumbling with the gate latch. He bent over the grindstone, trying to pretend he had not seen her. Vordar started whistling, to himself, of course.

Vrengnia had been there three times since his father's arrest. The first time was to offer her condolences following the arrest, and the second was to make sure that everything was going well in the smithy. The third was to bring Paca some fresh bread from the king's kitchen. Each time she had come alone, dressed in her comical colored outfit and looking more like a court jester than a right princess.

Her manner was always relaxed and open. Paca found it hard to see whether there was any other than her stated motive for her visits. She was not like other young women he knew who were always flustered or embarrassed over themselves, their conversation, their actions—over just about everything. The princess was completely at ease, even in the midst of the smithy. She asked intelligent questions with refreshingly true curiosity and listened to the answers as if she genuinely wanted to know. She looked into his eyes when he spoke, and her contribution to the conversation was articulate and useful.

In spite of her position as the princess of the kingdom, she carried no hint of this into her dealings with him. When she left, Paca found himself completely at ease with her having been there and completely at ease with her leaving. It was as if she had always been there when she was there, and as if she had never been there when she left. He guessed that she probably knew what was happening to his father, but she never spoke of having seen him, and it seemed improper to ask her.

As she approached the door, Paca was only curious as to the reason for her visit. He felt a remarkable calmness as he pumped the treadle on the massive wheel.

The princess seemed similarly disposed as she entered the smithy, hesitating only to adjust to its interior dimness. Her eyes found him quickly. She strode directly to him. He became aware of that fresh outside scent that always surrounded her, and he looked up, trying to act surprised. Laying the blade aside, he stood to his full height.

The princess spoke quickly. "We must talk." She was blunt, but polite.

Paca raised an eyebrow, but continued staring into her eyes quietly. He had learned this from his father; it was not something he would do naturally himself.

"Perhaps we can go outside—what I have to say is for you only," she continued, pausing to let Paca respond. He held out his hand in a "you first" gesture and then followed her to the door. He looked over his shoulder at Vordar and, with a wave of his hand, let him know he was in charge while he was gone. They walked out into the yard. He sensed that her easy disposition and confidence were displaced.

They left the smithy and followed the lane leading out of Shiloh into the barley fields behind the smithy's back fence. The road was quiet with few other people, and the air was fresh, warmed by the brilliant sunshine on the ripening grain. As he waited for Vrengnia to begin, Paca tried to absorb the infinite detail of the world laid out before him. Each gentle shift of the wind bore a glorious potpourri of warm smells: the pungent odor of ripe barley, the drying soil of the fields and the star flowers on the side of the road. Birds sang to one another as they feasted on the fields, embellishing the subtle cacophony of an unseen chorus of insects.

Vrengnia said nothing. Paca marveled at how strange it felt to be completely comfortable with this uncomfortable silence. "I need you to make that sword for my father's birthday," she said when they were well out of earshot of the smithy.

"No!" Paca stopped short. She took a couple more steps and turned back, looking straight up into his eyes. He stared at her, narrowing his own eyes.

"Did you say that, or was that your father?" she asked. Paca wanted to find a hint of offense in the question, but there was none, neither in her face nor his mind.

"What? Of course, I said it. My father is in prison, remember?"

"No—I mean—was what you said from *your* vorn, or was it tied to some obligation to be like your father?"

Paca wavered and dropped his eyes.

The princess was quick. "I thought as much—come on, we have much more to discuss."

"I'm not sure we do," said Paca quietly, unmoving in front of the princess. "At least not about this." He was finding it hard to be rude, although he thought it might even be appropriate in this situation. There was something about the princess that would not let him do it.

She took a step toward him until she was unusually close. "We are both much like our fathers, more than we are comfortable with sometimes. I often wonder if I even *want* to be exactly like my father. He is so strong, so disciplined, so organized—I am not sure I could bear it. In addition, he is sometimes stubborn to his own hurt." She paused and glanced at Paca. He did not want to let on that he understood what she was saying, not just the words, but the exact meaning. He had had similar thoughts, particularly in the last few days, as he wrestled with the reasoning behind his father's imprisonment. Vrengnia gestured that they should continue walking and they started down the lane again.

She continued: "I am not sure I would have imprisoned your father, for example. I mean—what good is it to imprison a man from whom you want a favor?" Paca stared into the distance but said nothing. "Maybe if my father had taken more time to explain the situation, *your* father would have been convinced to do his bidding."

She fell silent. Paca could feel her waiting for a response, but since she had initiated the conversation, he wanted her to lead it. He had nothing to contribute unless something were to provoke him. They walked a number of paces, each waiting, and each listening to the other quietly. "I also believe...I believe that if you examine your vorn, *you* would have agreed to make the blade." There was another silence. "I mean—as much as we are the same as our fathers, we are also different. We are not so stuck in our ways—"

"Perhaps."

"Perhaps?!" she exclaimed. "Perhaps? Come now. I know you love and respect your father, for he is a man worthy of both, but you must forge your own tools. My father is like that too, but there are some things that, when I am queen, I will definitely do differently."

"Why?" Paca shot back defensively. "Your father is a fine king! He is wise and thoughtful, kind and gentle, and has led us to great prosperity and peace. What would you do that would be better than this?" Vrengnia was gazing into the horizon. Paca continued, "Please understand me. I wrestle with the same thoughts about my father. There are things about him that I don't understand. I sometimes wonder whether it is just because he is getting older and set in his ways, or perhaps there is truth in his ways that I cannot comprehend yet. Maybe you, too, are underestimating your father's strength, Princess. Perhaps in judging your father, your own arrogance will lead you to miss the greatest gift he has for you."

Paca sensed that Vrengnia was clever enough to realize she had ventured into deep waters. She backed up. "Yes, I have had many such conversations with myself—about my father. But what about yours? Take, for instance, this obsession with not making weapons—where does *that* come from? What does it do for him? My father already has swords. His army has hundreds of them. One more will not make that much of a difference. Perhaps it is just arrogance. Your father's sword, were he to make one, might be fine, but should he suppose that it would be that much superior to those made by other smiths in Immerland?" Paca remained thoughtful. "I mean, would *you* be so arrogant? Are *your* blades so much superior?"

"If they aren't, then why are you so desperate to have one?" he returned, quietly. Vrengnia had made a good point. He found it curious that part of his mind wanted to retaliate, to defend itself against the attack, but some stronger part absorbed the sting and only wanted to return a sober, accepting answer.

The princess responded gently, "Don't get me wrong. I believe they are better. But are they *that* much better, that your arrogance would leave your father rotting in prison over this issue?"

Paca remained silent. He could feel himself softening. He felt rational clarity and full emotional acceptance at the same time. What was going on?

She continued. "Besides this, suppose I told you that this was more than just a birthday gift, that there was more at stake, that indeed the safety of the kingdom itself is in jeopardy."

"You hinted at this before," Paca replied. "Is this what you are going to tell me? If it is, I need to know. If you want my cooperation, you owe it to me to be honest."

"Well…it's not quite that simple." The princess paused. Paca felt her polling his response.

He looked at her thoughtfully. "Not that simple?"

"I made a promise to my father that I would not tell anyone—"

"Tell anyone what?"

"I promised."

"You mean that you have knowledge of a danger to the whole kingdom, that you think I could help with, and you are not allowed to let me know what it is so I *can* help. Why would your father make you promise such a thing?"

"You could help by making the king his sword."

"I cannot!"

"Why?"

"I promised—" Paca stopped short. He had walked right into the trap. The words had come out before he had time to think about the implications.

"Promised what?" shot back the princess. Paca remained silent. "You promised your father that you would not make any weapons, didn't you, that you would not make a sword for my father!"

The hint of triumph in the princess's voice should have galled him. "Yes, I did," he conceded. He wanted to feel angry. It wouldn't happen.

They had both stopped and were staring at each other in the middle of the road. There was a long pause before the princess continued. "Let's think about this situation: I made a promise to my father that I would not reveal this threat to our kingdom, and you made a promise to your father that prevents you from helping me. Are we not both just living out our fathers' stubbornness to all of our detriment? If I were to break my oath, and tell you the need, would you consider breaking yours to help me?"

Paca was defiant, but the words sunk into his vorn like a stone from a sling. He stared at the princess, not wanting to believe the situation unfolding before him. He stared unflinching outwardly, as his mind reeled and twisted. He had never been confronted on his own beliefs. It was so easy when his father was around, but now he was on his own. What were *his* convictions? What was it that *he* believed? "I might," he whispered hoarsely.

"Might what?"

"It depends on the seriousness of the situation."

"Then you would consider it, at least?" pressed the princess.

"Yes."

"Then as a measure of good faith, I will break my oath first—but you must tell no one of this conversation. The purpose of this revelation here is to convince you to help me. If you do, our kingdom can be saved, and your father will be freed from prison without having to compromise his convictions." The princess paused to make sure that Paca was still willing to go along.

"If all I have to do is make your father his sword, then go ahead." Paca was grave. He was still not sure if he wanted to do this. He was trying to weigh the measure of a greater good, the promise to his father, his psadeq or...he did not even know what rested on the other side of the scales. Psadeq weighed heavily. It was certainly not a thing to be taken lightly.

Paca understood that psadeq encompassed the entire nature of a relationship: trust, faithfulness, love, genuine concern, but it was more than all these things at the same time. It was something that everyone knew, that anyone could grasp and understand, yet it defied precise def-inition. Its essence encompassed and played into every relationship there was: husband and wife, doctor and patient, brothers, soldiers, tradesmen, father and son—it waxed and waned with the events in a relationship that drew two persons together or split them asunder. Psadeq was the measure of the "rightness" of the relationship: immutable and binding, but fragile and easily unraveled at the same time. Paca knew its value and knew his obligation to his father under its laws, but psadeq with the princess was strong also. Though he had known her but a short time, it seemed he should have known her all her life.

They walked a few steps before the princess began her revelation. "My father has received information from his scouts to the south that Verclan is amassing an army for another attack on Immerland."

"Verclan?!"

"The same," continued the princess gravely. "I think that my father is afraid. He believes our kingdom is facing a threat from Verclan we have not seen in many years, and there are complications on top of that: it seems that this is not the first conflict that your father has had with mine, but he would not tell me the details. Now he means to con-vince—or force—your father to make swords for him."

Paca listened quietly, trying to sort out the significance of the infor-mation being revealed to him. All around him, the world was bright, warm and at peace, but a darkness was creeping into his vorn, a dread, a fear that he could not shake.

The princess was talking, but he was only half listening. He thought about his father in prison and how, by giving in, he could free him. The cost, however, was to betray psadeq with his father. The alternative was betrayal of the kingdom in a time of great need, unless, of course, none of this was true. He wished his father were there to hear this; he would know what to do.

"So what do you think?" The princess's words cut into his thoughts like a stroke from a saber.

Paca shuddered. "I—I—I'm not sure."

"Not sure?" She said it gently, but even if she hadn't, he knew he would not have been angry.

"Not sure I can help!"

"Don't you see? You are the only one who can help!" The two stopped walking and were staring at each other in the middle of the road. A cart full of barley from the harvest was approaching along the lane. The horse ambled up, seemingly oblivious to the intensity of the interaction between the two people in the road. They stepped back to let the cart pass between them.

"G'morning," said the driver brightly.

"Good morning, good farmer," responded the princess with a smile. Paca said nothing. After the cart passed, the princess stepped forward. "Do you see this? Do you see how happy and content he is? This is the way it is throughout the kingdom now. People are secure; they are happy; they are busy. We cannot let all this be destroyed!" She put her hand firmly on his shoulder. "Come, good smith, let us return. You can think about this for a day or so. In two days, I will return and I will expect an answer. We have some time, but not a lot."

They started back toward Shiloh. Paca wanted more clarity. "So all you are asking is that I make a single sword for your father?"

"That's all."

Paca felt a sullen, irritating oppression, and sensed that this would not be "all." "Will you promise that you will ask no more from me if I do this?"

"I promise," said the princess earnestly.

Paca chose to believe her, because he did not want to think any further about where all this led. He sensed a sincerity and simplicity in her persuasion, but the doubt was there. How could he trust a promise from a woman who had just broken a promise she had made to her own father? What right had he to judge the princess when he himself was contemplating breaking a promise he had made to *his* father? He saw the trap he was walking into, and tried to ignore it. "In two days I will have an answer."

The princes smiled. "Two days it is!"

As they walked back to the smithy together, they talked of insignificant details of their lives, meandering in conversation between everything and nothing. Yet the princess seemed cautious, while Paca felt defeated and completely accepting at the same time. He did not want to face the reality invading his life, but did not want to run from it either. The thought that perhaps this was the purpose of his father's incarceration sank deeper and deeper into his vorn.

11

Decisions are temporal in nature and eternal in consequence. The path we walk in the Infinite consists of finite, decisive steps in the now.

The Tessarandin, Book 7

P ACA PURPOSELY AND CAREFULLY LEFT OUT THE DETAILS ABOUT THE SWORD when he told Vordar about their walk on the barley field road the next day.

Vordar laughed. "First she comes here to apologize, then to see how you are doing. Next it was that loaf of bread, which, by the way, was very good—"

"Vordar—"

"Then she wants to talk—"

"Stop it!"

Vordar stopped and stared at him, a smile lurking around the corners of his mouth. "All you did was talk?"

"Yes."

"For a whole hour?"

"Every minute of it. Look, Vordar, some of what we talked about was business. There is some work she wants from me, and I may need your help."

Vordar was rearranging his fire. "Okay," he said expectantly as he finished spreading the hot coal out around the rim of the firepot.

"I may have to work at night to keep up with the shop production, and I may need you to run the shop during the day...."

"Interesting." Vordar dropped the fire rake onto the rack beside the forge bed and wiped his hands on his apron.

"Most of all, I need you to cover for me and not let anyone else know what I am up to."

"What is it you are going to do?"

"I'm not sure I am—I have a couple days to consider the offer. It's tricky work...."

"Tricky?"

"I think it best not to actually let you know what I'm doing. Will you help me out?"

"I think I can do that." Vordar smiled.

Paca knew the smile was genuine; Vordar was a good friend and one to be trusted if the need for his help arose.

✠

Paca had had his two days to think about the princess's proposal, and today was the day of decision. Perhaps "think" was not exactly the right word. He mused as he rummaged around the wood room at the back of the smithy searching for stock to lay handles to the four scythes he was finishing for the barley harvest. The labyrinth of his thoughts seemed endless, but it always moved toward what seemed like the inevitable conclusion: the king's sword would be made.

Another thought burned in his mind: he wanted to make a second sword as a gift for the princess. The clarity of this desire was something that he was not accustomed to. On the surface, it was a bit forward. With anyone else, it would have been inappropriate, but it seemed right for the princess. It would be a work of friendship and honor, an expression of psadeq.

As he was extricating a candidate for one of the handles, the stack of wood leaning against the wall slid to the floor with a crash.

"Are you all right?" Vordar had poked his head into the storeroom. It seemed to Paca that he was looking for an excuse to intrude.

Paca looked up and shook his head. "I have never understood why my father has not come up with a better system for storing all this."

"Maybe you should. You're in charge now, right?" Vordar winked.

"Sure, maybe I should do it today," he said sarcastically.

"No, she's coming today, don't you remember?"

"I guess so...."

"Have you decided what you are going to do?"

"I think so...." Paca left Vordar hanging. They stared at each other for a long moment.

"Well?"

"I am leaving the finality of the decision to the moment. I feel I will know whether it is right or not then, not now; but in the now, it seems on the edge of inevitable."

"Okay...well, if you don't need any help, I have an appointment with a fire." Vordar smiled. Paca took comfort in his acceptance and reassurance and went back to stacking the wood as Vordar vanished from the doorway.

The real wrestling was more about the conditions under which this task would be carried out. The cost was not meaningless, but close to it.

How would he achieve this without his father knowing, or anyone else for that matter? What conditions would he put on the use of the swords? How could he make it clear to the princess that there would be no others after the two? How could he be sure that once he made the swords, his father would indeed be released?

Paca carried the four handle blanks out into the corner of the shop where the woodwork and handling was done. He knew it would take the better part of the day to prepare the handles. The balance and fairness of each was critical to the effectiveness of the tool in the hands of the harvester. He knew this all too well. He also knew that it would take a critical level of concentration to achieve it and was not sure he could gain that focus today.

The princess burned in his mind. It was not the silly attraction he had felt for women he had met on other occasions, but a curiously clear relationship of pure friendship that seemed timeless, not based on how long they had known each other, but simply that they *did* know each other. He had had only one other friend like this, Jarish, the baker's son, whom he had met at the first winter festival he attended. The two had become fast friends. They had much in common and they spent hours together through the years. They could tell each other anything, say anything, share anything. There was never an agenda with Jarish; the only important thing was being together. When they were apart, there was no fear and no anxiety, no matter how long the separation was. When they did find themselves together again, it was as if they had never been apart. His father had used the word "cymbic" to describe his friendship with Jarish. Paca thought he understood what it meant, but probably could not define it or even describe it very well. The best words he had for it were "comfortable" and "easy."

The drawknife was dull. He would have to sharpen it before he could begin. Where were the stones? There was a place for them in the small box at the end of the bench, but they were not there. Paca hated looking for mislaid tools.

The princess made him feel comfortable and easy, in spite of the vast social gulf that separated them. She did not seem to look down on him, and he sensed no desire in her to use her position to control his affairs. Even the pressure from her to make her father's sword did not seem to emanate from her position, but from her friendship, and although it seemed very demanding, it did not make him anxious. He felt more like he owed it to her as a friend, yet he did not feel he owed her anything at all.

He was wandering about the smithy looking for one of the sharpening stones when she appeared at the door. He had still not firmly made the decision about what to do. She was alone again. This time as she entered, she walked directly up to him and gave him a brief hug. Paca was surprised and not surprised at the same time. It actually seemed right. Vordar started with his whistling, and Paritan dropped a pair of tongs into his empty iron slacktub. The princess took no notice of either.

"Shall we go for a walk?" he asked.

She smiled comfortably. "Sure."

As they walked down the road, they chatted aimlessly about small things: the day, the perfect weather for the harvest, the affairs of the castle and the business of the smithy. Then came the inevitable pause. "So, what do you think?" the princess began.

"I have decided to make your father's sword, but I don't know why exactly."

Vrengnia listened when she could have said something to give him some indication that she heard him. Paca liked the silence.

"It's a matter of trust," he continued. "I don't know you very well, but I feel like I have known you forever. I have no basis on which to trust you or the things you have told me. I have suspicions that I am being manipulated—" Paca was sure that the princess would rush to her own defense. It was reassuring that she did not. "So I have decided to trust you and I will make the sword."

"Thank you." He knew she was looking at him. He was not ready to look back so he stared out to the horizon as they continued walking.

"There are some details...."

Vrengnia listened through the pause.

"I demand freedom to make the sword as I want it, by my will and design...."

She waited before she spoke. "Why would I ask anything else? It is your craft, not mine."

"You must not give the sword to your father until his birthday, and no one else must know that I am doing this." He wanted to add, "Is that clear?" but it seemed superfluous. "When I am done, there will be no more weapons to follow it. I am doing this to secure the release of my father and as a favor for you...out of friendship. Give me your word you will not offend me by asking that I do any more."

"You have my word." They walked on in silence. Paca knew that any restatement of anything already said would be distasteful.

"How will I pay you?"

"Hmmm...you know, I hadn't even thought about that. Perhaps it would be best if I just did the work. Do you feel comfortable deciding what you think it is worth to you when you see it?"

"Fair enough. I think you will be well enough paid."

"I am less concerned about the money than the eventual use of the sword," he ventured, still staring at the horizon. "That is what makes me afraid. And I am troubled by the promise I made to my father—"

"So am I. I mean with my father. However, it is a risk I will take for the greater good." She paused and looked at him again. He looked back as she continued: "To be honest, I do not know why I think this is good. Perhaps it is our friendship. I'm not sure I would have asked anyone else. I feel bad for your father, and resentful of my father for imprisoning him, but I have thought long and this path seems right. Perhaps we will look back someday and understand the significance of this decision, but I cannot regret it now."

Paca was encouraged by the clarity with which she explained things he was feeling but could not verbalize. She was "his friend and no more," as his father had said, and the friendship was genuine. What he feared was that he and Vrengnia, although wanting the best for both their fathers, were missing something that their fathers would have had them know.

She gave him another brief hug when she departed. It left him with an unusual sense of closure on the discussions of the day.

12

*When earnest beings speak, one may be
right, another may find he is wrong, but
all will learn something.*

Mortag of Horrinaine
Of Beings

T HE KING SAT ON A SMALL STOOL OPPOSITE THE SMITH. THEY WERE TALKING in the prison smithy over a simple but hearty lunch prepared by his personal chef. He was pleased. "Why did you decide to start smithing after all?"

The smith finished chewing on the bread he had in his mouth before answering. "There are a few things that I have to make."

"*Have* to make?" Sandihar found the smith's answer peculiar. Bits of shaped iron lay about on the table: simple in form, elegant, obviously the work of a skilled man, but obscure in purpose. The smith had started the forge for the first time only the day before, the fourteenth day after his arrest, despite the crude arrangement and supplies.

"I am a smith, good King. Sometimes I *have* to smith."

"But it sounded like there was something specific you have to make."

"Indeed!"

Sandihar had spent several lunches with his prisoner and was beginning to understand the way the smith sidestepped direct questions. He had the sense it was about to happen again. "Can you tell me what it is you are trying to make?"

"If I could, I would, but I don't know myself."

The king was suspicious. "Surely, you sport with me."

"No, I don't, good King. Have you ever had the feeling that you knew something that there was no way of knowing, but just the same, you knew it?"

"On occasion, but I never let it bother me. Such suspicions are as likely as not to deter real progress and knowledge."

"Hmmmm."

"What does that have to do with what you are making here in the smithy?"

"Well, I have learned over the years that it is possible and useful to listen to the things you may know-without-knowing. The more one listens, the more he hears, and the more he hears, the more certain he becomes. With practice one becomes sure of what one knows without seeing it."

"And…?"

"I know that I am supposed to be making something, but I don't know what. Part of my listening is to start working. At the right time it will become clear, and I will know what I am supposed to do."

Sandihar could not decide whether the smith might be mocking him. None of it made sense, but the smith himself seemed sure of what he was saying. The king watched him wipe his bowl with a piece of bread. It was a good time to change the direction of the conversation.

"My daughter has been to see your son," he announced suddenly. "Several times, I have heard—"

The smith looked up and smiled. "I expected that."

"You did?"

"Of course. They are primary cymbics," said the smith matter-of-factly.

Having meant to surprise the smith, the king himself was the one surprised. "How do you know?"

"I saw it in their eyes the first time—no, the second time you entered the smithy with her. They have been friends since birth, waiting to find one another."

"Hmmmm," grunted the king. The smith's confidence was irritating.

"In fact," continued the smith, "their friendship will serve as the resolution to our little impasse." The smith was wiping the last bit of stew out of the bowl with the last of his bread crust.

"Really," the king scoffed. "And how will that happen?"

"We don't know specifically and it doesn't matter that we don't, but this is the way with primary cymbics. Their trust and acceptance allows them to get past many obstacles that constrain others—they often find a path through."

The king's eyes darkened. A burgeoning suspicion that the smith must know something he did not about this situation made him uneasy. In fact, everything the smith said made it worse. Just by looking at him, the smith made him feel as if he were reading his mind.

"Come now, good King, you are acting like I know something I don't. You know that you have kept me cloistered here in your tower, that no man has spoken to me about what is going on out there." He gestured toward the southern window. "So I know nothing specific—but I know cymbics, and I have great confidence that all this will work out for the best, even though at first, it may seem to be wrong."

"What if they are plotting something?"

"What if they are? What are you going to do? You cannot break a cymbic connection, particularly in the primary sphere! Do you trust your daughter?"

"Do you trust your son?" retorted the king.

The smith paused, chewing the carrot he had just put in his mouth. The king waited impatiently. "I trust his love for me and his interest in my welfare. I trust his mastery of smithing, his ability and intuition. I am not sure I trust his judgment. I see this...situation as the time and the place where he must learn judgment for himself. After all, I *am* unavailable, am I not?"

Sandihar was not sure the smith actually wanted an answer, so he remained silent.

"A wiser man than I once said," continued the smith, "that 'good judgment comes from experience; and where does experience come from? From bad judgment.' Therefore, I see no reason to be alarmed. In the end, both your daughter and my son will be more of what we want them to be."

The king had come to respect the smith immensely, but found it a hard thing to learn basic lessons about life from his prisoner. "I have the same trust for my daughter," he conceded. "She will be a great queen some day, but she does not seem to be in much of a hurry to develop the character that she needs to reach that goal. I try to be patient, but it is most difficult at times."

"How old were you, when you became everything your mother wanted you to be?" queried the smith.

The king was silent for a moment, reflecting on his own life and the mistakes he had made, the errors in judgment and the experiences that had shaped his better judgment. He felt his vorn soften inside. "Your wisdom is fair and good," he said at last. "Do you think it is best not to interfere with this liaison between your son and my daughter?" he asked.

"I think it would be good to let her know you know, but not to interfere. She needs your trust now more than she needs your advice."

The king knew he was right. Only time would prove it, but somehow, he knew. He rose and extended his hand to the smith. "Thank you for your time—again," *Why am I thanking the smith?* "I am sure that you have things to do."

The smith rose and firmly grasped the king's hand, looking directly into his eyes. "It is always a pleasure."

Sandihar departed the prison smithy without looking back. He heard the guards close the door behind him and throw the bolt. He felt like he always did after a discussion with the smith: full, refreshed, inadequate... he couldn't find the word he needed to describe it. Maybe he didn't even have one.

13

By fire, by will, by strength of mind,
With focused blows, sure and full,
   not one errant,
Each delivered as the smith means.
By this is the ordinary transformed
Into the extraordinary,
Where it stands before the eyes of the king.

                            Timmanaeus

I START TONIGHT," PACA SAID IN RESPONSE TO VORDAR'S QUESTION ABOUT HIS task for the princess. Paca could tell that Vordar was consummately curious but respected him enough to ask no further. "I am not sure what will happen—I'm not even sure I will be able to do what I am being asked, but I know I will need your help. I expect a few long nights."

Vordar nodded and smiled. Paca knew he understood and could carry the load of the work that needed to be done when Paca was not there.

Paca found a new energy in making the swords for the princess. That night he stayed in the smithy after the other smiths had gone. It was challenging working the fire by himself and holding his own work while he welded the layers of steel and iron. It was certainly more diffi-cult working by the light of the lanterns than in daylight, meager as it was in the dimly lit smithy.

The aloneness also fostered a fierce concentration, a focus on the process that could not be had in the busy day's activities. He sang the forge poetry to himself out loud, without the self-consciousness he felt in the presence of the other smiths.

He worked each night until his eyes watered and would not stay open. When he left the smithy for the short walk to his small house, the street lamps had been extinguished, and the rest of the town was fast asleep. Each morning he rose early, arriving at the smithy before anyone else to examine the progress of his work in the daylight.

The days were filled with the tasks of running the smithy and producing the blades on order for other purposes. The routine was grueling, but the peculiar thrill of making the swords kept him pressing forward.

The princess came frequently now, nearly every day. She never asked about her father's sword and Paca never volunteered. They both seemed to understand that when the time came, they would speak about it. She brought food from the king's kitchen—none of the fancy delicacies that were the fare of the king and the advisors—but rich dark bread and hearty stews. There was not a lot of it, but just enough for Paca's dinner. Did she know he worked at night? He was not sure. He never asked.

"I remember the second day that I came here with my father," she said during one of these visits. "Your father was singing something when we interrupted him. What was it?"

"He was singing forge poetry."

"Forge poetry?"

"Yes." Paca looked up from the blade he was straightening on the bench to see Vrengnia's inquiring eyes. She was expecting more and he knew it. "It is a poetry that helps the smith who uses it to know his way. It's a map of sorts—no, more like a path."

"Where did it come from? I mean, did someone write it?"

"No, it is not written anywhere, I don't think. I believe it was Timmanaeus who first spoke it."

"Timmanaeus..." She said it like a statement, as if she were searching deep in her memory for a long forgotten piece of history.

"Timmanaeus was the greatest of all smiths, perhaps more of a legend than a real being. He lived among the Great Fathers. It is said that he learned smithing from the Eladra, that they gave it to him as a gift, for him to give to Tessalindria. Though others had tried working the metal, it was Timmanaeus who brought it forth as a viable trade and art."

"And he was the first to sing the forge poetry?"

"So it is said. I learned it from my father, and my father learned it from his. That's as far back as I know."

"I've never heard of it before."

"Not all smiths use it or even know it. Blacksmithing as a trade can be learned and passed on without it. My father insists, however, that one cannot master the smith's art without it."

"And you?"

"I...I'm not sure. When my father sings it, he changes, and the energy of his work increases...his focus, his precision...it's hard to describe."

"But that does not happen to you?"

"No, but the poetry helps me to concentrate and remember the steps." Paca bent to the task before him. The blade had warped slightly in the quench, and now that it had been tempered, it needed a precise series of blows from his straightening mallet to make it true. It was not a trivial task. Vrengnia sat still as if she suddenly knew that he needed to focus. Paca could feel her presence. It was not the uncomfortable intrusive hovering of someone watching over his shoulder, but one of patient appreciation. As he applied the first blows of the heavy wooden mallet, he marveled at how simple and clear it all seemed.

✠

There were few interruptions in the smithy late at night, so the work on the swords progressed rapidly. The initial stages of preparing the blade steel were no different than for any other knife, except for the quantity of it. The sword had to be a good deal longer than most common tool blades, except those of the great scythes used in the harvests, which he had never made.

The roar of the forge fire drawing breath from the great double-chambered bellows, along with the aloneness of the night smithy, engendered a queerness, a sense not of disproportion, but of a trueness which he had never before achieved. He sang the poetry of the firebed, and the fire obeyed his song. He sang the verses about welding, drawing and folding, and the glowing malleable steel obeyed the touch of the hammer without hesitation.

Paca felt his strength well up from deep inside, from a reserve he did not remember tapping before. His grip was sure and the tongs never lost their hold on the work. He found yet another new strength in imagining his father beside him at the forge, guiding him, encouraging him. Even in his utter solitude, he did not feel fully alone.

He could feel his strength and awareness growing, but it was on the sixth night, as he was drawing out the blades to their final length, that the sudden and sublime transformation occurred. He had the king's blade laid in the long, narrow fire as he worked the bellows, envisioning the hammer strokes for the next heat, when a gust of wind burst open the door of the smithy and blew out the lantern between the door and the forge. It backdrafted the chimney, blowing coal smoke and ash back across the forge bed. Paca had seen a backdraft before, but never quite like this. The hot smoke seared his face, and he stepped back reflexively, dropping the bellows toggle and shielding his eyes with his arm.

He tried to blink away the pain, uncovering his eyes as soon as he could see and quickly scanning the smithy through his tears to see if an errant coal or ash had landed where it could start a fire. A quiet uneasiness crept into his mind. Something was different. He re-lit the lantern, secured the smithy door against the night, and headed back to the forge. Without the bellows breath, the fire had cooled to red; and the sword still lay there, a black silhouette floating on the glow. He took hold of the bellows toggle and the fire was soon roaring again.

He waited patiently for the sword to come up to heat. It was taking longer than usual, so he worked the bellows harder and raked a few coals over the top of the blade. He had removed the clinker from the bottom of the fire only fifteen minutes before, and it roared like dragon's breath. But the blade remained black.

An echo of some unsaid phrase floated through his mind. *Sing—sing.* He opened his mouth to sing to the blade, to the fire, but he could not remember any words and no sound came forth. *Sing—sing the song of the sword,* his mind shouted. He opened his mouth again and a song burst forth:

"Argen tyven wi ri kiren
Kara toum a para kaant
Mira, Mira vola torren
Kenta kuolo viri paant."

The blade flashed as its blackness yielded suddenly to the bright orange of a forging heat. He dropped the bellows toggle and snatched the blade from the fire and stood trembling, the tongs gripped tightly in both hands and the sword quivering in the air above the forge bed.

Paca's mind reeled. He did not recognize the words. They were in a language he had never heard before, but he knew what they meant. Roughly translated they said:

"Put the blade over a deep fire,
The bellows steady and low.
Keep turning it over the embers
Until it resembles the sunset."

He stood transfixed as the blade began to cool. He dropped it back in the fire, his mind still racing. The words tumbled and turned, and the strange language receded, slowly being replaced by words from his own language:

"Lay the blade in fire deep.
Work the bellows firm, but low.
Turn it, turn it; let it steep,
'Til it takes the sunset's glow."

He recited the new words again and again, burning them into his memory as the original faded from his consciousness. He added music to it as he did so. He sang out, his voice strong and confident. He was sure he had never heard these words before. It was new poetry, strong and deep, welling up from an unknown source. It stirred his intuition; it stirred his vorn. He kept the breath of the forge steady, turning the blade slowly, over and over until it glowed like the sunset. He pulled it from the fire and laid it on the anvil. Suddenly, more new words flowed from the spring deep within him. He raised the sledge and began confidently hammering out the sword before him.

✠

The prisoner sat upright suddenly on his cot in the tower. For six nights now he had been able to hear the distant ring of an anvil late into the night. He knew anvils by their ring. He knew all the anvils in Immerland, who they belonged to and who was working them by their sound. As a blind man reads the footsteps of an approaching friend, so the smith knew that his son was working on *his* anvil late into the nights. No one else in the castle heard it except the smith. Each night he lay awake until the ringing stopped; then he would drift off to sleep.

Tonight there was a new sound. It was the sound of a voice long forgotten, suddenly stirring in his mind. At least he thought he had heard a voice. He listened intently, feeling the deep silence until the singing started again. It was a new voice, or perhaps one so old that he thought it might be new. He ran to the south wall of the tower chamber and threw open the window. Through the bars he could see the moonless night sky, brilliant with stars. Everything was in darkness and all but the voice was very still. Far away in Shiloh, there was one speck of light. He stared at it and it seemed to disappear. He looked a little to the side and he could just see it, far away and very small. He listened. The voice sang again. He gripped the bars for balance as from somewhere deep inside a voice rose to his throat. He began to sing:

> *"Waha olen ir con fira malen*
> *Winda ha o'la se vrama boren*
> *Korla hama, Korla vorna,*
> *Korla vinda hama sinden…"*

His voice swelled and resonated in the prison chambers. Unconstrainable, it flowed out the window and rolled down over the dark castle. It continued unwavering, lilting and somber at the same time.

The smith held onto the bars and sang as if, were he to let go, he would collapse from the weight of the song itself. He alone knew what was happening, and there in the dark stone chamber, he yielded himself to it.

14

Of all the curious and divergent capabilities of the beings of our world, the strangest of all would have to be the ability, without any previous exposure, to comprehend the original language.

Mortag of Horrinaine
Of Beings

THE KING ROLLED OVER IN HIS BED, OPENED ONE EYE, AND BOLTED UP. THE last watch had been at midnight, but what was this? A voice, a strong voice, was singing, flooding the castle with its haunting melody. It rose and fell like wind rushing through a forest, or like a waterfall—

"Lights!" Sandihar shouted into the darkness. Two attendants rushed in with torches and started lighting the lamps around the room. "What is happening?" he snapped.

The attendants flushed. "It started about ten minutes ago, Sire," one of them ventured. "We think it's coming from the South Tower, but everywhere we go, it seems to be coming from somewhere else."

"Guards!" he yelled. "Advisors!" He dressed hurriedly as he ran to the large window overlooking the castle courtyard and threw it open. Everything was black, except for the stars and a few other lights in the lower castle. He looked toward the South Tower. It was completely dark. The singing came from everywhere. All the walls resonated with the timbre of the voice; it filled the whole courtyard. It was deep and strong, light and melodious, sad, but full of conviction and power. He could hear the words distinctly, but recognized none of them.

The princess burst into his chambers, followed by Omberon, a second guard, Carnados, Cordas and Mindar. "What's happening, Father?" She showed her distress as she ran to him. Carnados and Cordas looked grave. Mindar was frightened. Omberon's brow was furrowed deep, his black eyes darker than usual, and his mouth in that perpetual sneer.

"I am not sure." Even as he answered his daughter's question, he looked wonderingly at the advisors.

Carnados bowed and took a step toward him. "By your leave," he started, "it seems that the prisoner is a taralang." He bowed again and stepped back.

The king felt his face flush red with anger. "Impossible! We have not had a taralang in Immerland since before my mother's time."

Carnados bowed his head, as if he did not want to look at him. "Well, we seem to have one now—and he is in the South Tower prison!"

The king understood better than he wanted to. "What is he saying?"

"He is singing in the original language. I did not hear it from the beginning, but the song is a great story about war and sorrow, of horror and fear, of bloodshed upon bloodshed. In places he is singing poetry about his forge—he is a smith after all."

"I know that!" snapped the king. He strode to the window again. "Who else can understand what he is saying?" An uncomfortable silence followed his question.

"I can," whispered the princess.

"So can I." Sandihar recognized the dark gravelly voice of Omberon.

He whirled to face his advisors, choosing to ignore his daughter and the captain for the moment. "Who else?" he demanded.

Carnados looked up at him. "We are not sure, Your Majesty. Supposedly, many still understand the original language, though only the taralangs speak it. Some animals understand it also, strange as that may be. Many believe it has to do with purity and simplicity of one's vorn, but most learned men consider this to be conjecture."

"Father, what is the 'original language'?" his daughter asked.

He shrugged, waving a hand in deference to Carnados.

"The original language, child, is the language that Mah'Eladra themselves gave to our world. All our beings used it at some time, but as the corruption of the vorn slowly gripped the world, people started making their own languages instead—out of pride—to separate themselves from others. They used them as tools to rule over other tribes and nations, to enslave the animals and to enslave one another. Eventually, they abandoned the original language altogether in favor of their own inferior inventions. They stopped talking to the animals and the animals stopped talking back. At certain times, the taralangs appear. Using the original language, they sing to those who can still understand it."

Sandihar felt the anger seething inside him. Why could he not understand but his daughter could? Why Omberon? Why was he, the king, left out of this? "What should be done?" he asked angrily, still leaning on the windowsill.

"Nothing can be done right now, Your Majesty," Carnados said gravely. "He must finish his song. However, in the morning, I would set this man free. It would not be wise to keep him in your prison."

The king turned to stare out the window. The sonorous voice rolled on, filling everything: gentle and strong, rising, falling, completely unintelligible to him. Everyone in the room fell silent.

After several long minutes, he sighed and turned back to face the small group. "We will let this taralang finish his song. Send word throughout the castle that no one should be alarmed. Those who understand should try to capture as much of what is being said as possible. Everyone else go to bed. We will make necessary decisions in the morning—" They all hesitated. Omberon's scowl had deepened, and Sandihar knew he wanted to say something, but as captain of the guard, did not speak unless addressed by the king.

"Omberon, you seem troubled."

"May I speak freely, Sire?"

"You may, Captain."

"The prisoner must be silenced, Sire."

Carnados's face fell. "Silence a taralang? Why, that—" He was cut short by a wave of the king's hand.

"I would like to hear my captain's view of this affair," the king said. "Why must he be silenced, Captain?"

"The song of the taralang is treasonous, Sire." Sandihar wondered why that rough voice grated on him so much. It seemed almost otherworldly sometimes, as if it did not belong on Tessalindria.

"Treasonous? In what way?"

"I would speak with you privately, Sire."

Sandihar suddenly felt very tired. He also wanted to hear the rest of the song, still cascading over the castle. "We will hear the taralang out, and we will speak in the morning."

Carnados spoke cautiously. "Sire, there are many strong images being sung here, but there is no treason in them." The king looked at him. Was it fear in his eyes? Betrayal? Defensiveness? He had never seen that look on Carnados's face. He looked around. The scene before him was too surreal to comprehend.

"Begone with you! All of you," he stormed. "We will discuss this in the morning!"

The guards and advisors moved at once. Vrengnia stayed until everyone else had gone. "I wish to stay here with you, Father," she said quietly.

He felt the tears well up in his eyes as he turned to face his daughter. "I would like that," he whispered hoarsely.

The mountain man, on a mountain horse,
is to be feared and respected.

Old Immerland Saying

STAND STILL!" COMMANDED THE LEAD HORSEMAN IN AN URGENT WHISPER. The rider following him stopped his horse. They were riding together along the ridge trail through the mountains on the southern border of Immerland. "Keep the horses quiet and wait here," the leader whispered. He dismounted silently, sprinting up the trail to a turn where a large pine tree rose above the others on the crest of the hill. With the grace of a cat, he climbed to a clearing in the branches near the top. The night sky was spangled with stars, but the countryside was dark, save for several points of light in the castle, far to the north.

Everything was silent. He held his breath, waiting in the darkness. He did this several times until at last he caught the sound he had been listening for: the ring of an anvil and a faint but firm voice. At this distance, he should not have been able to hear the sounds, but such is the nature of the original language. Such is the nature of the forge poetry to a smith. From the sound of the anvil, he knew that it belonged to the smith at Shiloh Forge. Listening intently, he strained to hear what was happening. After about fifteen minutes, he made his way down the tree into the darkness of the forest and sprinted back to the horses. "There is mischief at Shiloh Forge!" he exclaimed as he leapt onto his horse.

"What is it, Father?" the second horseman said as he mounted. They started back along the trail.

"I am not sure, but it sounds like someone is singing sword poetry. It is *not* the smith—the beat is wrong—but it's *his* hammer—on *his* anvil. We must find out what is happening."

16

It seems to come from within. It rises from the belly and bursts upon the lips, as if it is carried within you. It is, however, the gift of the Eladra.

Timmanaeus

PACA WAS ENERGIZED BY THE NEW POETRY THAT CONTINUED TO WELL UP inside him as he worked the swords deep into the night, each step bringing new verses into his mind and his voice. His thoughts focused them into the two blades. Each hammer stroke was new, each heat was different, and each placement on the anvil was unique. This poetry was very strong. He had little time to think about it, but in the back of his mind, he knew that it was the poetry for making swords and it was leading him along a path he had never traveled before.

At times, clairvoyant visions that accompanied the poetry burst upon him; bright, intense scenes of slaughter and carnage unfolded before his mind's eye. Fear tore through his mind, but to escape it seemed futile, so he worked on feverishly. His hammer hand froze, cramped onto the hammer while his tongs hand, gripping the blades like a vise, ached to his shoulder. He sweat profusely as the forge poured its heat into the blades. Exhaustion crept through him like a winter chill, but he pressed on relentlessly into the night.

As dawn broke, he finished forging the blades. Exhausted, but still driven by the fury of this peculiar night, he wrapped the blades in his apron, grabbed three files, and headed home before the first cock crowed in Shiloh. He stowed his secret under his bed and collapsed into a fitful sleep.

The presence of evil does often go unnoticed by those who refuse to acknowledge that it is not simply a void in the goodness; it is a presence all its own.

The Tessarandin, Book 12

MORNING BROKE IN IMMERLAND DARK AND WET. THE KING WOKE FROM HIS sleep at the first glimmer of gray. As he stretched, he noticed that he had inadvertently left one of his windows open the night before. He crossed the cold stone floor to close it. Looking out, he could barely see the lamps in the courtyard below, lit as the castle workers began their morning chores. Muffled sounds of their progress rose out of the fog that hid them from his view. A gentle, light rain fell on the windowsill from the wet sky that smelled of the sea and seemed to cling to his nightshirt, making it feel heavy and cold on his shoulders. He shuddered as he quietly closed the window against the dampness.

He had not slept well. He remembered the singing and remembered only vaguely when it had stopped. Vrengnia was fast asleep on the couch where she had chosen to stay the night, breathing peacefully under a quilt she had found in the wardrobe.

For her sake, he did not call for his attendants, but dressed himself quietly and slipped out of his chambers. He made his way toward the South Tower. The only sound along his short journey was that of the rain spattering on the windows of the hallway as he passed them. He wondered if the taralang and his singing could have brought on this cheerless morning. The mood it set seemed to match the darkness that had crept into his vorn. What had happened last night to trigger this event?

As he came around the corner of the corridor leading to the tower, he startled the guards at the foot of the stairs to the tower. They snapped to attention. "Omberon?" The king was surprised to see the captain of the guard there.

"At your service, Sire."

"I didn't expect that you would be here. Is there any trouble?"

"Only that which occurred last night."

The king sensed that Omberon held his tongue but would say more if bidden. It often seemed that way with the captain.

"The smith. He is still in his room?"

"Yes."

Sandihar looked at the other two guards for any hint that something else might be wrong. They looked scared. Undoubtedly, they had never heard a taralang. "Come on, I want to have a look—and a listen," he added as he slipped off his sandals, motioning to the guards to do the same. He looked at Omberon. That brooding I-want-to-say-more look clouded his dark eyes. The king looked away, motioning deliberately for the captain and his guards to follow him.

They padded quietly up the stairs to the smith's room. Everything was silent. *The smith must still be asleep,* thought the king. He motioned to the guards, and they followed him down the stairs to where they had left their footwear. As they knelt to help the king into his footwear, he looked at them. They were furtive and fearful. "What do you think happened last night?" he asked. He directed his question to the two guards, deliberately leaving Omberon out of the question.

They glanced at each other. "We are not sure," one of them said cautiously.

"Well, what did you see?"

"Nothing."

"Did you hear anything?"

"Yes, Sire, we heard a voice—singing in the castle somewhere."

"Somewhere?"

"Yes, Sire, but it was hard to tell where—it just was there."

"Did you understand what the voice was saying?"

The guards shifted and looked at each other again. "I understood a little bit of it," said the one on the right, "but I wouldn't say I knew what it all meant."

The other guard looked at the floor. "I didn't understand it at all," he said sullenly.

The king nodded and stood up. "Dismiss these men for the day, Captain," he said to Omberon. To them, he said gently, "Get some sleep."

They hesitated, looking at Omberon. He waved them on. He only had to do it once.

The king waited patiently, looking down at his feet until the sound of the guards faded away down the dimly lit, moist hallway. He felt Omberon brooding. He felt him staring, waiting for his king to allow him to speak his mind. Sandihar was not sure he wanted to hear it, but knew he would have to allow it. "What is it, Captain?" he said, looking up into the other man's dark face.

"May I speak freely, Sire?"

Why did he always ask that? "Of course, as always," said the king, pointedly. When he asked a man to speak, he expected nothing less than it be free.

"It is good, Sire, that you have imprisoned this man." Omberon leaned closer to the king, and his voice became strangely smooth. His closeness made Sandihar feel crowded and uncomfortable, but he held his ground. "If he is indeed a taralang, then it is wise to keep him here, for history has shown that the taralangs have always spoken against the rulers of a country."

"That is an odd way of putting it, Captain. My understanding of history is that they have always spoken when there was a need for change. Your words imply that change is always bad for kings and rulers."

"Well, Sire, when subjects of kings want change, there are usually serious repercussions against the kings themselves. You know that the lower classes do not have the capacity to separate the need for change from the one whom they understand to have created the situations they live in."

The king felt the touch of scorn in Omberon's smile. "You mistake yourself," he responded warily. "I have a higher regard for my subjects than that."

"You said I may speak freely, Sire. It is always the notion of kings that their minions love them. 'Tolerate' is probably more accurate. Search deep in history and make sure you are not deceived."

Sandihar respected Omberon, but underlying his words, the king sensed an agenda that extended beyond the welfare of Immerland. "How will keeping the taralang imprisoned stop him from singing? He was in prison last night, and the whole castle—and maybe even others—heard him."

"He must not be allowed to sing."

Omberon's imperious tone jarred the king; he suddenly wanted no more from the captain. Suspicious now of Omberon's motives, he knew he had to maneuver cautiously until he understood the captain's true purpose. "I will consider your suggestion, Captain."

Omberon bowed stiffly. "You will find it best, Sire," he said confidently.

"Perhaps so. You are dismissed."

Omberon hesitated.

"Is there something else, Captain?"

"By your leave, Sire, am I to post no guard on the prisoner?"

"Is the bolt secure on the smith's room?"

"Yes, Sire."

"Then he will require no guard today."

Omberon's eyes narrowed, but he saluted smartly.

"Thank you for your advice, Captain." The king strode off toward his chambers without looking back.

18

Three little wise men,
Attendants to the king,
He often called these three wise men,
And made them dance and sing.

Old Tessamandrian Rhyme

CARNADOS HUDDLED WITH MINDAR AND CORDAS IN THE KITCHEN, TAKING refuge from the cold, damp morning air with mugs of hot spiced tea, at a table most agreeably situated near the fire. They were having a hushed but spirited conversation about the events of the night before and what they would say to the king.

"We should have guessed," said Carnados. "I mean—look at the evidence. From the moment he set foot here, anyone could see the smith is obviously different. No one could stand up to the king as he has and keep his composure under such circumstances. He has been in control since the day he was taken. Of course, the king thought *he* was in control."

"Do you think the king will free him?" asked Mindar.

Carnados stroked his beard. "I think he *should* free him—but he probably won't." The others eyed him quizzically. "I don't believe the king understands what is going on. He is also a stubborn man some-times, as you know, and this is just the sort of thing he will continue to be stubborn about." They fell silent, brooding over their tea.

Mindar broke the silence: "What, exactly, is the role of the taralangs? I mean, who are they? What are they for?"

Carnados knew that one of his strengths was bringing clarity out of detail. "No one knows for sure. They are usually from the working class of the people, though sometimes not—the Great Queen is believed to have been a taralang, but it was never confirmed. She was so strong and directed; perhaps she never needed to reveal herself. They live ordinary lives, although they are not usually very ordinary people. When there is great need among the people, they reveal themselves—almost involuntarily, it seems. It is believed that their use of the original language draws together the strength necessary to face whatever is threatening. The threat is often obscure, to be revealed only in time—in hindsight it becomes very clear." He paused, staring into his tea and swirling it gently.

"So we just have to wait?" queried Mindar, a small irritation breaking through in his voice.

"Yes, we must simply wait," said Carnados, "unless…unless you have some clarity on this subject that I don't." He eyed the younger man keenly.

Mindar dropped his eyes, took a sip of the tea, and said, "No, I don't."

Cordas spoke for the first time. "There was one thing, though it's only indirectly related."

"What was that?" asked Carnados

"It seemed to me that Omberon took an unusually keen interest in what was happening."

"I didn't notice—" Carnados let his phrase hang to encourage Cordas to elaborate.

"First of all, he understood what was being said…."

"So did the princess—and you and I, as well."

"But the look on his face was different. You and the princess seemed to be hearing it and enjoying it. Omberon looked afraid. He always looks so smug and leering; but not then. It was as if he had seen a NarEladrim warrior."

"Hmmmm. That I did *not* notice."

Several minutes of silence followed. Carnados was absorbed in his own thoughts, his own fears and his own questions. It was during this reverie that the king appeared. His voice startled them, "Just the men I needed to see!" He had come looking for them without a summons, and Carnados found it strange to see him in the kitchen. The kitchen help were flustered.

Carnados rose to the occasion. "Sit with us, good King," he entreated. As the king sat down heavily on the fourth stool at the table, Carnados called, "Tea for the king!" sending several workers scurrying to the task. Carnados turned again to Sandihar. "It was an interesting night, was it not?" He did not forget that he addressed the king, but Carnados had known him from birth, so his familiar demeanor was not out of place at times like this.

"'Interesting' might be the right word; 'alarming' might be better. Tell me, each of you in turn. What should I do—and why?"

The three men shifted uneasily. A servant approached; Carnados waited until the servant had placed the mug of tea gracefully in front of the king and left. He leaned forward, "By your leave, Sire, you must certainly set this man free. There is something that he is supposed to do, and he must be free to do it. It is the way of the taralangs. You must set aside your differences with the smith and allow him to go back to his service at Shiloh Forge." He stopped and settled back on his stool.

"Hmmmm," rumbled the king thoughtfully as he turned his gaze to Cordas.

Cordas opened his mouth to speak and then stopped.

The king sipped his tea and gently set down the mug. "Well?"

"By your leave, Sire, I think you should ask the smith what he wants, what it is that he should be doing. Perhaps he thinks he should be in prison for some reason; maybe there is something going on that we do not understand—"

Carnados heard the king chuckle. He saw the quick, amused smile.

"I'm serious," continued Cordas earnestly. "If anyone knows what this means, it is probably the smith. After all, if he is a taralang and if he is as powerful as it is believed he should be in that role, why has he not left the prison himself? Do you think your prison could hold him? I mean, you never actually arrested him. He came along without shackles; he rode his own horse to the castle gate; he has never complained and has never tried to escape. Is he really our prisoner? Perhaps we are his."

Now it was the king's turn to shift uneasily. His eyes narrowed and he tapped his finger on the tea mug. "Well said, Cordas, well said." He turned his eyes to the youngest.

"I think we should wait!" Mindar said.

The king studied him. When it became clear that no more was forthcoming, the king leaned forward and said with a twinkle in his eye, "Just wait?—wait for what?"

Mindar looked for support to Carnados and then Cordas. He stared into his tea for a moment, then looked back to the king and held his ground. "By your leave, we should wait. We may not know what we are waiting for, but this is the way with taralangs. *He* may not even know what he is waiting for. For the good of the kingdom—for Immerland— we must wait and see what needs to happen." He looked up into Carnados's eyes. "Isn't that what you were saying only moments ago?"

Carnados could feel Mindar's stare, begging his support as the king turned toward him expectantly. Carnados thought for a moment and studied the king's face, pondering the appropriate response.

He was still arranging his next statement when the king slapped the table and stood up. The noise and the abruptness of it startled him and scattered his thoughts. Raising his mug of tea in a mock toast to his three advisors, Sandihar proclaimed loudly, "Wait we will, then. Wait we will!" Leaning his head back, he drained the mug and brought it down heavily on the table. Without another word, he turned and walked purposefully out of the kitchen.

19

Of acquaintances, we may have many; of close friends, a few. But in the one true friend, with whom the vorn holds no fear, and the mind needs no boundaries, there love is found in its purest and perfect form.

The Tessarandin, Book 4

W HEN SHE WOKE UP, HER FATHER HAD ALREADY LEFT HIS CHAMBERS, AND Vrengnia sensed an urgency to escape the castle without anyone seeing her. She went without breakfast, dressed in the clothes she had worn the day before.

Mahala stamped and snorted when she arrived in the stable. "Ready for a run?" she whispered as she slipped the bridle over his head. He tossed his head and snorted again. "We have to be silent," she added as she cinched his girth. "Silent." She knew he understood. As a retired Cortimane, a trained war horse from Mythinia, Mahala knew many things that ordinary horses did not. One of them was how to be quiet. She led him out through the courtyard to the drawbridge with hardly a sound.

"Going somewhere, Princess?"

The voice startled her and her heart raced as the looming figure emerged from the shadow of the portcullis. It was the suddenness that alarmed her, but not the huge man himself. It was Vishtorath, the gatekeeper. Vrengnia knew him well. "I am going to Shiloh to visit the young smith," she said without reservation.

"Hmmm…"

"I need to speak with him about the singing last night."

"The taralang?"

"How did you know?"

The giant paused, reaching up to stroke her gelding's ears. "I know many things, Princess. You know that." His voice was soft and strong. Vrengnia loved it. It gave credence to the fabulous legends surrounding this singular guardian of her father's gate.

"Mahala wants to run this morning. He will carry you to Shiloh quickly, but stay on the main road."

She had never asked Vishtorath for advice, but he always gave it as if she had. She knew he was sincere and purposeful. His advice was always worth heeding, even when she did not understand it. "I will."

He cupped his hand in a simple gesture to give her a lift into the saddle. She put one foot obediently into his massive palm and he lifted her as a man might lift a cat, as she swung her other leg up and over Mahala's back to find her seat in the saddle. "Please don't tell my father. I think he will worry," she said looking into his kind face.

"Only if I must."

Vrengnia knew he would keep her secret. He had a way of doing that sort of thing. "Thanks." Vishtorath turned his back and disappeared into the shadow of the portcullis.

She urged Mahala across the drawbridge. He *was* ready to run. As they left the bridge, he pulled at the reins and pawed the damp soil of the road until she gave him the go ahead with a gentle tap of her heels.

The off and on rain in the thick fog made for a wet ride, but the water brought out the subtle odors of the fields, and the wind blended them with the smell of the ocean and Mahala's wet body. His strong, confident gait surged beneath her as they galloped toward Shiloh, leaving the castle, her father, his advisors and the taralang far behind in distance and mind.

The gatekeeper burned in her thoughts. He had been the castle guardian ever since she was a child, since she could remember. He was the only gatekeeper the castle had and the only one it needed. He had a reputation for being a one-man army with "eyes that could read a being's vorn through armor."

He seemed to know every detail of every person that walked through the gate, and was thoroughly equipped to handle the toughest of assailants. On one occasion, he had been attacked at the gate by five men seeking entrance to the castle. One of the attackers managed to put a spear clean though his belly. He broke the spear in half with his bare hands and, pulling it out through his back, slew all five with the two pieces of the spear he wielded in both hands. He retired to his small room beside the gate and was back on duty the next morning.

Vishtorath seldom spoke, carrying out his business with silent precision. Most people respected him with a measure of healthy fear. Vrengnia loved him. He spoke with her often as she came and went. He was always interested in her destination, but never seemed to pry, and she always let him know where she was headed. Somehow, she felt his presence with her. It was he who had saved her on that one desperate occasion…he had never even told her father. Neither had she…she did not want to think of it any further.

Before she could see the smithy, she smelled the coal smoke through the fog. It was not a pleasant smell, as odors go, but distinctive, imbued with a sense of hard work and mannish things she liked so well. Breathing deeply, she tied Mahala to the hitching post outside the door and stepped into the shadowed warmth of the shop.

Vrengnia was well known and accepted there, and she looked around without hesitation. The main forge was vacant. She stopped, bewildered, leaning on the great anvil. It was still warm. She looked up to see one of the other smiths watching her. "He sent word that he would be out today."

"Who are you?"

"My name is Vordar, Princess, at your service." He bowed his head before looking up into her eyes.

"Where is he?" she asked. Her uneasiness crackled in her voice.

"Not sure—just not here." Vordar eyed her thoughtfully as he spread scoops of pea sized coal about the top of his forge bed between phrases: "He may be at home sleeping—his fire was just dying when we arrived this morning. It seems he was up all night."

"Where does he live?"

"He lives here," said Vordar with a hint of a smile. "He sleeps and eats in the last house on the right, on the lane leading to the barley fields. It's a small place—you will know it's his."

"How?"

"You'll know."

She was unsure what he meant, but the tone of his voice convinced her that she would find out.

After stopping several villagers and asking directions, Vrengnia found the lane to the barley fields. The last house on the right was indeed small. Designed more as a place to sleep and fix a little food than for living, it was neat and well kept, but lacked a front garden that decorated other houses in the town. As she slid off Mahala, she understood what Vordar had meant. The ironwork was extraordinary in its simplicity and function. The elegant hitching post put the one in the castle courtyard to shame and the iron gate swung noiselessly on its hinges and latched behind her with a solid click. The stout banded door displayed an impressive iron knocker. It seemed out of place on the simple dwelling, so she ignored it, choosing to rap gently with her knuckles.

The house remained silent. She waited and knocked again, this time with more resolve. There was no answer. She pushed on the door, but it was latched. With some trepidation, she tried the handle. It was sturdy but yielded easily to her touch, and the door swung open silently, stopping quietly against the wall. She peered into the darkened interior of the house. *This is clearly a man's place,* she thought to herself.

It was stark and simple. Three coat hooks decorated the wall by the door, one of which had a smith's leather apron hanging on it. She expected to see a vase with flowers on the small table just inside the door. Instead, it held several pieces of sculpted iron, each half finished, as if they had been dropped there after a long, unsatisfying day at the forge. Two pairs of boots lay on their side on the hall floor. A subtle mannish scent diffused over the threshold. It wasn't an unpleasant smell, but the exact word for it escaped her. It smelled somewhat like her father when he had been out hunting.

"Paca?" she called softly. The thick silence fed her discomfort. She hesitated before crossing the threshold, anxious, but resolved to find the smith. Straight in front of her, down a short hall was the kitchen. Just before the kitchen, on either side of the hall, two doors led to the left and to the right. The one on the left was closed and the other stood open. She walked softly down the hall. The manliness of the place enveloped her now, strong and quiet, with a stillness she could feel.

She looked cautiously into the open door. The bedroom was neat and empty except for a small bed, a nightstand, a chamber pot and several hooks hung with trousers and shirts.

She stepped back into the hall and then into the kitchen. It was a peculiar place. On the right was the fireplace, swept clean as if it were rarely used, with storage cabinets for food or dishes against the wall on either side of it. Straight across from where she stood was a long, low cupboard with a washbasin set into the top. It spread itself under six tall windows facing south. Along the left wall was an eclectic collection of pots, pans, utensils and tools, many of them unfamiliar to her. Except for a large sturdy table that filled the center of the floor, and two stools, the kitchen contained little else.

On the left end of the table, a small area had been set aside for eating, with the two stools pushed under it. Files and rasps, various punches, chisels and odd tools she had never seen before littered the other end. Massive iron vises, the kind she had seen in the smithy, commanded the two corners. Experimental bits of iron and steel; cut, punched and twisted, lay strewn over the table and floor. Some were grotesque in shape; others were beautiful. *A smith's idea of a kitchen,* she smiled to herself.

As she turned to go back into the hallway, she ran headlong into Paca. She yelped and jumped back. "Welcome to our home," he said as he stepped past her, sauntering around the table toward the washbasin.

He began splashing water on his face, and he spoke to her between splashes. "Your horse is lathered and shivering in the yard...I'll rub him down after I...get you something to eat...you must be hungry." He had grabbed a towel off a hook and wiped his beard. "*Are* you hungry?" He smiled as he put the towel back on the hook.

She wasn't sure what to say. Maybe it was a poor idea to have come here, after all, but she did not want to admit it; and she *was* hungry. Her hesitation gave her away.

"I'll take that as a 'Yes.'" He headed out the back door of the kitchen. Alone again, she sat down on one of the stools to wait. The uncomfortable feeling melted away as she reflected on Paca's ease at her unannounced arrival at his house. It faded into a quiet sense of acceptance that she realized she had felt nowhere else. In the castle, she was the princess. Outside the castle, she was still the princess. Paca had a way of letting her be Vrengnia. He did not fear her. He was not in awe of her, or wanting anything from her. She didn't know what to make of it, because it refused to fit into any of the jars she kept her feelings in.

When he returned, he carried a covered, clay pitcher full of fresh milk. As he rummaged through the cabinet beside the fireplace, he rambled off various contents: "Let's see, dried apples, dried peaches, oats...whole barley...cracked corn...figs...um, no...raisins...oh wow, an apple, well..." He kept going. She watched him from behind. He was out of his element, even in his own kitchen. She started to laugh. He turned. "What?"

"You."

He smiled, gave a little bow and gestured to the cabinet. "Your turn then. I'll go take care of your beast."

Vrengnia rummaged through the various cabinets and prepared a small porridge with oats, barley, a bit of cinnamon and some dried blackberries she found in a jar to the right of the fireplace. In the cupboard by the washbasin she discovered a collection of herbs in small glass bottles. She scanned the shelf quickly and selecting some spearmint, wolf flower petals and raspberry leaves, brewed them into a light tea. It was a recipe that Haniah had taught her to combat fatigue. *Paca might well need it,* she thought to herself as she puzzled over why the smith would have such a collection. Her thoughts were interrupted by Paca's return from grooming Mahala, with fresh cream to pour over the top of the mash. They sat down and ate breakfast together.

Vrengnia found a comfortable quietness in the smith's kitchen. She had the feeling that no one except Paca and his father had been in here in many years, but if Paca was at all uncomfortable, he hid it well. "I was expecting you—I mean not *here* exactly—and not this early but..." He trailed off.

"I had to come!" she exclaimed, looking into his eyes.

"Had to?"

"Yes, had to. I mean, after last night...I did not want to be around my father—and I wanted to see how it's going with his sword."

Paca sat silent for a moment while he sipped his tea, watching her green eyes. "What happened last night?"

"Why, didn't you hear it? The singing, I mean..." He stared at her, somewhere in the netherworld of confusion and disbelief. "Your father...last night...," she prompted.

"My father? What happened?" His eyes grew dark, but she sensed the darkness was not aimed at her.

She set down her teacup and related the story about his father's singing. She told him all the details: the comments by the king and the advisors; how they said he must be a taralang and how there had not been one in Immerland for many years; that it signified something serious, but no one was exactly sure what. She left out nothing. "I was afraid at first—it was so strange. Then I realized that I could understand some of it."

"What was it about? I mean, the part you understood."

"Some of it was about swords...like the forge poetry you described...."

"And?"

"Well, some of it was terrifying, about war and killing...." She felt Paca's eyes drilling into her, and she looked down as she continued, "and other parts were comforting and warm. But it was not just the words...it seemed to reach in and put the thoughts inside me. I could feel the words...I was living them." She stopped. She realized that she could still feel them, and a question loomed up out of them. She was not ready to ask it yet. She felt her hands trembling.

Paca reached down and took hold of them gently. "Go on." His hands were calloused and strong. She had never felt hands like this before. Even her father's were not like this.

"My father was angry because he could not understand any of it. I was afraid, but I could not stop listening."

"What were you afraid of?"

It was a simple and reasonable question. The answer was not as forthcoming. "I...I'm not sure. I have only felt it once before. I did not like it then; and I didn't like it last night." She paused as she struggled to articulate her thoughts.

"Have you ever been afraid to die?" Paca asked suddenly.

"We're all going to die," is what came out, sounding hollow.

"I know...I know, but have you ever feared that *you* would die *soon*...perhaps in the next few minutes?"

Vrengnia looked up into Paca's eyes. "Perhaps that one time...but last night it was something else...maybe it *was* the fear of death...but not my own."

"Whose?"

"I don't know." She felt his grip tighten on her hands.

"I had similar visions last night," Paca began. He was looking past her into the nothingness in the corner of the room as he spoke. "Some were ugly, and related to swords...to killing. Some were not. I felt the fear of death...I know that's what it was, and as you said, it was not my death, it was someone else's...I thought perhaps my father's. I have often wondered what will happen when my father dies, but I have never felt it...." His voice trailed off.

He rose and moved to the window and, leaning on the cupboard, stared out across the barley fields to the mountains on the horizon. She decided to wait until he spoke.

"Do you think my father is in danger because of this?" he asked, turning to face her again.

"I doubt it," she said quietly. "They all seemed to be quite afraid of him—even Omberon. Carnados wanted to set him free immediately."

"Who's Omberon?"

"The captain of my father's guard. The one with the sneer, if you ever see him."

"Oh, yes. He arrested my father. That face..."

"He doesn't seem to be afraid of anything. If he is, *that face* hides it well. But last night was different."

"Do you think your father will listen to...to..."

"Carnados? I don't think so. I think he is too stubborn."

"That's not good, but it adds urgency to what I must do to finish your father's sword." A sharp gleam she had never seen before came into his eyes. He told her what had happened in the smithy the night before, sparing no detail. "The two events must be related," he concluded. "The first song came to me just after midnight—but now, there's not a moment to waste."

"What do you mean?"

"I'm not sure, but I feel it. I only have tonight to finish it all. You must leave now, Vrengnia. Walk your horse for a bit before you ride him. The trip down was exhausting, even for him. Come back early tomorrow evening and I will have the sword finished. Don't let anyone follow you. Come here; don't come to the smithy. Is this clear?"

"But why...why the rush?"

"Again, I am not sure, but by tomorrow evening, if there *is* anything to explain, I will have the time then."

She hesitated. "Are you still my friend?" she asked suddenly.

He touched her arm gently. "Vrengnia, I will always be your friend." He stared into her eyes thoughtfully. For an instant, she thought she saw his father in his eyes. It was just a flicker, but it was real. "I think you have always *been* my friend—but now, as a friend, I beg you to go. The day is long before me."

She started for the back door, but paused before leaving, looking back at Paca. He smiled. "One more thing: if my father sings tonight, do not be afraid, but listen carefully." She turned and made her way through the door. The fresh air felt good. The rain had stopped, the fog had vanished, and the clouds tumbled eastward before the long thin line of blue that crawled upward along the western horizon. The sun would be a welcome friend for the journey back to the castle.

20

*Can you separate the smith from his
tools and still have a smith? Is not his
hammer only the extension of his one arm
and the tongs the extension of his other?*

Timmanaeus

SOMETIME FOLLOWING THE NOON WATCH, SANDIHAR DECIDED TO VISIT THE tower prison. The events of the night before burned in his mind, distracting him from all but the most necessary of his daily tasks. With these behind him, he wanted to talk directly with his prisoner. He drew the heavy bolt and opened the door slowly. The smith stood near the southern window of the room, gazing out over the landscape. He remained unmoving through several moments of uncomfortable silence, so the king cleared his throat. "May I come in?"

The smith turned his gaze in the direction of the door. "It's your castle, good King. You may come and go as you please."

The king was unsure what he wanted to say. So many questions remained and few answers were forthcoming—and there was no good place to begin.

"Good King," said the smith gently, easing the burden of the first word from the king's shoulders, "I want to start my smithing now."

"But you have been smithing."

"No, I have been scrapping iron. The time has come, but I will need certain things from my smithy."

"You will make my sword?" The king was as incredulous as he was suspicious.

"I did not say that." The smith was smiling. "I said that I will start my smithing, and I will need certain things from my smithy."

The king was annoyed, but kept his reserve. There were times to be annoyed, and there were times when it was best not to allow it. This was one of the latter. "What is it that you need, good smith?" he asked cautiously.

"I will make a list for my son, and he will bring the items here to the prison forge. I should meet him there at the noon watch tomorrow." The smith's voice was firm, but not threatening. The king felt a keen uneasiness. Something was not right, but he hadn't the nerve to say no to the smith today. Instead, he stepped out of the room and called for scribes. He heard his attendants hurrying up the steps below him.

As he waited for them to arrive, he broached the question that he now wanted to ask most of all. "My good smith," he said coming back through the door, "I will have arrangements made to have your goods delivered here, but I want to know what you plan to do with them. Has this new desire to start your smithing anything to do with the singing last night?"

"I do not know the answers to your question precisely," said the smith. "Much of what was sung last night I do not remember. Some of it was not about or for me. Of what I do remember, very little of it has anything to do with what I have to do in the smithy downstairs." He was staring out the window, so the king could not see his expression. His voice was gentle and genuine, so the king, though not wanting to believe him, felt compelled to accept his explanation for now. "As to my work downstairs, I do not yet know what I shall do. All I know at this time is that I need certain tools from my smithy in Shiloh."

The king remained silent. A moment later, two scribes came scurrying up the stairs behind him, armed with parchment, inkhorn, quills and sharpening knives. The king took them from the scribes and after walking across the room to the window, handed them to the smith. "By your leave, I cannot write," the smith said calmly. Carnados's suspicion about the smith's literacy was right. The king spread the parchment out on the small desk.

"Tell me your list." The king motioned to one of the scribes who promptly sat down on the small stool and took notes for the illiterate genius leaning against the window.

"Seven sacks of my finest coal. My two sledges and my large flatter (my son will know what these are). Three bars of steel from the bottom shelf. Four billets of wrought iron from last year's stock. My anvil—"

"Slow down, sir," interrupted the scribe. "Four billets...your anvil..."

"My flat blade tongs, the two small box tongs and a jar of welding flux—no, two jars." He paused until the scribe caught up with his dictation and looked up. "I will need my cross and straight peen hammers, the ones I use all the time—Paca will know."

"Hmmm...that's it?"

"For now."

The king took the list from the scribe and read the list back to the smith, who nodded with each item. "It will be done as you say," he said as he handed the list back to the scribe and with a wave of his hand sent the two men on their way. "Tomorrow at noon!" The king hesitated to see if there was anything else the smith would say. He was suddenly eager to get out of the room. He was afraid, not of the smith, but of the unknown that surrounded him. Sensing nothing forthcoming, he turned to leave.

"Good King!" said the smith softly. The king turned to meet his gaze. "The captain of your guards—"

"Omberon?"

"Is that his name? I was wondering how well you know him."

"What do you mean?"

"Have you known him a long time?"

"Four years and then some."

"How long has he been your captain?"

"A little more than two years. Why do you ask?"

"He does not seem like an Immerlander...perhaps Tessamandrian descent? Or Mooriman?"

"I'm not sure...I never asked. Does it matter? He has served me well in all things. I have had no reason to probe into his life's history."

The smith nodded to himself and shrugged as he turned back to the window.

"You think I should, don't you?"

"I was just curious." That was all. The king knew they were through. He turned to the door and left, pulling it shut and throwing the bolt securely behind him.

He stood for a moment in the semidarkness of the tower stairs and took a deep breath, closing his eyes and exhaling slowly, trying to cleanse his vorn of fear.

The voice sprang from the darkness to his left, "Sire."

His heart jumped within him. Omberon emerged from the shadows of the stairs. He must have been waiting there.

"You startled...me."

"I apologize. I did not mean to. May I speak freely?"

Sandihar cringed and nodded at the same time.

"Is everything all right?"

"Yes...yes, speak freely, my good captain, only let us walk as we do, away from this place."

"I sat on the steps outside the door because I knew you...were alone with the smith and wanted to be there if there was any...trouble."

"There is no need to explain, Omberon."

"Sire, I did overhear your conversation with the smith. May I speak freely?"

"By the lightning on the Crown, Captain, yes…yes, by all means, speak freely!"

"I think it unwise to allow the smith to have his tools—to let him smith at all."

They walked together down the stairs. Sandihar let the statement hang as he thought through an appropriate answer. What he felt for the smith was a peculiar blend of emotions that he had not fully unraveled. He was not afraid of the man. The smith had never even hinted at a threat of reprisal or violence. He had no grudge against the smith, save for his refusal to make the sword, and even that was more an issue of rebellion than not having the sword. He would have freed him in a moment, were it not for his determination not to let any man in his kingdom defy him to his face as the smith had. He respected the smith for his knowledge, his wisdom, his insight and his patience—many characteristics he wished he himself had in greater measure.

In addition, he had no particular fear of letting the smith ply his trade in the tower smithy. If there were any hope that he might make the sword, that would be the only way he could do it.

"I'm not sure I understand the urgency of your statement, Captain."

"The smith is up to some…treachery."

The king stopped on the stair and turned to face Omberon. "Treachery? Name it!"

Omberon looked him straight in the eye. "I can't—yet."

Sandihar raised his hands in a gesture of despair. "Well, when you can, I want to listen." He turned and started down the stairs. He could hear Omberon behind him. "You seem to have an agenda with the smith, Captain. You might as well tell me what it is."

"I fear for your safety, Sire."

The king stopped and turned to Omberon again. "That's the *right* agenda. That's what I pay you for. Now is there anything else, I mean, beyond that?"

Omberon opened his mouth to speak and then closed it suddenly, pausing briefly before he spoke again. "No, Sire, nothing else."

He does that a lot, Sandihar thought to himself. "I appreciate your concern. Why don't you take some time off, Captain." He deliberately said it in a manner to end the conversation and turned down the stairs. Omberon did not follow him this time. By the time he had gotten to the bottom of the stairs, it had occurred to him that Omberon had made no mention of the smith's question about his history. He wondered why the smith had even brought it up.

21

And where does one see his true self? Is it not in the darkness, when no one else is watching? When the full freedom of possibilities presents itself and he has to decide who he really is in that vast ocean of opportunity?

Oratanga
Passages

P ACA WORKED STEADILY AND CAREFULLY, SINGING THE NEW SONGS OVER AND over quietly while he filed the blades for the swords. The time flew by. In the middle of leveling the bevel on Vrengnia's sword, he heard the galloping hooves of several approaching horses. He hoped they would pass by, but they stopped at the gate. *What now?* he thought as he quickly wrapped the swords and stood the bundle in the corner by the mop and broom. The first urgent knock came as he rounded the table: five rapid strikes of the heavy knocker. Before he got to the door, it struck again seven times.

Two of the king's guards and a herald stood outside the door. "By the king's orders, we offer you this summons," said the herald and shoved a rolled parchment into Paca's face.

He stepped back. "Are you sure this is for me?" he said.

"Are you the son of the smith imprisoned in the castle?"

"Yes—"

"Then it's for you!" said the herald.

Paca took the parchment, broke the seal, and unrolled it, glancing at it for a moment before handing it back.

The herald's face showed his impatience. "Well?" he demanded.

"Well," Paca said with a smile, "I cannot read—if you would be so kind—"

The herald sniffed, and with a condescending flourish, unrolled the parchment and read:

"By order of King Sandihar of Immerland: Pacahara, the son of the proprietor of the Shiloh Forge, is hereby ordered to procure from the Shiloh Forge the following items, to be delivered to the smith at the Immerland Castle by the noon watch on the morrow..."

The herald read the list through.

"Can you read it through again slowly? I want to make sure I get everything ready."

The herald obliged with another sniff.

"How will it be delivered?" Paca asked.

He was told that a cart would be brought to the smithy by nine o'clock. He let the herald know that he needed to have men available to help move the anvil onto the cart, and he needed to be there to be sure that all the correct supplies got loaded. With these arrangements made, the herald and the soldiers left. He closed the door quietly.

He stood for a moment with his back against the door and his head thrown back in disbelief. Tomorrow, by this time, his father's great anvil and the best hammers and tongs would be gone. What was happening? Why did his father want these items? Was it to stop him from finishing? Whatever the reason, he had only tonight to finish his work on the swords. Now he understood the urgency he had felt the night before. Time was slipping away and there was still much work to do.

He moved swiftly to the kitchen and unrolled the blades again. He set to work, filing, grinding and polishing, perfecting the blades for the evening's work.

"Grind one way, then grind the other,
First one side, then its brother.
Grind toward the edge, but not too thin,
Grind this hollow, then its twin."

"File crossgrain, 'til scars are gone,
Cross-file again, 'til shape is won.
Polish the flat and polish the back
Leather and rust 'til leather is black."

The hours slipped away into twilight as he pursued the perfection of the swords, singing and filing, singing and polishing.

As twilight settled over the town of Shiloh, Paca stood up and straightened his back over the workbench in the darkening kitchen. He was done with the filing and sharpening. The task of finishing the handle needed to be completed before the blades received their final tempering. The swords would be made completely of steel; there would be no inlay, gold, silver or stones. He stretched again and bent down to look at the sky through the window of the kitchen. It was the perfect color, his favorite color. With the disappearance of the sun, the sky had slipped from deep blue to the rich blue green that appeared just before the darkness settled it into night. He sighed and stretched again.

It was dark when he arrived at the smithy, so he lit a lantern and set about preparing the forge for another long night. As he did, his thoughts drifted to his father. *A taralang! Could this be true? What was he up to? Why had he ordered that the tools from the smithy be brought to him at the castle? Was all this connected to his own work on the swords, and if so, how did his father know and what did he know?* He was sure that the princess had said nothing. Why would she? He had a strong feeling that all this was connected and that it would all be clear at some point. He also knew that something else would happen tonight, because the swords had yet to be hardened and tempered, the most critical steps of all.

As the fire developed, he selected the steel for the hilt, to be tempered to withstand the most brutal sword stroke. He also selected the iron for the handle, sculpted and swaged into the contour of the hand, shaped and textured so that any hand that gripped it would have control of the sword from the butt to the tip.

The poetry started before the process of forging, flowing up from deep within, erupting in the strange language, then slowly evolving into intelligible rhymes in Immerlander. Though he had hardly slept the night before or that day, he felt strong, and the energy he needed flowed from the poetry. Whenever the activity lulled, he slipped to the door, opened it and listened for his father's voice. He heard a dog barking once. Otherwise, no sound broke the stillness of the cool, clear night.

Some time after midnight, he finished the hilts, and three hours later, he found the handles satisfactory. His mind was flooded with the poetry involved in the making of the handle. He stared at his work in the lantern light. As he wrapped his fingers around the grip, it fit perfectly in the hand. As he held it, the sword came alive like an extension of his arm, almost as if it held itself to his hand. So sure was the grip, that he knew if ever he wielded such a sword, it would only be taken from his hand by death.

He picked up the princess's sword. It was smaller and lighter, but not by his design. He swept it from side to side. He had a vague sense of its superiority over the king's, but how? He wasn't sure and it didn't matter. He studied each sword carefully, making sure they were perfect. He had never seen anything like them. He had never *made* anything like them.

Selecting a small spot on the handle of the princess's sword, Paca engraved in miniature the three slashes and sunburst from the front of her tunic. He did not know what it meant, exactly, but he was sure it meant something to her.

He first heard the voice while waiting for the fire to mature for hardening. At first, it was faint. He laid the swords down on the bed of the forge and sprang to the door, throwing it open and stopping short to listen. Was it really there? All he could hear was his heart and the far-off barking of that dog. Then it came, almost imperceptibly, then clearer and clearer until he could hear every syllable. He could not make out the language, but he heard every thought. It was forge poetry, for the hardening and tempering of swords, mingled with other verses about war and death, life and wisdom. It was beautiful and haunting at the same time, far away, but clear, like a fine bell.

The hammering was over, so he wedged the smithy door open with an old axe head and leapt to the forge. The fire roared as he tugged on the bellows toggle, and it seemed to sing as he laid the king's blade into the long narrow trough of coals. Above it all, he heard the singing. He listened and watched, his gaze fixed on the steel. As it began to glow, the voice crescendoed. He turned the steel at the bidding of the poetry; he pushed it back and forth to even the heat. He turned it again—and then again. It was close to quenching temperature...another minute...a few more seconds...NOW! He raised the blade from the forge bed and held it vertically for an instant as it quivered in his hands and then, with a quick slicing motion, plunged it into the tepid slack tub.

The blade whistled as it hit the water, sending a cloud of sweet smelling steam into the shadows of the smithy. The blade's song blended with the distant voice for a moment, etching itself into Paca's memory forever.

Then the song shifted abruptly: it repeated itself. Vrengnia's sword! Into the fire it went, the tasks repeating themselves. Paca watched and listened. For nearly an hour, the voice guided him through the steps until both swords lay on the workbench, hardened and tempered for the king and his daughter. It was then that the singing stopped.

Paca ran to the door to listen again, but all was still. In the east, he saw the first hints of dawn. Dawn! Its presence seemed more like a threat than a blessing. There was so much more to be done. The king's wagon would be there in three hours to pick up the supplies for his father.

22

Psadeq is a concept so ingrained in the cultural fabric of our small planet that, were it not for the freedom we have been given to reject it, one might postulate that it is, in fact, an instinct. Its fundamental nature was confirmed by the progenitors of our dispersed languages, that they, finding no words suitable to capture its essence, left it one of the few words we have that is a direct descendent of the original language.

Mortag of Horrinaine
Of Beings

V RENGNIA STOOD OUTSIDE THE DOOR TO THE SMITH'S PRISON AND LISTENED. No sound came from within. She had carefully waited during her father's breakfast with the smith that morning, watching the comings and goings of the attendants, the waiter and servants, the clean-up crew and finally, the guards. Everything had been quiet in the tower for about half an hour, and she felt safe. She was not sure why she was there, but she wanted to talk with the smith alone.

She knocked gently and listened. There was no response. The door was bolted from the outside and there were no guards. Apparently, her father was unconcerned about the smith trying to escape.

She lifted the latch and slid the bolt back as quietly as she could. It creaked slightly and she stopped to listen again. The door swung open easily as she stood looking into the open doorway. Only yesterday, she had been standing in front of this man's house, looking into the silent hallway. She had the same feeling of intrusion, but knew she had to enter, so she stepped forward just enough to look around. It only took a moment for her eyes to find the smith. He was sitting on the bed looking back at her curiously.

"I thought it might be you," he said gently, a slight smile flitting across his lips as he spoke.

"You were expecting me?"

"Well, not exactly, but you certainly were not one of the guards—the way you waited at the door; the way you drew the bolt—something said to me 'Ah, the princess!' Come, sit down." He gestured to the sitting chair by the small desk.

She sat down and faced him. She kept thinking it strange that she was not uncomfortable. "I...I'm not sure why I am here," she started. The smith leaned back on his elbows on the bed and said nothing. "I visited your son yesterday—," she began again, but that didn't seem right either.

The smith smiled, "How is he?" His voice was gentle and full of warmth.

"He has tried several times to visit you here, but my father refuses to let him near." She broke eye contact and looked at the floor, ashamed as she said it, ashamed that her father would treat such a gentle man in this way.

"I miss him," said the smith, a faraway look crossing quickly over his face. "I most certainly would rather be there at the smithy than here." She looked up. His eyes gazed steadily into her own. "Your father has treated me well—in fact we had quite a breakfast together this morning."

"I know," she said, looking down at the floor again. She had observed how difficult it was to keep eye contact with someone when one felt embarrassed.

"And he *is* having some of my tools brought to the smithy he built for me below this chamber."

"Why?"

The smith smiled, "I asked him to."

The princess laughed. "You just asked him to?"

"That's right, and he seemed more than eager to comply. He thought I might make his sword after all. I think he was a bit disappointed when I told him I would not."

"Yes—I'm sure." The conversation paused. The princess wondered what to say, and the smith seemed content to wait for her. When she started feeling uncomfortable with the silence, he embarked on a new direction of his own.

"Princess Vrengnia," he began, standing up and walking to the southern window, "how well do you know my son?"

She was not sure whether to be angry or pleased with the question. "Why, I only just met him, really. The first time I ever saw him was the day my father and I came to your smithy about the sword...and then...well, we did not actually talk."

"But you have been to see him several times since then." The smith was so matter of fact that the princess was not sure whether it was a statement or a question. "Your father told me this," he continued, "but I could have guessed it would happen from the way you looked at him the next day."

"When my father had you arrested?"

"Yes—so how do you feel about him?" The smith was staring out the window at nothing. His voice told her she had a long time to attempt an answer.

"Well," she started tentatively, "it's a little different." The smith looked at her knowingly. She continued searching for the proper words. "I mean—the first time I looked at him and he looked at me, it seemed like I knew him—as if we were friends and had been for a long time. With other men, that look scares me, maybe it angers me, but with Paca, well, it...it accepted me—no those are not the right words—"

The smith listened carefully. She continued: "Ordinarily, I would never have talked to your son again, but I felt compelled to go back and find out what this meant. I was a bit nervous, but curiously, when I got there, it seemed like I almost belonged there. What was strangest of all, was that Paca seemed to feel much the same way. I haven't talked to anyone else about this—"

"Not even to your father?" interrupted the smith.

"Well, my father knows I have visited the smithy and spent some time with Paca, but I have never discussed this strange connection with him. He does not seem—or should I say—I do not think he would understand it very well." She looked at the floor again as she identified her own disappointment that she had not been able to tell this to her father.

The smith waited for her to continue. She remained silent. He spoke: "Have you ever heard the word 'cymbic'?"

Vrengnia gasped and looked up at him hopefully. "Do you know what it means?" she asked eagerly. "Yes, I have heard it, but have never really understood what it means. Can you tell me?" She saw her eager interest light a fire in the smith's eyes.

"Yes," he said softly. He eyed her thoughtfully for a moment and then stared out the window again. She waited patiently. "Are you comfortable?" he asked, turning his head toward her over his shoulder.

"I'm fine," she said. She wanted him to continue.

He turned to face her fully and leaned back against the sill, framing himself in the window. Crossing his arms comfortably, he began. "We are surrounded by other people. Everywhere we are, unless we have chosen to be isolated, there are people that come and go, passing through our lives, coming from all directions, going in all directions. Some are like props in a play at the theatre. We accept them as part of the scenery, but we never know their names, their lives, their being-ness—they are almost like shadows in our awareness, in our vorn."

She knew this vague, empty feeling of these shadow people. She nodded.

"With others, we have some commerce, perhaps they come into our shop to buy goods or they serve us our food at dinner. Still, we do not know their names and our relationship to them based on this commerce is purely functional and fleeting. You have seen this before?"

"Yes."

The smith shifted and began walking back and forth in front of the window, his left hand on his chin and his elbow cupped in his right hand. "At another level are those with whom the nature of the connection is more substantial. We know their names, perhaps where they live, what they do to survive. We may smile when we see them because we know this little bit, but in the end, were it not for some trivial circumstance, a twist of the path of life, we would never have this connection, and we would never miss it. In fact, when such a person disappears from our life, we may not even notice the event.

"This is not wrong, it is just the way of things. Our lives are arranged with many such layers of relationships and the involvement and concern for each level varies from person to person. Some people never experience layers that others do. Again, this is not wrong; it is just different."

The smith paused and looked at her. She listened intently. "Does this make sense to you so far?"

"So far," she responded tentatively, encouraging him to continue.

"At the other end of the spectrum of relationships are the cymbic relationships." He paused. "They are characterized by a certain timelessness, in two senses. First, they are timeless in that they seem to have always been there and second, cymbics know they *will* always be there." The princess looked up at him. She knew *this* feeling too. She had not known it had a name.

"Cymbics may not see each other for many years, yet they are able to pick up almost where they left off. The cymbics have 'natural' relationships, if you will. They do not need the approval of others, nor do they even expect it. There is a simple rightness to the cymbic relationship that others often do not understand. Psadeq is given and accepted from both sides without hesitation: it does not need to be earned; it does not need to be created; it does not need to be proven."

"Are you saying that I have a cymbic relationship with Paca?"

"It would seem so. Maybe you should tell *me*."

"Well…" Vrengnia tried to identify her feelings in this new context. "I wasn't sure what to make of it. Honestly, I thought I might be falling in love—but I have thought that before and it was a bit different."

"In what way?"

"Well, at other times it made me feel shy and foolish…. I did and said stupid things. That doesn't happen with Paca."

"The awareness of your self disappears?"

She had to think about that for a few seconds. "Yes, maybe that is it."

"It *is* part of it. The genuine love—that foundational personal concern for another being that transcends your own interests—is characteristic of cymbic relationships." The smith was looking at her curiously as he finished his sentence. "You have another question."

"I have many questions—"

"Ask."

"If this is so, why am I almost eighteen and have never been taught this?"

"Ahhh…" The smith nodded and turned to gaze into the nothingness outside the window. "In the course of a well-lived life, in the countless interactions that have the potential for such a relationship, we may only encounter a few—a small handful—of beings with whom we do have such a relationship. It is rare enough that it is often mistaken for something else, such as 'falling in love.' Other times, social dogmas prevent its realization. What if your father had forbidden you to go to the smithy to follow up on your first sense of the relationship? Hmmm?"

"He wouldn't have done that."

"Perhaps not. Many others have not been so fortunate. As a result, there are many—no probably most—who could have cymbic relationships, but don't."

"*Could* have?"

"Many people, even with the opportunity, cannot have such relationships. We don't know why. It seems to be given only to some. Perhaps it is the nature of the diversity of personalities…but those who lean toward cymbic relationships but never find them, live as strangers in their own cultures. They can be very lonely."

Vrengnia understood. She looked at the floor. The realization of what he was describing was comforting and disquieting at the same time.

"As a result of all these influences, many refuse to believe that cymbic relationships exist. They are treated like myths and met with disbelief and hostility when they are encountered—but you have another question!"

"Yes…" She looked up. "My father…does he…I mean, do you think he understands this?"

"I will never be one to categorize a person unfairly, but the fact that he has never told you any of this leads me to believe that he does not. My personal experience confirms this also."

She knew the smith was right. He stepped forward and sat down on the edge of the bed, leaning toward her as he continued his lesson: "Cymbics fall into three categories; they are the 'cymbic spheres': the primary sphere is the strongest, the most natural of them all. In the primary cymbic sphere of another, there is total acceptance, even across all kinds of boundaries. There is no fear; there is no hesitation. The psadeq is natural with no need to please the other, to prove rightness or wrongness in anything. It is the purest of friendships."

She listened intently. Pieces were beginning to fit together. "I'm beginning to see it," she said. "It makes more sense than how I have heard the word explained in the past...."

"But you still have questions?"

"Well...can cymbics be or become enemies?"

The smith raised his eyebrows. "Yes, under unusual circumstances. Beings change over time, and those changes, or perhaps a singular event, will turn cymbics into bitter enemies. Curiously, they remain close friends in the cymbic sphere, that is—they know each other, respect each other in the timeless cymbic way—but oppose one another in their pursuits and way of life. The conflict this fosters in their lives creates a bitterness that few people understand. They submerge it beneath a veil of goodness and false psadeq that makes it very hard to detect. It consumes them from the inside out. Unless there is reconciliation, it will eventually destroy them."

The princess found herself looking at the floor again. "Destroy them?"

"Inwardly at first. Psadeq is eroded and the peace it brings is lost. Sometimes this happens very slowly so that the individual does not know it is happening. If psadeq is destroyed, the consequences can be physical: ill health, fatigue, sickness."

Vrengnia did not want to look up now. She felt a growing fear that she wanted to escape, but did not know where to turn. She agonized. It seemed to have been sparked by the truth the smith was speaking, but was being fed from somewhere within. She feared the pain of it would overwhelm her if she were to look directly at him.

He redirected the conversation. "Yes, I believe that you have a cymbic relationship with my son in the primary sphere. Do not fear it, but you must be wise about it. "

"In what way?"

The smith was at the window again. He turned to face her, leaning back on the sill with his elbows. "The psadeq of cymbic relationships, though natural and easy, is more precarious—more fragile."

"I don't understand. If it is so strong, how can it be fragile—or precarious?"

The smith smiled. "I never said it was strong; only natural and easy. It is deceitfully weak at first, and this is what makes it fragile."

"I am still not sure that all this makes sense," she said, shifting slightly to make herself more comfortable. She was still sitting in the chair by the desk.

"You mentioned that you thought that you might be falling in love, but noticed a difference, did you not?"

"Yes."

"The closeness of the cymbic relationship can be confusing at first. Unless this confusion is clarified, it can lead to mistakes that violate psadeq. This is particularly true in a cymbic relationship between a man and a woman." The smith stepped away from the window and sat down again on the bed so that he was looking up at her. Her eyes met his. He continued: "The laws of psadeq in any relationship are immutable, even one which is cymbic. Cymbics seem to lose sight of this more easily."

Vrengnia looked down. "It seems backward," she said. "I mean, I would think that it would be stronger."

"And that is the danger, exactly," said the smith with a smile as he leaned back on his elbows. "Perhaps it is arrogance, self-confidence, a misguided understanding of what psadeq really is or belief that its laws do not apply. I am not sure. Either way, when psadeq is violated, much pain is brought into our world."

The talk of relationships with men and women surfaced new questions. "Does any of this change when people get married?"

"Cymbics remain cymbics," said the smith sitting up again. His eyes shone intently as he placed his elbows on his knees and leaned forward. "But the laws of psadeq are different in marriage, so cymbic behavior must change to stay within its boundaries. This is another mistake that cymbics make: they naturally feel that their relationship does not need to change, and this is a grave danger. The closeness and specialness of marriage must be honored and guarded. Cymbics often lose sight of this. It is not uncommon for cymbics to make the mistake of justifying the violation of a marriage relationship because of strong cymbic ties, but it is a violation none-the-less, and a grievous evil with equally grievous consequences."

Vrengnia thought she understood, but had to admit that she did not understand marriage very well, having never seen one up close. For now she did not have to think about it. She stared at the floor, and as her thoughts tumbled over themselves in the quiet chamber, she felt a silent fear closing in upon her, but could not identify its source or give it a name. Was it the fear of her relationship with Paca?

The smith reached over and lifted her chin gently, forcing her eyes to meet his. For a long moment, she stared into his eyes until she felt tears forming and a tightness growing in her throat. Not knowing whether to unleash her fear in a flood of tears or to turn and run, she stood up and stepped back, stammering, "Thank you...for your time, but I must be going. I'm not sure that my father would appreciate my being here."

He stood up, towering over her. "Love your father, Vrengnia, but do not fear him," the smith encouraged her gently. "He loves you deeply."

He opened his arms and she fell into them. She could feel his strength and warmth as his arms encircled her. It was brief and real, and it spoke comfort and relief without words. Nothing could be said to add to the moment she stayed there. When he relaxed his arms, she turned away without looking at him and headed for the door.

"One more thing," said the smith quietly. She stopped and faced him again, tears streaming down her cheeks. "I need a piece of leather, about two feet square. Could you get one for me?"

She wiped her face with the back of her hand. "Yes, of course."

The princess pulled the door to the smith's prison shut behind her. As she threw the bolt on the door, more tears flowed down her cheeks. As the iron bolt clanked into the hole in the stone doorway, she wondered whether she was locking the smith in, or the kingdom out.

23

There are few gifts greater than one into which the giver has vested his vorn and then has given without hesitation or expectation of like return.

Hispattea
The Essences of Corritanean Wisdom

PACA SAT AT THE KITCHEN TABLE, WHICH HE HAD TIDIED UP FOR THE princess's visit. He had taken the time to make a small vegetable stew and had picked up a loaf of dark rye bread from the baker just fifteen minutes earlier. It was still warm. The front door was open so she would not have to knock.

He had a vague sense of anticipation. It was a comfortable feeling, but it seemed a bit odd that he actually knew she was coming. Until then, she had always just shown up. This was different and he was not sure what to do, so he sat where he was at the table.

As he waited, Paca's mind drifted back over the day. The removal of the great anvil from the shop had had more of an effect than he had expected. He had purposely avoided involvement in removing it, having assigned Vordar to coordinate that with the other smiths. He could not remember a time that the anvil, the centerpiece of the whole smithy, had not been there. The hammers and tongs, the familiar ones, the best ones, had all been taken by strangers to a place he was forbidden to go. It hurt inside when he thought about it. The pain was a blend of helplessness, emptiness and anger, fueled by the unforgettable image of the captain of the King's Guard, leering as he entered the smithy to appropriate the tools. Paca was not sure where the line was drawn between hurt and hate, but if he were ever asked if he hated anyone, the captain would probably come to mind.

He had tried to fill the emptiness left by the anvil's removal by focusing on the task of finishing the two swords. It had taken nearly three hours to grind the edges onto the swords. The steel on their edges was harder than any tool Paca had ever worked. The polishing process was equally arduous. Try as he might, the best he could achieve was a dull sheen. It was beautiful, but not the mirror finish he had hoped to produce. He etched and pickled the handles, buffing them off to produce a contrast of bright steel highlights with dark lines and features. By four o'clock he had finished both swords and rolled them carefully into the muslin cloth, the bundle that stood in the corner of the kitchen against the back wall.

The princess arrived as close to six o'clock as Paca could guess. The slow and measured cadence of the horse's hooves echoed gently as they came down the lane. She did not seem to be in a hurry, almost as if she had arrived a bit early, but did not want to show up at the door *too* early.

She entered without knocking. As she stepped over the threshold, he heard her call softly, "Paca?"

"I'm in the kitchen," Paca said warmly as he stood up and pushed his stool back. By the time he got to the kitchen door, she was already there. She held a large basket in both hands.

"I brought some supper from a friend," she said, handing him the basket. "We should eat it while it is still warm."

Paca smiled. "You must thank your friend for the kindness," he said as he carried the basket to the table, laughing. "Why don't you unpack it while I get some dishes?"

Vrengnia hesitated. "What's so funny? Do you not want dinner?"

"Oh, no," he said, amused. "I am relieved that you do not have to eat what I prepared."

"You made dinner?" she asked incredulously, as she raised her nose and inhaled tentatively.

"Well—" He laughed at the comical sight of the Pied Princess sniffing the air.

"C'mon, get it out. We will eat like kings and queens tonight," she said as she began unpacking the basket onto the table.

"You should know," he said and set about finding his best silverware and bowls.

They sat down to dine together, the princess of the kingdom with the son of a smith, on lentil stew, corn bread, cranberry raisin jelly on dark rye bread, fresh pears dressed with fresh cream whipped with honey, and oat cakes drizzled with tamarind syrup. They talked about everything and nothing. They laughed at each other and with each other. They laughed at all the people who never laugh because they are so serious about their lives. They laughed about princesses, kings and queens who had never tasted oat cakes and tamarind syrup, about blacksmiths who had never met princesses. They enjoyed their time together in spite of how serious the world around them seemed.

It was not until the dishes were clean and the lamps had been lit in the kitchen that Paca turned to the princess and said solemnly, "I have a gift for you."

"A gift?" she teased.

"Yes, a gift," he said as he started unrolling the muslin bundle he had fetched from the corner. The first sword to appear was Vrengnia's. Paca stopped. So did the princess. There on the soft cloth, dully reflecting the dim light of the lanterns, lay the simple sword. Paca reflected that it was not the kind of sword a king would wear, but he was still enamored with its elegance. Vrengnia stared at it, as if frozen for a moment. Paca knew it was his job to break the silence. "Well?"

"May I touch it?" she whispered.

"Yes, but be careful—it's *very* sharp."

She touched the blade gently and jerked her hand back. "It's deathly cold!"

"Try the handle."

She reached out gingerly and laid two fingers on the handle. Paca saw her pause with a surprised look on her face before she wrapped her hand around it. As her fingers settled around the grip, the sword lifted from the table. "I...I've never felt anything like it." She swung it back and forth gently. It hummed as it moved through the air. "I...it...it sort of...well, I'm not sure whether I am holding it or it's holding me," she said, her eyes bright with excitement. She held it straight out in front of her toward one of the lanterns. It gleamed in the light. "It's...it's perfect—" Her eyes fell, "Well, for me at least—but my father's hand is so much larger—"

Paca put his hand gently on her shoulder and guided her to the table. "Look carefully at the handle," he said. She held the sword close to the lantern to examine the details of the grip. He watched every movement of her eyes as she scrutinized it, turning it this way and that to get the best light. She gasped suddenly and stood up straight, her eyes wide. "I told you I had a gift for *you*." Paca smiled. "This is *your* sword."

For a moment the princess was speechless, then she managed to stammer, "What about my father?"

"His is right here." He unrolled the remaining muslin. A second sword appeared under the folds. It was of the same design, but a little larger and heavier. The details were perfect. She laid her sword carefully on the muslin, stepped toward him, and hugged him tightly around the neck. Stepping back, she started fumbling for her purse, which she had tucked under her tunic.

Paca stepped forward and took her by the arm, stopping her. "Vrengnia, my friend, this is a gift—for my friend. The other is a gift for my king. There is no payment to be made." She pulled away and started for her purse again.

He grabbed her hand more forcefully. "I meant what I said."

She heard it this time and stopped. Tears formed in her eyes as she stood looking into his. "Thank you, thank you, thank you!" she said. Paca knew that she knew that the words were unnecessary, but he nodded in recognition of her gratefulness.

"Come now, it is time for you to be getting back," he said. "I will wrap the swords in something more fitting." He left the kitchen to fetch an appropriate wrap for the swords. Under his father's bed he found a piece of finely tanned leather. It was soft and supple and would serve well to protect the swords on their way to the castle. He brought it back to the kitchen, laid it out on the table, and started putting the swords in place to wrap them.

"What are all the markings on the leather?" she asked.

Paca stopped and flipped the corner of the leather over, glancing at it matter-of-factly. "It's a parcel leather—have you never seen one before?"

"No—I don't think so."

"Hmmmm..." He started to roll the edge of the leather around the king's sword. "My father uses them all the time to deliver things to others. The markings are the glyphs of individuals who—" Suddenly, he stopped and looked up.

"What is it?" she asked, puzzled.

"There is one more thing," he said slowly. "Hold out your hands."

He picked up her sword, and balancing it deftly before him, he faced her. He lowered the sword into her outstretched hands and said slowly, with all the conviction he had:

"Bless this sword to this woman's hand.
Bless it to work at her command.
Bless her to use it as she should.
Bless its edge for a common good."

"It's beautiful," she whispered. "I mean—the poem. It's similar to something my father says to his dors when he appoints them."

"I think it a very old blessing. My father always says this when he delivers a tool. I never understood why. But I think I do now."

"What about my father's sword?"

"I don't know what to do. My father always delivers his tools in person...I guess it will have to wait...or maybe you can do it."

"I will try." She laid the sword back on the leather wrap and Paca rolled it up, tying it securely with a short leather thong.

After they had safely stowed the bundle on the back of Mahala's saddle, Paca walked the princess to the edge of the last stand of trees before the castle gate. They chatted about everything and nothing for the whole hour's walk. When they finally stopped, she gave him a quick hug, and then, with the grace of a trained horseman, she swung up into her saddle and set Mahala into a canter across the field to the castle gate.

He saw her stop at the gate and get off her horse. She stood for a long while talking to the gatekeeper. It was longer than a simple, pleasant hello, and he wondered what it meant. A twinge of jealousy was working its way up to his throat from somewhere in his belly, an ugly feeling that he hated and relished at the same time. He knew it was not right. He had no claim on the princess; she had given no indication of anything except appreciation and pure friendship. He continued watching, slowly forcing the ugliness back into its lair by sheer will of mind.

He watched until she vanished into the dark throat of the castle, then he turned and headed home. Tal hung low in the sky to the east as Paca walked toward Shiloh in the quiet starlit night, pondering the everything and the nothing of their recent conversation and celebrating the relief of having delivered his burden into the princess's hands.

24

He who seeks understanding without a true willingness to find it, is like a man who seeks water everywhere but in the stream.

Hispattea
The Essences of Corritanean Wisdom

T HE HAMMER HAD BEEN SILENT FOR ABOUT HALF AN HOUR. SANDIHAR, HAV-ing listened all day to the taunting ring of the smith's enormous anvil, concluded that he had finished for the evening. He had ordered that the smith be escorted back to his room and dinner taken to him.

Now another hour had passed, and the king headed for the tower. The guards were still outside the smith's door. The king said nothing, but waved for them to follow him. He led them down to the smithy door. "Did anyone visit today?" He tried to speak casually.

"No, Sire."

"Did he take anything with him to his chambers?"

"No, Sire...uhhh...except for his tools."

"Tools?" The king stepped closer to the guard.

The guard took a step back. "Yes, his two hammers and his tongs and...I think that is all, Sire."

"Why would he take his tools with him? Is he going to sleep with them?"

The taller guard frowned. "I surely would not know, Sire."

"Open the door!" Sandihar wanted to see what the smith had been doing. The warm, acrid smell of the fire lingered in the air as he strode through the door into the dim interior. A curious assortment of worked pieces, all beautifully detailed but completely unrecognizable, lay about on the small table. There were hooks and pointed spikes with barbs on them, many of them finished with small eyes in the end as if they might be fishhooks or spear points. On one end of the table, an array of flattened loops with curled-over ends paraded across the surface, each one slightly larger than the last. Another pile of unfinished or perhaps rejected pieces and several small blocks of stacked plates that were fused together with a short rod sticking out of them sat together in the middle of the table.

"Does this make any sense?" he asked the guards.

They shrugged and shook their heads, stepping to the table as if a closer look would reveal the answer.

The pieces were arranged in some odd pattern. The king tried to imagine how they might fit together, if they were meant to fit at all, but he dared not touch them. He did not want the smith to think he had been snooping around. "I give up," he said in exasperation. "Let's go. Check that the door upstairs is bolted, and you can leave for the night. The smith isn't going anywhere."

Before he started down the tower steps, he faced the guards one last time. "You let no one in, correct?"

"Yes, Sire, no one went in and no one came out until we escorted him to dinner upstairs."

"Good," said the king. "Now, in addition to this, I do not want him taking anything in or out of there either, is *that* clear?"

"Yes, Sire. Nothing in or out," affirmed the taller guard.

"And his tools?" asked the shorter guard.

"He may take his tools, but nothing else."

"Nothing else," echoed the guards.

The taralang did not sing that night, and the king slept well for the first time in three days.

25

Who is the greater prisoner: the caged
man whose mind transcends his physical
boundaries or the untethered being
whose mind holds him in a cage?

Hispattea
The Essences of Corritanean Wisdom

V RENGNIA DISMOUNTED IN THE DARKNESS ON THE DRAWBRIDGE. SHE SECRETLY
hoped that Vishtorath would speak to her as she led Mahala slowly
under the portcullis.

"Good to see you, Princess." His voice was vibrant and rich, full of
warmth. She wondered why so many people feared this man. He
stepped forward just enough so that he was not in the shadows. "Was
your trip worthwhile?"

"Yes, it was very pleasant." Mahala had stopped when Vishtorath
spoke. She had stopped also. She had a question. "Has my father been
looking for me?"

"No, Princess. I have not seen him today. He seems preoccupied
with the smith."

"I know. Do you think it odd, this preoccupation?"

"He is the king; he may do as he likes."

"I know that too." She paused. "But—it seems, well…unusual."

Vishtorath remained silent. He seemed to know that she had more
to say, and he waited for her real question.

"What do you know about the singing the past few nights? Have
you ever heard a taralang before? I mean, no one seems sure that that is
what he is." She felt the giant shift slightly and waited for him to
answer. It came slowly.

"I have heard…many taralangs."

The way he said it was more of a confession than a statement.
Whatever it was, it startled her. She pressed him carefully. "Many?"

"I am old, Princess. You know that."

"How many times have you heard a taralang?"

A long silence shrouded the huge man. Was he counting? Was he weighing the truth or fomenting a lie? "Twenty."

"Twenty?! How old *are* you?"

"I don't know."

She had to imagine his eyes in the darkness as she found herself staring up into the shadow where they should be. "Did you understand when he sang—"

"Every word. Every thought. Every intention."

Was he quoting something? It sounded familiar. "Can you tell me what—"

"It is forbidden." He interrupted her again.

There was something about the way he said it that made her feel like she should not ask anything else. He seemed to be telling her the truth as if he were compelled to do so, despite his strong personal reluctance. She wanted to move the conversation to another place before leaving him to his post.

"Have you met the smith's son? He said he came here three times looking for his father and was turned away at the gate."

Vishtorath shifted again. "Princess, the king forbade his entrance."

"But you did meet him?"

"Yes. He is a fine young man. He is standing now in the shadow of the trees on the road. I think he is waiting to see you safely into the castle."

Vrengnia turned to look. She saw the horizon, shaped by the dark line of trees between the field and the sky with the snaking ribbon of road disappearing into it. There was no detail to be distinguished in the bands of black that formed the night landscape. She turned to face him again. "How can you see him?" she blurted.

"I see many things, Princess. Please come in, I was waiting for you to return before I lowered the portcullis for the night."

Mahala suddenly started walking toward the stable. "Thank you, Vishtorath," the princess said as she fell in step beside her horse. The portcullis creaked softly as it dropped slowly into place behind her in the darkness. As she crossed the courtyard, she pondered her unusual conversation with the strange, gentle giant.

✠

Vrengnia took her parcel to her chambers as soon as she left the stables. She was thankful that there were very few people about and that no one asked her about the package. It was a rather unusual package to be carrying around the castle, but she *was* the princess, and while she seldom exploited it, she had rights to a certain privacy.

When the swords were stowed safely in her wardrobe, behind the bright pantaloons and pied blouses, she left her chambers to deliver the leather to the smith. Vrengnia had acquired a different piece of leather for the smith, but left it behind, under her bed, thinking that the piece that had wrapped the swords was his anyway.

She pondered how she had come to have this piece of leather. She was beginning to discern patterns in things that happened; she found herself discounting congruent events as coincidence less frequently, and she was seeing a grand design slowly evolve out of the linear perception she had had of her life.

It did not matter that she had no idea why the smith wanted the leather. What was most striking was that just when she was to bring him some, this piece had fallen into her hands as part of an unrelated sub-plot of her life...or was it unrelated? There was no way to know. Her father maintained that he did not believe in coincidence; she knew that, but she was not so sure.

There was no one around. Perhaps everyone was sleeping, catching up after the last two nights of singing, or maybe...maybe what? She climbed to the tower completely unchallenged, in fact, unencountered. When she got to the smith's door, it was bolted securely. She stood for a long time, wondering whether the smith would know that she was there. Finally deciding that it did not matter, she threw the latch and drew the bolt hastily, pushing the door open as abruptly as she could.

"Come in, Princess," said the warm voice of the smith.

She remained outside the door. "How did you know it was me?" she asked incredulously.

"You waited so long and then drew the bolt so quickly." There was a smile in his voice. She gave up and walked into the smith's chambers. He was gazing out the window.

"Come here, Princess." He waved gracefully and she walked over to the window where he was standing. "Do you see the mountains on the horizon?" She stared into the darkness for a moment.

"Barely!" she exclaimed. "My eyes are not used to the darkness."

"Keep looking. When you can see the mountains, look for the lights that shine out from them periodically. I just noticed them for the first time tonight. Do you have any idea what they might be?"

"I think...no...yes, I see," said the princess. "They are very far away; they are probably outside the boundaries of Immerland. They could be anything."

"Or something," rejoined the smith.

The princess looked at him sternly. "Why do I get the feeling that you know what is going on there?"

"I do know, Princess—and so do you; and so does your father for that matter...but come, why are you here?"

She held out the leather and pressed it into his hands.

"Ah, the leather." He unrolled it and snapped it briskly to straighten it out. "Hmmmm…this looks familiar." He glanced knowingly at her. "You were there today?"

She nodded.

"And he just gave you this?" He had walked over to his bed and spread it out flat on top of it.

She leaned against the wall by the window with her hands behind her. "He made a gift for me and wrapped it in this so I could bring it back here safely."

The smith raised his eyebrow. "A gift for friendship?"

"Yes—pure friendship." She was suddenly dreading the direction this conversation was going.

"And what sort of gift was it, exactly?"

The "exactly" part was most annoying. She was not ready to tell him about the swords. "May we leave this for some other time, good smith?"

"Of course," he said gently. "Whenever you are ready."

She was beginning to like the smith almost as much as his son, although the connection was different somehow. His gentleness, confidence and ability to defuse the stickiest of situations were amazing.

"So, when is your father's birthday, exactly?" asked the smith, adroitly redirecting the conversation.

"Eight days from now, when Tal is full. There will be a great feast. He will be fifty, you know."

"Yes, I knew that. It's rather remarkable, is it not, to live fifty years…." He was staring out the window again. "And how old are you, Princess?"

"I'll be eighteen on the equinox," she replied.

"So soon?"

"Uh huh."

"Have you chosen your name?"

It suddenly occurred to her that she had not even thought about it. The eighteenth birthday was important. It was the time when the child name was shed and a new name was chosen to carry into adulthood. The child name was given at birth. One had no choice in its designation, but the adult name was by choice, a chance to stake a claim in the adult world. "Not yet…I kind of like my name as it is…I…I guess I have just been putting it off."

"I see. You may want to give it a bit more thought. You know how important it is." The smith walked slowly to the window again. It seemed almost like a magnet to him.

"I know. I guess I'm not sure I am ready to be an adult."

He looked at her squarely. "An adult? Or a queen?"

Vrengnia felt herself flush, caught somewhere between embarrassment and anger. She held her tongue for a moment, trying to find the right words. The smith turned to gaze out the window. She said, "I will give it due consideration...and you? How old are you?"

"I'm not exactly sure. By my closest accounting, I am about fifty-five; my son is twenty-three." He stopped, concentrating on the scene out the window. "Princess," he said suddenly, "come quickly!" She ran to the window. "What do you see now?"

She strained to see into the darkness. One of the brighter spots on the distant mountain was flashing on and off, in an irregular sequence of light and darkness.

"What is it?" she whispered.

"I am not sure. It may be a message of some kind," said the smith, "but I think you should go tell your father now."

"Why do you want *me* to tell him?"

"In spite of what he thinks of me, I am not his enemy, but he will hear this better from you. Do not tell him that I pointed it out to you."

As he walked her to the door, he said quickly, "I will need your help two nights hence about this time. Will you be able to come?

"Yes, of course," she said affectionately.

"And Princess..." She turned to look at him again. "Do not fear." She was not afraid, but wondered if perhaps she should be as she threw the bolt on the smith's prison, locking him away again, so that the rest of the world would be safe from his wisdom and gifts.

26

The value of the man who speaks sincerely
to his king is weighed on the barley scales
and not on the gem cutter's balance.

Mindar Colloden
The Great fathers

KING SANDIHAR DID NOT LIKE WHAT HE WAS SEEING, BUT WAS NOT SURE exactly what it was. "When did you first see this?" he asked his daughter.

"About ten minutes ago…from the windows in the southern hall-way near my chambers. What are they, Father, and what do they mean?" she asked. Her voice was calm.

"I do not know the answer to either question, but I think that they are not good. Advisors!" he shouted. He could see the irregular pulses of light, now coming from two places. It seemed to be some kind of sig-naling. What and who were they for? The king and princess were watch-ing the horizon when the advisors arrived.

Pointing to the window the king asked, "What do you make of all this?" Just as he asked the question, Omberon appeared at the door.

Carnados, Cordas, Mindar and Omberon stood at the windows and watched for several minutes in silence. The advisors scratched their heads and stroked their beards, stealing glances at one another. Omberon smiled. The king hated his smile. It was always arrogant, though there *were* times when it almost seemed genuine as well. After a short and hushed conversation, the advisors turned toward him. "May we speak freely in front of the princess?" Carnados asked.

"Of course!"

"We have had more reports from the field, Sire. Verclan is station-ing many men in the southern mountains. They seem to be scattered here and there in the hills, not as an army, but more dispersed, in small pockets—highly mobile bands, if you will, possibly small raiding par-ties. Our scouts have also seen these fires but have not been able to determine what they are for."

The king felt his anger rising to fury. "Why was I not told of this earlier?" he demanded.

"We were on our way here to inform you when we were summoned," replied Carnados. "The scouts came in only about half an hour ago. There was much confusion—we had to piece it together as best we could."

The king stared out the window. "What do you think should be done?"

"They are signals, Sire." Omberon's gravelly interruption rang with confidence.

"What kind of signals?"

"It's an old Tessamandrian fire code. Someone from the mountains is in Immerland now. He will be able to read these signals from anywhere that they are visible, which is probably most of Immerland."

"Do you know what they are saying?"

"I only caught the end. 'All clear, Mordan, Shiloh, Yendel.' There were a couple of words I did not recognize." Omberon stopped. No one else seemed ready to speak.

Sandihar urged them, "I'm open to suggestions." He turned back to the window.

"We suggest that you prepare the army for skirmishes along the southern border," Carnados paused, steeling himself. "We also believe that you should try to establish some communication with Verclan himself."

The king felt the word rising as he whirled to face his advisors. "No!" he shouted. Carnados stepped back. "He is a brigand and a murderer. He cannot be reasoned with. And I told you before to never make that suggestion again."

"But, Sire—"

"Don't 'But, Sire' me! Do you understand? Do you understand?!" he thundered. The advisors backed away.

"The area surrounding those three towns is quite large," graveled Omberon. "We may be dealing with just one or two persons—it may be a small army—it may be a scattered group, and it would be useless to search for them in the dark...."

"Go on," pressed the king.

"We should send the scouts out to investigate in the morning. By afternoon we will know if there has been any mischief."

Sandihar eyed the captain warily. Omberon stood his ground, his impassive face unmoved by the royal scrutiny. "So it will be," he said slowly. "Find Rapahoogin. I want him here tonight."

Every event in life, every peak and every valley on the path we choose, strengthens us or weakens us according to whether we live in the Psadeq of Mah'Eladra and the inevitable collection of beings that surrounds us.

Karendo Marha
Journey to the Infinite

EXHAUSTED FROM TWO LONG NIGHTS AND THE FOLLOWING DAYS' ACTIVITIES, Paca stood idle in the gloom of the silent smithy. He felt a dark melancholy setting in. The delivery of the princess's sword and his blessing of it were troubling his mind. He had returned to the smithy after leaving her near the castle.

Sometimes he liked to sit and think. Right now, he wanted to just sit. As he lit the lantern over the slack tub, his mind wandered through the events of the day, and his eyes gazed into the darkness to the left of the forge. He sat down on the empty anvil stump. Time dissolved; so did the world around him as he listened to his vorn, not sure whether he could trust it. Something had been violated, but he was not sure what. Maybe he was just tired. Perhaps it was merely the letdown after all the intensity. Somewhere inside he knew that this was not the end of the matter. However, if this was not the end, what was next?

The quiet knock on the window at the back of the smithy startled him. The tapping had been gentle, nothing to cause alarm or fear, so he took the lantern and walked toward the window to see what it was. When he got there, he held up the light, shading his eyes from the lantern's reflection on the smoky glass. He could see nothing. Perhaps he was imagining things

He made his way back toward the front door, holding the lantern in front of him to make sure he did not trip over anything. As he passed the forge he looked up to see a man sitting, exactly where he had just been, on the anvil stump. Startled by the unexpected appearance, Paca jumped back, grabbing a fire rake from the forge bed. He stood facing the stranger. The man was motionless and calm. He appeared to be tall, but Paca could not see how tall because he remained seated and his dark cloak mostly covered his torso and legs. In the dim light the man looked gaunt and tired, but also well built and powerful. His face wore a sad, kindly expression, yet his eyes sparkled. Neither man moved.

"Where is the smith?" asked the stranger.

"Who is it that asks?" Paca replied cautiously. He did not intend to cross this quiet stranger.

"An old friend." The voice was gentle and sad but carried a deep sense of affection.

If this man knew his father, then he could not get away with calling himself the smith. "And this friend's name is?"

"That is not important now. Where is the smith?" The tone was more commanding, but still soft and accepting. Not a muscle of his body moved except in his face. "I must speak with him now!"

Surely this stranger was not from within the kingdom because he would know about his father's incarceration, but how did he get here, and what was he after? Paca remained silent. The man rose off the anvil stump to his full height and dropped his cloak backwards in one simple motion. Paca took a step back and raised the fire rake. The other turned his palms toward him in a gesture of openness, and Paca could see that he was unarmed. He wore a simple brown linen tunic with a black silhouette of a crow across the front, girdled with a belt that supported neither dagger nor sword, and leather leggings with soft leather shoes laced up to his calves. The two men stood facing each other. It was the stranger who spoke first.

"If you are the smith's son...are you?"

Something about the stranger's manner calmed his mind and quelled the natural fear he should have felt. "Yes, I am."

"I have known your father for many years. Your father served as a farrier in the service of the Great Queen, the mother of your king. You knew this?"

"Yes." Paca noted the "your king," as though Sandihar was not this man's king also.

"I and your father were close friends and worked together on the farrier's staff in the queen's stables." He leaned back against the stump again, stared into the dead forge coal, and crossed his arms across the black crow on his tunic. "Your father had a gift with steel. He could make anything, and his talent was wasted on the farrier's forge. He taught me more than you can imagine. We were separated when I was sent off by the prince to serve the cavalry in the wars for the southern sector. Your father refused to go and was dismissed by the prince. Your father set up here in Shiloh to work his craft, still within the queen's domain, but a fair distance from the prince." He paused, continuing to stare into the dark fire pit. Paca remained motionless, still holding the lantern and the fire rake.

Suddenly, the stranger's eyes darted up to meet his own. "I need him now."

Paca took a step back. He felt himself tensing again.

"Lay down your weapon, son," the stranger said gently. "You have nothing to fear from me."

Paca hesitated as he eyed the man then laid the rake carefully onto the forge bed and raised the lantern to a hook on a ceiling beam. "If you tell me your name, I will tell you where my father is."

The stranger eyed him thoughtfully. "If I tell you my name, will you promise not to touch that fire rake?"

Paca was uneasy. Why would this stranger ask such a question? The dark man continued. "If you do, you will be shot through before you get it off the forge bed."

"I will not touch the rake."

The stranger paused, then said impassively, "My name is Verclan. Now, where is your father?"

Paca glanced about uneasily, straining to see through the windows and the door. Verclan! The leader of the rebellious mountain clans. What did he want with his father?

"You promised. Where is my friend?" The voice seemed to be coming from somewhere far away. Stunned, Paca sat down heavily on the swage block beside the forge. Looking hopelessly down at the floor, he uttered, "He's in the king's prison."

Verclan unfolded his arms; his eyes narrowed and burned with anger. "Is there a reason?"

The young smith looked up. "He refused to make a sword for the king. So the king has imprisoned him until he does."

Verclan threw his head back and laughed heartily. Paca was perplexed at the outburst, but also more than a bit relieved. "That would be your father!" Verclan exclaimed with a wide smile on his face, his arms open and a smirk twisted into the words as they came out. "He never would make a weapon. Not ever! That is why the prince—who is now the king—discharged him. And with good reason, mind you. He always said that his blades would be too dangerous as weapons." He shifted his weight on the stump and faced Paca full on, his eyes gleaming in the light of the lantern. "We just thought he was prideful and arrogant. It cost him his job. But looking back," Verclan ran his left hand through his thick, dark hair, "he probably made the wiser decision." There was a faraway look in his eyes as he sat motionless for a moment.

The vague forebodings Paca had been mulling over before Verclan's arrival coalesced. Would he have had the courage to make such a decision? In light of the sudden revelation of this odd stranger, he regretted the path he had chosen.

Verclan clapped his hands onto his knees and stood up suddenly as if he were finished with his business. "It is good to know that he is still as stubborn about this as he used to be, though I wish he were not in prison for it—but that would be the king, too!"

"You know the king?" Paca was incredulous.

"Of course. We were friends, also, but in a different sphere. I served under him when he was just the prince. He was in charge of the cavalry. I shod his horses. As your father is with blades, so am I as a farrier. Only the best for the prince, don't you know?"

"He regards you as an enemy now," ventured Paca uncertainly.

"Yes, he does. We have our differences, to be sure. Someday you will learn that every man has a story. Unfortunately, history is often determined by who gets to tell his story. Perhaps some day I will get to tell you mine." He paused and looked keenly into Paca's eyes. "And you, young smith, what is your story? Do you understand the steel and the fire as your father does? Can you forge an edge and breathe into it the blessing of peace, or do your blades threaten the lives of honest men?" He paused. Paca felt the heat rising under his collar. He shifted his weight and looked down at the floor. "Do you carry the banner of your father, seeing the wisdom in refusing to participate in the study of war? Or do you yield to the king in his pursuit of my life?" Paca looked up again. The dark eyes flickered brightly in the dim light of the smithy. Verclan was standing at full height, waiting pensively for a response.

"If you were friends with the king, why does he seek your life?" Paca tried vainly to throw Verclan off the track.

"That is one of the strange paradoxes that surround our lives. Suffice it to say that we are friends *and* he seeks my life. Now, answer my question!"

Paca pointed to the sign that hung above the forge, but said nothing. Verclan glanced at the sign and smiled. "Why do I have a sense that you are lying to me? But, for the honor of your father's name, I will press this issue no further." He raised his hand, glanced at the door, and snapped his middle finger smartly into his palm.

Through the door came a tall young man, powerfully built and proud in bearing, carrying a woodland bow with a long arrow nocked on the string. Paca guessed that they were about the same age. "This is my son, Patira," said Verclan. "He is a smith like you. You will employ him in your smithy for a time to make sure that no blades for the king are forged here."

Paca's eyes narrowed. "I don't need another smith!"

"Yes, you do," said Verclan matter-of-factly. "I know that without your father, your work is lagging. Patira is a fine smith; as good, if not better, than any you have in your employ already. He knows the art of the blade and much of the forge poetry—and he knows that no blade made by you or your father should come into the hands of the king."

"I will not have him here!"

Verclan leaned forward. "Let me tell you part of my story, then—but only part. Your father knows the blade and the edge, but have you ever wondered where he gets his steel? Have you ever wondered where he gets the coal to make his fine blades?" Paca stared at him silently. He did know. His father bought them from the old trader who came through Shiloh about once a month. He was a strange man who never spoke. His father selected what he wanted from the cart and paid the man in iron-ware from the smithy. "Have you?!" commanded Verclan.

"No...I mean...yes," stammered Paca. He felt the intimidation of Verclan's close intense energy.

"He gets them from me. It is my hand that provides the blade steel that your father uses and my mines that provide the only coal he wants." Verclan paced back and forth before the forge. "And besides his impene-trable determination not to use his extraordinary gift to make weapons, he has vowed to me that he would never supply them to the king!" He stopped pacing and turned to face Paca squarely. "I don't think that you have fully accepted the character lessons that your father undoubtedly has been giving you, and I don't trust you. Therefore, Patira will stay in your employ until I need him to come back to my service. Otherwise—" He raised his hand and slowly drew a finger across his throat.

Paca got the message clearly enough. He leaned on the forge heavily, wanting to break eye contact, but not daring to do so. Verclan turned to leave, then hesitated. "One more thing! No one is to know who Patira is or why he is here. Is this understood?"

Paca wanted to just nod his head, but decided that a complete verbal answer would be best. "It is very clear," he said, trembling.

"Then Patira will start in the morning." Verclan wrapped himself in his cloak and addressed his son. "Check the fires."

"I have—we are clear for now."

Verclan and Patira disappeared silently into the night. Paca sat for a long time on the anvil stump. A great storm was gathering. Between the king and the princess, his father, Verclan, Patira and undoubtedly the mountain men that followed them, he was now a common link. He just sat, staring at nothing, hearing nothing, seeing nothing, trying to feel nothing.

28

The handiest tool of a good smith is an able assistant who moves and breathes to the rhythm of his master's stroke.

Timmanaeus

Patira was sitting on the stone step outside the door of the smithy, leaning casually against the doorframe, when Paca arrived. "Good morning," he said cheerfully.

"So it is." Paca was early—earlier than the other smiths, but he was now wishing he had been there even earlier.

Patira stood up and shook his hand vigorously. His grip suggested extraordinary strength. "It is good to be here." His voice was gentle and reassuring, more like a genuine friend than a spy. Paca could not say how good it all was, but accepted Patira's sincerity.

In the daylight, he could see Patira better. He was a handsome young man, with black eyes and short hair so dark that Paca could not be sure whether it was black. His face was perfectly featured, thin and delicate but strong at the same time. The breadth of his smile extended over his whole face, and his teeth flashed white behind an olive flesh tone. His clothing was dark; a black tunic with brown leggings and soft leather shoes molded tightly around his feet. Sun-darkened, muscular arms, bare to the shoulder and banded at the wrist with wide leather braids, heightened the visage of a lithe and agile youth.

"Come," Paca said, pushing open the smithy door. He hung his light coat on the hook just inside the door. "The other smiths will be wondering what is going on. I haven't been here the last two days, and the soldiers came only yesterday to take my father's anvil and some of his tools to the castle."

"Hmmmm…" Patira mused, reassuring Paca that he was listening and interested.

"Not sure why, really. They said that my father needed them. Anyway, we need to get another anvil. C'mon." Paca led the way through a door behind the main forge to the storeroom at the back of the smithy. "So the other smiths—I'll introduce you to them—we will just have to ignore their curiosity."

"By the fires of Timmanaeus himself!" Patira whistled softly when he saw the pyramid of anvils stacked against the back wall.

"My father believes that a blacksmith can never have too many anvils. Whenever he can, he picks them up and stores them in here. C'mon, help me find one suitable for the main forge."

Paca thought he knew anvils, but Patira proved to have a strong sense of selection. "Too small." "Not enough ring." "Not flat enough." "Too worn." It took nearly an hour of heavy lifting and three narrow escapes with their fingers before they finally found one that suited them both. Patira agreed with this particular choice because of the sound. "All things being equal, the sound of its ring is the final arbiter for the integrity of the anvil," he said.

Paca liked it more for the quality of the surface. It was smooth, though not perfect, and the horn still had the right shape to its point. They set it aside and re-stacked the other anvils.

By the time they hauled it out of the shed and set it on the stump, the work of the smithy was in full swing. As Patira and Paca adjusted the anvil until it was level and solid, they could feel the furtive, curious glances of the other smiths. A voice at his right queried cheerfully, "A new assistant?"

"Vordar! This is Patira," he said heartily as Patira took Vordar's hand. "He is the son of an old friend of my father, a farrier and blade-smith. I thought we needed the help. He'll be working my fire."

Vordar's eyes narrowed with a slight suspicion, but addressed the newcomer graciously. With a shallow bow he said, "Welcome to Shiloh Forge. We can always use the help." He turned and started pointing out the other smiths, calling them by name and introducing them briefly to Patira. Each nodded and started back to work with no further acknowledgment of his presence. "If you need any help, be sure to let me know," Vordar said in closing and with a wink delivered his final remark, "Paca can be a bit tiresome to work for, and he has a bad habit of drinking out of his slack tub."

Patira was quick. "Does he stir it first?" Paca felt the flush in his ears as all the smiths guffawed. Patira smiled in amusement.

Paca had to admit he was beginning to like him already. "C'mon, we have to work sometime."

For the rest of the morning, they worked the anvil, grinding and polishing, polishing and grinding, filing the horn, and then polishing so that the anvil's newly exposed surfaces fairly gleamed.

Paca busied himself with preparations for the day's work while Patira cleaned out the forge and laid the fire. He watched Patira as he worked. He had an easy manner and a quick mind, particularly related to the forge work. He was younger than all the other smiths, but seemed to have a curiously broad grasp of details. The fire was burning bright and clean as quickly as Paca could imagine doing it himself; and Patira had several tricks that Paca had never seen, as if he had learned his trade in a different country altogether.

As he laid the first blades into the fire, Paca struggled to resolve his emotions about having Patira there. There was nothing offensive or arrogant about his presence; in fact he fit in rather well. He could not likely have found a more apt and eager worker. Patira knew how to be quiet, he knew when to speak, he listened well and he offered his opinion only when it was appropriate. *All in all*, Paca thought, *this is not going to be so bad.*

Patira worked the bellows and the fire with great skill, anticipating every move that Paca made. He was always in the right place; he worked the fire perfectly around Paca's needs, adding coal at the right time and never disturbing the flow or timing of the work.

✠

It was late afternoon when they heard the clip-clop of a horse's hooves in the lane. Paca knew it was the princess. A quick wave of panic fled through his mind about the princess meeting Patira. It was a fleeting thought. He decided not to worry about it, then thought it strange that he could make this decision so quickly. There was not much he could do anyway, and Vrengnia had never embarrassed him before. He must wait and keep working.

Vrengnia entered the smithy gaily, striding up to the great forge without hesitation. "I brought you a raisin cake from the kitchen…well, actually I *stole* it from the kitchen." Patira looked at Paca quizzically, wanting to know who this curiously dressed person was. Paca had gotten used to her peculiar fashion habits, but Patira's look made him realize all over again how unusual it was.

He bowed slightly and smiled. "Thank you, my friend." He gestured to Patira who was watching intently. "Princess Vrengnia, this is my new assistant and fire keeper, Patira. Patira, this is Princess Vrengnia, daughter of King Sandihar of Immerland." He glanced at Patira to see if there was any surprise. If there were, he did not show it. Patira nodded his head and smiled. Vrengnia stuck out her hand and she shook Patira's vigorously, saying, "You could not have chosen to work for a finer smith than my friend here." She paused before she looked at Paca and said, "Do you have time for a piece of this purloined cake?"

"I am sure we do. Is there enough for everyone?"

Vrengnia scanned the smithy quickly and laughed as she walked out the door. She returned with a large bundle in her hands. Paca was amazed. "You stole *that* from the king's kitchen?" he asked incredulously.

"Well, I *am* the princess, don't you know—got a knife?"

Patira laughed. "That's like asking your father if he has a page." They all laughed. Paca took one of the mostly finished blades from the workbench, washed it carefully, and handed it to the princess. All the smiths took a break and had raisin cake together in the smithy.

For a few minutes, they all talked about everything and nothing. Paca was thankful for his friendship with the princess. It never seemed to go wrong, even in the awkward places.

"I saw your father last night," said Vrengnia in the midst of the gaiety. Paca looked at her. She had caught him with his mouth full of cake. "He had asked me to get a piece of leather for him, so I gave him the piece you gave to me yesterday. I hope you don't mind."

Paca swallowed his cake. "Not at all," he said. "And how is he doing?"

"He seems quite content and at peace—I mean, my father is treating him rather well—for a prisoner." She took a small bite of cake. "He recognized that piece of leather instantly. I hadn't noticed how beautiful it was until he shook it out."

"What did he want it for?"

"He didn't say," said the princess. "He just said he needed a piece of leather."

The smiths had devoured the cake, and the princess busied herself with cleaning up the crumbs. "Did you come all this way just to bring cake to the smith?" asked Patira suddenly.

"Why, yes," Vrengnia smiled. "It isn't really that far, on a good horse." She hesitated. "You seem suspicious, Patira."

"Just curious; it seems a bit...I mean, the Princess of Immerland bringing a raisin cake to a smith?"

"Paca is my friend and has been for some time. This is what friends do, is it not?" Paca detected her defensiveness mingled with a touch of resentment.

Patira looked at her thoughtfully. "Yes it is, in fact," he said. "I was just curious."

The conversation drifted back to the mundane as the smiths returned to their work. Patira, Paca and the princess chatted for a few more minutes, and Vrengnia bid them goodbye. She left as she came, without fanfare.

Paca was silent for a while as he worked. At a pause in the work, he looked up at Patira and said, "You made quite an impression on the princess."

"Oh?"

"I have never seen her react so quickly to anything."

"Does she come here often?"

"Fairly—usually just like that. She drops by, chats awhile and then goes back to the castle. She's just like that. She is not your ordinary princess."

"That, I could see," said Patira with a slight smile.

They went back to work and for the rest of the day spoke no more of the princess.

29

Wrap your soul in a mountain cloak,
Close by a mountain fire,
In hemlock stand, in shadowed night,
Warmed by flame, and drawn by light.
Let no one speak, that each one may
Discern the truth, the mountain way.

Dorvatica
Mountain Song

THE SCENTED WIND THREATENED TO CHILL THE MEN SITTING AROUND THE fire. Wrapped in their cloaks, they sat shoulder to shoulder on makeshift benches in a clearing in the dense hemlock canopy. Shadows cast by the roaring fire danced on the dark trunks of the surrounding trees as they waited. The usual banter had run low, and no one moved as they stared into the fire.

At the first faint sound of hoof beats, Verclan sat up straight and listened intently. He rose as if to hear better. "It's my son," he announced confidently. "At least it is his horse." He smiled as he sat down again. Everyone remained quiet as the sound of the approaching horse grew louder. As Patira emerged from the darkness into the light of the fire, Verclan rose again and greeted him with a hug. "Come, sit down and have something to drink."

"That sounds good," said Patira. Verclan watched patiently as his son tied his horse to a nearby tree and joined the ring around the fire. Verclan knew that Patira was familiar with everyone there; they were his most trusted advisors. He handed his son a jug with a diluted apple cider mixed with spices. "Maclin?"

Patira took the jug, paused, and took a long draught. It was a drink concocted by mountain herbalists to strengthen the mind and stimulate clear thinking in times of fatigue. Bitter to the taste and burning slightly as it ran down the throat for the first time, it was what Patira would need after the long ride from Shiloh.

Verclan would not have to ask his son to start. Patira would know that this is why they were gathered; and Verclan waited patiently, staring into the fire without moving, for his son to begin.

"I saw nothing unusual at the smithy today. There was no indication that any of the smiths are working on any kind of weaponry, offensive or defensive—not any armor either." He paused and took another drink of the maclin. "I waited for two hours after the smithy was shut down to see if there would be any night activity, but there was not. It seemed like a rather ordinary day at the forge."

"How was the young smith?" interjected Verclan. Patira took another sip from the jug before continuing. "He is very talented. He has a strong intuition for the steel. He is easygoing, good with the hammer, and fast. He can do more in one heat than most smiths would do in two or three." No one spoke so he continued. "He has a curious style. I was trying to figure out whether that might be because he is left-handed, but I think not."

Verclan took advantage of the pause: "Did he accept you? Did he seem suspicious?"

"Well at first it was a bit awkward—he had me working the fire. I think I did a passable job, and after a while we fell into a rhythm that seemed to suit him. We actually got a lot done. At the end of the day, he thanked me for my help." Patira smiled into the fire. "It was good."

"So there was nothing unusual or suspicious that happened?"

"There was one curious thing. I would not call it suspicious, just unusual."

Verclan raised his eyebrows. Several of his advisors shifted slightly in their places, but said nothing.

"We had a visit from the princess," Patira announced casually.

"*The* princess? Vrengnia?" Verclan leaned forward intently, his eyes sparkling in the firelight. "You don't call that suspicious?"

"Well, at first I did think it was odd, but it seems that she has some sort of friendship with the smith's son. She visits him often, riding down from the castle just to say hello and stay at the smithy for a while. Then she goes back to the castle. Today she stole a raisin cake from the king's kitchen and brought it down. We all took a break and ate it right in the smithy. Then she left."

"That *is* odd," mused Verclan.

"The other smiths confirmed that this is *not* unusual. Occasionally she will convince Paca to go for a walk down the lane to the barley fields, but never for very long. It seems that they are friends. Don't know how long they have known each other. I got the impression it's been a while."

Verclan took a minute to think before he spoke. "Perhaps we will learn more tomorrow," he said quietly. "In the meantime, everybody get some sleep. My son and I need to talk. We will hold council one hour after daybreak for a discussion on these things."

None of the advisors had spoken since Patira had come into the circle. Most of them were wise men who knew that listening was of much greater value than talking. There was always a time to talk. They got up. Some of them stretched as they pulled their cloaks around them and disappeared silently into the woods.

Verclan waited several minutes, allowing time for both him and his son to think privately, watching the fire and waiting for the right moment to continue the discussion. "Tell me about the princess, son," he said when the moment came.

"I don't know a whole lot. I mean, I only just met her today."

"No, I mean your impressions. What is she like?"

"Well, she didn't act like a princess. She was unpretentious and accepting. She came into the smithy almost like a child. It's as if she doesn't care that she is a princess. And the way she was dressed, she wasn't even like a woman, much less a princess, in baggy men's trousers and a blouse streaked as if someone spilled dye on it. And this gray tunic over it all, with blue slashes and a bright yellow starburst...very peculiar."

"That was her grandmother's crest," said Verclan distantly.

"And the hat was the strangest; green and purple leather, more like a cap, but larger and flopped over to one side."

"Was she attractive?"

"She was not...let's see...it's hard to say. She would not stand out in a crowd, except for her clothes, but she wasn't ugly, if that's what you mean." Patira fell silent. Both men continued staring into the fire together, comfortable with the silence between them. Verclan knew there was more to be said, but he knew his son, and he waited.

Several minutes passed before Verclan spoke. "Do you remember the other day at the smithy? I offered to tell the smith my story some time." He looked Patira in the eye.

"Yes."

"It occurred to me then, that I have never even told *you* my story. I wanted to do this on numerous occasions, but your mother and I agreed that we would not tell you until the time seemed right. Now I feel you need to know.

"Why now?"

"Today you met the princess. As I told the young smith, the person who gets to tell the story, defines history. Every story has two sides. I want you to hear my side first."

"What does the princess have to do with it?"

"Well, the princess, undoubtedly, has only heard the other side of the story, and—"

"You know the princess?"

Verclan looked up into his son's questioning eyes. "Let me start at the beginning."

30

The ever-expanding tapestry of true history is far too complex to be represented by the linearity of a single man's understanding of one of its threads.

Mindar Colloden
The Great Fathers

PATIRA WATCHED HIS FATHER, WHO SAT TO HIS LEFT, HIS EYES FIXED ON THE flames. In the firelight Verclan's visage was accentuated by the sharp contrasts of the orange flames against his olive skin and the dark folds of his mountain cloak, wrapped around him. His face looked tired, and he suddenly seemed old in a way that Patira had never noticed.

His father pushed at the base of the fire with a stick and a shower of sparks leapt into air. How many times had they sat like this under the mountain sky? Five hundred? A thousand? Patira couldn't even begin to count. His eyes followed the shower of sparks down into the heart of the fire.

They were silent for a time, waiting and listening to each other as only mountain men do, breathing deeply of the moist, hemlock-laden air and the dry, faintly acrid smoke from the burning wood.

"I worked for the King of Immerland once—," his father began.

Patira shifted on his bench without taking his eyes from the fire.

"It was many years back—before you were born. He was still the prince at the time; and his mother, Vorania, the Great Queen, ruled Immerland.

"I was a farrier in her stables." His father looked up from the fire. Patira could feel his gaze but did not return it. "It was there I met the smith. We were about the same age. He just showed up one day. I'm not sure where he came from. I never asked. He needed a job and there was plenty to do. Queen Vorania had dozens of horses. She loved horses.

"I realized that the smith was an extraordinary craftsman, particularly when it came to blades. I've never seen anyone like him anywhere.

After hours, when we were done with our shoeing, he would work into the night on his blades…."

"What kind?"

"Anything: shears, knives, scythes. He became known and his reputation spread quickly." His father paused, then pursued his story. "We were friends from the moment we met. I remember our first handshake. I can still feel his grip. Something inside me latched onto him. It seemed as if I had known him all my life in that instant.

"It was in this service that I met your mother. She was a riding instructor to one of the queen's handmaidens, Viarda. We became close friends because of the hours we spent together in and around the stables and the horses. It was through your mother that I was able to meet Viarda. Viarda and I had a special friendship. It was different from any relationship I ever had with a woman. We spent many hours talking about everything and nothing. I shod her horse—she often brought me little gifts from the kitchen. The smith called it a cymbic relationship— it was…it was so different.

"The prince also liked Viarda and set his eye on her to be his queen. I loved your mother—she was the one to be my wife, and Viarda was…well, she was part of the court and understood royalty. She knew what it meant to be a queen from her service to the prince's mother. All in all, the prince made a good choice, and she fell very much in love with him. Viarda and I had never thought of being anything but friends."

His father paused and stretched, adjusting his cloak around him. Patira thought he saw a greater sadness settling into the lines on his father's face as he rocked back and forth gently on the small wooden bench. He seemed to be struggling with what to say next.

"When the queen died, the new king took Viarda for his wife. That was good for both of them, except that the king was insanely jealous. Though she loved him deeply, Viarda and I remained friends. It was soon after that I asked your mother to marry me.

"Your mother understood my friendship with Viarda, but the king did not. I had several discussions with him about it." His father was staring past the fire into a vast nothingness behind it and his voice grew distant. "Each time he grew more hostile. Though I had no romantic desire for Viarda, he could not understand it or tolerate it.

"Finally, he forbade Viarda to have any communication with me and in a fit of spite, ordered me to serve in the cavalry with his army, fighting the mountain people for the foothills to the south of Immerland.

"He did the same to the smith…but *he* refused to serve in the cavalry, so the king released him from his service in the stables. The smith left and settled in Shiloh. I think he did this to be comfortably far from the king." Patira saw his father shake his head and smile at the irony of the current situation between the king and the smith.

"I continued to court your mother. Whenever I could, I got back to the castle to see her, and whenever I did, I always ran into Viarda. We never did anything wrong, at least not in a certain way. Your mother will attest to that. But we were young and I was arrogant and unmarried. I did not understand the special psadeq of marriage, nor did I have the wisdom to know that our relationship needed to change because of her marriage. The smith warned me, but I did not have the sense to respect Viarda's new position as a queen and as a wife.

"Anyway, after Viarda had become pregnant with Sandihar's first child, I took a small gift for her during one of my visits to the palace. I do not know to this day how the king knew about our meeting in the stables. Viarda had just opened the gift when Sandihar attacked me. She tried to intervene on my behalf; and Sandihar, in his jealous rage, pushed her out of the fray. She tripped and fell against a hitching post—"

Patira felt the pause—and saw the sadness settle onto his father's shoulders.

"The king had a sword. I was unarmed. Your mother saddled a pair of horses while we quarreled, and she and I barely escaped; to this day, I don't exactly know how. I do remember the king's last words: that he would kill me if he ever caught me."

"Kill you?" Patira echoed in disbelief.

"Yes…kill me. Queen Viarda went into labor and died in childbirth. She named the princess Vrengnia just before she died. Sandihar blamed me for her death and banished me from the kingdom of Immerland. He has never forgiven me."

His father's voice trembled at the last sentence and trailed off, gripped by some deep pain. Patira knew there was little to be said, if anything, and little to be gained by looking at his father. He kept his eyes in the heart of the fire.

His father breathed deeply and sighed. "I fled to the hills to the south. Life was hard in the mountains. The mountain people were suspicious and independent. Fortunately, being a farrier, I had not been engaged in direct warfare with them, or they surely would have killed me. I earned their respect because of my skill as a farrier, and your mother, because of her skill as a horse trainer. Through a series of curious opportunities, we ended up serving princes of the mountain clans. They all wanted me to do their shoeing.

"The hard life became harder when Sandihar discovered where I was. He captured the foothills and took all the arable land up to the base of the mountains. There was no land for the mountain people to grow food. Winters were lean and challenging and many people starved. Resentment for the king grew strong here in the mountains. Because all the mountain warriors and princes came through my smithy for shoes, it became the central meeting place for raiding parties that marauded the lowlands for food at harvest time." His father stirred the fire absently as he talked.

"Sandihar viewed these raids as attacks on his kingdom, and blamed all of it on me." A smile appeared on his father's face. Patira could feel his amusement as his father looked up into his eyes. "Not wanting to be blamed for something I was not doing, I began organizing the raiding parties myself. I knew Immerland, and I knew the king and his army. We became so successful that I was able to unite several clans. The king, in his folly, created a greater enemy in the mountain people than he ever would have had if he had left us alone. Curious, is it not? Interestingly, our cause was not so much to oppose the king as it was a fight for survival of the mountain people. Sandihar has never understood this." He smiled sadly, shaking his head and looking up into the trees.

"By this time we had opened the mines, finding our own supply of iron and coal. I kept in touch with the smith, secretly of course. He is the best there is for testing my new alloys and forge coal. The smith, in return, has provided food and other goods that were hard to come by in the mountains.

"I have not spoken to the king since the day he drove me out. I have a hope that we will be able to speak one day, that we can resolve this. That is why whenever we catch one of his scouts, we send them back with that same message. The king has never agreed to meet."

"Ever?"

"Never. He keeps sending his army."

"Yes, I know."

"Perhaps the princess is the key to reaching the king," Verclan mused at the end of his story.

"Perhaps," said Patira, "but she is a feisty one, and although she may seem a bit odd and small, I dare say she has some fight in her."

"Knowing the king, she is probably pretty handy with the bow and the sword. I have heard that he is raising her more like a son than a daughter—she is his only heir."

"She did not seem to recognize my name when the smith introduced me to her," said Patira.

His father looked up with a hint of a smile. "Well, I know that the king knows about you and undoubtedly he knows your name. Either she did not recognize it because she did not expect it, or the king has not told her his story yet. Soon, however, he will have to do that."

"Hmmmm," said Patira. "Yes, I suppose so."

There was a long pause. Patira sat and pondered what his father had said. Finally his father peered up through the trees at the stars. "Time for bed," he said slowly. "Past time for bed. We will speak more after we have slept."

31

We are forever doomed to suffer with histories defined by those who are able to shout the loudest.

Mindar Colloden
The Great Fathers

THE PRINCESS EYED HER FATHER THOUGHTFULLY. "YOU HAVEN'T EVEN touched your dinner," she said matter-of-factly. He had invited her to a private supper, saying he had not had much time to see her lately with all the worries about the kingdom. Now he was sitting at the other end of the table, preoccupied with his own thoughts and hardly acknowledging that she was there.

"It's hard to be hungry these days," he mumbled as if he knew that was not true, but had to say something.

The princess took advantage of his attention. "Was there something particular you wanted to talk about?" she asked as she raised a glass of wine for a sip.

"Well, yes—and no—I mean, it just seems like I have not seen you around a lot lately and, well, it is nice to spend time with someone who does not want something from me."

She set down her glass and looked at him.

He continued hastily: "I mean everyone who comes to see me wants something. They all have their schemes, and many of them pretend to be after something entirely different from what they really want. It's exhausting and frustrating trying to figure it out." Vrengnia waited. "You don't come with an agenda, so it is nice to spend time with you." She let herself smile appreciatively. "So that is the 'no' side of your question. But yes, there is something specific."

She was not surprised. Although he appreciated her straightforwardness, whenever he wanted time with her, it was usually because he did have an agenda. He was the king, after all; his whole life was an agenda and hardly anything was spontaneous. Sometimes she wondered if it *could* be. Now when she became queen—

"I hear that you have been sneaking off to visit the smith's son down in Shiloh." He was trying to be stern.

"I would hardly call it sneaking. I mean, I didn't have anything else I was supposed to be doing. And I didn't try to hide it either."

"And you stole a raisin cake from the kitchen?"

"Yes," she hesitated, "but there were seven of them, and I thought the smiths at Shiloh would appreciate them more than your advisors and attendants—and I think they did, honestly," she said with a faint smile. It was her way of letting her father know that she thought his sternness was unwarranted.

He backed down. "All right, all right—just tell me what's going on."

"I will. Do you promise you won't laugh?" she looked pleadingly over the flowers in the center of the table.

The king laughed. "Yes, I promise."

"But you are already laughing," she pressed.

"I'll stop—right now." He tried to put on a serious face and ended up laughing even harder.

Vrengnia saw the opening and jumped up, grabbed the heavy arm-chair she had been sitting in and dragged it the length of the table to the spot just to the left of her father. "I always hated this long table," she said brightly as she sat down. "Now I can tell you. Where should I start?"

"At the beginning—no, wherever you want," said her father.

So that was where she started, from the first encounter the day the king first visited the smithy, all the way to her last visit with the raisin cake; that is, everything except about the swords. *That* had to remain a surprise until his birthday.

"So anyway, yesterday when I took that raisin cake down to the smithy, there was a new assistant there. Paca introduced him to me, but didn't say much else." She reached for a cluster of grapes on the table in front of her father. "He had an odd name. I think it was Patira." She began eating the grapes. She saw her father's eyes narrow but otherwise he didn't flinch.

"Hmmm. That *is* an odd name," he said thoughtfully. "Was there anything else odd about him?"

Vrengnia thought she detected a slight shift in his attitude, but she kept going. "Well, his clothes were a little strange, but then I suppose that I am not one to talk about that."

"Indeed." A flickering smile faded quickly into seriousness again.

The princess was sure now that she had hit some nerve. "Let's see, they were more like clothes you would see on a man who lived in the mountains, dark; no—"

"Have you ever seen a man from the mountains?" he interrupted.

"No," she said cautiously, "but it just seemed that way, if you know what I mean."

Her father stroked his chin, a habit he had when he was not ready to say what was on his mind.

"And he seemed a little suspicious of me," she continued. "He wanted to know why I had come all the way down to the smithy just to bring a cake to Paca. He actually had the nerve to almost interrogate me about it."

"And well he might," said her father angrily, standing up and walking to the window.

"You know him?" she gasped. It all dawned on her in an instant. She stood up suddenly at the table. Her father was looking out the window at the mountains in the distance.

"Not personally," he said. His voice was peevish. "I am not sure. That is, I have no proof yet, but this might be the son of Verclan himself."

"Verclan?"

"Yes, *the* Verclan. He has a son by that name and he would be from the mountains." He was resigned and thoughtful. "The question is, what is he doing in the smith's shop? There is something…in the back of my mind…I…" he snapped his fingers as if it would jog his memory. He did it again. "Yes!" his eyes lit up. "The smith and Verclan were friends; they served together as farriers in my mother's stables. I sent them off to serve in the cavalry, but the smith refused to go. I figured that they had lost contact when I exiled Verclan, but perhaps not."

Vrengnia was still standing by the table. Her father turned to her and spoke gravely. "You must not go to the smithy until I find out what is going on, no matter what else you do. Promise me this!" The command was firm.

She wanted to say no as firmly as he had issued his edict, but something inside told her to take a wiser direction. "I need some explanation before I will agree to that."

The king walked back over to the table. Resting his hands on it heavily, he leaned forward. "Explanations about what?" he asked, his countenance brimming with rage.

Vrengnia felt the intimidation. She had seldom seen her father so angry, but she decided to hold her ground. She leaned across the table to face him. "You can start by giving me an honest story about Verclan. I mean, why did he have to leave? What happened between you and him?" He turned away and walked back to the window. She pressed her advantage. "*You* have never told me." She followed him to the window. He was staring at the lights in the mountains. "You kept saying that you would someday, well—*now* would be fine!" She said it as forcefully as she could. Her father was silent. They stood that way for five minutes.

He was wrestling with his emotions, and she waited, knowing that she had to, but unsure whether her father would break down or explode.

She saw a tear roll down his cheek, and she stepped forward and laid her hand lightly on his left shoulder. He shook it off and sniffed, and gesturing to the table, he said, "Sit down. It's a long story."

They walked to the table and sat down again. After pouring himself some more wine, he leaned back and slid down in his chair with the flagon sitting on his belly. The posture he took suddenly made him look weak and old. Was she changing or was he? Something was happening between them that she did not understand. He looked vulnerable and broken in a way she had never noticed before. Perhaps it was that *she* was growing up and gaining strength. Vrengnia was not sure she was ready for either one.

Her father's words cut into her thoughts. He was in mid-sentence before she noticed he was talking. "...at the beginning, but I am not sure exactly where the beginning is," he said. His eyes looked far away and filled with a sad anger. She leaned forward, not wanting to miss what he was about to say.

"It started when I was still prince and my mother ruled Immerland. My older brother had disappeared, and I knew I would be king eventually."

"You had a brother?"

"He was four years older. He left one day when I was fourteen, heading for the coast. We never saw him again." He looked up into her eyes and took a sip of wine. "So I knew I would be king, but did not know how I could possibly learn how to do it. I followed my mother around and watched carefully, but it was very difficult to figure out what she did. It seemed so effortless for her." He paused and sat staring into the nothingness just to the left of his feet stretched out before him. Vrengnia waited.

"She would meet with various people, the dors, her advisors, friends—whomever—and just talk. She might ask their opinion, maybe advice. She seldom told them to actually do anything. Somehow, it all just worked. Everyone seemed to know what to do, and did it." She detected a quiet frustration in his voice, almost desperation. "She never seemed to be busy and always had time for doing things she wanted to do.

"She loved riding, just for the joy of it, and never needed a reason to go riding. She would just take the time and do it. Her stables had the best horses, the best groomsmen, the best stable hands and the best farriers." He paused. The way he had said "farriers" carried an angry edge. "She paid them handsomely to maintain her horses and the stables. Her sense of the best—on which she insisted in everything—included character as well as skill. She once dismissed the best cook in the castle because of a small indiscretion.

"When I asked her about it, she simply said that the nature of the lie he told her indicated a corruption she could not tolerate in the castle. Frankly, I never understood it." He stopped and looked into her eyes. She nodded to reassure him she was listening.

"Anyway, there were three workers in the stable that are significant to this fragment of history: first, there was Verclan himself, the finest farrier in the kingdom, though I never understood how she tolerated him on her staff. He was as arrogant as the day is long. I don't think she ever saw it that way. It was said that he could take a horse he had never seen and shoe him blindfolded, and if you asked around, you could probably find someone who would claim they *saw* him do it." Her father shook his head sadly and lapsed into a faraway stare.

"And?"

He shuddered and sat up, taking another quick sip of wine. "Well, working the forge beside Verclan was the older smith, then a young man, with talent to make the blade that was unsurpassed. He knew a good shoe and how to fit it, and the queen paid him well to forsake the blade-making to work her stables. My mother had an odd relationship with the smith. He was somewhat of a favorite in the stable when she would visit, and they often spent extended time in conversation talking about everything and nothing at all, so it seemed. I think I understand that better now. He is a very compelling individual."

"Where did he come from?"

"I don't know. My mother found him somewhere. She had a knack for attracting talent. Anyway, the smith and Verclan also had a peculiar relationship. They were always together and always stood up for each other. They seemed to have the sense of twins. They worked together as a team on the farrier's forge and could shoe a horse in a third the time that any other team could do it. The horses they shod never threw their shoes. I have never believed in magic, but this pair was the closest thing to it I have ever seen. They were the best." He took a thoughtful sip of his wine before continuing.

"Now, one of the finest riding instructors in my mother's service was a young woman by the name of Mordara. The stable hands joked that she was born on a horse. She knew the ways of horses and was particularly skilled at teaching others what she knew. She was selected as the instructor for the beautiful Viarda, your mother, who was my mother's handmaiden at the time."

"When my mother went riding, Viarda was always there and Mordara would ride along with her. The two became best friends and spent many hours together beyond the riding lessons." There was another pause and another sad, faraway look. Vrengnia guessed that her father was remembering many things that were not directly part of the story he was telling, but were part of what had shaped him. She waited silently.

"All this was well within the ordinary, but the odd thing that came out of it was that Verclan and Viarda also developed a relationship. It would have been of little consequence, except that as handmaiden to the queen, he should never have been nearly as forward as he was with her."

"Your mother was extremely beautiful. I was often in her presence, obviously, and we fell in love. We tried to be discreet. I don't think my mother would have approved."

"Why?"

Her father sighed deeply and looked into her eyes. "Your grandmother was very traditional in certain ways. She loved Viarda, but Viarda was still a handmaiden. Princes do *not* marry handmaidens." He took another sip of wine.

"Did you ever talk to her about it?"

"No, it would have been useless."

Vrengnia decided not to press it further.

"I knew she loved me too. I wasn't in a hurry, and mother was getting old. We secretly decided to wait until she died to marry. The only hitch was Verclan."

"Verclan?"

"Your mother kept insisting they were just friends...."

"You were jealous—"

"Yes, yes. I suppose so, but with good reason. A woman who has agreed to marry someone should *not* have that kind of friendship with another man." He drank deeply, quelling his anger behind the rim of the flagon. Vrengnia's thoughts drifted back to her conversation with the smith.

"I tried desperately to reason with Verclan—to keep him away from Viarda. And I tried to reason with Viarda, but to no avail. They insisted they were just friends. Finally in desperation, I had Verclan reassigned to the cavalry. We were engaged with the mountain people over the farming rights in the foothills to the south. I sent him there, to be a farrier for the cavalry."

"When mother died, the stables were not used nearly as much, so I tried to reassign the smith also. He refused to serve in the cavalry, so I dismissed him from service to the castle."

"So that's how he ended up in Shiloh?"

Her father nodded. "Your mother and I married, but somehow the connection between your mother and Verclan continued, through the agency of Mordara. I knew it was there, but tried to ignore it. It was beyond resolution, so I just tolerated it."

"Just before you were born, Mordara arranged a secret meeting between Verclan and your mother in the castle stables. Ostensibly, it was so that Verclan could deliver a small gift to honor her expected child, which of course was you. I heard about it through one of the other attendants who had overheard a conversation between your mother and Mordara. I accosted them in the stables and challenged them. Verclan grew violent and attacked me. He was much stronger than I. Fortunately, I had brought my sword. When your mother tried to intervene, Verclan pushed her aside. She tripped and fell into a hitching post, where she was mortally wounded.

"Verclan fled. I pursued him, but the treacherous Mordara had already saddled two of the best horses for their escape, and they fled to the mountains. The castle doctors delivered you, but your mother died in the birthing." The faraway look returned to her father's eyes. "I have never been able to forgive him for the death of your mother." He sat unmoving for a long time, collecting his thoughts which flitted across his face, never surfacing in words. Vrengnia waited. The weight of her father's story descended on her; a weight of anger and hatred, pressing from all sides. If his tale were true, then his loathing of Verclan could be justified, but she found, in her vorn, a peculiar strength pushing back and repelling her fear. It was doubt, working from the inside out; doubt that this was the whole story; doubt that the simplicity of it could lead to the level of fear and resentment he carried.

Her father continued. "Verclan was a very clever man, and it did not take long before he had aroused the mountain people against me and begun raiding the border villages, systematically rallying the outlying boundaries of Immerland against me also. Many of my scouts disappeared, tortured and killed by the outlaw and his followers. I knew that there could be no peace in Immerland unless this man was brought to justice and his followers disbanded."

Vrengnia felt her father's shift from sadness to anger. She wanted to sympathize. It would have been easy to do a month ago, but having met the smith and Patira and being engaged with Paca in his endeavor to make her father's sword, she found a tangle of emotions woven so tightly around her inner doubt that she could not. Even the idea, buried in her father's vorn and withheld from her for so long, that Verclan had killed her mother, seemed like a restless cloud, driven overhead by the gale, but powerless to drop its rain. A new determination was awakening in her vorn, a determination to move forward rather than sympathize. "Father," she queried, "have you ever tried to seek peace with Verclan? I mean, talk to him, find a better solution than fighting?"

"Impossible," he snorted in disgust. "He is a madman, a renegade and a traitor. He killed my wife and *your mother*. He cannot be trusted and he deserves to die. Even now, our scouts are reporting a massing of small bands of men, waiting in the hills. That is what all the lights are—their fires. They will attack again. It is just a matter of when and how."

He rose from the table where they had been sitting and walked to the window again. "So, my darling daughter, that is why you must not go to the smithy until we know why Patira is there."

Vrengnia bristled inside. She hated that appellation. Her father only used it when he was trying to get some unwarranted control over her. She knew that there was a time to show one's anger, but this was not it. "Father, you have no proof that this Patira at the forge is one and the same as the son of your enemy." The king glanced at her with a mixture of disgust and anger, but she pressed on. "Secondly, I do not see a reason to fear. Patira gave me no indication, no threat—"

Her father interrupted her in a burst of rage. "When Patira went to the forge, he had no idea that you would be going there. By now, he has undoubtedly conferred with his father, and they are laying a plan of what to do if you show up again. Open your eyes! This is the real world. Though we are royalty—the *king*, the *princess*—in many ways we are just pawns in the vast scheme of things, and you must trust my intuition about this man Verclan." He turned back to the window.

Vrengnia was furious, but she also saw the wisdom in what her father was saying. She waited until she could answer appropriately, more like a queen than a child, then said evenly, "I will refrain from visiting the smithy—and the smith—out of respect for your authority as king, until you have ascertained the truth about Patira. However, I wish to send a message to Paca explaining that I will not be visiting."

"Why?" asked the king without turning from the window.

"Because he is my friend. He would wonder if I did not come to visit for some time."

"That's fair," said the king quietly, his anger subsiding, "but it must not say why."

Vrengnia thought she understood and said firmly, "It will not state why. Good night, Father." She turned and headed for the door of the great hall; dinner remained uneaten on the table.

She headed straight to her chambers. Anger raged inside her, but she knew that her father was right, in spite of his fear. She stared out the windows at the mountains. The lights were still there. She wondered what they really were, what they really meant. Then she looked up to see the sky, full of lights, peaceful, eternal. *They* were no threat to her or Immerland. Should the lights on the mountains really be any different?

She called for an attendant and made her way to her writing desk and wrote a simple note:

"Paca, because of certain obligations here at the castle, I will not be able to come to the smithy for several days. I look forward to the time I will be able to come and see you again. I hope that it will be soon. Vrengnia."

She rolled it carefully, sealing it with hot wax and impressing it with her ring. When the attendant arrived, she handed it to him. "See that this is delivered to the smith at Shiloh Forge first thing in the morning." The attendant bowed and disappeared down the hall.

It was already late, so she prepared herself for bed and lay down. She knew she was exhausted but she could not sleep. She was still half-awake when she heard the midnight watch called from the parapet across the courtyard.

Somewhere in the nether world between wakefulness and deep sleep she heard a peculiar sound she had never heard before. It was a slight creak and a click just outside her door. It was curious and different, but she fell asleep without making the effort to discover what it was.

32

Courage is not found in the one who does not fear. It is born in the heart of the one who knows fear, but does not allow that fear to dissuade him from his course.

Pratoraman
The Middle Way

PATIRA WAS SITTING ON THE STOOP OF THE SMITHY DOOR WHEN PACA arrived. Paca could feel the uneasy conflict between the simple joy of seeing a new friend and a subtle fear emanating from who this friend was. He greeted Patira casually. "How long a ride is it to…to wherever you are staying?"

"Perhaps an hour. Maybe a bit longer. I had to be more careful today. The king's scouts have been snooping around since early this morning."

"Do you know why?"

"No, but it doesn't matter." Patira seemed completely relaxed. He stepped in front of Paca and opened the door. "What's on the slate for today?"

"We have to finish those barley scythes." Paca hung his coat. "We need an edging fire, long and not too hot." He knew Patira would do exactly what was needed. They had worked together only one day, but Patira had proven himself well. He headed for the forge as Paca gathered the four roughed-in blades from the previous day's work. He took them to the window to examine them while Patira cleaned the firepot and laid the new fire.

Paca could not help wondering what the king's scouts were up to. He wondered if Vrengnia had mentioned Patira to her father, though he doubted that she knew who Patira was, and nothing had been said to give him away. If this were the case, then Patira's cavalier attitude seemed out of place, particularly if the scouts were after *him*.

He looked toward the forge. The fire was already burning. Patira was focused on arranging the coal on the forge bed. "Long and low!" he called as a reminder. Patira turned and smiled.

Paca worked the blades in and out of the fire; four at once. Patira tended the air and the coal perfectly while Paca pounded out the details of the blades. Paca sang; Patira listened.

It was mid-morning and Paca had all four blades cycling through the fire under Patira's expert care, when suddenly, as he looked up, Patira had vanished. The bellows toggle was still swinging where he had left it. Paca hesitated and glanced quickly around the smithy. There was no sign of his helper. He was about to say his name when the door of the smithy burst open, and the captain of the King's Guard lurched through it. "We're looking for Patira," the captain growled, squinting in the dimness of the smithy.

Paca thought quickly. "There is no one here by that name," he said as he put the blade he had been working back into the fire carefully, reaching up to work the bellows himself. The captain seemed to know little about smithing, so the absence of an assistant to the head smith was apparently not noteworthy. The other smiths were good men, wise and perceptive, and they kept working without a hint of hesitation.

Paca felt the captain's eyes narrow. Those ugly eyes. Where had the king found a man with such ugly eyes? The edge on his attitude only made it worse. Paca could feel the resentment of the interruption rising in his vorn, and it made him more determined not to let this rude man take advantage of him.

The captain continued: "There was a man here by the name of Patira. He is a sworn enemy of the king. I want to know where he is!"

"So do I," said Paca casually. "If I did, I would hand him over to you, and you would get out of my smithy so I could continue my work."

The captain scowled. He strode toward the main forge and stopped close enough so that Paca could have touched him.

Paca kept his eyes focused on the man as he spoke. "Perhaps you could describe this scoundrel, and I could tell you if I have seen him."

The captain leapt at Paca and pulled the bellows toggle from his hand in desperate anger. "I am not fond of games," he growled.

"Neither am I," said Paca, reclaiming the toggle from the captain's hand by sheer strength and quickness. "Now. I am late delivering these blades for the barley harvest, and I do not need any further interruptions. Describe the man you are looking for, and I will tell you whether I have seen him. I have no quarrel with the king about this, but if these blades are any later—"

The captain put his fingers in his mouth and whistled. Four more guards, armed with swords, bustled through the door. The captain motioned with his hand and they began a search of the smithy, poking their swords into every space that they could not see. The captain turned to face Paca again. "We do not have a very good description. None of us have ever seen him. All we know is that he is tall and dark, and dresses like one from the mountains."

"Hmmmm," said Paca, turning one of the blades in the fire and pulling again on the bellows. "There was a man like this here the last two days. He came in volunteering to help to make up for time lost since my father was imprisoned—I never turn down help like that. But I had no idea he was so dangerous to the king. I have not seen him recently, and I have no idea where he might be. Feel free to poke around."

Paca could tell that the captain wasn't sure whether he was teasing him or not. The captain eyed him coldly for a moment and then joined his men in the search. Paca went back to work, working only two blades and tending his own fire. When the guards were satisfied that there was no place in the smithy that had not been thoroughly searched, they filed out into the yard and circled the building, checking everything again.

The captain, still brimming with irritation and suspicion, came back inside to speak to Paca: "One of the king's scouts saw this man enter your smithy this morning, before you or the other smiths were here. He did not see him leave. We will be watching. If you are lying, we will take you in as well."

"So be it," said the Paca coolly. "Fare thee well, Captain."

The captain stepped through the doorway into the sunlight, dragging the heavy door closed behind him. The frame of the smithy shuddered as it slammed shut. Paca shook his head and went back to work. He was as mystified as the captain, but in a different way. He really had no idea what had happened to Patira, and he was not sure he wanted to know. He figured Patira could take care of himself.

33

The sum of what one is and does
cannot be held in Hjarvin's Jars.

Tessamandrian Proverb

THE BEAM PATIRA WAS LYING ON SHOOK WHEN THE DOOR SLAMMED. HE HAD not seen the man's face but could tell from the voice and the attitude that it was someone he did not want to know.

He lay comfortably on the beam above the smithy pondering the events of the last few minutes. In his mind he could picture Hjarvin's jars, lined up in rows on the shelves in front of him. He was searching for the enemy jar. He knew it was just a couple of rows down and a little to the left of center. The jars were numerous and all looked the same except for the hand lettered marking on each one. As soon as he found the enemy jar he could safely put that voice in it. Hadn't the man claimed him as an enemy, and could he not justifiably put him in the jar?

His father had said many times never to do this; that the story of Hjarvin and his famous shelves of jars showed so clearly the injustice in our desire to quickly and prematurely categorize beings.

Patira tried to imagine the great philosopher coming home to find his precious jars all rearranged and all the scraps of white bark, on which he had so carefully recorded his observations about each person he had met, scrambled and re-sorted into different jars.

If it had no true basis in fact, the story was a good one: Hjarvin lived shortly after The Beginnings, and was given the gift of clear thinking by the Eladra. His fame as a philosopher brought many wise men and truth seekers into his presence. To keep track of all beings he encountered, he took to writing his observations on scraps of white bark, which he then stored in clay jars. Each jar was loosely categorized with characteristics that Hjarvin developed based on his observations.

After a while there were many such jars, and he spent innumerable hours rearranging them and creating new ones to accommodate his changing understanding of beings.

One day, when he returned from his trip to the market, he found that someone had come into his home and shuffled the jars as well as the scraps of bark that were in them. As he began the process of sorting out the confusion before him, he realized how impossible and unfair it was to create such categorizations, that beings by nature are unique and deserve to be treated without prejudice of being placed in a jar with any label on it.

The smithy below resumed its rhythm as Patira reflected on this. No one was talking, and it gave him some space to think. He knew that "jarring" the captain of the guard based on his voice and his attitude was wrong. The king had undoubtedly sent him. It was his task to make an arrest. All he would know about Patira would have been told to him by someone else who had put Patira in the "enemy jar" of his own mind. Now he was in the enemy jar in the captain's mind. Everyone knows that enemies are dangerous, that enemies are to be treated in a certain way, that enemies have lots of characteristics that Patira did not consider himself to have.

Patira did not want to be in anyone's enemy jar, but he had no control over how others categorized him. The only control he had was not to jar other people unfairly: the king, the captain, Paca and the princess were all individuals who deserved fair treatment in his mind about who they were.

"So, where do you think he went?" Patira recognized Vordar's voice, and he heard Paca breathe deeply. They were not ten feet from him, though he could not see either.

"I haven't a clue," said Paca. "I was hammering out the edge of one of my blades, and when I turned back to the fire, he was gone."

"I didn't see him go either," added Vordar. "I didn't even realize he had disappeared until the captain said his name. I looked over and he just wasn't there."

All the hammering stopped immediately. Paca must have given some sort of signal. "Did anyone see where Patira went?" he asked, addressing the whole smithy.

"No."

"Not me."

"Me neither."

The responses came from all the remaining forges.

"Thanks for not letting on to the captain that he had been here," said Paca. "I am sure we will find out sooner or later what happened."

"What I want to know is how he knew they were coming," said Vordar.

"Me too," chimed a voice from the corner. "I mean, when they crashed in here, he was already gone."

"We'll have to find out—but not now; there is a lot to be done." The rhythm of the five forges resumed.

Patira smiled to himself. *Flatlanders!* These people had grown up without having to be aware for their life in every second of existence. He had sensed the danger several minutes before it threatened him, and he knew exactly when it became a real threat. He had surveyed the smithy early that morning and had found his escape route and how to get there should any danger arise.

The smithy was post and beam construction, with heavy timbers supporting its thatched roof. It was a tricky thing to have a thatched roof on a smithy, and so, large animal skins had been stretched across the ceiling just under the roof beams to prevent any sparks from getting to the thatch. The gap between the skins and the thatch was several feet thick with large support beams crossing between them. Away from the forges, near the walls of the shop, the skins ended, and one could climb up into this space, which offered numerous places to rest undetected from the smithy below.

One of the characteristics of flatlanders is that they never look up when searching for anything. It was a common failing when they were in the mountains. If a man were just a few feet above eye level, he could remain unseen as long as he was quiet. None of the soldiers searching for him had even considered that he might be "up" somewhere.

Patira had decided that he would not come down until everyone had left and it was dark. Whatever mystery there was to his disappearance, he wanted to preserve. Besides, if Paca thought he was gone, he might find out things he would never know if he were working there. He settled in to wait. Perhaps he would nap a little. His mind drifted to the princess.

He found himself drawn to her in a peculiar way. Interestingly, he had not put the princess in a jar. He had not even struggled with it. That morning on the ride in from camp, many of his thoughts had been about her. They were good thoughts, most of them centered on the connection they had through their fathers. He wondered how different life would have been had that singular encounter between them in the castle stables not happened. He and the princess might have known each other since they were young. As it was, now they had met only one time, and that was notably brief and unremarkable. How was it that this single, short encounter carried so much weight in his thoughts?

His father had taught him that coincidence was never actually coincidental. There was always a point, a reason. His encounter with the princess the day before was significant, but he would probably have to wait to discover why. *Romance is out of the question,* he reasoned. In the whole of Immerland and the mountain realms, there could not be a more unlikely pair than the son and the daughter of these men. Still, he found himself attracted to her and to the idea of getting to know her better. But how? He would have to wait on that thought also.

Somewhere in the thought circles about himself and Vrengnia, of his father and the king, of romance and friendship, he drifted into a shallow sleep, stretched out comfortably on a rafter above the ceaseless, chaotic din of the smithy below.

34

The twilight of childhood descends upon
us when we begin to understand the weakness and failing of our elders, and realize
that we may be walking the same path.

Oratanga
Passages

V RENGNIA WOKE LATE, AND THE SUN HAD BEEN UP FOR SOME TIME WHEN SHE
opened her eyes and sat up. She walked to the door of her chambers to call for an attendant, but as she pushed on the door to open it,
it would not move. She pushed harder. It seemed to be latched, from
the outside. She sat down on the stool by the door, stunned. She had
not even known that there was a latch on the door to her chambers. It
was engaged from the outside, making her a prisoner in her own room.
This is ridiculous, she thought to herself. She knocked on the door and
waited, but there was no answer.

She was not one for self-pity or grieving her circumstances, so she
checked each of the windows. They could be opened, but each was
barred on the outside. She had always thought this was for her own protection—to keep others from getting in—but the bars suddenly seemed
different. For half an hour, she searched for a secret door in the back of
the closet, a loose brick in the wall, or a floor tile that could be pried
up, but found nothing. She threw herself onto her bed. How simple it
was to become a prisoner in one's own bedroom!

It did not take long for her to reason that her father wanted to make
sure that she did not warn Paca and Patira. The realization that he did
not trust her surfaced the slowly rising anger within her. Something was
happening to him. She had never seen this dark side of him before, and
it unnerved her.

While she was getting dressed, she had time to think through other
details of this unusual turn of events. She remembered that tonight was
the night she had promised to help the smith with something. She did

not know what it was, but knew somehow that she must honor her commitment to him.

There was nothing to do but wait, so she sat down at her desk and tried to think of something to write. Shortly before the change in the noon watch, she heard the gallop of horses approaching the castle from the south. From the window she saw Omberon and four other horsemen approaching the castle at a full gallop. There was no one else with them. If they had been to Shiloh to find Patira, they had failed. She sighed, and went back to her desk to write, but no words volunteered to be laid on the paper.

The sound of shuffling feet in the corridor and the soft click of the door latch awakened her where she had fallen asleep at her desk. The door opened, and her father strode in with his arms wide and a warm smile on his face. "My daughter, Princess of Immerland."

Vrengnia bristled like a cat cornered by a dog. "Don't you 'my daughter' me," she raged. "What is the meaning of imprisoning me in my own chambers like a common criminal?"

"There are times—," began the king, as she ducked past him into the hallway. "Wait!" he cried.

She shouted over her shoulder as she rounded a corner in the hallway, "There are never times for the likes of this."

She wanted something to eat and could feel the hunger gnawing inside. Her father was unlikely to look in the kitchen, since he seldom went there himself, nor was it one of her usual haunts. As she entered, the head baker smiled and raised his eyebrows. "Ah, the princess herself—" She knew that the baker liked her, so the look in his eyes evoked an immediate twinge of guilt about the raisin cake. "I'm sorry about the cake the other day," she apologized.

His eyes smiled and twinkled at the same time. "I knew you needed it—just let me know next time." The way he said it made her laugh. "You seem troubled, what do you need now?"

It caught her off guard. "I just need something to eat," she stuttered, "and to stay away from my father, I think."

The baker smiled again, wiping his hands on his apron. "Both should be easy." There was always a pot of something-or-other soup on the oversized stove and extra bread on the table for the kitchen help, so he found a bowl and served her. She sat on one of the large stools by the loaving table to eat and to think about her new situation. The table was tucked in the back where no casual visitor to the kitchen would see her, especially if she was sitting down. It was a warm, comfortable place to be right then.

He left her with her thoughts. They were not happy ones. She was having a hard time identifying the terror that was crouching just beyond the horizon of her mind. As her thoughts swirled around her, she found that she was not completely surprised at the recent turn of events. She should have been angrier than she was, but somewhere, lurking just behind that unseen terror, she sensed a greater strength that overshadowed it all—surrounding and engulfing her, the castle and even her father. There was no name for it, no jar into which to drop it in her mind. It had a vagueness that should have made her uneasy, but instead, was giving her courage and peace. Somewhere in the middle of it all she sensed the presence of the smith.

She ate slowly, savoring every mouthful and waiting for a clarity that was being denied her. It seemed to take forever, and when the last drop of soup had been mopped out of the bowl with the last crust of bread, she was not sure she was any better off except for her full stomach.

Thanking the baker warmly, she took her leave. *To the stables,* her mind said. That was the one other place that her father would not come to look. Although she knew how to ride well, horses for her were utilitarian, and she was not one to waste time in the stables. As she crossed the courtyard, she realized that this was only part of the reason she wanted to go there. She needed to find out more about Verclan. She knew somehow that she had only heard a small piece of the story; there *was* more, and the most likely place to find it would be the stables.

There were about twenty people who worked at the stables, and during the day, there would likely be about fifteen of them around. She found several of the grooms, still brushing down the horses of the king's captain and his men. "They look tired," she said casually, stroking the chestnut mare softly down the nose.

The head groom was angry. He spat on the ground. "They should never have ridden them this hard—all the way from Shiloh without a break—and for no good reason, mind you. Trying to catch some mountain man outlaw! They failed and took their anger out on the horses."

She felt the terror on the horizon inching closer. She knew what the party was for. "That's part of the reason I'm here. I was wondering if anyone here knew anything about Verclan." The head groom spat again and turned away. They all fell silent, not wanting to look at her. "I think they were after his son," she said. One of the older grooms looked up suddenly, caught her eye and winked, but turned back to his work without saying anything else.

Vrengnia pitched in, uninvited, to help with the various chores. She was sure that the old groom had something to say and just needed a place to say it. There was plenty to do and lots of time. The work was a good way to forget the specter in the distance, and she also thought it might be encouraging to the stable hands to see royalty carrying oats and shoveling manure.

Just before the dinner break in the stables, the old groom shuffled past her and with an almost imperceptible wag of a finger beckoned her toward a small door at the back of one of the stalls. He drew the latch on the heavy door and pulled it open. She followed him out through the low doorway, glancing over her shoulder to see if others were watching. No one seemed to notice or care.

The small passage led through the castle wall, and when they emerged, they were in a small courtyard just outside the wall that looked like it had not been visited in years. There were closed gates on either side, overgrown with vines, and the lane between the gates was filled with untouched grass. "The Great Queen used to have her buggy pick her up here when she went riding," said the old groom as he stepped to the right and sat down heavily on a small bench propped up against the wall. "It has not been used since she died." He patted the seat beside him. She sat down. "I come here when I need a quiet place. No one will disturb us. Few people know this even exists." He stared out into the fields beyond the courtyard, resting his hands on his knees, and sighed heavily. Vrengnia guessed he was probably eighty years old. "Now, young lady," he began in a low voice, tired with many years, "what is your interest in Verclan?"

She honored his age with a brief pause. "Well, let's see. Last night, my father told me the story of Verclan for the first time. I mean, I knew he was an outlaw from the mountains, but never knew that my father knew him personally...I never knew how my mother died either. I thought perhaps someone here might know something more about what happened. I get the feeling that no one wants to talk about it, or maybe they are not allowed to or something."

The old groom smiled. It was a slow, sad smile, and then he began, staring far away to the horizon as he spoke. "Verclan was a remarkable farrier, and he was well liked by all of us in the stables. He was very strong-willed and had a reputation for it. He had what we called 'Verclan's way,' but he would smooth it over so that it was not distasteful to people who knew him. He loved the horses, he loved the forge, he loved his work, and he loved all of us. He got crossed up with the prince—your father—somehow. Not that your father is a bad fellow, mind you, but he never had been able to understand Verclan's way and let him *have* his way. Verclan never did your father wrong. He gave him the best he had and the prince knew it." The old man shifted, putting both hands down on the edge of the bench and leaning forward. With his eyes still staring over the low wall in front of them he continued:

"The final straw between Verclan and your father was his relationship with the Lady Viarda, your mother. Viarda was your grandmother's handmaiden and was being instructed in her horse handling by

Verclan's sweetheart, the beautiful Mordara. Viarda and Verclan had had a special relationship. Do you know the word 'cymbic'?" he asked suddenly, turning to look at her. She nodded. "They had a strong cymbic friendship about which your father took issue with Verclan at every opportunity. When the old queen died and your father became king, he married Viarda and dismissed Verclan from the stable."

The story went on, more or less as her father had described it to her, except that the old groom was much more sympathetic toward Verclan. From his perspective, it was her father who had pushed her mother in the fateful confrontation in the stable.

"And you witnessed this yourself?" she said.

"I was in the corner cleaning a saddle. I was a ways away, but I saw most of it. It was quite a ruckus."

"Would you call Verclan a 'ruthless villain'?" she asked.

"Ruthless? Well…" The old groom hesitated then turned suddenly to face her. "Aside from the smith who used to work with him at the forge, I have never met a more peace-loving man. His lack of wisdom and his stubborn refusal to listen to the smith's advice about his relationship with Viarda when she got married, cost him his place in Immerland. They say when he was banished that he went bad, but I have never found that easy to believe. A man of his character and strength does not go bad like that." The old man shook his head sadly.

"There must be other help around here who remember Verclan. Why won't any of them talk about him? I mean, everyone got so quiet when I mentioned his name."

"Well, the king—your father—doesn't want us talking about it. I've never understood why though. It just seems like he has this obsession with Verclan. Everything else he does is wise—kind—kingly if you will, but his strangeness toward this one man, his unwillingness to forgive, seems much out of character. Some say it will be his undoing."

"I am beginning to wonder myself," Vrengnia said, trying to coax more talk from the old man.

"If he were to come and ask me, why I'd tell him to forget the whole thing." The old groom seemed pleased with the idea of giving advice to the king. He leaned forward and pushed himself up with his hands. "If you have any other questions, you know where to find me." He winked again at her. "Make sure you throw the bolt on the door," he said and shuffled back through the wall.

Vrengnia sat still in the courtyard. The pieces of the strange puzzle were starting to fall into place, but the picture that it was making was not what she expected, and there were still parts missing. Where would she find them and how? Where could she go next?

She decided to remain where she was until it was time to visit the smith. She could hear his anvil ringing in the tower. Her terror, held at bay by the conversation with the old man, began creeping back in, but each round of hammering from the tower seemed to drive it back. She remained in the gathering twilight, sensing the pulse of a world surrounding her that she had never allowed herself to see.

She had watched the stars come out one by one before the hammering stopped for the last time. The sky faded through its colors from day to night, and the warm grass mingled its scent with the ubiquitous lavender of the small, unused courtyard as the air chilled into evening. No one disturbed her reverie in this tiny, private spot. No one would ever find her if she came here again.

✠

She sat until she was sure that the smith had moved upstairs and the guards had left, then made her way softly through the hallways to the tower, trying to avoid contact with anyone. Though the rage about her imprisonment had subsided, she was not yet ready to meet her father.

There was no one in the tower, as she expected. This time when she got to the smith's door, she only paused for an instant and drew the bolt in an ordinary way. When she pushed the door open, the smith said, "Good evening, Princess." He was sitting on his bed with a knowing smile. "I was expecting you this time," he said softly.

When she was safely inside the door and it was shut behind her, the smith stood up quickly. "We do not have much time," he whispered urgently. "I am also expecting your father, and I am expecting that he will be very angry." He reached under his bed and pulled a leather parcel from underneath it. She recognized the leather as the piece that she had brought back to him from his own house. It seemed smaller, and it was wrapped into a parcel that she could slip into her tunic. It was carefully stitched so that one of the odd symbols on the leather was centered on the front: four simple lines that looked like a pair of mountain peaks. He handed it to her.

She nearly dropped it. The smith's strength was deceptive and so was the weight of the package as he held it. She could tell that it contained several pieces of his work. "You must take this to Haniah, the hermit, who lives off the southern road to the mountains past Mordan—do you know of her?"

"I should be asking that of you!" she exclaimed. At every turn, the smith amazed her. "Haniah is a dear friend; I know her well."

"All the better," continued the smith rapidly. "There will be less suspicion about your going there. Give this to her and tell her I sent it. Do not give it to anyone else. Is this clear?"

The princess nodded.

"If she is not there, leave it under the writing table to the left of the door. Leave a note—you can write, can't you?"

She nodded again.

"Leave a note saying it was from me, but do not sign *your* name. If you do speak to her, give her my best. Go quickly now; before your father arrives." As she started to turn to the door, they heard the muffled voices of the king and his guards coming up the stairs.

The smith moved quickly. He leaned forward, took her arm and whispered in her ear. She did exactly as she was told. The smith seemed to know that her father would stop in the smithy first.

She waited until her father's party had entered the smithy, and she slipped through the door, closed it, and threw the bolt quietly. Then she headed up the stairs outside the smith's prison to wait until her father had left.

35

Mah'Eladra sit on the staircase to the Infinite and close their eyes to listen. In the midst of the relentless cacophony below, the true nature of each being is found and proven.

Karendo Marha
Journey to the Infinite

VRENGNIA FELT STRANGE SITTING UP AND OUT OF SIGHT FROM THE ACTIVITY developing just below her. Because of the stone walls and stairs, she could hear everything clearly, but could see nothing.

Several sets of footsteps plodded up the stairs. She guessed it was her father and perhaps a couple of guards. "Keep your voices low; we don't want to disturb the smith." It *was* her father.

The bolt was drawn on the prison smithy and she heard the door creak. What followed was a series of noises that indicated that they, whoever they were, were rummaging through the articles on a wooden table. She could hear iron hitting iron and wood intermixed with shuffling footsteps. The conversation was hushed and intermittent.

"Look at this."

"I wonder what it is."

"Don't know." Carnados! She knew his voice well. Her father had his advisors with him.

"Hmmm…curious."

"What?"

"This thing—"

"What a strange shape."

"Do you suppose that this—"

Something fell to the floor and the clang echoed up and down the stairway.

"*Shhhhhh!*"

"Sorry."

"Did you damage it?"

"Don't think so."

"Be careful."

She supposed they had lanterns. What they were doing would have been impossible in the dark.

"Sire," Carnados said, "I looked into Omberon's history as you asked."

"And?"

"Well, it's a bit cloudy."

"Cloudy?"

"Clouded, perhaps…as if he did not have a history at all."

All the noises stopped. "Exactly what do you mean?"

"Well, the earliest record of him in Immerland is only from about ten years ago, Sire."

"Ten years?"

"Yes. He has no birth records, no family. He just appeared."

"Appeared where?"

"His first records are in the army, Sire. There is no record of his joining the army or being commissioned or conscripted. He was just suddenly there—in with all the other foot soldiers."

"That's very, very odd, indeed!"

Vrengnia could visualize her father stroking his beard with his eyes cast down, staring into the infinity of the floor as if it were glass.

"What do you suppose it means, Carnados?"

"I have never seen anything like it."

"Yes, well—we will have to keep an eye on him." The conversation dropped off and something else fell to the table. "Something seems different here tonight, I—" Her father paused. In her mind, she could see his face as he stood thinking.

"How so?"

"Well…the pieces look almost the same, but there seem to be fewer of them…."

"Or perhaps different ones."

"You see what I mean?"

"I was thinking the same thing—"

"Ow! O-oh…ah-h…ow-w-w!"

"What happened?"

"My toe…"

"Are you hurt?"

"Not really…just stubbed it on—hey! Look at this!"

There was a sudden commotion, and she heard her father swear angrily. "Guards!" he yelled. "Guards!" His voice boomed up and down the tower staircase, echoing several times in the otherwise still castle. There were rapid footsteps coming up the staircase.

She heard the guards scrambling up the steps, tripping over one another in their haste. Her father was furious now. His rage seemed palpable to her.

Her father accosted the guards verbally. "What is this—do you know what this is?" his voice was condescending and angry.

There was a hesitation. "It's the smith's tool bag, Sire," said one of the new voices.

"Yes—I know it's the tool bag—so what is it doing here?" Her father was trying to get the guards to come to a conclusion that he had already made. It did not seem to work.

"Well," said the second guard cautiously, "he must have left it here tonight."

"And why would he do that?" pressed the king.

"Well, maybe he did not need it."

"Why did he ever need it?" he shot back. The guards were silent. "Why didn't he take it with him tonight? He has every other night, right?" Her father was leading them to a disturbing discovery.

"I thought he did take it with him," said one of the guards, "but I could be mistaken."

The king closed the trap. "I think he did take it with him, only it wasn't *it!*" The guards were silent. "Did you check his tool bag to make sure it was actually his tools? Did you?"

"I think we did," said one of the guards. "We always have, but since the bag is obviously here, I guess we didn't."

"No!" shouted her father. "Don't you get it? Sure he took his tool bag, only it wasn't his tool bag—it just looked like it. It was full of whatever he was making—and you let it slip through the door."

One of the guards spoke to defend himself. "I don't think so, Sire. Look! All the things he was making are still on the bench."

"Yes, except they are not the *same* things," said the king. He was frustrated and angry. "Come on, let's check the smith's room upstairs. It cannot have gone far."

The hushed voices were mingled with their hurried footsteps as they came up the stairs. The bolt was drawn and the smith's door was kicked open by someone. The princess guessed it was her father himself.

"Where is your tool bag?" demanded the king.

"Why, I left it in the smithy tonight. I was done with my work later than usual, so I just left it there." It was the calm, even voice of the smith. There was no fear, no resentment, and not even a hit of worry.

A long pause followed. Vrengnia guessed that her father was trying to get a grip on what to do in the face of the smith. "Search the chambers," he said forcefully to the guards. "You—sit on your bed."

No one spoke as the guards rummaged through the sparse accommodations of the smith. Someone closed the door in the process of the search. She seized the opportunity and crept past, carrying the burden that the smith had given her. She fled down the remaining steps and headed for her chambers.

36

Under Tal's pale light they sat,
And wept again, for knowing
That if they ever met again
'Twould be in Meekar's glowing.
With friends as foes, their families' feud,
Such time would not be soon,
That they would meet to speak again,
Under a different moon.

Ramonmara
The Legend of Mishla Mira

As she approached the hitching post in the lane, Vrengnia realized it was the only indication that anyone lived near there at all. She was south of Mordan by several miles, on the seldom-used road to the mountains. They seemed to loom closer than usual. On this trip they made her uneasy.

She turned Mahala to the right at the post, and he stepped over the broken down stone wall onto the path to Haniah's house. There was no hurry. No one would see her now and it did not matter anyway. Haniah was her friend and she came here often.

The strange brilliance on entering Haniah's land caught her off guard as it always did. She had no word for it; no way to describe the sensation, but everything seemed a little lighter, a bit fresher. Each time it was as new and refreshing as the first.

Her thoughts drifted back to the first time she had ever visited Haniah. She had found out about her from one of the royal physicians. He had given her some herbal concoction for an illness she had, and her recovery had been just short of miraculous, so she had asked where the good doctor had gotten his herbs.

He was given to long rambling conversations, particularly with patients who would listen, so the doctor spoke freely. "My friend Haniah, she lives south of Mordan, you know. She makes the best herbal remedies in Immerland," he had said. "Been at it for years, don't rightly know exactly how long, but a good while. She makes the best herbal remedies in Immerland, don't you know."

"You said that."

"Yes, yes, well, she does."

"I believe it, if they are all like the potion you gave me."

"They're the best."

"Do you suppose she would mind if I visited her one day? I mean, I am often out and about, and always looking for a new place to go, and herbal treatment has always been an interest of mine."

"It *is* a bit of a hike—"

"Oh, I would ride my horse." She smiled to herself when she recalled the silliness of the statement.

The doctor had chuckled. "I can give you directions—perhaps a map would be best. Do you have a piece of paper?" He had droned on as he drew the map: "You go down the lane south of Mordan past the old wooden barn, the only one in those parts, you know, and you come to this hitching post on the right—it's the only one around; you won't miss it. You cross the broken down stone wall...let's see..." He began counting on his fingers, "and then go across a field, don't you see, then you go across another field, and there is sort of a path through the woods that leads to another field, which you also cross. Then there is a crooked little path through another wood, and there is *another* field. Haniah's house is on the other side of *that* field." She remembered thinking, *How many fields was that?* It was all somewhat vague, but when she got there, she managed to find it. She had been there many times in the three years since she first met Haniah. Mahala knew the way.

As they ambled through the second field on the way to the first path, she pulled the bundle out of her tunic. Mahala's gait was easy and confident so she dropped the reins and took the time to scrutinize the strange package. How would the smith have known Haniah? "Of course—the vials of herbs in Paca's kitchen. Strange connection," she said aloud. Perhaps it was not so strange after all. The smith was a remarkable man, seeming to know almost everything. If Haniah was the best in the land, it stood to reason that the smith would know of her. It was a small step to imagine he knew her personally. Another question crossed Vrengnia's mind. What, exactly, was it that she was carrying to her?

There were markings all over the leather, some of them apparently dyed into it, and others pressed in or stamped. Still others seemed to have been lightly burned in and some carved with the tip of a knife. Many were very old. In the center of the side away from the stitching was the freshly burned mark resembling the mountain peaks, and just below it a small bow drawn back. The bow had no arrow in it and there was a small, five-pointed star just to the right and above it. They were glyphs of some sort.

There were many people in Immerland who had glyphs, personal marks that were used as signatures. It was an old tradition, predating written language and generally only used as ornamental symbols on letters and personal clothing. They spoke of something simple, fundamental. The package in her hand represented the genuine use of glyphs. She had never seen these before and could not tell what they were or to whom they might belong.

There were at least two pieces inside, maybe three, but the leather was wrapped so tightly that she could not tell what they were. The whole thing was a little larger in diameter than the flat, spread hand of a large man. It was stitched together neatly using strips of the leather. The smith must have made a needle to do such fine work.

Mahala stopped suddenly and dropped his head to eat. She was there. Everything was still, and the sun cast a brilliant warmth across the field. There was no breath of wind to move so much as a blade of the grass, and the air was heavy with the scent of drying grass, mint and hazel breath. The stillness made it like a painting in the great hall at the castle.

She slid off Mahala and left him to graze in the rich grass in front of Haniah's small sod house. As she walked toward the door, she passed Haniah's outside table. It looked as if it were set for dinner. There were bowls and flagons and cutting boards, hand carved scoops and stoneware plates all neatly placed as if Haniah were expecting a dinner party. It seemed odd for a person who was so removed from the mainstream of people, but the princess had to admit that she did not know all of what Haniah might do in her remote habitat.

She made her way to the door of the house and knocked gently. "Haniah?" There was no answer. She knew that she was always welcome there so she did not wait to knock again. She pushed on the door; it yielded gently, and she stepped into the semidarkness of the peculiar dwelling. "Haniah?"

The hut was made of sod, from top to bottom, stacked in such a way as to make a solid wall about a foot thick, except for the occasional window openings that lit the interior. Inside the floor was dirt, but packed so hard that it was almost polished with the wear. There was a small stove for heat in the winter, but today it was covered with nuts and small bowls of grains that were drying. Beside one of the windows to the left of the door was the writing desk. There was no sign of Haniah. The princess guessed that she was off foraging for nuts or roots in the woods on the other side of the stream.

She wanted to stay and wait, but decided that it was best to leave the note as the smith had directed and get back to the castle. She had not seen her father since he had freed her from her chambers the morning before, and she was feeling that it was time to find him and resolve the matter. The thought made her shudder.

There was a small scroll of bark on the floor next to the stove, so she took the quill pen from the desk and wrote simply and neatly:

"To Haniah, from the smith at Shiloh Forge." It was odd, not signing her own name. She figured that this must be what it was like when the king's messengers carried her notes to others, being held as of no account by both the sender and receiver.

She left the house slowly, wishing that Haniah would have been home so they could talk together, even for a short while. Under the circumstances, she knew it was best to leave. She closed the door gently behind her.

Vrengnia walked the few paces from the door past the neatly laid table and looked up. Another horse grazed calmly beside Mahala. It was a beautiful black mare, fully saddled and the bridle neatly draped in her mane. Vrengnia whirled around, looking about uneasily for any sign of a second rider. Nothing moved. The peaceful stillness was suddenly threatening. She made her way to her horse quietly, as if being quiet made some difference.

She stroked the gelding's mane and swung up into the saddle. The horses were so close that she could hardly get her right leg between them. As she swung her leg over the saddle, there was a sudden movement on the other horse, and the other rider appeared as if from nowhere onto his saddle.

The princess would have shrieked had not the other rider reached out with his left hand and covered her mouth, while deftly grabbing the reins of her horse with his right. It all happened so fast that she did not have time to do anything. "It's all right, Princess," said a voice that was calm and much in command. It was Patira!

She did not know whether to be afraid or not. He had a firm command on her horse, though she was not sure how, and he had grabbed her right arm. She stammered, "Where did you come from?"

"It's an old mountain trick," he said casually. "I was hanging off the other side of my horse waiting for you."

"How did you know it was me?"

"I recognized your horse, a fine beast and well bred. He did not even move when I rode up beside him."

She remembered that Patira's mother was a master horse trainer so Patira would likely know a good deal about it also. This would explain how he had gotten control so quickly.

"I'm glad you are here," said Patira softly. "I was wondering when I would see you again. I am sorry I made such a brash introduction at the forge. It really was not me. Do you have a few minutes to talk before you leave?" Although he still had control of her horse and a vise-like grip on her arm, he didn't seem like he was threatening her at all; he genuinely wanted to talk about something. "If I let go of your arm and your horse, will you promise not to try to get away?" he asked half mockingly.

"What do you want to talk about?" she asked.

"Well, after meeting you at the forge the other day, I asked my father about what he knew of you. He told me quite a story. It seemed to me that we ought to know each other and should have long before now. Were it not for the stubbornness of our fathers, we might already be good friends. I decided if I had the chance, I would like to make up for some of that lost time."

"I promise I will not try to get away." Vrengnia had had similar thoughts about Patira.

Patira let go of her arm and slid from his horse effortlessly, never letting go of Mahala's bridle. He held out his hand to help her off the horse and she obliged, sliding to the ground beside him. He dropped the bridle and they left the horses to graze. He led her to the table and sat down in one of the places. "This is my seat," he said blandly. "You can sit wherever you want."

"Your seat?"

"Sure, whenever we come to eat with Haniah, I sit here. My mother sits there, my father sits there and my two sisters sit on the end. Haniah sits on this end." The princess was stunned. "And now, good Princess, why are *you* here today?"

Vrengnia could not quite grasp what was unfolding before her. Patira was so polite and disarming. Even if she had anticipated such a meeting, it would all seem upside down. She decided not to worry about it until there was something specific to be alarmed about. She started by telling him about her relationship to Haniah over several years and how she came here occasionally just to visit. She told him about the discussion with her father and the old stable groom.

He recounted his escape from the captain of the King's Guard and how Paca had snuck him out of the smithy in the dark later that night.

She shared about her encounters with the old smith and how wise and knowledgeable he was; how he refused to make the swords for her father and his imprisonment for that refusal.

He explained about his father and how he developed his steel and sold it to the smith.

She related how she had come to know Paca, but she did not tell him about the swords.

He told her about his mother, and that if she were able to stay a little longer she could meet her. They talked about odds and ends for nearly an hour. Patira's honesty and simple view of life refreshed her.

Finally, she stood up to leave. "I must really be getting back to the castle," she said slowly. "My father has been in a bad temper lately, and I have not seen him since yesterday morning."

"Yes—the king," said Patira curiously. "You know, I have been thinking, that were it not for the king and my father...Is there some way we could get them to talk to each other?"

Vrengnia looked at the ground. She felt a slight flush of embarrassment and a twinge of fear. "I don't know," she said slowly. "My father is consumed by his hatred for your father. I tried to talk to him about it...I can try again," she said, looking up. As she spoke the words, she sensed the struggle within her between the strange, natural trust she felt with Patira and her responsibility to her father and the kingdom. It was similar to that which she felt toward the smith, that though both of them were at the very center of her father's conflict, they also seemed to be at the core of its resolution.

She walked over to her horse. Patira walked alongside and she could feel his presence. He helped her up into the saddle. She felt his strength. It seemed as if she had known him somewhere else, although that would have been impossible. She smiled warmly. "May we meet again, under a different moon." It was an old Immerland saying, fitting in this situation.

"A brighter moon!" he said obligingly. She pulled the gelding around and set him into a gallop across the field and into the trees at the far edge. She wanted to look back but decided against it as the line of trees between the two fields eclipsed her view. If more time were to be had together, it was not for her making right then. It would have to be a different moon, a *much* brighter moon.

37

When pieces of the puzzle that is our life do not seem to fit, should we deny that they are, in fact, part of the puzzle? Should we not suppose, instead, that perhaps we are trying to put them in the wrong place?

Hispattea
The Essences of Corritanean Wisdom

W HAT'S IN THE PACKAGE?" MORDARA ASKED AS THE HORSES WALKED SLOWLY across the field, leaving Haniah's hut behind them.

Verclan looked up at his wife. They rode beside each other as they often did when traveling together, and close enough to touch one another. "I'm not sure, but it *is* from the smith."

"Isn't he in prison?" Her eyes sparkled and widened as she said it.

Verclan loved watching her face. She was a beautiful woman by everyone's account, and he often wondered how she had chosen him from all the men she could have selected in and around the castle. Part of her peculiar beauty was the expressiveness of her face when she spoke. She had a dark complexion and coal black eyes that complemented her long, straight raven hair. Today she had it pulled back from her face and tied behind her neck with a purple leather thong, but the long tresses still draped forward over her shoulders.

"I believe he is. I'm not sure how he would have gotten this to Haniah, however."

"How do you know it is from the smith?" asked Patira thoughtfully.

"It has his mark—the bow and the star; and it's wrapped in parcel leather. The Immerland merchants do not use parcel leather."

"Perhaps it was the princess," Patira mused absently.

Verclan turned in his saddle and stopped his horse. "The princess?"

"Yes. She was there today," Patira continued, "in the soddy when I arrived. I hid side-slung until she came out. You should have seen her face when I came up into the saddle."

"You said that the princess had been to the smithy in Shiloh. Perhaps she knows the smith and did this as a favor," Mordara interjected.

"Perhaps. Did she tell you anything?"

Patira shook his head and smiled. "Nothing about the parcel or any such errand. We talked for perhaps an hour."

"About what?" Mordara's voice was deep, sonorous and gentle with her son.

"Oh, lots of things. She says she has known Haniah for several years and comes to visit quite frequently. We talked about events at the castle. Her father's birthday is coming up. There's going to be quite a celebration. The king is very busy with preparations."

"The king's birthday...hmmmm."

"She said it is to be his fiftieth. He wants it to be a grand occasion."

They had reached the trees and had moved to single file. Verclan led, followed by his wife. Patira's sisters, Verice and Tangar, fell in behind their mother and Patira brought up the rear.

"I think Pati likes the princess," Verice announced as they crossed a small stream. Verclan smiled to himself.

"How do you know?" asked Mordara.

"He smiles when he talks about her."

"I don't think he can have her though," chimed in Tangar. Then she added with a snicker, "Besides, she is probably very ugly!"

Verice giggled. Verclan looked over his shoulder at Patira. His son knew when to be quiet.

"Yes, really ugly, I bet," said Verice.

"Girls!" chided Mordara.

"And she's a *princess*. Pati couldn't marry a princess." Verice giggled again.

Verclan turned in his saddle so he could see the discussion behind him. He smiled. "Why not? Your brother is a prince. It would be a perfect match."

"Well, I don't think the king would like it one bit," said Tangar.

"Why do you think that?" asked Mordara as she looked into Verclan's eyes. She had a hopeful look; that special look that men know in their wives' eyes.

"The king doesn't like you, Father, and I don't think he would like Pati either."

"All right, all right. I think it's time to be quiet now." Verclan spoke with his fatherly authority. He was sure that they wanted to continue the discussion, but there were strict rules about being quiet in the woods. When it was time to be quiet, no one spoke. He turned to look at his son, ten paces behind him.

Patira sat straight in his saddle. He smiled but said nothing. Verclan turned back to the path in front of him. He knew that look also. His thoughts drifted back to the first time he had seen Mordara. They were friends in the stable, but she was always so busy with the castle staff and the queen that they seldom spoke.

One afternoon, she had some free time and asked him if he would like to go riding. Although he was a farrier, he did not consider himself much of a horseman at the time, but the invitation from "the beautiful Mordara" as she was called, was enough to make a horseman out of anyone. They had gone out riding for perhaps two hours, and they chatted about the castle, its people, Immerland, the queen, the prince, the stables and the horses. The time flew by. As they returned over the crest of the small rise obscuring the stable, she spurred her horse to a gallop.

He followed, about twenty feet behind. The horses were fast and the fresh crisp air whistled past him as he rode. They were about a hundred yards from the stables when she reached back and pulled the hair pin from the knot of hair on the back of her head. A shower of black hair leapt into the wind and streamed out behind her. Verclan had never seen her without her hair neatly tied back for riding and working around the stables. It was a moment he would never forget and the moment he first *saw* his wife.

The family rode on in silence until they came to a turn in the path where it met a swift stream. "We'll take a break here," said Verclan, "and take a look at the smith's wares."

They tied their horses to a small birch tree by the bank and sat down beside the swift water. Patira opened his riding sack and brought out some cheese, dried apples and two small cups for water. He handed them to his sisters. "Find the best water in the stream for your mother and father." The girls giggled as they headed to the edge of the stream.

Verclan studied the package, knowing it was significant because it was from the smith. He turned it over several times, weighing it in both hands.

"If you open it, you can see what it is better," Mordara said as she draped her arm around his neck and shoulder. She was sitting beside him where he could feel her closeness.

"I know. I just…hmmm." He had unsheathed a short knife to cut the stitching in the parcel. "Whatever it is, he wanted to make sure no one knew until it was delivered." After cutting the thongs carefully, he unfolded the layers of leather neatly encasing the pieces inside.

He held up the first piece. It looked like the hilt of a sword but there was no sword in it. On one side, it was polished smooth and the bare metal shone. On the other side, it was hollowed out, as if something

was made to fit into it. He examined it carefully and handed it to his son. "What do you think?"

"It's a sword hilt without a sword," replied Patira. "It seems a little odd, don't you think?"

"Yes, at first sight. However, knowing the smith, there is a precise purpose to it, no matter how odd it seems."

Verclan lifted the second piece slowly out of the leather folds. It had the handle of a sword, but where the blade was supposed to be, there was a fan of metal tines, each very close to the other, and all emanating from the place where the base of the blade of a normal sword would have been. Each of the tines was sharp at the end, but not dangerously so. Between the tines were tiny barbs, facing each other, so that if anything entered between the tines, it would not be able to get back out. Verclan picked it up and held it by the handle. It balanced perfectly in his hand.

"What is *that*?" asked Patira.

"It looks like an eel spear," interjected Mordara, "like the ones used by the fishermen along the western coast—but the handle is too short."

Verclan marveled at the piece as he held it up. He knew *what* it was. The question in his mind was why? "It's a sataliin," he said slowly, waving the piece evenly back and forth, allowing the sunlight to glint off its faceted surfaces, "a Tessamandrian sword trap—but I have never seen one quite like this."

He snapped one of the tines with the back of his finger and it rang like a bell.

"A sword trap?" Mordara and Patira spoke at the same time.

Verclan leapt to his feet and pulled his sword from its scabbard, which hung from his saddle, and handed it to Patira. "I'll show you. Take a swing at me—not very hard—as if you were trying to strike me down."

He saw Patira hesitate. "Go on."

Patira took a step back and brought the sword over his head as if to strike him diagonally across the shoulder. Verclan had used a sataliin before. At the last moment, he raised it up into the path of the descending blade. It slipped between the tines of the sataliin and jammed tight, and with a quick flick of his wrist, Verclan had flipped the sword out of Patira's hand and into his own. In the next instant, he had the point of the sword planted against Patira's chest. Patira blinked, but did not move. Mordara gasped, raising both hands to cover her mouth.

Verclan was smiling. "Tessamandrian warriors developed the sataliins to carry on their belts in case they ever lost their own swords. I would never have guessed that the smith had ever seen one. He took his knife and scratched one of the tines with its tip. It left no mark. "This steel is hardened beyond my knowledge," he said softly with a hint of incredulity in his voice. "I wonder..." He handed the device to Patira. "This other thing..." he continued, picking up the first piece again. He tried to slip it over his sword blade but it did not fit. "Get me your sword," he commanded suddenly.

Patira stood up, unsheathed his sword, and handed it to his father. Verclan took the strange piece and carefully slipped it over the blade of his son's sword. As it came down the blade, it fit perfectly over the hilt and jammed around the butt of the blade, covering the existing hilt as if it belonged there. He tried to remove it, but it would not move. He lifted the sword by the handle and waved it back and forth. It had remained perfectly balanced. He looked up at his son and smiled. "I believe we found out what it's for—we will have to wait to find out why it was made." He looked at Mordara. He could see the fear in her eyes.

"I don't like this," she said quietly, looking down the stream where the girls were throwing water at each other using the cups Patira had given them.

Verclan handed the sataliin to Patira and sat down beside her. Putting his arm around her shoulder, he drew her to him. "I don't either, but we will have to wait to see what it is all about. In the meantime, we cannot fear. Life must be lived and we must trust that Mah'Eladra are working; that there is a plan, and that it is all for the best."

38

For many, the greatest fear is that of looking at oneself in the glass and being as ruthless with our own reflection as we are with those who challenge us.

Pratoraman
The Middle Way

S ANDIHAR FELT MUCH BETTER. AFTER HE ACCUSED THE SMITH OF SPIRITING away some of his work, the smith refused to do any more in the prison smithy. The lights in the mountains had disappeared the night after the smith stopped. This mystified the king, but also relieved him. It was now only four days before the celebration of his birthday and the less aggravation from all these little details, the better. There was still much to be done. He wasn't responsible for most of it, but he had to make sure that those who were in charge did their jobs.

His birthday party was to be the greatest celebration that Immerland had ever had. The best of the best was being prepared for the celebration, and there was an excitement in the air as everyone did double duty in preparation. The mayors and elders from each of the nine towns surrounding the castle had been invited and had confirmed that they would be there. The entire castle staff was included, though not everyone was invited to the main banquet. Food was flowing in from all over the kingdom. He had declared a two-day holiday following the "big night"—as it had come to be called—in which everyone in the kingdom was relieved of their tasks. Gifts were being readied, not just for the king, but for everybody.

In spite of all this, he was troubled. The smith was still in prison, having refused to make the swords, and Sandihar was not sure what to do about it. Perhaps he would free him for his birthday. Patira had not been caught, though the frustration of that was fading in the growing excitement of his party. He had not seen the princess in the two days since he let her out of her room the morning after he had locked her in. She had been around, because other people had seen her, but she had somehow avoided him. He thought he understood what she might be feeling, but he was unsure; and he *did* want an opportunity to explain himself. Perhaps "explain" was not the right word.

He had often told his daughter that one should never explain: "because your friends don't need it and your enemies wouldn't believe you anyway." He thought that the princess must be his friend, but he *had* treated her rudely in locking her up without giving her a real reason. She wasn't an enemy (at least he didn't think she should be), so now he was not sure what to say when he finally found her.

He was in the middle of breakfast when she sauntered into the hall. "Good morning, Father," she said brightly. She sat down at the other end of the table. Her place was not set because she had not been expected. She seemed as if whatever had happened was past, so he smiled warmly, and played along.

"Did you sleep well?"

"Well enough, thank you. May I have something to eat?" When she entered, Sandihar had motioned to the servants, and they were already bustling about in the kitchen getting together the table setting and foods they knew she liked for breakfast.

"I'm sure it's on the way," said the king. "I haven't seen you in a couple days," he continued, not looking directly at her but at the eggs on his plate.

"Well, it certainly wasn't any fun being imprisoned in my *own* room by my *own* father." He knew he had to look up. She was staring at him.

He looked down again. "I'm sorry, but I had to make sure that no one, not even you, tipped off the young smith or Patira. I had a feeling that you might."

"It's not much of an apology when you have to say 'but,' Father."

The king was feeling very small. She continued to press her position. "Can't you just admit that it was a ridiculous thing to do? I told you that I would not visit the smith or send a warning!" The king said nothing. "So, in the end, did you catch the scoundrel?"

He was beginning to get irritated. "No," he scowled. "He tricked us and got away."

"Tricked you? Maybe he wasn't there at all," she said with disgust. "And maybe he isn't the enemy you think he is anyway."

"What are you saying?" he shot back darkly as he stood up.

"What I am saying is that just because Verclan is your enemy, it does not necessarily make him mine."

"He is an enemy of our kingdom—of Immerland!" thundered the king, bringing his fist down hard on the table to emphasize his point.

The princess continued evenly, ignoring the interruption, "And just because *Verclan* is your enemy does not mean that his *son* is your enemy.

When all is said and done, if Patira is *your* enemy, it would not necessarily make him *my* enemy. And even if Patira is *my* friend, it would not make *me* your enemy, would it?"

The king was silent with rage. He could not argue with her logic. "You're missing the point," he said sullenly, trying to deflect the conversation to anywhere else.

She held her ground. "Just what *is* the point, Father?"

He threw up his hands. "Someday you will understand," he said, trying to find a way to end the conversation. He was begging.

"You could die tomorrow. Then I would have to be queen—I want to understand *now!*"

The king sat down heavily in his chair. There was nothing to say. This had been happening a lot lately, not only with his daughter but also with the smith, with his advisors, with—everyone. Was he changing or were they? He needed time to think.

The princess would not let him have it. "Father, why will you not meet with Verclan and try to find a resolution to all this? You won't listen to your advisors—you won't listen to the smith—" He felt the last phrase hanging above him, suspended like the executioner's sword before the final downward stroke.

Ordinarily he would have dodged the strike or fought back, but he did not want to engage his daughter any further today. There were too many other things to do, and deep within he knew she was right. "I will give due consideration to your request after my birthday celebration. Until then we will speak no further of it." He looked at his daughter, trying to guess what she was really thinking. She remained still, opaque to his gaze.

She stood up without breaking eye contact. "Thank you, Father," she said softly and strode out of the hall without eating. The king sat silently in his chair for a long while. Now he had his time to think, but he did not want to.

A being whose psadeq is mature cannot be mocked.

The Tessarandin, Book 2

Sandihar stood in front of his wardrobe staring vacantly into the welter of clothing that hung there. It was the morning of the big celebration. The festivities were supposed to begin about noon and he was getting ready for his part in it. He had to select his best royal garb, something that would be fitting for a fifty-year-old sovereign. This was no easy task for a man who had never had to select his own clothing. Today he decided that he would, and he found himself in a quandary. Since this was the only thing he had to do that morning, he felt ridiculous. He had been at it for an hour already. He was wondering how he ever accumulated such a collection of silly clothing when someone knocked on the door.

It irritated him because he had given specific instructions not to be disturbed until he was ready. As he strode over toward the door, ready to give the intruder a sound piece of his mind, it opened by itself. "Father?"

By the time he could see her in the doorway, he felt the irritation ebbing. "Come in, come in," he said, opening his arms to hug his daughter.

"Father," she said as she accepted his embrace, "I have a special favor to ask."

"Will it cost me anything?" he quipped as he sent a smirk across his face, trying to look impish. He was actually in a good mood this morning (except for having to choose his clothing).

"Only a few minutes of your time. By the way, what are you planning to wear to the celebration today?" He must have frowned. She caught it and laughed. "Oh, I see. I'll help out in a few minutes, but come, I have a gift for you.

"The gifts are to be—"

"—given after the cake," she answered methodically, "but as your daughter, I wanted to make mine special and give it to you before everyone else, and I didn't really want everyone to see it."

"Are you worried that I won't like it?"

"I hadn't thought of it that way. I mean, it's different. Come on!"

"All right, but no more than ten minutes."

He followed her into a small sitting room just down the corridor from his chambers. In front of him on top of a small polished oak table was a folded blue velvet cloth, embroidered with silver thread. It was bathed in full morning sun that streamed through the window. It was a magnificent piece of cloth. The king was not sure what to do. What was it for? His daughter seemed to catch his bewilderment and jumped forward, grabbing the cloth and lifting it free of the table. There was a flash as the sunlight struck something on the table. He blinked and looked more closely. It was a sword, shimmering in the light, and he had to move to the side slightly so that he could actually look at it.

In many ways, it was a very ordinary sword, in fact less than ordinary. It had no gold or silver, nor ivory or jewels; it seemed to be made completely of iron or steel. As ironwork, it was superb, beyond any imagination of what iron could be. Not a single surface of it was fully polished, but it glowed softly wherever the sun struck it.

"Be careful, Father. It's very sharp," she warned in a whisper, as if talking aloud would be irreverent.

The king reached out and touched the blade, and instantly pulled back his hand. The blade was as cold as ice. "The handle is warmer," she suggested.

He touched the handle. It *was* warmer. *How can this be?* he wondered to himself. The sword seemed to float into his hand as he wrapped his fingers around the handle for the first time. It became a part of him, an extension of his arm. He stepped back. The sword hummed softly as he moved it slowly through the air. He had never felt a weapon so perfectly matched to his touch.

He stared at his daughter, who was smiling back at him. "Where did you get it?" he whispered.

"I had the young smith make it for you," she responded softly. "For your birthday. And he made this for me on mine." He watched as she stooped down and pulled a second sword from under the table.

The king gazed at the second blade. "But how? Why?"

"He is a friend of mine. I asked him to do it and he did."

"You just *asked* him!?"

She nodded and smiled.

The king looked back at the blade in his hand. He did not have time to play with it just now. That would have to wait. He laid it gently on the table, and the princess laid hers beside it. He stepped forward and embraced her. "It's the best present I could possibly have gotten," he said exuberantly, He stepped back suddenly, his hands on both her shoulders. "The smith," he exclaimed, "I meant to set him free this morning in honor of my birthday. Come on—to the tower!"

He started off down the hall, the princess close on his heels. "No, wait!" He stopped short and she plowed into him. He laughed. "The sword! I want to bring the sword."

The princess caught his sleeve. "No, Father. Please don't bring the sword."

"Why not?" he could see an intense earnestness in her eyes that pleaded with him.

"There is no reason to mock the smith. I mean, he does not know about it and wouldn't—"

The king thought for a second. Mock the smith? Why, the smith had mocked him, had he not? The sword had been made in spite of him. He *was* the king, after all, and it was fitting that the smith should learn that one should not mock the king. He pulled his sleeve out of her hand and turned back to get the sword.

"Father, please!" He ignored her. When he got to the end of the corridor, he turned to look at her. She had disappeared.

The swords were still on the table where they had left them. The king paused for a moment as he laid his hand on the larger of the two. Should he take both? No, out of respect for his daughter he would not bring hers. He felt a little foolish, but only a little. As he turned and headed back to the tower, he shook off the foolish feeling.

His guards snapped to attention at the bottom of the stairs. They fell in behind him as he led the way up. After drawing the bolt on the door himself, he pushed it open. The smith was standing by the window, watching the preparations in the courtyard below; and as he entered, the smith turned to face him.

The king smiled. He was happy for the smith and he was happy for himself. He had always felt uncomfortable having this man locked up and it felt good to be setting him free. He held the sword casually but conspicuously in front of him to make sure the smith would notice it.

"Good smith," he began, as if he were about to make a proclamation of some import. "You are hereby free to go, in honor of my fiftieth birthday." The king bowed slightly and, stepping aside, flourished his new sword toward the door.

He could feel the smith studying him; neither moved.

"Do you not want to leave?" he said as boldly as he could.

"Good King," said the smith quietly, "if you will leave the door unlocked and unguarded, I will take my leave when I am ready. But not right now. To leave hurriedly would insult Your Majesty's hospitality, which has been more than adequate. In the meantime I would like to examine your new sword."

The king felt a curious mixture of emotions. He was delighted that the smith took an interest in the sword, but frustrated that he did not seem to even feel inconvenienced by his imprisonment. He had felt a gloat thwarted within him, a silent victory that should have been there but never came to completion. It left him with a strange sense of emptiness, and there was something else. It was not fear, for the smith had never given him cause to fear him personally. It was a more groundless apprehension.

After a moment's hesitation, he decided that there was no substantial reason not to fulfill the smith's request. Perhaps in doing so his unease would be allayed. He stepped forward, both hands outstretched with the sword laid across them, the uncomfortable coldness of the blade in his left hand and the warmth of the handle in his right.

As the smith stepped forward to take the sword from his hands, he felt the smith's eyes engage his own and locked on them. The eyes did not let go until the smith had the sword in his huge left hand. He thought it was best to take a step back and let the smith have some space with the sword. A wave of genuine fear rolled over him as he realized he had no idea what the smith would do.

The smith waved the sword slowly from side to side. It was not a casual movement, but choreographed, sweeping through some sort of strange ritual that the king had never seen.

Sandihar sensed that the sword was in the hand of a master swordsman. One hand on the handle, then two, waving the blade this way and that. He would stop, holding it still in various positions, examining details of its construction and design. He lifted it high over his head and stared intently down the length of the blade. He stepped and turned this way and that, and each time the sword swept through the air, it sang an eerie song.

The smith paused and stared. The king followed his eyes to the door. It was of solid oak, and swung into the room on massive iron hinges. It stood a little more than half open. Suddenly, the smith raised the sword straight above his head and looked up its length.

"Woren dorren, vahat barra." The words sprang from his mouth. Sandihar was startled by the abruptness of the eruption, but he understood the meaning. "Vegen sor ahurat marra." Without warning, the smith sprang past the king. The sword's song was followed by two bright blue flashes as it sliced both hinges at the knuckles in a single, driven stroke. The door dropped onto its bottom, hesitated for a moment and then, losing its balance, crashed face down into the room with a thundering slap. The guards had to jump out of the way to keep from being flattened by it. As the smith turned to face him, holding out the sword in the same way that he had held it, Sandihar felt himself trembling.

"My son did a fine job for his king," said the smith calmly. "May the king, in his wisdom, bear it for good and not for evil." The king reached out and took the blade. The smith turned to the window again. "Now get out of my chambers!"

The king felt himself flush with anger as the smith delivered the command, but he knew that it was time to leave. He waved to the guards and they followed him out of the room eagerly, leaving the smith as they had found him, staring out the window into the courtyard and the door lying flat on the floor.

Halfway down the tower stairs, when they were safely out of earshot of the smith, one of the guards said, "Sire, what was it that he said?"

"Open door, may you stay this way, may you never imprison another," said the king hurriedly. Nothing more was said. Nothing more needed to be said.

The turns we encounter on the path of life can be as abrupt as those on a steep mountain trail. How we accept such unexpected re-directions tests and reveals who we really are.

The Tessarandin, Book 8

VRENGNIA SAT AT DINNER WITH HER FATHER. THE DAY HAD BEEN LONG. Festivities had started at noon with a grand parade through the courtyard of the castle, followed by a proclamation by her father concerning the festival and the two-day holiday. For those who knew her father personally, there had been a huge banquet. Mayors and dors, alderwomen and prominent merchants from throughout the kingdom, many of whom Vrengnia had never seen, sat at the enormous banquet table. They ate food that she had only heard about in legends and washed it down with an endless flow of wine and ale. The cutting of the huge cake was followed by a long parade of gifts to the king, as the nobles competed with one another in the extravagance of their gifts.

Vrengnia had spent most of the time ignoring all the formal posturing and wandered about the crowded courtyard with the townspeople. She tasted the wares of every food hawker's cart that had been squeezed into the castle. She sang with the musicians and danced with the actors on the makeshift stage by the drawbridge. Having wandered out into the field outside the gate, she had run in the three-legged race, competed in the spear-throwing and archery contests and helped build the huge bonfires that would be lit when darkness descended on Immerland.

Now she sat alone with her father at the dinner table in the dining room. Having encouraged others to continue in their revelry, he had withdrawn after the banquet. Vrengnia eyed him thoughtfully. After all the food, this "dinner" seemed to be but a time and place to escape. There was no need for a meal so she was trying to figure out why they were even there. The king did not look unhappy, but he did not look happy either. He was simply quiet.

"Are you content, Father?" she asked at length.

He looked up. "What?"

"Are you happy? I mean, it *has* been a great day hasn't it?"

The king smiled. "It's been wonderful. But I was just thinking, of all the things that were given to me today—and some of them *are* very nice—the best was definitely the sword."

"Thanks," she said. It had been a genuine compliment.

"I took it to show the smith. He seemed pleased with the work of his son."

"I should think that he would be; the sword is beautiful."

"He did not seem surprised though. It's almost as if he knew about it already."

She was not sure if he was probing or making a simple observation. "No one knew of either sword except Paca and me," she said simply. "Even the other smiths at the Shiloh smithy."

"Even Patira?"

"He did not even show up until after Paca had given me the swords. I am sure he did not know, unless Paca told him—but I doubt it."

Her father was thoughtful. "I have been giving considerable thought to the questions you had about Verclan," he said at length. "Perhaps it *is* time that we met." Vrengnia was not sure she had heard correctly. Her father continued, "I mean—I'm fifty now and I am weary of all the conflict."

She remained quiet. There was a time to talk and this was not that time. She listened.

"Do you suppose that he would come and talk with me after all these years? I mean, if he were willing to meet me, do you suppose that we could work things out?" Vrengnia was still not sure what to say. "Come my dear, what are you thinking?"

She held her tongue for a moment. "Father," she started cautiously, "it seems to me that any attempt at reconciliation would be good. In the worst case your fears, your thoughts, your position would be confirmed, and in the best, they would be proved wrong. The only thing it would cost you is your pride." She looked directly into her father's eyes.

His eyebrows rose and a hint of offense flared in his nostrils, but he backed down. "Yes. Yes, that would be all right." He shifted uncomfortably in his chair, looking at the floor as he spoke.

Vrengnia was encouraged. "Think of how much—" She was interrupted by a sudden commotion in the corridor outside the dinner hall followed by an urgent pounding on the door. The king sat up in his chair and set down the glass he had been holding. "Enter!" he commanded.

One of the king's attendants burst through the door followed by a short wiry man dressed in black from head to foot. The only thing that was not black was his face. It was Rappahoogin, head of the king's scouts.

He made straight for the king, glancing suspiciously at the Vrengnia on the way. "Sire," he whispered urgently, "we must speak." He was gasping as if out of breath.

The king stood up. "Speak freely my good man." The scout looked again at the princess. The king clapped him on the back. "Speak man, it is appropriate that she hears."

Vrengnia did not like the scouts. They were beings who were by nature suspicious, whom her father paid to be even *more* suspicious. All in all, they were a strange lot, well suited to snooping around to the king's advantage. She had never liked them—any of them, and for the most part, they were suspicious of her.

Rappahoogin bent over and put his hands on his knees, breathed deeply to try to catch his breath, and began speaking in that nasal, droning voice that gnawed at Vrengnia's vorn: "Reports started coming in about an hour ago of large scale raids on the barley and wheat fields along the southern border of the kingdom, Sire. No one was hurt; in fact, no one was even there to see it. Everyone was at the festivities here at the castle. When the crowds went home, they came back with the news. We think Verclan's men raided the fields and harvested large amounts of the ripe grain. It was all very neatly done, and there is no damage to buildings or fences; and no animals were hurt.

"As soon as I heard, I sent whoever I could find to confirm the reports before we came to you. I myself went down past Mordan." The little scout continued, "It seems that all in all, about fifteen acres of wheat have been taken and another twenty-four of barley. In addition, many vegetable gardens were raided. How many, it is hard to tell. It was all done very subtly."

The king sat down hastily. Vrengnia could see his rage, though he was trying to hide it. He looked at her with cold angry eyes, then turning to the scout, said, "Do we have any evidence that it was indeed Verclan?"

"No proof, Sire, but perhaps in the morning—"

"I want proof. Put the best men on it. *Now!*"

Rappahoogin did not need to be told twice. "The best men. Now." In an instant, he was out the door leaving the king, the princess and the attendant.

The king waved to the attendant, who dismissed himself without a word and shut the door behind him.

As her father turned toward her, his eyes were narrowed. "I think I have underestimated his gall again, and one time too many. Should I really try to reason with such a—" He stopped suddenly and a smile played briefly on his lips. He raised his hand as if he was going to speak and gesture somehow at the same time, but no words came out of his mouth. A peculiar look flitted across his face as he stared at her.

He put down his hand. "It is time to meet this man face to face and resolve this once and for all." His voice was quiet and resolved, but the glint in his eyes was full of anger and passion. He strode out of the room without so much as a glance back at her. She stood speechless behind the table. There was nothing more to be said to him anyway.

Vrengnia sat down heavily. Was there no relief? Was there no justice, that just when a small flame of progress seemed to be catching, it would be mercilessly snuffed out by this coincidence? What was it the smith had said? "There is no such thing as coincidence," and "All things work together for the good." How could this possibly be good?

She sat and stared into the candle on the table in front of her. She thought she understood her father's anger. Certainly, if Verclan had indeed perpetrated this insult on the kingdom, then her father would be justified in his anger, but there was something twisted in the way he had ended the conversation. The sudden shift and resolution he had shown as he walked out of the room were disquieting. She had a vague sense of foreboding. She thought that it had something to do with the sword, but she did not know what.

She *had* wanted to give him the sword. It had been made for him, and *she* had convinced Paca to make it. She remembered the twinge of fear she had felt just before she led him into the sitting room to give it to him, but in the end, she had decided that the reluctance was not based in sufficient clarity to justify withholding the gift. However, when he had insisted on taking his new sword to show the smith, she had left, driven away by a deep shame in her father's desire to gloat over his victory over the smith.

Now she wondered what it all meant. The only thing she was sure of was that she had tried to do something special and good, but now, what was good was being twisted beyond her control. It made her dizzy to think about it.

She sat alone in the huge room for a long time, the events of the recent weeks tumbling and cartwheeling through her mind. Like so many gymnasts on the lawn outside the castle that afternoon, they never stopped to rest.

Quite suddenly, noticing how alone she was, she stood up. "Somewhere, anywhere, but not here," she said aloud and headed for the door.

41

The heart of a man is fully revealed in how he looks upon his children.

Hispattea
The Essences of Corritanean Wisdom

VERCLAN SAT BY THE FIRE IN THE CLEARING WITH PATIRA AND HIS ADVISORS. The air was damp with the first dew of evening as the cool wind flowed down from the heights of the mountains towering over them. "Chronista?"

"Seven acres of barley sir, from the fields south of Mordan, from the edge of Haniah's land south and to the mountain road. We also gathered thirty pumpkins, four sacks of cucumbers, four baskets of beans and two pigs."

"Pigs?" Verclan smiled.

"*Two* pigs, sir. The grain is being transported to the eastern camp behind Mount Martak."

"Well done, Chronista, well done. And where are the pigs?"

Chronista smiled. "They are in a small pen beyond the rise over there. We thought we might have them for dinner."

"Let it be so," said Verclan. "Phartang?"

The small circle of men erupted in applause for the prospect of pork for dinner as Phartang stepped forward. He was a huge man, nearly a head taller than all the others and known for his feats of strength and daring. His hair was long and tied behind his shoulders. Two long scars ran diagonally from his left ear to his chin where he had been attacked by a bear as a young man. He had escaped by killing the bear with a stone. Of all the leaders of the clans, he was the most highly respected.

"We worked the fields south of Shiloh, sir. Two acres of barley and nine of wheat." The men cheered. "It is stored in carts in the foothills awaiting direction about where you would like it taken. We were also able to get fresh melons—to go with Chronista's fine Immerland pork—a cartload of apples, tomatoes, several sacks of late corn, and about half an acre of merrinath."

Verclan was genuinely surprised. "Merrinath? Are you sure?" Merrinath was a rare grain, and usually only grown far to the south and even then with great difficulty. It was valued for its unique flavor and herb-like qualities.

"Yes, sir, I am sure. It was hidden in the middle of a large barley field." A ripple of applause ran through the men.

Verclan stood up, bowed briefly and held his hand out to Phartang, saying merrily, "To Phartang. Should we have expected less?" Everyone laughed. Verclan sat down again. "Mortaga?"

Mortaga stepped forward, sweeping his cloak back over his shoulder. He was the oldest of the clan leaders, with a full head of white hair and a white beard. His eyes were fierce and keen, and he spoke with a rasp. "Seven acres of wheat. Some radishes, celery, peppers and eggplant—and a cart of rutabagas, sir."

"Well done, old man, and where is it now?"

"Most of it is also being taken to the eastern camp. Some of it is on its way here for the celebration."

"Celebration?"

"Sir, we are going to celebrate tonight, are we not?" Mortaga's eyes sparkled as he held out his hands in a questioning gesture to the group surrounding him. Several men hooted and everyone applauded.

Verclan bent to write the amounts and smiled. Looking up he said, "Of course, a celebration. Tonight. Patira?"

Verclan looked up as his son stepped forward. He felt his pride in his son. Patira was the youngest of the raid leaders by at least fifteen years, but he had earned his position among them. Verclan had struggled carefully to not favor Patira, but Patira had proven himself many times over in cunning, skill and courage. His mind drifted back to the defining moment for both of them in their place among the mountain people.

Acceptance of outsiders by the mountain people was slow and hard to earn among these fiercely noble clans. Having gained their trust as a farrier and having built the mines that supplied the clans with coal and iron, Verclan had established his place in their midst. Patira had been less successful at being accepted by his peers, the sons of the mountain warriors. As a result, he had taken to spending his spare time in the woods alone, tracking the warriors and learning on his own about how they lived.

It was spring, four years ago, that Patira had been following four trackers as they wove their way along the foothills on the Immerland border. The trackers were ambushed by a band of the king's men. There were about twenty soldiers in all who had been waiting for the mountain men who, in spite of their skill, were all captured. They had been bound and gagged in a small clearing and awaited the march into Immerland. Their captors made sport of them while they ate their lunch.

Through a series of clever distractions and daring maneuvers, Patira had scattered the soldiers, wounding them and frightening them to the point where they fled back into Immerland without their captives.

Patira never spoke of what happened or what he did. However, the four trackers told and retold the story in the fine oral tradition of the mountains, and Patira became a legend of daring and cunning, unmatched by any woodland hero of his generation.

"Nine acres of barley, sir, loaded and on their way to the Urland store houses."

Verclan smiled to himself as he wrote.

Patira continued, "Six bushels of white beans, some cucumbers, a cartload of apples and six kegs of Red Talion Wine…and no injuries."

"You found them while you were harvesting?"

"They were in the town hall at Yendel. We went to get a drink at the well there and a couple of the men—well—I think it should be very good wine."

All the men laughed. Verclan smiled at his son.

The reports were good. Forty-five acres of grain had been harvested and moved up into the mountains where they would feed his people through most of the winter. No one had been hurt. As far as he could tell, no one had even been seen. Carefully planted clues would tie the raid directly to his hand, but there was no direct action the king could take except to meet personally with him. There were no scouts to capture, no army to rebuff, no risks to be taken by any man. He had left a specific request for the king, an invitation to meet him on neutral territory, without fanfare and without an army. A personal meeting to discuss differences and possible solutions.

"So all we have to do now is wait—and thresh the barley." Verclan smiled and the all the raid leaders laughed.

Patira popped the cork from a jug of mountain mead and took a sip. "There will be plenty of this, this winter," he called as he wiped his mouth with his sleeve. "To the barley harvest—Long live the King!" Everyone laughed again while Verclan proudly took the jug from his son. He raised it to his lips and drank freely to the applause of his raid leaders. He knew this was where he and his family belonged.

42

Sometimes, silence is an answer all to itself.

Old Tessamandrian Proverb

PACA STROLLED DOWN THE LANE THROUGH THE WOODS IN THE DARKNESS. He had been at the castle for the entire first day of the festival. He had seen enough jugglers and minstrels for one day and had eaten enough for all the next. It was a magnificent celebration, and he had enjoyed the energy of the crowds and the joy of the people, most of whom cared little about the king's birthday, but had gone to be part of the event of a lifetime. He had stayed late, watching the people and hoping he would get a glimpse of the princess.

By now, she would have given her father the sword. He tried to imagine what the king's reaction might have been. More than that, he wanted to know if the king had freed his father and whether he had been at the feast. Paca had not seen him. Somehow he knew that his father was not at home yet, so he was in no hurry to get back, but the subtle disquiet of all these unknowns dominated his thoughts.

The night was warm, so the walk was invigorating and helped alleviate the quiet melancholy that had set in since he left the castle. Meekar hung over the mountains to the east. She was nearly full and Tal's glow could be seen faintly behind the distant peaks. It would not be long before she too, would be casting her light over all Immerland. The twins always gave a sense of comfort to the night, and Paca was looking forward to having both of them up.

He wasn't alone on the road; many revelers streamed away from the castle, heading home. Many still rode the energy of the crowds, silly from having had too much to drink and tired from the endless activity. In spite of the crowds, Meekar and Tal, he felt lonely. He wanted to talk to someone he *knew*.

As he neared the line of trees that would swallow the castle behind him, Paca heard the voice. Wondering for a second how he heard it above the hubbub of the people moving along the road, he stopped. No one else seemed to notice. He headed back toward the castle, and as he did so, others seemed to suddenly hear it also. They stopped and looked back, as if there were something to listen to, but nothing they could hear.

Paca knew it was his father. The voice rang like a clarion call above the throng. Every syllable was uttered with the utmost clarity, penetrating the murmur of humanity with a curious vigor.

An old donkey, carrying empty pack baskets from the festival, stopped suddenly in front of him and turned to face the castle, her ears standing straight forward. The elderly merchant who held her bridle was a short, stocky man with a permanent scowl creased into his face behind his beard. He swore and switched the animal with the stick he was carrying. "Stupid beast, come on!" he yelled, yanking on the animal's halter.

Paca strode over to the man and grabbed his hand. "My good merchant, let your animal listen to the taralang," he said firmly.

The merchant pulled his hand from Paca's in a rage. "You insolent dolt," he replied angrily, "what right have you to interfere with my affairs? Listen to the taralang. Rubbish!"

"Can't you hear the voice?" Paca was incredulous but firm.

"What voice?" The merchant asked, still angry. Paca could tell now that he was drunk; the smell of mead was heavy in his breath.

"The singing—from the castle."

"They've been singing at the castle all day, why should this stupid donkey want to listen now—and no, I do not hear any voice!" The merchant tried to pull the donkey's halter, but Paca had a firm hold on it.

"No!" said Paca to the merchant. "You will let this animal listen until she has heard what she is to hear!" The donkey's ears were turned toward the castle, and she seemed to almost be in a spell, listening intently and oblivious to the two men arguing over her.

The old merchant lashed out at Paca with a clenched fist. Paca saw it coming, caught the fist in his right hand, and began to squeeze. The old man had never felt the crushing power of a smith's grip and fell to his knees, begging the smith to let go. "You will let this animal listen as long as she likes," said Paca angrily. The merchant begged again and Paca let him go. Paca and the donkey stood silently beside each other, listening to the voice sing out its lilting and somber melody. The merchant sat heavily to the ground, nursing his hand and his grudge as the crowds swept by, most of them oblivious to the taralang's song.

43

Kor-Alura, the original language, speaks to the deep corners of the vorn.

Mortag of Horrinaine
Of Beings

WHEN THE SINGING STARTED, SANDIHAR WAS SITTING BY HIS BED IN HIS chambers, examining his new sword. He leapt from his seat and ran to the window in anger. *How dare he sing tonight,* he thought. *Why didn't he go home after I freed him?* It occurred to him that he had never gone back to check whether the smith had left after ruining the door to his room.

The king's anger melted as he realized that he understood some of the words. Parts of it remained unintelligible, while whole verses painted their understanding on his mind. Beautiful and powerful, it rose and fell like the West Sea on the shore at Minsora, lilting like the waters of Rinort in the spring. Sometimes it sounded like the wind in the tops of the forest trees.

Because he could understand some of it, he listened.

....
....

*"The swords of war are lifted high
Royal banners carried forth
Warriors in battle array,
Listening, listening,
Waiting for a different Moon."*

....

Several lines the king did not understand followed; then more that he could.

....

*"Not to stand by peace alone
Waiting until they see all men standing*

Waiting for a sword to crush the enemy
So that fighting would cease.
Not that death of any man is the answer
But that sometimes necessity lives
To be the reminder of forgiveness
In the face of timeless wonder."

His advisors burst into the room as if they all wanted to get there first. "Sire—, Carnados started."

He held up his hand indicating for them to be quiet and listen. They obeyed and stopped. More lines followed that the king could not understand. The rhythm of the verse was perfect in tone and tempo, and the words rhymed meticulously in the strange tongue.

There was more he could understand; at least the words themselves:

"Peace, peace there must be before,
Strong the ruler of the people stands;
Righteous, wise and equal to all who listen.
To lead in unity, to quench the famine,
Light the fire that shows to all who wonder.
Power, strength and virtue in hand."

....

The king found himself held in its grip. In the courtyard below the celebration stopped when the singing started, and a calming stillness hung over everything. He watched people sit down to listen as others started to leave, as if Immerland itself swayed under the voice of the enchanter. What did it mean? Why now, and how long would it last tonight?

Sandihar held on to the windowsill and closed his eyes, trying to make sense of what he heard and felt. It felt good to understand. It was terrifying at the same time, as it seemed to reach parts of his vorn that had remained untouched for years. Tears formed in his eyes and rolled down his cheeks, and he felt his shoulders trembling. He lifted his chin and breathed deeply, as if inhaling the song helped him understand not only the words, but perhaps himself.

He felt his advisors breathing behind him. They could wait; they needed to wait. As he opened his eyes again to look up, Meekar filled his vision; and the stars—how long had it been since he had looked up to see stars? He shuddered again as the voice rolled over him on the cool, dew laden evening air. He didn't move. He didn't *want* to move. Some distant longing made him just want to stand there forever.

The gravelly voice of Omberon crashed into his solitude. "Sire?"

Sandihar whirled to face the intruder. Omberon stood beside Carnados, as impassive and smirking as ever. "What is it, Omberon?" he asked, trying to convey his irritation as forcefully as he could.

"I wanted to know if you want us to stop him?" As if in response to some strange synchronicity, the voice halted.

"No! Not tonight." As Sandihar turned back to the window, the singing started again.

"He should be stopped, Sire." The voice paused again, this time as if it had been cut off suddenly.

As he turned again to look at Omberon, he felt a wave of disgust mingled with anger flow over him. His gut was torn by the pull of Omberon's words against the unrelenting desire to hear the rest of what the taralang had to say. Near perfect silence closed in around him, as if Immerland awaited his decision. Few times had he felt such anguish. He understood neither of the forces waging war within him. His mouth would not open so he turned back to the window, hoping to loosen the grip on his throat with the fresh air. As he did so, the voice resumed.

Something about it unleashed the power to speak. "No," he shouted, "the taralang must finish tonight!" He did not turn back, but he sensed Omberon's retreat as the voice continued singing—to Meekar and Tal, to the infinity of stars in the bright Tessalindrian sky, to his people, and to him, the King and Sovereign of Immerland.

44

*The power is not in the words themselves,
but in that they are words given by
Mah'Eladra.*

Mortag of Horrinaine
Of Beings

V RENGNIA HAD RETIRED TO HER CHAMBERS AFTER HER DISCUSSION WITH HER father. She was wondering about Paca. Had he come to the celebration? She had wanted to see him, or for him to see her so they could talk. Amidst all the nonsense and gaiety, she had longed for his friendship. She was holding his sword in her hands, marveling at its craftsmanship, when the first lines rolled out over the courtyard.

She did not understand much of it, but the lines she did understand were very clear. It cascaded out of the tower as it had the other nights, settling gently over Immerland. After laying the sword down on the nightstand, she moved to the window, captivated by the words. She had remained unmoving for a long time, when one of the phrases sprang into her mind with unusual clarity:

....

....

*"Standing in the lane, listening, waiting
The father speaks to his son freely.
Come close to listen, listen, listen
Wait now, wait until all is said properly."*

....

....

In an instant, she knew what she was supposed to do. She turned from the window and left her chambers, running down corridor and stair as fast as she could. She sped through the thinning crowds of people in the courtyard and out through the open portcullis.

"Princess!" Vishtorath's voice arrested her flight.

"I must find him," she gasped as she leaned over with her hands on her knees before the giant.

"He passed here not twenty minutes ago. He may be past the trees." She looked up. She could not see his eyes in the darkness, only a deep shadow under his helmet. "Do not go beyond the trees, Princess. If you need help, I will get him for you."

"Thank you," she gasped again.

She could feel the people staring at her as she sprinted down the lane toward the woods, the warm evening air streaming around her. Somehow, she knew she would find him—she had to find him, but how? Meekar's light helped to illuminate the road but there were people everywhere.

She slowed to a trot as she came to the woods. It was darker here, and she needed a little time to adjust to it.

A vise-like grip caught her short suddenly, on her arm. "Vrengnia!" It was Paca. "Where are you going?"

He was holding the bridle of a donkey with his left hand and her arm with his right. She could not see his eyes in the darkness but she knew they were looking at her. "I...I...was coming...to find...you!" she gasped. She threw herself on him in a hug. "Quick, you must...come with me!"

"Why?"

"Come on!" She grabbed his hand and pulled.

Paca looked at the old merchant, still sitting in the road in frustration. "Let the donkey listen!" he commanded.

"Hurry!" said Vrengnia. "We have to get to the castle."

Paca yielded to her tugging and started trotting along beside her. "What's going on?"

"I'm...not sure." Vrengnia was still out of breath because of her run from the castle. "But you need...to come and talk...to your father."

"But he is in prison."

"My father...set him free...this morning."

"Why didn't he leave?"

"Don't know that...either."

The voice continued its singing as they slowed to a walk at the portcullis. She thought she saw Vishtorath nod, but he said nothing. They walked quietly through the courtyard together. As she looked up, she saw her father standing in the window of his chambers. *Please stay there a little longer,* she pleaded silently.

The voice rolled on, ever changing, singing out words that were heard throughout the kingdom by those whose vorns were meant to hear them, whose minds were open to the direction they gave. She and Paca hurried on, the only movement in the immense stillness of the castle as it listened to the taralang.

Our world tires quickly of a being who gloats.

Mortag of Horrinaine
Of Beings

Paca struggled to breathe as they started the final ascent to the tower. The rapt attention of the entire castle on the voice of the taralang had allowed them to arrive there unnoticed. The stamina of the princess amazed him. She never slowed on the entire journey and now seemed to have a burst of energy as they approached the last set of stairs to his father's prison.

Without warning, the singing stopped; they kept running. As Paca came through the doorway, he saw his father standing by the window, holding onto the bars as if he were faint with exhaustion. He ran to him and wrapped his arms around him. The big man almost fell, but Paca caught him under the arm, supporting his weight. He helped him over to the bed, where the smith sat down heavily. "Father, are you all right?" he gasped. The older smith smiled slightly and nodded his head indicating that he should look toward the door.

Paca turned his head to see Vrengnia standing on the heavy oak door, examining what was left of the hinges fastened to the wall. He jumped up and started toward her. "What happened here?" he whispered as he saw her staring and in the next instant realized exactly what had occurred. The knuckles of the hinges were polished bright as if they had been sawn, exactly like the iron piece he had sliced in the kitchen with Vrengnia's sword. He grabbed her by the arm and pulled her back toward his father.

He was standing now. "The sword you made is a terrible weapon—flawless in its design, and terrifying in its purpose and power." His voice was strong. It cut into Paca's vorn like a dagger.

"Did the king—?"

"No," continued the smith, "I did that." Paca stared at him incredulously. "The king came here gloating over his new weapon—I borrowed it from him to examine it. It's a fine piece of swordcraft, and its first act was to keep this room from being a prison." His father had moved to the window and was staring out into the courtyard. He turned back to Paca and the princess, beckoning them to sit on the bed. "Come, we haven't much time. Your father will be here shortly."

"Son," his father began, "you must sleep at the top of the stairs tonight. Take this blanket for warmth. Princess, you must return to your chambers. Paca will visit you later this evening to confirm your plans. Do you both understand?" He looked from one to the other as they nodded their heads.

The smith continued: "Paca, we will talk more after the king has left. You will both meet at sunrise outside the gate to the castle for an errand that I will explain to *you*, Paca. Now go, quickly!" There was an intensity and urgency in his voice that would not be denied.

Paca rose and held out his hand to help the princess stand up. They headed toward the door. Paca was used to taking orders from his father, and he started up the stairs, but the princess hesitated. Paca heard his father say firmly, "Princess, there is not time now. You will know in the morning."

46

Silence creates a deafening roar in a troubled vorn.

Mortag of Horrinaine
Of Beings

To the king, in his chambers with his advisors, the taralang seemed to stop very abruptly. He was not sure if this was his own paranoia, but he did not remember him stopping like this the other two nights he sang—yet, he could not remember those nights clearly either.

He turned to his advisors questioningly. They seemed confused. He *was* confused. "I understood some of it this time," he said quietly, watching them intently. "And you?"

All three nodded gravely, but said nothing.

The king continued, "At first I was angry that the taralang was going to ruin the festivities—" He stared out the window to the courtyard. "But it seems that much of Immerland stopped to listen. Perhaps it was a fitting end to the day. Still, I am not sure I know what it all meant."

His advisors shifted on their feet as he looked back at them. "Come," he said firmly, "we must visit the smith once again."

He waved for them to follow, and they headed out into the corridor. As they rounded the corner to the tower stairs, he ran headlong into his daughter.

"Father," she burst out excitedly, "did you hear the singing again tonight?"

"Yes, I did—and I actually understood some of it!" he said. Inside he was suspicious. Where had she been? He guarded himself against a thought he did not want to have.

"I hardly understood any of it, but it seemed so beautiful!" She smiled and gave her father a hug. "Anyway, I am going to bed. It's been a long day." She brushed past the king, and he watched her head off to her chambers.

The king loved his daughter, though he had to admit that he did not understand her very well. She seemed to be changing and growing beyond his reach. He was having a hard time putting his finger on it, but the best he could figure, she was becoming more and more like her grandmother, the Great Queen. She seemed to take everything so easily. The king sighed and shook his head involuntarily. "Someday she will have to learn the burdens of being a queen." He smiled to his advisors as they proceeded up the stairs.

47

We must be gentle when we speak hard truth. There must be much love, for this is the Way of Psadeq.

Sessasha
It Is Written

PACA HEADED SOFTLY UP THE STAIRS TOWARD THE TOWER'S PARAPET. HE HAD taken about six stairs when he heard something drop on the stairs above him. It made a small metallic sound like a coin or a key. He stopped to listen. All he could hear was his heart beating wildly, and from below he could hear the king's entourage making its way toward his father's chamber. He dared not speak.

He moved softly upward against the inner wall, wanting to get far enough up so that he could not be seen by the king, but not so far as to encounter whoever was there. When he thought he was high enough, he sat down, trying to listen upward. There were no other sounds in that direction, but he had the feeling he was being watched. The skin on the back of his neck crawled. He wanted to run down and he knew he could not.

He turned suddenly. There was nothing there except the gray stairs climbing into the darkness above him. For a moment he sat still, unsure what should be done, then with careful movements, turned himself so that his back was to the inner wall so he could see up and down the stairs easily. As he stretched his feet out in front of him on the stairs, his left hand brushed something small and loose on the stair above him. He picked it up and felt it. It was a disk of metal, about two inches in diameter, with a hole through the center and small blunt points around its edge. It had various details stamped into its surface that he could not see in the darkness.

Whatever it was, he was sure he had never seen anything like it. He thought for a moment that this must have been what had fallen while he was climbing the stairs. He clamped it into his hand. He would show his father when he had a chance. If anyone would know what it was, he would. For now he had to concentrate on the events evolving below him. The king, and whoever was with him, were almost to the door of his father's chambers.

From where he sat, he could hear the entire conversation. He found it curious to listen without being able to see the expressions of the people involved.

"Good evening, good smith!" called the king.

"Good evening, good King," his father's voice returned evenly. It startled Paca to hear the difference between the voice with which his father addressed the king, and that with which he had addressed the princess. It was unguarded and accepting, but empty of warmth, as if he had little to give to the man before him.

If the king noticed, he ignored it and continued jovially, "You sang again tonight—it made a fitting end to the first day of the big celebration!"

"Perhaps," said the smith calmly.

"But that is not why I—I mean we—are here." A moment of silence followed and Paca imagined his father's eyes penetrating the king in that peculiar way he had of asking a question without saying anything. "No, we came to get some advice from you." A hint of triumph echoed in the king's voice, as if in asking advice he had overcome some grand obstacle.

"I have told you before. I cannot reveal what the taralang has said."

"No—no. This is real advice," smiled the voice of the king. He paused as Paca's father asked another silent question.

"Listen, good smith, I know that you were friends with this brigand Verclan—"

"Brigand?"

"Well, with Verclan—many years back in my mother's stable."

"Yes, I remember it well," said his father with a remote warmth.

"Well, this Verclan has taken it upon himself to organize the mountain clans into a significant threat to the peace of Immerland." There was another pause. "Most recently, in fact this evening, he took advantage of my festival. He apparently raided the barley and wheat harvest and disappeared with forty acres of grain."

"Apparently?" Paca could see his father raising his eyebrows to the king.

"Well, we don't have proof, but I am sure it was him." Another pause followed. "So, I am at a little bit of a loss as to what to do—and I thought you might have some insight for me."

"Are you seeking my advice, or are you looking for an accomplice?" came the blunt reply.

"Accomplice to what?"

"The question was rhetorical, good King. I am simply trying to discern whether you really want my advice or whether you want me to play into your plans somehow." Paca detected a new warmth in his father's voice; a hope, perhaps, that the king really wanted his advice. "I only give advice to people who sincerely want it."

In the pause that followed, Paca felt it again. Someone *was* watching him. Waiting in the darkness; silent and without a name. It created a kind of terror inside him that he had never felt before.

The brief pause gave way to the king's measured voice: "Good smith, I have come to have the utmost respect for your wisdom. I see that you have much to offer, and I sincerely need your advice in this situation."

No one else had uttered a word. Paca wished he knew who they were and could see their faces to know what they were thinking.

"My good King, do sit down." A chair dragged across the floor. His father's voice flowed with warmth and confidence. "My advice to you is simple: Make peace with Verclan. This is the road to peace for all Immerland. The way of the sword leads only to death and oblivion."

"How is it that you are so sure about these things? We have successfully repelled Verclan's minions with the sword in the past. You speak of peace. Well, we have maintained peace with our swords."

There was another pause. His father sighed heavily. "My good King, let me tell you my story. Perhaps I can convince you of your folly."

"Perhaps." The king's tone was facetious.

"My father was a great smith. He was the head blade maker for Lutaka the Great."

"Lutaka?!" The king must have stood up. Paca heard a chair fall onto the floor. "Lutaka was one of the Great Fathers. He lived before The Grayness—"

The commanding voice of the smith interrupted the king. "Sit down, Sire, and let me finish my story! Indeed, what you say is true. And if you will accept the impossibility of that being true *and* what I will tell you as *also* being true, you will be much the wiser.

"One of Lutaka's commanders came to my father's smithy and asked my father for swords for himself and all the generals under his command. The order was for thirteen swords of the finest steel to be used for the defense of the kingdom of Tessamandria. The Grayness had started to appear at that time, although we were not aware of its power or the awful toll it would take on Tessalindria.

"My father was not accustomed to making weapons, because up to that time weapons were of little need in Tessamandria. My father had been taught his smith craft by the Eladra, who had instructed him to never use his skill to make weapons, but at the commander's request, my father, beguiled by the convincing words of the commander, made the thirteen swords. Twelve were made together and the thirteenth forged after the others had been completed. The thirteenth was by far the best. No one, not even my father, knew the danger that he had unleashed into Tessalindria with that sword. The commander's name was Mankar—"

Paca felt a movement above him on the stairs. It was subtle and vague, but something had moved, as if the name "Mankar" had unsettled the watcher. He wanted to scream.

"The Sword of Mankar is a legend," interrupted the king with a sneer. "You speak as if it were real!"

"The Sword of Mankar is *very* real. My father forged it. I watched him do it. In doing so, my father broke trust with the Eladra. Mankar came with his generals to acquire the swords, and after they had been delivered to him, he slew my father with the sword he had made."

"Why? How?"

"In that sword lay Mankar's key to power and he knew it, so by killing my father, no more such swords could be made. He hewed my father to pieces in his own smithy. So began the reign of terror that Mankar brought to Tessamandria and all Tessalindria in the end; the dawn of The Grayness."

"And how did you escape, good smith?" The king's voice hinted that he was humoring the smith. Paca found himself infuriated by the king's attitude, and fascinated by his father's story. His father had always taught him that there was fact behind the fiction in the legends. "One man's fact is another man's fiction," he had often said. "Discerning the difference is always the challenge." The king seemed unwilling to treat the legend as anything but fiction.

"I fled out the back of the smithy; the Eladra protected me as I escaped. I was sixteen at the time. Mankar and his generals pursued me relentlessly. He knew that I alone had the knowledge to destroy the swords. I eluded their search for four years, living in the caves in the mountains, and watching the destruction of Lutaka's kingdom at Mankar's hand. I made a solemn pact that I would never make a weapon designed to inflict pain on another man.

"Finally, Mankar found my hideout and trapped me in a cave in which I had taken refuge. I fled back into the cave, farther and farther. One of Mankar's generals was on my trail, but, having lived in the caves so long, I was able to elude him. It was in my efforts to escape that I fell through the Trestal Portal. When I came out of the cave, I was in a different time and different place."

Paca could hear the muffled and hurried voices of the others, but could not understand what was being said. His father continued…

"It took me a while to understand what had happened, the legend of the portals being but fiction to me at the time, until I fell in with Sessasha—he helped me to put it all together."

"You knew Sessasha?" There was mocking incredulity in the king's voice.

"I saw him die," stated his father. "For two years longer I stayed with his followers. With the help of an old friend who had one of Lonama's maps, I came through another portal to Immerland. Shortly afterward, I began serving under your mother with Verclan."

"Why Immerland?"

"That is my business, good King—but my advice to you is still the same: make peace with Verclan. The way of the sword will lead to death and more death beyond that."

"So, why did you let your son make the swords for me and my daughter?" He sounded genuinely curious.

"Swords?"

"Why yes. He made a second one for Vrengnia. Didn't you know?"

"I was in your prison, good King. I asked my son to promise me when I left the smithy that he would not make any weapons, but it was his decision to do so. Given that he has, he, along with your daughter, will have to learn its consequences. It's part of his education. He would not have done this had it not been for some greater good, which none of us can see at this time."

"You are saying that there is some fate waiting for Vrengnia and your son for violating his promise to you? Are you saying that someone will die, and that is a greater *good*?"

"There is no such thing as fate, just as there is no luck or coincidence. Nevertheless, there are consequences for every decision. Each being must take responsibility for the decisions that he makes. Vrengnia and Paca will someday have to take responsibility for theirs, just as you must assume full responsibility for yours in regards to Verclan.

"Every being is destined to die, good King, the only question is when. Swords are designed to kill people. Should it surprise you that some being's untimely death would be associated with your new sword? Or with Vrengnia's? Are you in a position to say that that untimely death might not be part of a greater good? That the death of *one* might not prevent the death of many others? That the death of *one* might not save but one other, through whom a greater goodness is brought to many? Surely you do not set yourself up in judgment of history before it has happened and question the leadings of Mah'Eladra." His father's reasoning hung in the long pause that followed.

"The man is a murderer and a thief," said the king evenly. "There can be no peace while he continues to plague my kingdom!"

"My good King"—his father's voice was still gentle— "the decision is yours. I have only offered my advice. You may take it for whatever you think it is worth. But you will own that decision."

"Exactly what is your current association with Verclan?" asked the king, shifting the direction of the discussion.

"He is my friend, a cymbic in the first sphere. We love each other deeply and respect one another. He provides me with his finest steel and coal from the mountain mines, and I provide his family with food so that they do not starve in the winter. The sword you possess, and Vrengnia's too, were made possible by Verclan's toil." There was silence for a brief moment. "Believe it or not, good King, Verclan is not the enemy you have made him to be."

"What are you saying?" asked the king.

"Have you ever been to the mountains? Perhaps you have spent a night there? Have you ever tried to imagine what it must be like to *live* there?"

"That is ridiculous!" The king was indignant.

"So you have no personal understanding of what you inflicted on Verclan when you banished him from Immerland, am I correct?"

"I suppose—"

"Why do you *suppose* that Verclan raided the barley and wheat harvest last night? Was it to spite you? Was it to start a war with you?"

"Yes, I think it was."

"No, it was not!" said his father firmly. "Verclan raided the fields because his people would starve this winter without that grain. It's as simple as that. You, O King, have taken all the arable land up to the mountains and have left nothing for these people to live on. The attack was as simple as survival! Though you are seen as a good king in Immerland, you are viewed as an oppressor of the poor in the mountains."

There was another long pause. The watcher shifted again, a silent movement in the non-shadows of the black stairway.

"Verclan murdered my wife, the Queen of Immerland," began the king slowly. "The princess barely survived."

"If this is about a personal vendetta, then settle that with Verclan himself." The smith's voice was becoming stern. There was silence again for a moment. "You have heard my advice, good King, There is little else to be said."

"Yes, I suppose that is true." The king's dark voice was sullen. "Come, let us go," he said to the others in his entourage.

Paca listened as the royal party left the smith's chambers and shuffled down the tower stairs. They said nothing as they descended. He sat frozen, listening until the sound could no longer be heard and everything was quiet again.

"Pacahara!" His father's voice was quiet, but it shattered the stillness like a taskmaster's whip.

Paca scrambled to his feet and leapt down the stairs. Was the watcher following? It seemed so, but there was no time or need to find out now. Rounding the corner in the corridor, he saw the light of the doorway beckoning. It seemed like only an instant before he was through the door.

His father pointed to the chair by the reading table. "Have a seat, son," he said as he turned himself to sit on the bed. "There is much more to be said.... What's the matter?"

Paca held out his hand with the small disk in it. He could not speak.

His father stepped up and looked down into his hand. "Where did this come from?"

He motioned toward the doorway and up the stairs. His father grabbed the disk and bolted past him. He had never seen his father move so quickly. In two steps he had reached the door. In another two he had disappeared up the stairs. Paca tried to follow, but he was shaking and his knees felt weak. Before he got to the door, his father was back.

"There is no one up there now," he said. "You found this up there?"

"Yes, I heard it fall as I was going up. I found it when I sat down."

"You think that someone was up there?"

"I am sure of it. But I did not know what to do—I mean the king was coming—"

His father stared at him intensely. "Did you hear anything else?"

"I thought I did, but I was never sure. I had the feeling that I was being watched several times." His father was turning the small disk over and over in the light of one of the lanterns. "Do you know what it is?" Paca could see that it was iron, inlaid with gold on both surfaces. It was about the thickness of two coins and shaped like a star with a hole through its center.

"It's a signet star, used by the kings of Tessamandria to prove that the messages from the king were genuine. The hole through the middle fit only certain keys which the recipients of the messages had. By matching the key to the star, the bearer was assumed to be delivering a royal message." He held the star up to the lamp, and Paca noticed for the first time that the hole was irregularly shaped. "The only time I have ever seen these, they were carried by Mankar's generals. They wore them around their necks, on small chains. In Lutaka's kingdom, they were the messengers. It brings back memories I would like to forget."

There was a faraway look in his father's eyes for a moment before he shuddered and looked back at Paca. "Whoever it was seems to be gone now. We will have to wait for an answer on this—and not be afraid—as I was saying, sit down, there is more to be said."

More to be said? Paca had so many questions. Most of what he had heard in the corridor was as new to him as it must have been to the king. His father had never told him much of his history—only what related to him directly. Now his father was staring at him calmly as if he was expecting Paca to initiate the conversation. Paca decided to wait.

His father broke the silence easily. "Tomorrow morning at dawn, you must meet the princess outside the castle gates. The coming and going will be easy because of the festival. The gates will be open, but you should not be seen together inside the castle. The princess should go on foot. A horse would attract too much attention. She should dress as normally as she can." He smiled as if he had made some kind of a joke. Paca smiled back and shrugged to show that he had understood the humor of it. "You must travel together to Haniah's soddy. The princess can show you the way; she has been there many times. Wait there until you know it is time to return." The smith stood up, moved over to the south window, and stared out into nothingness.

"How will I—I mean, *we*—know what are we supposed to do there?"

"I'm not sure. I have told you all I know. You are to wait there. You will know when it is time to return." The way he spoke indicated more was coming. Paca listened.

"There are many things happening right now that are all falling together according to a great plan. I know only what is given me, and you know only what is given you." His father turned toward him and leaned casually against the wall by the window. His tall frame seemed even larger than reality as the soft light of the lanterns on the table threw his shadows up on the wall behind him. "It is a time to trust the El in you, and time to act on this trust; to see that our lives are much bigger than just us, our minds, or even our imagination; that history is being formed and that the greater good of all Immerland hangs in the balance."

Paca knew vaguely what the El was, but he had never thought he possessed it. It was the piece of the vorn that formed the connection between the nephus and Mah'Eladra. There was much controversy about the El, and few people he knew believed it was real. His father was one who believed, but it was more like a knowledge than a belief. He had always encouraged Paca to believe, but had never said it quite like he just did.

His father shifted his weight and peered out into the vast darkness behind the window. Paca waited again. He knew his father wanted to talk and he had to let him. "Did you hear my conversation with the king?" he asked suddenly. "All of it?"

"Yes, I—I did," Paca stammered. He had not been ready for the shift in the direction of the conversation.

"And what did you make of it? Was there anything peculiar about it?"

It seemed to Paca that there were a thousand unanswered questions, but was there anything peculiar? Anything odd? "Only that the king did not ask many of the obvious questions that I would have had!"

"Would have had? Or *do* have!"

"Well,—*would* have had if I were the king—but that I *do* have as your son."

"And what do you make of the fact that the king—as the king—did not ask them?" There was an intensity and penetration in his father's voice that made Paca uneasy. If he had not known his father, he would have been intimidated into silence.

"Perhaps the king is afraid of your apparent knowledge about a situation that he cannot grasp?"

"Afraid? Yes!" His father's animation heightened as he turned from the window and stepped toward him, his hands starting to get involved in the conversation. "But not of me or my knowledge. He is afraid of believing the truth about me, afraid that if he finds out this truth, it will make him *less* rather than *more*!" There was a glint of strength in his eyes that Paca had never seen before. "There are many men who spend their lives trying to fabricate their own truth by hiding from the truth that surrounds them. It is a terror to them and they are trapped by their own fear. One can see it in their eyes, in their faces, in the decisions they make, in the simple act of not grasping for the truth when it is offered to them so plainly." He was standing two steps in front of Paca, with his hands clenched, eyes full of the forge's fire. "Paca, never be afraid of finding truth!"

Paca met his gaze and they locked eyes. "I will never be afraid of finding truth!" he said firmly.

His father turned suddenly, walked back to the window, and leaning against the sill, faced into the room with his legs crossed comfortably in front of him. Paca was still not sure what this was all about.

"Now—ask me the questions that the king should have asked!" his father demanded. It was more of a challenge, a test of truth seeking.

"Can I start with a question he did ask, that you did not answer?" Their eyes met. The answer was all in the eyes. Paca continued: "Why did you come to *Immerland* through the portal after Sessasha's death?"

His father crossed his arms and a dark expression spread over his face. "When my father was slain by Mankar, I escaped, and I carried with me the singular knowledge of how those swords were forged and how they could be destroyed. That is why Mankar hunted me so ferociously. In my vorn I had made two vows: First, to never make another tool that had as its design the injury of another man, and second, to track down the swords my father made and destroy them. When I fell through the portal into The Dawning, I escaped his pursuit, but also left the swords behind."

He turned to gaze out the window again, as if looking into the far distant past. "Remember I mentioned to the king about my friend with Lonama's map?" He turned again to Paca. "Well, using the map, we were able to track the swords to the Age of Waiting, that's now. They are somewhere here in Immerland. I knew exactly where they were, but the trip through the portal plays tricks on the memory, or at least it seems to, and when I arrived, the specifics were cloudy. I was twenty-two years of age, and needing a job, I managed to sign on with the queen's stables while I set about tracking them down. It was my hope that my blade smithing would eventually lead to their whereabouts. This has to be done before they fall into the hands of the wrong beings. In the wrong hands, they could once again terrorize Tessalindria."

"What is needed to destroy them?"

"Another sword, forged as a destroyer. Fearful it will be, and not meant for any other purpose. Since I had taken a solemn oath never to create another sword, I was never quite sure what I would do when I found the others."

"Does any one except you suspect that they are here in Immerland?"

"Not that I know of. Only I—and you—and Verclan."

"Verclan?"

"Yes, he knows. It is partly why he continues to supply me with his finest steel and coal. We have to be ready when the time comes!"

Paca was curious, but he thought he saw a flaw in his father's plan. "Have you ever wondered whether Verclan's purpose in helping you is pure, I mean, perhaps he is just hoping to find the swords and use them to *his* advantage?"

The smith was staring out the window. "I have wondered that. It would be a fearful thing, but I trust Verclan, more than any other man I know. I do not trust the king." He turned to face his son. "The king and the princess must never, not ever—never, never, never know what I told you here tonight, do you understand?" There was that look again, only this time it *was* intimidating.

"I understand," said Paca.

"Never ever!" whispered the smith and turned again to the window. He stared silently. He seemed to be waiting. For what? For the next question? Yes, the next question!

"Why didn't the king ask you about what you discussed with the princess?" queried Paca.

"This is a good example of not wanting to know the truth. I would have gladly told him, but he fears that his daughter is betraying him. Instead of confronting and being guided by the truth, he would rather let *suspicion* drive his actions. The suspicion belongs to him—he owns it—so he justifies himself in its use. It is a vicious circle. It leads to nowhere but trouble."

Paca knew the next question that needed to be asked, but was dreading it. Perhaps he did not want the truth any more than the king. He had to fight for it now. "Why have you not reprimanded me for breaking my oath to you about the king's sword?"

His father turned from the window, stepped to the bed and sat down on its edge. His eyes were level with or slightly below Paca's and they locked into his. Paca noticed how gray they really were as he was waiting for the answer. It was slow in coming. "There was much confusion that day. I really did not expect the king to take me as a prisoner. In a moment of distrust, I tried to get you to commit to a conviction that you did not have the basis to accept."

"Distrust?"

"Yes, distrust of how the vorn of a man must be shaped. It cannot be done with promises. It takes time and experience. I did not have time, you have not had the experiences. I tried to shortcut your education by extracting a promise. It was doomed to fail, and fail it did."

Paca broke away from his father's eyes and looked down at the floor. "You said something about learning from the consequences of what I did."

"Yes." His father stood up. He turned and headed toward the window again. There were not that many places to go in the small room, and the window seemed like a magnet to him. Perhaps it was just a force of habit, from being imprisoned for some time. "When a weapon is designed for the destruction of another person, it will not be long before that intent is realized. Someone will die! Who? How? When? Where? For these, we must wait." He was leaning against the window frame and facing Paca again. "And wait we will. But there is something much bigger happening here. I can sense it. Some purpose in all this that I cannot identify. The El in me tells me it is good, but it is too vague to see. This is often the way it is in the making of history."

"Did you ever see the Eladra that trained your father?" Paca had only heard of the existence of the Eladra as legends, stories from ages past to give credence to the incredible exploits of the Great Fathers. According to the legends, it had been at least seven hundred years since Lutaka died, but his father claimed to have been born then and believed in the Eladra. Out of respect, any question should acknowledge that belief, no matter how strange it seemed.

His father didn't even flinch at the question. "On occasion—although one does not really see them most of the time. It is more of a luminous presence—better seen out of the corner of one's eye than looking directly at them. Occasionally they take the form of a fully present being, no different in appearance from you or me."

His father was staring out the window as he spoke. "Paca, come here."

Paca rose from the chair and made his way to the window.

"Look at the tower on the opposite side of the courtyard—where it meets the wall, on the left. On top of the last merlon of the parapet—do you see anything?"

Paca shook his head. He was not sure whether his father wanted him to see anything specific.

"Don't look directly at it, but look a little to the left, but concentrate on what you see on the merlon."

Paca tried to do what his father said. There was a faint wavering luminance, dancing on the top of the stone. "I think I see something."

"How about over to the left, in the corner of the drawbridge tower, just to the left of the door. Don't look directly at it."

Paca looked a little to one side of where his father had indicated. "Yes, yes. I see it!"

"Eladrim warriors," said the smith calmly. "They have been here since I arrived. There are about twenty of them guarding the castle. If you look around, you will see most of them."

Paca was astounded. "Why are they here?"

"I am not sure, but it is a great comfort that they are. It means that we are well protected. If this signet star represents what I think it may, we would be in grave danger without their presence. They may be watching to keep evil out of the castle or contain it within."

His father turned from the window and continued his description of the Eladra. "They speak the original language, and one only hears them if they are addressing you directly." The faraway look in his father's eyes returned, and his voice softened into almost a whisper. The description came in fragments with long pauses in between. "My father saw them often, sometimes in groups. They would visit his smithy, mostly at night. It was they that taught him the forge poetry, in the evenings. It was then that he did his greatest work. The Mankar swords were all done after the other smiths had left—in the stillness—in the darkness."

Paca stood patiently by the window, not moving as he allowed his father to continue his soliloquy. "As I recall—though it is not very clear—the Eladra stopped visiting him when he started the swords. The poetry for the swords came from somewhere else. It just welled up, almost from within himself, perhaps from his own nephus. I do not know for sure how, or where it came from."

It was time to speak. "I...I think I know that feeling. That is what happened to me in the smithy—when I started the sword for the king."

"*And* the sword for the princess!" His father turned, and his words cut deep.

Paca could not look at him; he stared at the floor. "Yes, and the sword for the princess," he said, realizing his shame for not admitting to it earlier. He looked up again to meet his father's eyes. "How did you know?"

"I was the one who sang the poetry for the swords as you were making them the second night," he said matter-of-factly. "I also got a chance to handle the king's sword—he brought it here to show me—and it was a fine blade, but it is not the blade that was the object of the poetry that night."

"How do you know?"

His father's intensity had risen again, and he was pacing back and forth in front of the window with his left hand on his beard; he was staring at the floor. At Paca's question he stopped and looked up. "There are things that we know without knowing how we know them. This is part of trusting the El. The person who refuses to acknowledge this type of knowing limits his possibilities. He always wants proof. Consequently, he always doubts. This doubt scares him into something less than he could be. The realization of the existence of the second sword was unexpected, but once it occurred to me that it might exist, it was obvious that it had to."

His father opened his mouth to continue and stopped suddenly, as if what he was going to say needed to remain unsaid. Paca waited. "It's late and we have talked enough for this time," he said after the pause. "There is more, but it must wait. You need sleep for tomorrow's journey. Do you remember what needs to be done?"

Paca recited back to his father the plans for the next day's trip with the princess.

"Good," said his father, "you must tell the princess before the morning. Now go! Go quietly, let no one see you. Return here to sleep."

Paca hesitated.

"You are thinking that you do not know where to find the princess! Paca, you do know! Do not fear your apparent ignorance—it is false."

Paca knew it was time to go. He hugged his father and left without another word. He knew somehow, that he would find the princess, but was unsure exactly how.

48

Whose folly is greater, the fool who shouts
"Aha" when he has learned nothing or the
blind man who says, "Now I can see," but
refuses to open his eyes?

Hispattea
The Essences of Corritanean Wisdom

THE KING DID NOT LIKE WHAT HE WAS THINKING. HE HAD TRIED TO THINK about something else, but it was not working. Why had his daughter been to visit the smith? Was she in league with him? Had she just been to see him because of the singing? Was there something she was supposed to do for him that he had communicated through the singing? He did not like these questions because he was afraid that he would not like the answers either. Instead of asking the smith directly, he was now left to avoid them himself, which he was finding very difficult. He changed the subject on himself.

"Why do you suppose that the smith so carefully avoided my question about why he had come to Immerland? I mean, if, in fact, he really did." His advisors were shuffling along behind him quietly as he headed back to his quarters from the visit with the smith. "Well?" he pressed, glancing back over his shoulder to see if there was any reaction from his entourage.

Carnados saw his glance and began to answer. "Sire, it was a most peculiar and informative conversation. Apparently, we not only have a taralang, but a portal walker as well—"

The king whirled to face his followers. Carnados stopped and the others ran into him from behind. "And you believe that?! The portals are but legends. The portal walkers are just the same. Son of Lutaka's smith, indeed!" The king was peering keenly into Carnados's face. He held the other's gaze for a moment before continuing. "You believed him, didn't you? I mean, all that nonsense about his father making Mankar's sword, falling through the portal, seeing Sessasha's death, Lonama's map. Come now, my trusted friend, we—"

"Sire," Carnados interrupted severely, "may I finish speaking?"

The king was not used to being interrupted, and his face must have shown it clearly. Carnados stood firm. The king read his eyes as they stared at each other. "Yes, you may," he conceded, "but in my chambers." He turned and beckoned them to follow, and they walked in silence the rest of the way through the dark halls.

They sat facing each other. The king was sitting on the edge of his huge bed with his shoulders drooped and his chin in his hands, his elbows resting on his knees. He was staring into the eyes of the three advisors in turn as they sat on stiff-backed chairs facing him. "Well?"

"Sire," said Carnados, "I would speak of legends more as a plausible history that has never been confirmed." The king eyed him passively. The advisor seemed to be setting up a scenario without saying anything, a common tactic for delicate conversations, but the king allowed him to go on, in spite of his disgust for such maneuvers. "Lutaka is an historical figure. We know he was the last of the Great Fathers, and that it was during his reign that the usurper and unraveler Mankar rose to power and ushered in The Grayness. It has never been clear how he managed to wreak such havoc on the fabulous achievements of the Great Fathers. The only explanation ever propounded was his acquisition of the great sword and the swords of his generals—"

The king shifted, stretched and resumed his baleful chin-in-hands position. Carnados continued: "His killing of the smith that made the swords is part of the legend. As to whether the smith had a son, there is no written record. Indeed, after Lutaka was deposed, any written history would have been under the influence of Mankar; and it is likely, given the way histories are written, that if such a son did exist and eluded Mankar's grasp, it would be a sufficient embarrassment that it would not be recorded. Is this not true?"

"It could be," said the king, leaving his sentence to hang in such a way that it was clear that Carnados should continue.

"The existence of the portals is woven into every great legend we have. Our lack of direct experience with them would never be a valid criterion for rejecting their existence." Carnados paused as he considered which branch of his argument to present next. "We have done some checking on our smith and have found no genealogical history. The first record of him in Immerland is his service to your mother. He seemed to have been about twenty years of age. There is no record of any smithing apprenticeship, but when he came to the stables, he was quickly recognized as one of the best smiths ever seen in Immerland."

The king rubbed his face wearily. He did not like what he was hearing. He had no logical reason to reject it, and he had no historical fact to contradict the advisors' research, but the truth pointed in a direction he did not want to face. "So now we have a smith with no history and a captain of the guard with no history. Who's next? You, Carnados?"

If Carnados noticed the sarcasm, he did not show it. "No one has ever disproved the existence of Lonama's map, but almost all portal-walker legends attest to it."

"What, exactly, is Lonama's map?" the king interrupted. He stood up and started pacing back and forth in front of the bed. He genuinely wanted more details. Perhaps this was the clue to the frustrating riddle that was developing before him.

Mindar spoke: "Details are scanty on this subject. It is not clear whether there is one map or perhaps several—but it seems to be a sort of detailed map of Tessalindria that includes temporal information—"

"Temporal?"

"Yes. It is a map of Tessalindrian time as well as geographical details. We don't know much about it because those who possess it, or them, have kept the secret from all but a small number of select persons. The map somehow includes the location of the time portals and where they go, both in location and time. The smith's claim, that a "friend" who had such a map helped him to come to Immerland, is certainly plausible if such a map exists."

"Yes—if!" said the king, stroking his chin. "If!" He disliked what he was hearing more and more because it gave credence the smith's story. "If this is true, then it is likely that the smith is on some sort of mission, wouldn't you say?"

"Exactly, Sire," the older advisor rejoined. "The smith's implication, that Immerland-now was a conscious selection, was subtle but real, in my opinion." The others nodded gravely. "This would indicate a mission."

The king sat down on the bed heavily. "Give me some reasonable scenarios for such a mission."

"Well, we have all found it peculiar that given his claim to have witnessed his father's death and his refusal to make a weapon of any kind, that he continues to pursue the development of his blademaking craft."

"That is what he does well. Why would we not expect that he would enjoy it and pursue it?" asked the king.

"We think that there is more to it, that's all," said Cordas. "We do not know why, but we think this is part of his mission."

"Why?"

"We are not sure. It is simply an idea to consider well."

The king could feel his frustration and fear subsiding in the pursuit of the logical explanation for the smith's presence in Immerland. His mind was clearing, and a sudden thought occurred to him. "Missions are often quests, aren't they?" His advisors looked at him thoughtfully, but said nothing. The fog suddenly cleared completely and he snapped his fingers. "He's looking for something perhaps—but what?" He was pacing briskly back and forth. The advisors waited for him. "Maybe another person, another portal walker—maybe an object, lost in our time—in the map!"

His pacing had carried him from the bed to his dressing table and back several times, when suddenly, he paused, leaning on the table itself and looking down. He picked up his new sword and smiled. "He is looking for the Sword of Mankar!" he said triumphantly. He laughed aloud at the expressions on his advisors' faces. "He thinks it is here, in Immerland! He may make me a believer yet. I mean, I'm not sure I believe all this, but if the sword of Mankar is here—now, then...come, we have little time to lose!"

"Sire?" It was Carnados.

"What?" the king shot back impatiently.

"If the Sword of Mankar exists and is here now, it would be best to leave it alone. Its terror is legendary, and it is a terror we would not want to unleash on Immerland."

"On Immerland? Hah!" laughed the king. "We would unleash it on that NarEladra Verclan!"

"Sire—"

"What?" said the king. There was so much to do. He did not *want* to stop and listen.

"Sire, you have seen the influence of the smith in all these events. The singing, your birthday and Verclan's activities—may be a confluence of some sort—the culmination of the smith's quest. It would not be prudent to interfere—"

The king interrupted his advisor. "Interfere? Can't you see? I am part of this confluence as much as the smith! How could I interfere? Perhaps my finding of the sword is exactly part of the plan!"

Cordas spoke, "Yes, Sire, perhaps. Nevertheless, Verclan seems to be part of this confluence also. Perhaps he already has the sword. It would make him a formidable enemy!"

Sandihar suddenly realized that there were many possible paths to the future from the present. He knew that Cordas was right. He had to be careful. He felt a wave of fear that he associated with his doubt about the future. If there were just some way to know with a little more certainty what path was best...

Then another thought occurred to him. His sword! It was right in his hand. He had seen its power, now it was time to show his advisors. There was large iron lamp stand on the dressing table. The king put both hands to the handle of the sword and swung it suddenly at the lamp stand. There was a flash of blue light as the blade slipped through the thick vertical shaft of the stand as if it were a cucumber. The top of the heavy stand hardly moved under the impact. It tottered momentarily and then crashed onto the desk.

With both hands on the sword, the king turned slowly toward his advisors and smiled. They were speechless. Holding up the sword so that it divided the chamber between him and the others, he slowly scanned its perfection from hilt to tip. "It was a gift from my daughter, forged by the smith's son. It, too, is part of the confluence!"

Carnados opened his mouth to speak, but the king held up his palm. Carnados stopped before any sound came out.

"We will confer at dawn. We need to sleep on this. Get some sleep!" It was a command, uttered in such a way that when the king pointed to the door, the advisors knew there was nothing more to be said, and filed slowly out of the room.

The king still held the sword as he stared out the window toward the mountains. "Verclan, my friend—my enemy—soon we must meet." He uttered it slowly, not even sure where the thought came from. He turned, laid down the sword and strode to the door of his chambers, and looking both ways down the corridor, stepped out unattended into the semidarkness.

49

Tears are drops from the bottle of pain within us, poured from the open window of our nephus to be washed away forever.

Old Tessamandrian Saying

PACA SAT ON THE GROUND LEANING AGAINST A STONE PILLAR ON THE OTHER side of the moat from the main castle gate. It was about half an hour before sunrise, and the sky to the east behind the mountains was a collage of colors: yellow at the horizon, then orange mixed with pink and vermilion which faded into an indescribable blend of blues. Overhead there were still a few brilliant stars in the deep violet of the retreating night sky. The air was damp, but warm, and bore the gentle scent of the newly-cut grass on the fields on either side of the road winding into the low fog in front of him.

In his mind, he was reviewing the details of the night before. Everything seemed far away and incredible except that he was indeed sitting outside the castle waiting for the princess. He had found her chambers the night before by some sort of miracle, though he was sure his father would have postulated otherwise. The door had been bolted from the outside. He had unbolted it and informed Vrengnia of the plans for the morning. He left the door unbolted so she could escape in the morning to meet him.

Sleeping on the stairs had been fitful and he still felt a bit stiff from the cold stone, even with the blanket his father had given him. There had been no sign of the watcher, but the memories of the experience had kept him from sleeping well.

One other curious thing had already happened since he left the tower at the first hint of dawn. He had made his way out to and across the courtyard and was passing through the portcullis to the drawbridge when he felt someone watching again. He stopped. The feeling was acute and this time he knew where it came from. Turning his head quickly to the left, he met the eyes of the gatekeeper directly. He was a huge man, dressed head to toe in heavy armor, and he stood unmoving at his post by the trigger to the portcullis.

He didn't speak, but Paca could feel his eyes boring into him. For a moment they stood, with eyes locked, until Paca dropped his and continued out onto the drawbridge. The keeper made no move, but Paca felt his eyes following him until he had crossed the drawbridge. Then quite suddenly, the feeling was gone. He looked back at the gatekeeper. He was standing erect and strong at full attention, staring directly across the gateway at the nothingness on the opposite wall. Paca turned and sat down to watch the sunrise while he waited for Vrengnia and tried to forget the gatekeeper.

In the middle of a mental review of his father's history, he heard the slow, ambling hoofbeats of what he thought was an approaching horse. At first, he could not tell where it was coming from. The road from the castle stretched out in front of him for several hundred yards before it descended over the edge of a small rise, disappearing into the morning fog that blanketed the land around the castle. There were other people about, merchants, mostly, working their way into town, anticipating the festivities of the day. This horse, however, was coming from inside the castle toward him.

He stood up to get a better view. It was not a horse, but a lone donkey, wandering across the drawbridge on her way out of the castle. "How peculiar," he thought. He looked at the gatekeeper. He hadn't moved. Paca turned, sat down again and leaned nonchalantly against the pillar, facing the sunrise. Whatever the beast was up to, he did not have to worry about an unattended animal; she probably just got loose from the hand of a drunken merchant and decided to leave the castle to feed on the lush green grass in the field outside the moat.

The animal was just even with the gate pillar when she stopped. When Paca turned to look at her; she was looking straight back. He turned away quickly. The donkey started moving, but instead of heading down the road, she made straight for Paca and, coming around in front of him, swung her head down and began grazing on the grass beside the moat. He tried to ignore her, but every few mouthfuls, she would pause and look up, as if she were studying him.

Was this the same donkey that he had encountered the night before? He had not taken note of any distinct feature that would identify this one from any other donkey. The next time she interrupted her munching, Paca made the point of looking straight into her eyes.

She looked like the same animal, but what would she be doing here? When he caught her eye, she stopped chewing and swung her ears forward so that her full attention was focused on him, and this time, instead of lowering her head to resume grazing, she ambled right up to Paca and nuzzled him gently with her nose. *It must be,* he thought to himself. But why was she here and where was her owner? She returned to refreshing herself with the grass by the moat, leaving Paca to his own thoughts.

"Good morning, my friend." Paca jumped at the sound of the Vrengnia's voice. He had not heard her coming. "I brought some water and a couple of sweet rolls from the kitchen for the trip. It's likely to take a while without horses—Hey! Why is this donkey here? I shouldn't bring my horse—but you brought this donkey?"

"I didn't bring her," Paca protested. "She just showed up a few minutes ago. Probably just wanted some fresh grass outside the castle." He did not want to tell her about the encounter with this animal the night before. "So, are you ready for a hike?"

"Let's get on with it. There will be plenty of time to talk along the way."

They started off; the princess and the young smith, walking side by side in the cool light of pre-dawn. It was glorious and refreshing; unthreatening, as if the whole world were safe and peaceful.

They had not taken ten steps when Paca heard the hoofbeats of the donkey behind them. He turned and the donkey stopped, looking at him attentively. "Come on," he said to Vrengnia, turning away from the beast, the irritation in his voice overshadowing his determination not to be irritated. The donkey started following them immediately.

The princess laughed. "It seems she wants to tag along," she said thumbing backwards with her hand.

Paca was brooding. It was not so much that the donkey was following, but that he had misled the princess about knowing the donkey previously. He was not sure how to explain it now. He turned back to the animal and walking up to face her, told her to go back to the castle. She didn't flinch, and kept watching him, her ears turned forward. He knew that she heard him, but he had no way of knowing whether she understood.

The princess laughed again. "Perhaps she is supposed to come with us." Paca whirled around, embarrassed by the whole encounter. The princess continued, "I mean, what could it hurt if she tags along? She may have heard the taralang and this is what she is supposed to do."

Paca threw his hands in the air. "All right, let's go—again! If she wants to follow, let her follow!" Paca was expecting some sort of ribbing from the princess, but she seemed content to let him work through his embarrassment alone.

They walked for some time before Paca broke the silence. "Actually, last night, just before you came out of the castle to find me, I did meet this donkey on the road. She was trying to listen to the taralang, but her owner was giving her a hard time about it. I forced the man to let her listen."

"So it was the same animal."

"Huh?"

"Well, when I found you on the road, you were standing right beside her. I thought it looked a little odd, but there have been so many odd things happening lately and getting you to your father was so urgent, I paid it no mind. So when I saw her this morning, I was a bit curious."

"How did you know it was her?"

"I know horses—and donkeys, Paca. I never forget an animal. That's just the way it is."

"Well, I wonder what happened to her owner. He was a bit sore when I drubbed him last night and made him let her listen."

"Who knows," said the princess quietly, "but it seems that when the taralang speaks, and tells someone, or some-animal, to do some thing, it always works out for them to be able to do it, no matter how strange. I think we should be satisfied that, if she is now free of her owner and following us, it is proof enough that it is in response to the taralang's message. Otherwise the whole situation doesn't make sense."

Paca was quiet for a moment. He could not refute her logic in the face of the evidence, and there was no acceptable reason for doing so. He forced himself to change his attitude toward the whole affair and said warmly, "Your wisdom exceeds your years. It is a queen's wisdom, and worthy of full acceptance. The donkey is a welcome member of our traveling party." He reached behind and waved to the animal to follow, not knowing whether she could even understand the gesture. She seemed to take heart and quickening her pace, came up close behind them.

They had passed through the first stand of trees heading south on the road to Mordan when the sun broke over the horizon of mountains. More travelers were appearing on the road, streaming toward the castle for the second day of the king's birthday festival. They took little notice of the threesome: a young man, dressed in ordinary work clothes, a young woman, dressed in very ordinary young men's clothing and a gentle she-donkey, walking just behind them.

As they walked in the warm sunshine, Paca felt their familiar, comfortable friendship as he and Vrengnia laughed and talked about everything and nothing, oblivious to whether the donkey heard, understood or cared about the conversation. They were in for a long walk; there was no hurry to talk of anything significant just yet.

It took several hours before they could see the small town of Mordan on the road ahead, nestled in a dip in the endless carpet of fields and clumps of trees. As they came over a rise in the road above the town, Vrengnia grew quiet.

"Is everything all right?" Paca asked, wondering if he had offended her in something he said.

"Everything is fine, but I need to talk to you about the swords—" A hint of anxiety wavered in her voice. "I want to apologize for convincing you to make them."

Paca paused before answering. He felt a twinge of embarrassment that he had not had the courage to bring up the discussion himself. "Did your father not like his sword?"

"No, he did like it—but a little too much, I think, or maybe in the wrong way."

"What do you mean?"

Well, I'm not sure, but the whole business of showing it to your father, right away. There was something wrong with that. His attitude seemed to shift slightly, and not in a good way." Paca could see Vrengnia struggling to understand the situation developing around them. She was staring at the mountains as she spoke. "I almost didn't give it to him, but I didn't have anything else for his birthday and decided that I should finish what I started."

Paca honored her struggle with a thoughtful, momentary silence. He was not sure what to say himself. "I spoke with my father about all this," he said quietly.

"Was he angry?"

"I think he was disappointed. *I* am disappointed, I mean, in myself. I feel like I let him down."

"Me too."

"Interestingly, *he* seemed to think it was actually part of a much bigger—some grand plan that is much larger than any of us can know."

"I have felt that also, but wasn't sure about my feelings—what to make of them."

Paca continued: "He said that someone will die because of the sword; perhaps there will be more than one death—that you and I will have to face the consequences for our actions."

"Maybe it's going to be one of us."

It wasn't a new idea to Paca. He had thought the same thing several times. They walked quietly for a while, absorbed in their own thoughts, until the princess opened the conversation again. "Are you afraid of dying?" she asked suddenly.

Paca had to think for a moment. "Afraid of dying? Yes. Afraid of death? No."

The silence that followed begged the question.

"What I mean is, the process of dying can be very painful. I fear the pain of dying. But death itself...well, there's not that much to fear, I guess."

"I think my father is afraid of death." She looked up at him. They were walking beside each other with their arms almost touching.

"Your father?"

"Yes. I mean, it's the only explanation for his behavior. I have been thinking that this whole obsession with his fiftieth birthday party and with Verclan—I think he is afraid of death. This fear has a strange power over him. He does not believe that there is anything after death, so his life is all there is. He wants to hold on to it with all his might. That's easy when you are young, but there comes a time when this fear begins to eat at you—you know what I mean?"

"I think I do." Paca was trying to understand. He had always believed in the Infinite: the afterlife for those who understood and walked in the way of the Psadeq of Mah'Eladra. His father had taught this to him since the first day he could remember. It was difficult to grasp the thinking of someone who thought otherwise. "What about you?" he said, looking down at Vrengnia.

She was staring at the mountains. She and Paca were closer now and could see the details of the individual rocky peaks. He kept watching her as he gave her time to think.

"I'm not sure. I think I am more afraid of my father's death than my own," she said.

"Why is that?"

"Well, if my father dies, then I have to become queen, and I am not ready to face that."

"You don't want to become queen?" Paca was genuinely surprised, but he tried to express it gently.

"I did at one time—when I was young. Since I am the only heir to the throne, my father tried to raise me as a son. For a while it was fun. I got training as a warrior—swords, bows and all that. My father was determined to make me like him, but I do not think I *am* like him and don't want to be *made* like him." She turned to look at him. "Does that make sense?"

Paca nodded. "So when did you realize you *didn't* want to be like him?"

Vrengnia was staring at the mountains again. They walked on quietly. He heard her sniff and looked over to see tears running down her cheeks. When he took her left hand, she squeezed his, wiping her eyes with the sleeve of her tunic and sniffing again.

"It's all right, Vrengnia."

"No! It's not," she said. "I need to tell you why; what happened."
She looked up through her tears. Paca nodded to reassure her and she
squeezed his hand tightly. "It was about four years ago. I had gone riding on Mahala early one morning, out along the road to Minsora. I
wanted to see the ocean before the winter set in. I was alone—I
thought." She was sobbing between phrases.

Whatever it was, Paca could tell it was painful, and he knew he
needed to let her tell her story. He squeezed her hand.

"I came across four boys, about my age...they were around a bend
in the road, hidden by a small grove of trees. They didn't hear me coming and I surprised them." She sniffed again. "I was as surprised as they
were. They were standing over a fifth boy, who was badly beaten. He
was very still and may have been dead. I thought they were trying to
help him. " She looked up and grimaced through her tears.

Paca shook his head at the irony of the situation developing in her tale.

"I dismounted and asked if I could help. Before I knew it, they had
surrounded me and began shouting." A new wave of tears flooded her
eyes. "I reached for my sword and one of them hit me in the face and
knocked me down...I think he broke my nose...I could hardly see for
the pain. I drew the dagger from my boot and when one of the them
bent over to grab me, I stabbed him in the shoulder...I still remember
the feeling of the knife hitting the bone...it makes me sick to think of
it.... In all my training, I never had to actually hurt anyone." She looked
directly into his eyes through her tears. "I don't ever want to have to do
that again."

He nodded. "What happened then?"

"He yelled and lurched back...I remember his blood pouring down
my arm...and then they started kicking me...it all became a blur of pain
and fear. I must have passed out.

"The next thing I remember, I was lying on a blanket in a field. The
sun was perhaps an hour from setting, and Mahala was grazing on the
grass in front of me...through his legs I could see the mountains to the
south. I tried to move and couldn't...and I was *so* cold.... It was then
that I thought for the first time that perhaps I had died and I panicked.
I wanted to yell, but I could not open my mouth.... I remember the fear.
I was utterly alone.

"I lay there—it seemed like forever—unable to move, unable to
speak, when suddenly, I felt his hand. It was very cold...colder than I
was. 'Be still, Princess' was all he said. It was Vishtorath."

The way she said it made Paca think he should have known who
Vishtorath was. "Vishtorath?" he asked.

She was surprised. "The gatekeeper at the castle...the giant at the portcullis." She wiped her eyes with her sleeve again.

Paca thought back to that morning and his strange encounter with Vrengnia's giant.

"I don't know what happened, or how, but Vishtorath had found me and rescued me. I found out later that all four of the boys had been killed. They were found tied to a tree limb by their ankles. No killer was ever found—no one was ever accused. The boy on the road lived, but did not remember anything. I was so badly beaten, that I would not have survived, had not Vishtorath intervened. He did something...it must have been some kind of miracle, I think, and by nightfall, when we arrived at the castle, I was completely healed."

"You never told anyone what happened?"

"You are the first."

"Even your father?"

"I couldn't tell my father. He would not have understood. He would have imprisoned me in the castle. I was so ashamed of my weakness. I decided that night that I did not want to be queen. The more I think of it—becoming queen, I mean—the more I see of it, the less I like it."

"Couldn't you be a queen like your grandmother? Isn't that her crest on your tunic?"

"And who will teach me to be like my grandmother? My father? I am beginning to see that he has no idea about how my grandmother was. His idea of making me a queen is to become like him. I can't do that. I don't want to do that!"

Paca wanted to say something, but his father's teaching about allowing people to talk restrained him. They continued in silence, still holding hands. Vrengnia's tears had subsided, and she was walking calmly beside him. He could sense her warmth. Her story and her openness about it to him had drawn her close to him.

"That night I decided that there had to be more to life than what we see around us, more to life than what my father was teaching me. I didn't know where to go to find answers. No one I knew seemed to really know or believe anything for themselves. Carnados and Cordas know a lot; they know philosophy—and about spiritual things, but I can't tell if they *believe* any of it. Vishtorath knows more than he will say. It's almost as if he is not allowed to tell me what he knows." She paused and took a deep breath, exhaling slowly. Your father has given me new hope," she said quietly. "If I could be like him, I think I could be queen."

Paca smiled. "Yes, if you could be like him, you would be a *great* queen," he said, and squeezed her hand. A comfortable silence settled between them. Nothing else needed to be said for a long while.

The donkey ambled along, five steps behind them. Paca found himself wondering whether the animal could possibly have understood what had been said, and if so, what she might think about all the strange and hurtful things that people do to one another.

50

Suspicion is a harsh mistress.

Old Tessamandrian Proverb

CARNADOS COULD FEEL THE KING'S IRRITATION BEFORE HE EVEN OPENED THE door to the great hall. How was this? He was never sure how, but he could often sense the mood of the king, and he had learned to pay attention to it.

His sense was right. As they entered the throne room, he could see that this was not going to be an ordinary meeting. Two of the king's best dors, Galar and Windarad, stood facing one another in an earnest, hushed conversation. The king was leaning almost off his throne, face to face with Rapahoogin, the wiry scout clad in black. The king's face was almost as black with anger; in his hand, he held a rolled up parchment. The scout's little black eyes sparkled, telling of what was probably another juicy discovery about the raids from the night before. Carnados felt a wave of revulsion as the scout glanced at him quickly.

There were no chairs. This was going to be one of the king's standup meetings, consisting more of command giving than advice seeking. These were usually short and to the point.

The king stood up rapidly and strode forward to meet him as he stepped through the doorway. The sun had just risen, and the king's shadow was cast across the floor almost to Carnados's feet. The halo of the morning sun backlit his silhouette and made his approach a little larger than life. Carnados waited with the others just inside the door.

"Come in, come in, my good advisors," boomed the king. His voice carried no trace of the anger Carnados had seen in his face only moments before. The two dors turned to face the door and the ever-furtive scout hovered just to the right of the throne, as if he would disappear behind it at the first sign of trouble. "There is more news from the fields," continued the king, "good news and bad." He fairly pulled the advisors into the room, closing the door behind them himself and beckoning them all into a circle in the middle of the room. "Rapahoogin, come, tell them what we found at the edge of the barley field on the western flank of the raids."

The king's scout came forward, peering suspiciously at each member of the circle in turn with a sneer just forming on his lips. The king handed him the parchment. Carnados had never liked the chief scout. He was certainly good at what he did, but he had a sneaky, guarded, superior air that made Carnados uneasy, and Rapahoogin's voice reminded Carnados of the edge of a knife dragged sideways on slate.

The scout fixed his gaze on Carnados and snapped the parchment open without retreating his eyes. Carnados stared back, not wanting to yield to such childish manipulations. "To the Good and Noble King Sandihar of Immerland," began the scout, that same mocking sneer smearing through his voice as he read what opened like a proclamation.

"We, the people of the mountains, and outlanders to the prosperous and glorious Immerland Kingdom, have gathered a tiny portion of your fall harvest so that our families will have bread through the winter. No one was hurt. We did no damage to the land. We took only what we could not provide for ourselves."

The king was pacing back and forth in the circle stroking his chin feverishly, his eyes darting from face to face of those gathered round him. "Go on, go on," he said impatiently when the scout hesitated.

"If the good king and his court find this offensive to his sense of justice, be it known that we will gladly meet with him in person to discuss such injustice, at a time and place selected by the good smith of Shiloh." Rapahoogin paused again.

"Read the signatures!" snapped the king.

"Verclan, Omisar, Chron—"

"Verclan!" thundered the king. "By the darkness of the caves of Tessalindria! This murderer's gall is only exceeded by his insolence! Something has to be done to stop this madness. The question is what?" The king was pacing furiously. "I want to hear from each of you. I want an honest answer, so don't patronize me! Galar?"

The dor shifted his weight and straightened before bowing slightly to the king. "Good King, we have tried to apprehend this brigand on numerous occasions, but their horses are bred and trained for use in the mountains. Our men are unfamiliar with the land and unaccustomed to hunting there. There is little avail in pursuing him yet again."

The king eyed him sharply. "I don't want to hear what we shouldn't do. I want to know what we *should* do, Galar."

The dor was quick to the point. "We should accept his offer then, except for the selection of the time and place by the smith, and set an ambush for him and his men. It seems that he is willing to get together after all."

"Dor Windarad. Your favored action?"

"I would favor the thinking of Dor Galar," he said calmly, "but another option would be to challenge him and his men to a more open battle."

"Open battle?" the king pretended to be stunned. "Open battle, did you say? And why would he do that? What incentive would we give him to confront us in open battle, eh, good Dor? He holds all the cards. I need a solution! Rapahoogin?"

Carnados could tell that the little scout was nervous, but he spoke up quickly, hoping the king would not notice. "Sire, we should hold the meeting as the enemy has suggested. When the meeting is over, my best scouts will be able to trail the brigands. We will be able to find where they are so the dors can capture them later."

"You have never been able to effectively trail them before," said the king thoughtfully. "What would be different this time?"

"They would all be together. Our chances are much better that we could follow at least one."

The king cut off the scout unceremoniously: "Carnados?"

He was not quite ready. Usually, he spoke for all three of the advisors. He was not sure whether this was expected this morning. He decided to try to get the others off the hook. "Sire, we believe that the best course of action is to accept the offer to meet with Verclan, to try to settle differences between Immerland and the mountain peoples, and between you and Verclan." The king put an "I knew you were going to say that" scowl on his face, but he allowed him to continue. "We should seek peace for Immerland without bloodshed first."

"And what about the Sword of Mankar?"

Dor Galar and Rapahoogin gasped. Carnados wished the king had not brought this up. "The sword is only legend, as far as we know," he said calmly. "The existence of the sword in Immerland is conjecture on top of that legend. We should not concern ourselves with it in this context, Sire."

"The Sword of Mankar is in Immerland?" interjected Galar in disbelief. Rapahoogin's eyes were dancing. Carnados knew that such a mystery would be a delightful diversion for his scouts from the daily grind of spying on various suspicious characters whom the king had fingered.

"What do you know of the sword, good Dor Galar?" asked the king abruptly.

"What I know is legend, but the legend is terrible. If the Sword of Mankar is in Immerland, it is a much bigger threat to all of us than a thousand Verclans, Sire."

"What if this whole play by Verclan is somehow connected to the revealing of the Sword of Mankar?" queried the king.

"Why would it be?" interjected Dor Windarad.

"Well," the king began, "it is obvious that Verclan and the smith are in league with one another at some level, exactly how, we do not know, and we have reason to suspect that the smith is on some sort of quest to find the Sword of Mankar—"

Carnados felt compelled to interrupt the king's logical progression: "That part is purely conjecture, Sire. We have no proof."

The king stared at Carnados and continued pointedly. "In fact, he may already have revealed the sword to Verclan, which may be why he has suddenly become so bold. This also is conjecture...but it seems to me that we must play into Verclan's hands somewhat until we can find out what is going on."

Carnados sensed that it was time for the king to start issuing his orders. He was right.

"Galar, go to the smith in the prison tower and see what he has to say about a time and a place for such a meeting with Verclan. He has been set free, so if he is no longer there, find him and set up the meeting. After that, find Omberon. I have something to discuss with him privately."

"Windarad, take four of your best and find the young smith. Put him under house arrest in his smithy so he can continue his work, but do not let him go anywhere. And do not let my daughter visit him there."

"Rapahoogin, I locked my daughter in her room last night. Go unlock the door, but do not let her see you. Follow her wherever she goes today and see what she does. Whatever it is, do not interfere."

"Carnados, Cordas and Mindar: Make sure the festival is uninterrupted today. We will all meet here tomorrow morning at the same time to see where we are. You are dismissed."

Carnados was relieved that he had been given a job that was unrelated to the king's obsession with Verclan; that what he and the others had been given to do was to enjoy the day and make sure all the people of the kingdom did likewise. He smiled secretly to Cordas and Mindar, and led the way out of the throne room behind Dor Windarad.

51

True grace and genuine beauty are matters of character.

Hispattea
The Essences of Corritanean Wisdom

PATIRA LAY ON THE MOSS UNDER THE LAURELS BY THE STREAM ON THE SOUTH-ern side of Haniah's field. From atop the slight rise that separated the stream from the slope into the field, he could see the breadth of it and watch unseen all comings and goings. The sun was high and he could tell that out in the field it was hot, but in the shadows where he lay, the cool, smell of the soil and the moss filled his nostrils, and the semidarkness under the canopy made it quite comfortable.

The woods were quiet, and that was always a sign that demanded caution. Four of the king's scouts had been caught the night before. The surprise harvest had brought an onslaught of the clever little men, dressed in black, and probably quite good at what they did in Immerland. Fortunately, they had never understood the woods and eas-ily fell prey to the many woodland tricks that the mountain guards set for them. Two of them had been caught in snares, one in a man-pit, and the other had been spotted and treed by a guard triad. They had to cut down the tree to capture the poor fellow. Each of them had been stripped, dressed in a bright red loincloth, and sent back to the king unharmed. Patira smiled as he recalled the look on the face of the one he had seen when they sent him off. He knew the scout would be back someday, but probably none the wiser.

Still, caution was the wisdom of the day. It was the wisdom of everyone who lived on the border of Immerland. More than wisdom, it was a way of life. Even in the quiet seclusion of his carefully selected vantage point, Patira's mind was half tuned to every detail of the forest around him.

Patience was another well-bred characteristic of the mountain people. Patira knew that his father had sent him for a purpose and though it was not clear exactly what it was, even to his father, Patira lay quietly waiting.

He would know when it was time; and he would know exactly what to do. "There are times to trust one's instincts and the El and wait, in spite of the urgency of the situation," his father had often said; he knew that this was one of them.

For about three hours, he had watched. Haniah had come out of her hut several times. She had gathered some food from the field, washed some clothes, and hung them to dry on the drying sticks. She had gone back into her hut, come back out again to get water from the stream and so on. It was probably a daily routine. He knew her well, but had never even wondered what she did when no one else was around.

Suddenly she appeared again with a bright cloth under her arm and a platter, laden with tableware. She went to the large table in the field just in front of the hut, set the platter down, and busied herself with setting the table. Patira was curious. Someone must be coming for a meal.

Patira knew Haniah's meals. They were simple and hearty, always enough but never anything left over. Though they had the aroma of the woods and the field, he knew somehow that they would be considered delicate to even a better trained palate than his own.

Haniah finished setting the table and headed for the stream for more water. The place where she got her water was a bit over to the right from where he was. He could not see exactly what she was doing, but he was confident that she could not see him because of the shape of the ground and the thick foliage between them. He busied himself with watching the empty field with its flowers and sunburned, late-summer grass.

"Master Patira..." It was one of those moments when one feels as if he could jump out of his own skin, if it was not fitted so tightly. He was on his feet almost instantly and in the same instant knew that there was no danger. Haniah stood not five feet to his right, leaning over to peer through the laurels to where he stood. "It is almost time. You should come out and make yourself presentable to our guests."

He started brushing the bits of moss off his tunic. "How did you know I was here?" he asked without looking at her.

"Well, it *is* my land, and I make it my business to know what is happening on it. Now come, we haven't much time."

Patira followed her as she went back to her water baskets by the stream. She lifted the yoke, as if it were empty and laid it on his shoulders. It was much heavier than she made it look. Without a word, she started toward the hut. Chafing under the load, Patira followed.

Haniah was his friend. He knew that she would never do anything to embarrass him. His pride melted away as he walked back to the hut behind his hostess. As she walked silently in front of him, he watched her.

She was a study in contrasts. She had a simple beauty that he had always admired, but she was not the type of person one would compliment on it. Her hair was the color of the autumn hayfields, with strong hints of sun just before sunset. Its tightly curled mass cascaded over her shoulders and glistened in the brilliant sunlight of the open field. She was as slender as a steel blade, with a strength forged of experience. Her clothing was simple, functional, clean and perfectly matched to her place in the fields, to the extent that it was wholly unremarkable.

Haniah worked with her hands. They were her tools. They showed a firmness, a ruggedness of their labor, but still carried a feminine quality that bespoke gentleness.

Patira could not see her face as they walked up the path from the stream, but he knew it well. The slightly chiseled cheeks, thin nose and fine straight lips. Her blue-gray eyes were more like windows, but into what? He wasn't sure. He sometimes felt that her eyes made his own eyes seem more like windows into *his* vorn. If this were true, she never seemed to take advantage of what she learned when she looked in.

He guessed that she was about his age, but he thought he remembered her being somewhat older when *he* was younger. It was very difficult to tell. All in all, Patira saw in her a quiet beauty that did not come from her outward appearance, but more from the firmness of character; her love of life and the gentleness of one who knew her place in a large world and lived there at peace.

They were almost to her hut when she broke the silence. "I had a strange dream last night, Master Patira," she said as she helped him get the yoke off his shoulders and the water safely to the ground. She always called men "master" and the women she called "mistress." It was just one of her peculiarities. Patira paid it little mind.

Haniah did not talk a lot. Patira guessed that years of living alone might do that to a person, or perhaps that was why she preferred to live alone. Either way, he waited for her to elaborate if she wanted to as he rubbed his shoulders and neck where they had borne the weight of the yoke.

"I will tell you more, but only after the others have come."

Patira found himself looking into those infinite blue-gray eyes.

"I am not sure who they are, but there are three—one of them...it's all very vague at this turn, but there will be five all together."

"Five what?"

"Five for lunch," she responded, sweeping her hand toward the table. "Why are you here, Master Patira?" she turned to busy herself with paring the beets he had watched her harvest from the field earlier that day.

"May I help?" Patira offered.

"Of course. There is another knife on the table by the berry bowl."

Patira picked up the knife and joined his hostess in the preparations. "My father sent me here. He said to come and watch—that I needed to be here, but he was not sure why. I arrived perhaps an hour after sunrise."

"So you saw those two Immerland scouts rounding the far edge of the field not an hour and a half ago."

"What?"

"Two of the king's scouts, short, dressed in black. They cut the corner on the far edge of the field and headed up into the mountains, I would say."

"No, I didn't see them."

"You are slipping, Master Patira."

They worked together in silence for a while. Patira wondered how so many people could know so little about what was going on and yet be so confident that something right was happening. It seemed to be a matter of trust: trusting in one's sense of psadeq and trusting in the El and the leading of Mah'Eladra. He thought that his *father* understood what this meant, and perhaps Haniah, but he was sure that he did not, at least not in the same way that they did.

He looked up at Haniah. She looked up at him as she continued paring the large beet in her hand. She said nothing, and her eyes bored into him, probing earnestly and gently. Patira looked back to the task of peeling the beet in his own hand. Neither of them spoke.

When all the beets were peeled and had been placed in a small pot of water, Haniah broke the silence again. "The others are almost here. Come, we should wash our hands and gather some fresh parsley and ginger before they arrive. We have just enough time."

She rose and turned toward the soddy in a graceful movement, purposeful and resolute. Patira watched for a moment before falling in behind her as she wended her way around the side of her hut to the large herb garden behind it.

52

In that brief moment, where he stood
When she, with lighted eyes did fire
His vorn, as match is set to wood,
Consuming all with bright desire.

Ramonmara
The Legend of Mishla Mira

Paca, Vrengnia and the donkey had been walking all morning. Encounters with other travelers had become rare, partly because they were so far from the castle and partly because many people had gone up to the festival. When they had passed through Mordan, they found it almost deserted. Since leaving it to the north of them, they had met no one.

Vrengnia had told him everything she could about Haniah. From all the stories, she seemed a little larger than life, and Paca was looking forward to finally meeting her. The threesome had made their way up the old dirt road to the hitching post at the trailhead to Haniah's fields. The last couple of miles had been in the full sun so they were sitting in the shade of the large chestnut tree hanging over the small gap in the stone wall. "Do you have any idea why she has chosen to live so far from everyone else?" Paca asked.

Vrengnia smiled. "I have wondered that myself. I don't know, but I'm sure she would tell you if you asked."

"Maybe it has to do with her relationship to Verclan. I mean, my father chose Shiloh when he left the castle. It's kind of on the fringe. I am quite sure now that he moved there so he could have contact with Verclan without endangering him. Perhaps Haniah is the same."

"Perhaps. I am surprised that you have never met her. Your father seems to know her quite well. Isn't that where he gets all those herbs he has in your kitchen?"

"I believe so, but he never spoke of her at home, at least not in a personal way. He always spoke of her in a remote, 'there is this person' kind of way. I don't recall her ever coming to Shiloh or him mentioning that he came here."

"Well," Vrengnia laughed, "you are about to meet her in person, if she is here."

"Why wouldn't she be here?"

"Sometimes she isn't. Even when she's not here, it's a wonderful place to visit."

Vrengnia stood up and stretched. "Time to go." The entrance to Haniah's land consisted of an uneven break in an old stone wall. It was clear that few people passed this way, for the path was covered with deep grass that showed little wear. Vrengnia stepped through the gap in the stones, with Paca close behind, and the donkey ambling easily behind him.

As he first set foot on the path, a vague uneasy thought caused him to look up suddenly. In the deep shade to the left of the trail, an unnatural brightness caught the corner of his vision. When he turned to look at it directly, it vanished. Without a second thought, he plunged toward the spot where he had seen it, not knowing what he might find. In four quick steps he reached the spot and looked around quickly. Nothing stirred. The cool tranquility of the forest shade surrounded him and left no hint of what he had seen.

"What are you doing?" The princess was standing on the path, with the donkey behind her. They were both staring at him.

"I...I'm not sure!" he stammered. "I thought I saw something moving in the trees here." He started back to the path. "It must have been some trick of the sunlight piercing the shade. Let's go." He stepped onto the path behind the princess.

Paca was still uneasy. He was sure he had seen something in the woods. Now he detected a slight shift in the air...no, in the lighting...no—what was it? There was some very slight, but tangible difference between the surroundings here and in the place before they stepped onto the Haniah's trail. "Wait here," he said quickly. He sprinted back up the path to the trailhead, a matter of ten running steps. At the entrance to the trail he turned.

The donkey, as unconcerned as ever, had leaned down and was munching on some of the grass by the trail. The princess was facing him with a bewildered look on her face. "What is it?" she called, a hint of alarm rising in her voice.

Paca stood for a moment and listened. He breathed deeply and held out his hands, trying to grasp some elusive ambiance of the place. He stepped back onto the trail and took several steps. He stopped again, listening, and then, taking a deep breath, he held out his hands again. He could feel the difference. Perhaps feel was not the right word; he sensed it, but he was not sure how. There was more clarity; the colors were a little brighter, and the air a little cooler and drier. Every detail was sharper and more penetrating; more *real*, perhaps.

He eyed the princess thoughtfully, as he made his way down the trail toward her. He knew he needed to offer some explanation. "Something is different here—on Haniah's land. Can you feel it?"

"Yes," said the princess. "I have been here many times and each time I notice a slight difference in the air when I enter, or in the light or something"

The trio resumed their journey. "I…it is hard to explain," Paca continued. "It's as if we are being watched…or protected…or no—surrounded by something. Something a little larger or maybe stronger—something more real than before we entered." The princess said nothing. The intensity of the tranquility seemed to pervade everything. It was quiet beyond quietness; almost un-Tessalindrian, yet there was nothing specific that he could identify as different. He suspected that he may have seen one of the Eladra, but since he had only seen them for the first time the night before, he was not sure. He was not confident enough to say anything about his suspicion to Vrengnia. If they were here, he reasoned, it was a good sign.

They walked in silence along the edge of the field, through a small stretch of thinly wooded forest, and out into another meadow. The smell of the drying grass, intermingled with occasional breaths of wildflower scents in the still air of the late summer field, was almost overpowering. Paca decided to change the mood by asking a question. "What do you suppose we will find here; I mean at Haniah's place?"

"If your father did not tell you, then he certainly did not tell me. Perhaps our four-footed friend knows. She has come for a reason, I am sure; it's too bad that she can't talk." Vrengnia glanced back over her shoulder and smiled. "I think we will find peace here."

"What do you mean?"

"Well, I have never seen any kind of conflict on Haniah's land. I had not really thought about it until you mentioned it back there at the trailhead."

"When?"

"Whatever you said back there—about feeling protected or being surrounded by something. I think it is a unique peace that is only found here. I'm not sure, but I *have* felt it here before. It touches my vorn in ways that no other place does, perhaps in the nephus, though I would be first to admit that I am not sure what that means."

Whatever it was, Paca would not have described it as peace. *Perhaps she is right*, he thought. He couldn't argue that he knew peace well enough to refute her, nor did he know for sure what something that touched his nephus would mean. The nephus was the most elusive layer of the vorn. There were many who did not believe it existed at all. To those who did believe, it was the extension of the vorn, one step beyond the hjarg—it was not tied to their life on Tessalindria. The nephus was a layer of existence that transcended time and death; that piece of a being that made one different from an animal. Perhaps she was right because while both he and Vrengnia pondered this sensation, the donkey seemed wholly unaffected as she casually munched mouthfuls of the green grass bordering the path.

They passed through the last stand of trees and into the large open field that surrounded Haniah's hut. Paca had never seen anything like it before. He had expected something different, but how it should be different, was not clear. The field was wide and still and filled with wild flowers and patches of cultivated plants, which were scattered unevenly across it. To the left was the small sod hut, barely big enough for someone to actually live in it. In front of the hut, in the open field was a long table, set for five and begging for someone to sit down and eat.

They stopped to assess the scene laid out before them. Nothing moved except the donkey who nudged between them and plodded slowly toward the little hut. If Haniah were home, she would surely hear her approaching. She was almost to the door of the hut when Paca decided to break the silence. "Come on—let's see what's going on here."

They started forward again, glancing about to catch the first sign of any movement. The donkey approached the front door of the hut and, with a light shove, opened the door and plodded in. "Now that is peculiar," said the princess over her shoulder. "Perhaps she has been here before."

"Could be," said Paca quietly. "Let's find out." They were almost to the door when Haniah and Patira rounded the far corner of the hut, startling all of them.

"Haniah!" gasped the princess.

"Patira!" Paca nearly choked on the name.

Paca stood staring at Patira. Haniah threw her arms around Vrengnia's neck. "Mistress Vrengnia, I was hoping it would be you," she said warmly, holding the embrace tightly. She stepped back suddenly and looked squarely at Paca. "But you must introduce me to your friend."

At the same moment, the donkey emerged from the hut with an ear of corn held between her teeth. "Which one?" asked the princess with a smirk, nodding toward the door of the hut.

Haniah whirled and dashed over to the donkey. "Meshabo, my dear Meshabo..." She threw her arms around the donkey with a tight squeeze and turned back to the princess. The light sparkled in her delighted eyes. "Did she come with you?"

"Well, she sort of followed us. Do you know her?" asked the princess.

"Know her? Why of course—but now you must introduce your other friend."

Paca studied Haniah briefly. He detected the same sense of hyper-realness in her presence as he had first felt when he stepped onto her property. Her eyes had a depth and clarity that defied identification. She came up to him as she spoke.

"This is my friend, Pacahara, the—"

"—the son of the great smith at Shiloh Forge!" Haniah finished. "It is a great honor to meet you, Master Pacahara. Your presence does justice to your father's name." She stepped closer and gave Paca a gentle hug, standing on her toes to lightly touch her cheek to his and then retreating to arm's length. Paca felt the overwhelming sense of realness again, lingering in his cheek where she had touched him, and a wave of emotion rolled over him as she stepped back. It was an immediate sense of closeness and desire that he had never felt before, a flush of embarrassment that he should feel such intimacy with someone whom he had known for less than two minutes. He was speechless.

"Come," she said brightly, "it's time to celebrate. We will eat together before we discuss our reasons for being here."

Haniah's presence had made Paca forget about Patira. He remembered suddenly, and looked to Patira to find him staring back curiously. Paca guessed he was thinking the same thing, so he stepped forward to break the ice, embracing Patira. Patira hugged him back. They both stepped back, holding each other's arms, and started laughing. "We meet again, my friend, my foe," said Paca with a smile. "Shall we not make the most of our short times together?" He beckoned to the table.

Haniah was busy removing the fifth place setting while Vrengnia poured water into a large bucket for Meshabo. "I knew there were five," she spoke joyfully, "but I never guessed that Meshabo would be the fifth."

They sat down at the table, the princess and the smith on one side, with the woodland prince and Haniah on the other. Patira brought the food from the hut. He served the party with a style and grace that would have honored the king's best table. There was much food, but not what Paca had expected. There were small quantities in a variety of tastes and textures: wild vegetables, roots, nuts and berries. They were chopped, cut and brought together, then uniquely flavored with herbs to produce a subtle experience for the palate of a man who was used to eating stew, dark bread, porridge and dried fruit. There was plenty of fresh water and a light ginger mead that burned slightly as it went down the throat.

They spent most of the meal talking about everything and nothing, joking and laughing together as old friends. When at last they finally sat back, each pleasantly full from the meal, Paca realized that there was almost nothing left on the table, but no one seemed eager for more. He was full, yet alert and felt ready to do almost anything.

It was at this point that Haniah turned the talk deftly toward the business at hand. "I had a dream last night," she announced casually, "and I think it concerns all of you, including Meshabo."

53

*Our dreams hang from threads of reality
and truth that must be sought without
fear and without hesitation.*

Mortag of Horrinaine
Of Beings

VRENGNIA THOUGHT SHE SAW PATIRA SHIFT SLIGHTLY IN HIS CHAIR AS Haniah began to recount the dream. It was very strange, as dreams usually are.

Haniah had gone to bed earlier than usual and had slept soundly through the night until just before the birds in the south woods began their morning songs. She remembered sitting up abruptly. At the foot of her bed stood a man dressed in an ancient warrior's garb. The stranger told her not to move and reaching behind himself, pulled out a parcel: a large roll of leather with ancient markings on it. As he laid it on the foot of the bed and unrolled it, a line of fine swords appeared, one by one. There were seven in all.

"Seven?" interjected Paca suddenly. Vrengnia saw Patira's eyes narrow as Paca said the word.

"Yes, there were seven swords and one of them a little larger than all the others. They glowed faintly against the dark leather. When I moved my hand to touch them, I could not reach them. They seemed close enough but too far at the same time.

"The man spoke again, this time asking me to prepare a dinner for him. I got up to prepare it, and as I was setting the table, I realized that I had set places for five. I ran back into the soddy; the ancient man had disappeared, and there were four others in his place in an animated discussion over the swords...in the original language. There were two women and two men, but I could not see their faces. The odd quartet wore ancient tunics that gave no clue to their origins; their faces remained dark and unidentifiable.

"I bid them come to dinner, and they all filed out of the hut, leaving the swords on the bed. They all ate in silence. After the dinner was over, the two men stood up and began a discussion, and as it grew heated the two drew their own swords and began fighting. The two women stood up, one of them turned into a man; they joined into the fight.

"Suddenly the first two fighting men vanished, one at a time, but very close in time to each other. The man and the woman who remained stopped fighting and embraced, then, holding hands, walked back to the hut.

"I tried to follow them, but by the time I got into the hut, they had vanished, and the original warrior stood by the bed. He told me to lie down again, which I did. Suddenly he burst forth in song in the original language, but this time I understood exactly what he was saying. It rhymed; its meter was perfect. He said something like this:

"Swords for the ancient sword master
Hidden in time for no one but the master.
When he comes, by his birthright
Shall he hold them, bend them to his will.
Nary another man should touch them.
Lest in death and wanton destruction
He beat a path into the darkness
A darkness that lasts forever and ever."

"He touched my forehead with three fingers. They were cold as ice, but they seemed to burn the words into my mind. He turned and looked straight at me and told me to set the table today—for five, then he strode out of the door, leaving it open.

"In my dream I fell asleep again, but only for a short time. When I woke the door was open. I went to shut it and I noticed his boot prints in the soft soil just to the left of the path."

"His boot prints?" said Patira, sitting up suddenly then jumping out of his seat and running to the door of the hut with Paca right behind him. Vrengnia followed as quickly as she could. Looking back she saw Haniah seated quietly at the table, watching.

The prints were clear. They were a hand's width longer than her own foot and made by an abnormally heavy person.

"Now this is odd! They lead this way and then vanish," Patira exclaimed. Vrengnia tracked the prints. The ground got softer to the east of the beaten path from Haniah's door, but the prints became shallower and smaller so that after about ten steps there was no trace of the heavy stranger's passage.

She saw Patira's eyes meet Paca's. They stared at one another for an instant before Patira swiveled and ran back to the table. "Are you sure this was a dream?"

"Well I thought it was—but there were parts that were so real—it is all very clear and very vague at the same time," said Haniah quietly, "but here we are, five of us and the footprints of the warrior are still there. I don't know what to make of it any more than you."

"How big was this warrior?"

"He was no taller than Paca—a bit more robust, but not exceedingly so."

"Did you see how large and deep those footprints are?" Patira's eyes sparkled with alarm. "The person who made them had to weigh twice what Paca does!"

"Yes," said Haniah, "that is probably true, but did you also notice that they get shallower in the softer soil and then disappear altogether?"

"Yes, I have never seen anything like it."

Patira paused and Paca took the opportunity to shift the angle of the discussion. "So, why are we here then, and what might it have to do with Haniah's dream?"

The reality of the strange footprints had put a crack in the quiet simplicity of Haniah's hospitality, and Vrengnia was eager to mend it. "Well, there are two men and two women, besides Haniah—if you count Meshabo. And we certainly have enjoyed Haniah's fine meal." Everyone nodded and smiled at Haniah. She flushed slightly and smiled back. Vrengnia continued, "I, for one, am in no mood for a fight; I left my sword back at the castle—I'm not even sure if Paca owns a sword—"

Paca picked up when she hesitated: "—but there is trouble brewing, in which all of us, except possibly Haniah, are involved." He looked at Patira who, glancing back, raised his eyebrows in expectation of being addressed. Paca seemed to be choosing his words carefully. Vrengnia guessed that he did not want what he was about to say to sound inflammatory. "The unexpected harvest in the southern barley fields has raised the king's ire. Even now he is seeking a resolution to the insult he has incurred." The carefully selected phrasing seemed to be doing its job. Patira sat and listen thoughtfully. It was difficult to know what he was thinking.

Paca continued, "My personal preference, were I the king's advisor, would be for the king to resolve the matter quickly by seeking an audience with his offender. To settle the matter without bloodshed would be the primary objective."

Vrengnia had to fight back a smile at Paca's formality. Patira answered in kind. "Were I the sole confidant of the mountain people's leader, I would suggest the same," he said gravely.

"Then I propose," responded Paca, "that in spite of not being so positioned—any of us—that we craft such a scenario and make it our business to persuade the leaders to meet for that purpose." As he spoke he stood up and raised his flagon for a toast. "To peace—to justice—to psadeq."

Vrengnia watched Patira rise to match Paca's stance. The nobility and grace in that simple action caught her off guard. Everything slowed almost to a stop as a wave of...what was it...something she did not understand swept over her. Patira echoed Paca's toast, clashing his flagon gently against the other's, but the movement, the sounds were distant; surreal. She watched him take a draught and sit down.

There was silence for a moment as reality swirled in around her, bringing her back from wherever she had been.

"So now that that is over, what are we really going to do?" said Paca brightly. They all laughed. It shook away the last vestige of the silent, tumbling reverie that had overcome her.

Paca stood up again. "May I suggest that I let the son of the Mountain Leader, and the daughter of the Immerland King craft such a plan. You know your fathers best. You have their best interests at heart, and you wield, might I say, more influence than you think. Haniah and I will clean up." He began loading his arms with bowls, plates, flatware and crumpled napkins, watching to see if the idea would take.

Patira leaned forward and rested his elbows on the edge of the table opposite her. "It sounds workable. What do you say, Princess?"

"I applaud Paca's wisdom," she said, turning to face him briefly. "To your duties, good smith—there is man's work to be done here."

She felt Patira's eyes tugging at her. Bringing her forearms up onto the table, she leaned forward to meet them. She thought she heard Haniah laugh, followed by the distant clinking of flatware being gathered from the table. She knew that what they decided would affect the course of history for Immerland and the mountain people, but part of her also wanted to just spend time with Patira. The strange attraction and the conflicting motives made her feel weak, immature and shy, yet empowered, bold and important at the same time. She waited for Patira to begin.

54

Mah'Eladra define the nature of psadeq and, at the same time, are completely confined by psadeq's nature.

Karendo Marha
Journey to the Infinite

VRENGNIA AND PACA LEFT HANIAH'S PROPERTY DISCUSSING THE ARRANGE-ments that she had made with Patira for their fathers to meet. They chatted through various events of the day, the meal, Haniah's strange acquaintance with Meshabo, and that they had forgotten to ask her how they knew each other. It was light and easy and seemed fitting for the return to the castle in the warm glow of the mid-afternoon sun.

"What did you think of her?" Vrengnia asked eventually.

"Who?"

Vrengnia laughed. "What do you mean 'who'? Haniah, of course."

"Oh. Well, she is quite different, much different than I expected."

Vrengnia was not sure whether Paca was being evasive or if the peculiar male tendency that made him unable to identify his feelings was beginning to surface. "You spent a fair amount of time with her cleaning up in the soddy."

"I know."

Vrengnia bit her tongue. She knew that the best way to get him to talk was to not talk herself. It always worked with her father, and although Paca was quite different, he was very much the same in this.

"It was a bit strange...I mean, I found myself just wanting to watch her."

The phrases were coming in stilted, insecure bursts. Vrengnia nod-ded and said nothing.

"Everything she did...every time she moved, it was graceful and easy. She never seemed...well, she never was in a hurry. It's almost as if her land is an extension of her...no, maybe that she fits it so perfectly...." His voice trailed off and stopped.

They walked on silently. Vrengnia was determined to let him talk.

She had seen his first reaction to Haniah and was convinced that he had been quite taken. Haniah's energy was compelling and contagious, and she dove into the vorn of anyone she met. She seemed to be completely free of fear, suspicion and selfishness to the extent that anyone with those weaknesses could easily misread her intentions. Paca was also a very open person, with an honest vorn and simple motives. Vrengnia was consummately curious about his reaction to Haniah's spirit.

"How old do you think she is?" he asked suddenly.

"I don't know. I would guess that she is a little older than we are, but that doesn't make sense. According to the old doctor who first told me about her, she has been here a while."

"What do you mean?"

"Well, he implied that he had always bought his herbs from her."

"Hmmm..." Paca fell silent again.

They walked together for twenty minutes without talking. Vrengnia had plenty to think about herself. She wondered about the warrior and Haniah's dream. What were the swords all about? Why had Paca reacted to the fact that there were seven swords? Did the four other warriors represent real people and if so, who might they be? The woman who became a man and joined in the fight and the two who remained holding hands after the battle; what could it all mean?

She found herself particularly troubled with the two fighting warriors and their sudden disappearance. Perhaps it was linked to the smith's statement that at least one, and maybe more, would die because of the swords that Paca had made. She knew she was not sure about death and what happened following it. The Infinite was hard to comprehend, and she was not ready to accept oblivion as the finality of all things. The awareness of her ignorance about death crept up slowly and then stood up in front of her suddenly. She must have reacted to her own thoughts.

"Are you all right?" Paca was looking directly at her.

She shook her head and shivered as if she could shake off the feeling. "I think so."

"You looked as if you were about to...as if you had seen a ghost."

"I was thinking about Haniah's dream. It seems to be another confirmation that someone will die. There were four of us there today and four warriors. Two of them die, I think."

She looked up at Paca. He was staring at the horizon to the north. "Hmmm," was all he said.

"What do you think happens when you die?" she asked.

"That depends."

"It depends? On what?"

"Well, my father believes that the life of a being is the essence of what he really is and is contained in the layers of the vorn. Our bodies, though part of the vorn are sort of like containers into which the vorn is placed, where it is nourished and protected, like an eggshell that contains the egg and is part of the egg, or a woman's womb. How we develop our vorn—how we think about our life while we are here—the things we do, determines what happens when we die."

"So?"

"Well, we were created for something much greater than this, just as the chicken develops in the egg and was created for something much greater than remaining in the egg. Our bodies anchor us to the linear progression of time we call our life span. When the vorn is developed, or when our bodies fail us or are taken away, the deeper layers of the vorn move either into the Infinite or oblivion. Our bodies are changed somehow and then reunited with the rest of the vorn wherever it is."

"But what *is* the Infinite and what *is* oblivion?" Every being on Tessalindria knew the terms and had vague sentiments about what they were, but she had found no one with a good explanation of them.

"My father thinks that they are different types of time experience. I don't understand his description very well, but he seems to think that oblivion is a state of being completely bound in time and space, sort of like a time prison. One cannot go anywhere or do anything. Whatever we are when we enter it, we are trapped alone with ourselves forever, in both the past and the future, from our current point of view."

"The Infinite is the opposite. The Infinite, he describes as a state of boundlessness in both time and space. That is the state where we will understand Mah'Eladra, and we will be there with all the others from the past and future who are there."

Vrengnia was not sure that Paca was answering her question but gave him the benefit of the doubt that he was trying. "Do *you* believe that?" she asked.

"I *believe* it, but I'm not sure I understand it. I'm not even sure whether I need to or not."

"So who decides whether you end up in oblivion or the Infinite? Mah'Eladra?"

"No, you do."

"Me?"

"Well, yes, for you anyway. Every day you face decisions about who you are going to be. You choose, actively or by inactivity, what kind of person you are going to be at the moment your body is taken from your life. The cumulative choice that you make through your life, is your path, if you will. I mean—if you choose to go in a different direction from someone else, don't you end up in a different place?"

"Well...yes."

"Every step, then, is a decision point at which you either stay on your chosen path or step off it, is it not?"

"And?"

"And if you step off, say by accident, or even on purpose, the next decision is simply whether to step back on or step farther away. The farther you get away, the harder it is to get back, right?"

Vrengnia did not feel she needed to answer. She kept listening as Paca continued.

"So at some point, when your body is about to be taken, your vorn is in a state that you have created or allowed to be created for you; you have brought yourself somewhere, and—there you are."

"But I don't understand. I mean, do you believe...I guess I thought Mah'Eladra had something to do with it?"

"Well, yes, many think Mah'Eladra decide what happens to them. I think that's because many beings don't want to take responsibility for the path they've taken. It's always much easier to blame their final situation on something other than their own poor decisions."

"So do Mah'Eladra have *anything* to do with it?"

"I think what Mah'Eladra want is for us to be where they are, but they do not want people to be there who do not *want* to be there. The path to the Infinite is simply following the path of psadeq with Mah'Eladra. This demonstrates that we want to be with them. When we step off the path, we damage that relationship with Mah'Eladra and with other beings. Mah'Eladra are constrained by psadeq as much as we are, and if we choose to break psadeq, by our own decisions, Mah'Eladra cannot intervene. By the very nature of that path, we have chosen oblivion."

Vrengnia began to realize that what she was hearing encompassed a whole different way of thinking about her life. Taking responsibility for every decision in an active and thoughtful way was something she had never faced, and she was not sure she wanted to. She realized that it was related to her fear of becoming queen. "I need some time to think about this," she said as she looked up at Paca.

He nodded and smiled back, "So do I."

They were passing through a small stand of trees in a shallow valley in the middle of the huge grain fields north of Mordan. It was quiet and secluded in the shade of the trees, and Vrengnia was thankful for the respite from the brilliance of the sun.

She was still pondering how everything that Paca had said fit together. The smith came to mind. He was the source of all this. Paca seemed to be but a conduit for ideas that he had not fully made his own yet. This in itself should not be a reason to doubt. Perhaps if she had heard it from the smith himself, she would understand it better, as if in the translation and the incompleteness of his understanding, Paca was unable to transmit the real essence of what he was saying. It was in the midst of this pondering that her thoughts were interrupted by a sudden sense of danger.

Paca stopped and grabbed her arm. Apparently, he had felt it also. They stood silently in the path and waited. Paca had his finger up in front of his lips, warning her to be quiet. Vrengnia could feel her heart pounding as they waited for some indication of what it might be. It was so still under the trees that she wondered how she could possibly have known there was something to be afraid of. Paca's grip on her arm was beginning to hurt, and as she reached across to loosen his fingers, a huge form sprang from the foliage just in front of them.

Paca let go of her arm, stepped in front of her, and in the next instant sprang into the brush where the animal had emerged. Mahala stood before her on the road, looking directly at her. She was stunned. Somewhere in the back of her mind, she heard Paca thrashing through the underbrush as she stood staring at her horse. He was fully saddled and as fresh as if he had just been readied at the stables. He tossed his head and snorted. She knew he wanted her to mount him.

Paca crashed back onto the road. "What's going on?" she asked.

"I don't know," he gasped as he leaned over to catch his breath. "Someone was holding your horse in the wood. I thought I saw him, but there is no one there now."

"Not anywhere?"

"No. This grove is not that big. There is no one here. It's very strange!"

"I think I am supposed to get on and ride. I also think that you should not come with me, though I wish you could." She did not know how she knew, but she did. Paca was looking at her thoughtfully.

"Then that is what you should do," he said after a moment's hesitation. "I think that it is only about an hour to the castle on foot. I will follow. There must be some reason that you need to be back."

She swung onto Mahala's back and looked down. "Maybe I'll see you at the castle."

Paca nodded. She swung Mahala around and cantered up the small rise out of the valley. As Mahala emerged into the sunlight at the top, he broke into a full gallop. Vrengnia turned to look back. Paca was standing in the middle of the road, staring into the woods where Mahala had emerged. She looked forward, wondering how this piece fit in the huge, evolving puzzle of her life.

55

The evil they spread is like an adder's venom in the society of beings that share Tessalindria.

The Tessarandin, Book 12
(Referring to the NarEladra)

THE LAST DYING RAYS OF THE SUN FELL OBLIQUELY ACROSS THE STONE WIN-dowsill as Paca looked down from the tower window at the evening revelries. People were coming and going continuously through the huge open gate. Some were heading home after a long day; others were returning for the evening bonfires that had been lit and were burning brightly in the courtyard. It was an ordered chaos, bright with the sounds of shouting, singing and the hubbub of many people with no agenda, bathing in the warmth of the fires and the late afternoon sky.

After Vrengnia had left on Mahala, Paca had remained in the small grove for some time hoping to find a clue as to how Mahala had gotten there and who had been in the undergrowth holding him. He had only seen a brief movement and heard a couple of quick footsteps, but when he had entered the undergrowth, the noise he made would have masked the sound of anyone else who was there. He waited in the road, hoping that he might hear or see something that would give him a clue to what had happened. Having detected nothing, he headed back to the castle.

As it came into view, he had decided that he should make his entrance as inconspicuous as possible. He found a pack of young men about his own age who were returning to the festival along the road from Mordan. Anticipating a riotous time in the castle that evening, they were already overflowing with eagerness and wit and making it known to everyone within earshot. There were six in all, and Paca made an easy seventh. As they had approached the gate, Paca suggested that they enter the main gate arm in arm, so they marched through the archway in a line, seven across singing a bawdy song about the boredom of life in a small town. It was not Paca's style exactly, but it was good cover.

There were additional soldiers standing under the portcullis, eyeing each passerby. Paca was not sure why, so kept his head down and sang loudly. As they swept through the gate without breaking stride, Paca felt the watcher again. He looked up briefly to see Vishtorath staring straight at him. He looked down quickly. There was something in the giant's stare that scared him and comforted him at the same time. It frightened him that he was clearly singled out by this man, and comforted that he did not seem to be the object of the search by the increased vigilance at the gate. If he had, surely Vishtorath would have stopped him.

Once inside the courtyard, he had made his way carefully to the tower. No guard had been posted on the stairway or at his father's chambers, so his access to his father had been undetected, as far as he knew.

Now he was with his father again, hoping there would be enough time to sift through the events of the day. There was much to discuss. He did not know where to start, so after giving his father a hug, he opened with the first and most innocuous thought he had. "I met Haniah today—she was different than I expected."

His father had seated himself on the bed. An amused smile flitted across the corners of his mouth. "Really? What did you expect and how was it different?"

"I'm not sure. I guess, well, I figured that any woman who chose to live alone in a sod house in such a remote place would be a little strange. I mean, perhaps she was hiding something, or there was something wrong—but it wasn't like that."

His father raised his eyebrows, but said nothing.

Paca continued, "She seemed very normal, confident, at peace with herself, and…it was…maybe as if she actually belonged there…in the field, I mean…and she was beautiful!" Paca could feel himself flushing as he said it. He felt he should qualify it a little. "It was not the artificial beauty that so many women try to make for themselves, but it was simple, straightforward. It was not on the outside, is what I am trying to say…. She was very attractive, but what made her so was her character, her spirit, if you will."

His father laughed. "Yes, that is true. Haniah is a remarkable woman—but what you say is true. Real beauty is a blend of spirit, body and mind. If any of those are ugly, then a woman cannot be truly beautiful. Painting the outside, when one is devoid of character and strength inside, produces no lasting beauty."

"We got to spend some time together while Vrengnia and Patira talked. I'm not sure I would choose to live that way, but she made it seem very appropriate…for her, I mean." Paca often had a hard time choosing words. He felt that either he did not *know* the right word or perhaps the right word did not exist. It was so difficult to be precise, especially when trying to describe feelings. "Her land seems to be an extension of who she is. I could almost feel it when I set foot onto it. A different kind of reality, a…a brightness, a…clarity that I had never sensed before." He looked straight into his father's eyes. "It was almost as if she lives in a different world there."

"Did you see anything unusual, anything *specifically* different?"

"Well, a number of things happened that seemed odd. When we started down the path to her house from the road, I am sure I saw an Eladrim being in the woods, not five steps from where I was—like the ones you showed me last night. When I looked directly at it, I could not really see it." Paca saw his father's eyes grow bright with excitement.

The older smith stood up, strode across the room to the door, and listened intently. Then, turning back, he lifted the heavy oak door and stood it up on end. "Help me," he said, "we must put this back in place for the time being." Paca helped him move the base of the door back into place, and they pushed it into the doorframe so it blocked the corridor from prying ears.

His father grabbed him by the arm and pulled him across the room where they sat down on the bed. The fire was still flickering in his father's eyes.

"What is it?" Paca asked tenuously.

"What I am about to tell you, you must tell to no one else. It is part of your education and is for you only. Do you understand?"

Paca could not remember ever seeing his father's face so serious and full of intent. He knew he had to promise this to him. "I do," he said confidently.

"Haniah's land is a special place. It is the first place I set foot in Immerland when I came here. The entrance to one of the portals opens out onto her land. It is the portal I came through to get here." He stood up and started pacing back and forth between the window and the bed.

Paca was confused. "How old is Haniah?" he asked a bit incredulously.

"I'm not sure, but she did not own the land at that time. I believe it belonged to an old cobbler who lived in Mordan—it had been in his family for years. Haniah purchased that property about twenty years ago. I'm not sure why she selected it, but it was a good choice, for both Haniah and the land."

"What do you mean?"

His father stopped pacing and looked straight into his eyes. "The portals are carefully guarded by the Eladra. Their presence gives the area surrounding the entrance to the portal the slightly altered intensity that you sensed. What you saw in the woods was probably one of these guards."

"I know I saw something. I think I may have seen another one later—in a grove of trees just an hour's walk south of the castle." He related the events surrounding Mahala's appearance on the road to his father in detail.

His father frowned and remained silent.

"What else do you know about them?" Paca continued. "I mean, most people think they are only mythical—part of the ancient legends."

"No. They are very real, perhaps more real than we are."

"Then why do they appear so vague, so fleeting?"

His father came over and sat down close beside him. "It is not well understood how it all works together. The Eladra are a race of beings, not unlike us. They are servants of Mah'Eladra and have certain abilities that we do not. They can appear and disappear, seemingly at will. No one knows exactly how they do it, but *I* believe that they can walk through time as you would walk through this castle. For us, time moves in one direction—its inevitability carries us along, as I have told you before. I believe the Eladra move through time in all directions, forward, backward, up, down, left to right. Infinity for them can be navigated. As you might visit a single place many times, they can visit many places at, what seems to us, the same time. They live in what one might call the eternal present; in the Infinite, with Mah'Eladra."

"If they go in the same time direction as we are going, they become visible for the time they are doing that. When this happens, they appear just like us, as I said before. They are heavier, stronger, denser— more...more *real*. They can remain that way if they choose, or are so commissioned. When they do, they are undetectable as Eladra, and appear as you or I."

Paca did not want to interrupt his father. He sat still.

"If they just cross our time stream, we often get a fleeting glimpse. When moving slightly faster or slightly slower or just in front or behind our time, they appear shadowy and vague. Their voices like whispers— a hissing—timeless and remote."

"They speak the original language," his father continued. "In the eternal present, nothing changes, so the language is unchanged. I was going to say, 'always the same,' but words like *always, never, then, now, before* and *after* don't really apply to the Eladra."

Paca was intrigued. He had no idea that his father knew so much about these matters, but it seemed to fit. Knowledge produces power in authority, and his father did have that. "Can the Eladra carry things from our world through time, like objects, or people?"

"I'm not sure." The older smith stroked his beard and thought for a moment. "We don't know a lot, but I think that is what the portals are all about."

"What do you mean?"

"Well, we know there are seven portals. As far as we can tell, they were made by Mah'Eladra so that we can move, or be moved, about in time in a limited way—and things, people, animals *can* be carried through the portals. The Eladra guard them, so that they are not abused. When I came through the portal into The Awakening, I was being pursued by one of Mankar's generals. He did not make it through, if he even tried. It seems that the portal travel is restricted to those whose vorns fit an acceptable pattern of psadeq and peace as determined by the Eladra, but that is conjecture on my part. Whether the Eladra use the portals I don't know; they seem able to time walk without them."

Several incidents on the day's journey suddenly became clear. "If what you say is true, I think I saw yet another one of them in Haniah's hut." Paca spoke evenly, though inside he was overly eager to tell his father what had happened.

The smith looked at him soberly. "Another Eladra?"

"A warrior. At dinner, Haniah had told us a very strange dream she had last night," Paca said slowly.

His father looked at him curiously, but encouraged him to go on. Paca related Haniah's dream to his father in as much detail as he could remember, while the older man sat and listened thoughtfully. Paca saw his eyes flash at the mention of the swords.

"I became suspicious about the dream and whether it was really just a dream when she showed us the footprints the warrior left outside the hut. Haniah and I went inside to clean up while Patira and the princess colluded on how to best bring their fathers together. Once inside, Haniah whispered to me, 'Come quickly, there is something you must see.' She was very urgent. She reached under her bed and pulled out a large roll, like the one she had described in her dream—"

"The swords?" His father leapt to his feet.

"Yes. She unrolled the package on the bed. There were seven swords all together, one a little larger, the others as perfectly the same as is imaginable."

"Only seven?" asked the smith. He was pacing now, back and forth, his bearded chin buried in his huge right hand.

"There were only seven," Paca confirmed. "The craftsmanship was astonishing. It was hard to tell, but they seemed to glow against the dark leather wrapping." His father was deep in thought, but Paca knew he was listening as he thought. "I reached out my hand to touch one of the swords—on impulse—they were so beautiful. Suddenly a gloved hand appeared and grabbed me by the wrist. The grip was painfully powerful and as cold as ice. I cried out and pulled back and the hand let go. As I stood back, I faced a man—a huge man—fully dressed in an ancient warrior's leather armor. He stared at me for a moment then he turned to Haniah and said something I did not understand. When I looked at her, she told me that I could not touch the swords; it would be too dangerous."

"An Eladrim warrior," said his father matter-of-factly. He was standing at the window now, staring out into the dusk. "Then what?"

"I turned to Haniah. She knew what I was thinking 'Some of it was not a dream,' she said. I asked why she did not tell the others. She responded that she had been told to only show them to the smith who would visit her that day. 'He would know what to do,' she said. Then she rolled up the swords and put them back under her bed. She told me I was to tell no one else except you. *That* was…difficult."

His father looked at him calmly. "It is essential that you do not tell anyone, especially the princess." Paca reasoned that his father trusted the princess, but she was the king's daughter, and he was not sure whether she could be trusted with the knowledge of the swords.

"They are undoubtedly Mankar's sword and six of his brothers'," he continued. "Why they were brought here, at this time, is mystifying. We must watch carefully and wait. That they are on Haniah's land makes them safe for the time being—" Suddenly he changed the subject.

"You know that old signature star you found on the steps last night?"

"Yes."

"It disappeared from the washstand last night some time."

"This washstand?" Paca said, pointing beside the bed.

"Yes."

Paca opened his mouth to speak, but his father held up his hand. "It seems that we may have a personified Eladra walking among us. Your watcher may have been such. And it may not be a friendly one."

"A NarEladra?"

"Perhaps."

"Wouldn't the Eladrim guards on the walls know; I mean, wouldn't they be able to see one of their own."

"I'm not sure, but I think that when they personify, they become as one of us for that time and may not be recognized, even by their own kind."

"Is it dangerous? For us? Or Vrengnia?"

"Yes and no. Yes, in that the NarEladra always will pose a serious threat. They are dangerous and full of evil intent. Their presence never bodes well. However, if your watcher is a *clandestine* NarEladra, he knows that his cover is precarious with the force of Eladrim guards about the castle. He will be very careful. I am surprised at his carelessness in dropping his signature star, if that is the case. Something big is brewing. Each day I see more evidence of forces and activities that move us closer to some significant event. We have to be more vigilant. Keep your eyes and ears open, Paca. Undoubtedly there is much at stake."

Paca sat silently with his thoughts as his father continued to stare out the window. Less than a month ago, he could never have imagined the situation that was unfolding before him. Everything was happening so fast and escalating into something completely unknown that would undoubtedly change his life forever, and he had no way of knowing whether that would be for the better or the worse. He would have to wait and trust. His father always said that waiting and trusting with sober awareness was the key to a positive outcome for any situation.

His father interrupted his thoughts: "Do you know the details that the princess and Patira worked out for the meeting between their fathers?"

"Vrengnia and Patira are to convince their fathers to meet at Haniah's field two days hence at noon. It will be the autumnal equinox. No more than seven people are to accompany each of them onto Haniah's land, and they will not be allowed to bring any weapons. The table will be set for the king, the princess, Patira, Verclan and Haniah, who will serve as hostess and mediator. They thought about having you as the mediator, but feared that the king would be too suspicious."

His father stared out the window. "Hmmm…that is also Vrengnia's birthday; her eighteenth. Did she tell you whether she has chosen a name yet?"

"No, she hasn't mentioned it at all. I didn't even realize that was her birthday." Paca suspected that his father saw something significant in this discovery from the way he stood. He was thinking deeply.

"You need to go home tonight," he said slowly. "Sleep in your own bed; you need the rest after a long day. Meet me at dawn on the morning of the meeting, at the Yendel Fork, north of Shiloh. Be well rested; it will also be a long day."

Paca hugged his father. He felt his strength surrounding him and warding off the fear that was creeping around the edges of his consciousness. They said nothing as they pulled the door from its frame and laid it carefully on the floor where it had fallen before.

"Paca," his father said, "do not fear, and do not let anyone know where you are going."

"I won't," Paca replied and slipped down the darkened stairs on his way to the courtyard.

56

Today bounds your life. Do not miss its fullness by worrying about tomorrow, or fretting over yesterday.

Sessasha
It Is Said

VERCLAN SAT STARING INTO THE DYING FIRE IN THE STONE FIREPLACE BEFORE him. He loved fire. In all the years of smithing, he had never lost the delight of sitting and watching its steady, consuming nature and feeling the heat on his face and eyes. It was a form of meditation for him; a place to wash out the events of the hours and days behind him and set the course of his life onto a well thought out path of appropriate action, instead of reaction.

Tonight he needed his time with the fire more than usual. Patira had gotten back from his trip to Haniah's just before dusk, and had related the events of the day briefly. The family had eaten dinner together, as they always did when he and Patira were home, and they had worked to clean up the kitchen for the end of another day. The girls had been put to bed and now he sat with his wife and son, facing what might be the biggest challenge of his life.

"Do you think the king will accept the terms of the agreement?" asked Mordara, without looking up from the spoon she was carving in her lap.

She sat to the left of him and he could feel her presence with almost the same intensity as he could feel the fire. Her question was not an intrusion, but more of an echo of his thoughts, set into words and reflected back to him. He was not sure he knew the answer, so he waited.

Patira sat cross-legged on the floor to his right, playing idly in the fire with a long thin stick. It was a habit of his, part of something he had never lost from his childhood. Verclan thought back to his own childhood in Immerland. He had few happy memories. It was mostly work, as he remembered, and lots of busy-ness and hurry trying to help his father make enough money to feed the family. His father never had the time to enjoy the fire, and he never had time to talk to his only son. They would come home, eat dinner, and go to bed, day after day, week after week, year after year until his father died. His mother had died a year later from grief. That was when he was seventeen.

Patira interrupted his reflection. "I think the princess will convince her father," he said slowly as he stared at the smoldering tip of the stick he had pulled from the fire. "She has a remarkable character and a strong desire to see this happen."

Verclan looked over at his son, now a strong young man. "Do you like the princess?" he asked.

Patira poked one of the logs in the fire with his stick. "I do," he said. "Our first meeting was a bit awkward. But I think she…well, when we met at Haniah's that afternoon before our last dinner there, we were able to talk alone. She will be a fine queen some day, but right now she ·is living in the shadow of her father. It's almost as if she has not been allowed to find out who she is yet."

"Hmmm…I have yet to meet her. Perhaps if we can come to some reasonable terms with the king, you will be able to know her better."

Patira looked up at him. "I am hoping that is true. I think we have a special connection. At first, I thought it was simply that of being the son and daughter of two important men who should have been able to be friends themselves, but now I think it is more than that."

"I'm sure it is," Verclan replied. His son's comments could easily have been taken as offensive, but he knew they were not meant that way. He turned to his wife. She was busy with the carving, but he was sure she was listening intently. She looked back at him and her eyes sparkled in the fire. "What are you thinking?" he asked gently.

"I was thinking that I would like to go with you to the meeting with Sandihar."

The thought took him by surprise. She was looking straight into his eyes as she spoke, and he could tell that she said it in complete earnestness. "I don't think that is best. I can only take seven—"

"I know. I want to be one of the seven." Her eyes shone with an intensity that Verclan knew well. It only appeared when she was afraid or when she was determined to have her way. Neither happened often. Mordara had an unusual strength of character and did not seek her own way without reasonable cause, nor was she easily frightened. Verclan could not tell which it was tonight. He turned back to the fire and stroked his chin.

Patira spoke first. "This could be a dangerous trip, Mother. The king has already increased the number of scouts along the border, and we do not know what treachery is planned. We are hoping for a peaceful meeting, but we have no guarantees."

Verclan turned to look back at his wife. Her busy hands had stopped. The carving knife and the spoon lay still in her apron on her lap, and her hands were on her knees. She was as beautiful as ever, and the firelight accentuated her fine features. Her black hair was tucked back around her ears and then hung forward over her shoulders. She too, was staring into the fire. She spoke slowly, but with an undaunted resolution.

"It is no more dangerous for me than for you. In fact, it is likely to be more dangerous for each of you than for me, since you, my husband, are the target of the king and you, my son, are his only male heir. We will be in the mountain woods until we enter Haniah's land, and once we are there, we will be as safe as we are here. By agreement, there will be no weapons at the meeting. That will make it safer yet."

As she paused, Verclan listened into the silence, hoping to hear something that had not been said. All that she said was true. He knew that she was right, but he was trying to understand his own reluctance to agree. Was it simply because she was a woman, or maybe that he had not thought of it himself? He had always assumed that he would take Patira, his close advisors and fill out the party with warriors. But why? If it was to be a peaceful meeting and there were no weapons, what would be wrong with having his wife with him? She was by far his best friend and his closest ally. Dependable, strong and insightful, she was particularly useful in diplomacy. "What about the girls?" he asked.

"They could stay with Corrada and Minstar for the day and even the night if necessary."

"Hmmm." Corrada was one of the village elders. He and his wife had no children, and had adopted the girls as their grandchildren.

"Besides, I want to meet the princess as much as you do. This may be my only chance. Haniah may need my help. You may need my support."

Verclan smiled into the fire. "Hopefully not. But we should sleep on this tonight and make a decision tomorrow." He looked over to his wife and she nodded and smiled back.

It was as if she knew the answer when she spoke. "It's been a long day. I'm going to bed; if you need to stay up a little longer, that would be fine." She stood up and laid her hand on his shoulder.

"I'll be in in a few minutes."

She bent over and kissed his ear, then left without another word to disturb his thoughts.

Patira threw his stick into the fire, stretched, yawned and stood up. "Me too. I'll see you in the morning."

The deep silence of night settled around him as Verclan sat alone, staring into the fire. His feelings eluded him. It wasn't fear exactly, and it was not joy, although there was a significant sense of accomplishment in having provoked the king into finally meeting with him. It was more of a sobriety in the realization that the event for which he had worked so long was coming to fruition, yet it was still complicated by many unknowns.

He had not seen the king in nearly twenty years. He had never met the princess. Passions and vendettas do not die easily, and he was not sure what the king's real motives might be, nor what his capabilities and resources were. Why had Sandihar changed his mind so quickly, and had he *really* changed? He had seen men who fought for something for years, suddenly give up and head home, and the king *had* just celebrated his fiftieth birthday. Perhaps that had triggered a recognition of the folly of his hatred.

Patira had told him all about Haniah's dream, leaving a trail of questions. What were the swords about? Could they be some of the Mankar swords that the smith was looking for? The vanishing footprints of the dream warrior had particularly disturbed Patira. Verclan suspected that it was an Eladrim warrior. There seemed to be an increase in Eladra activity lately. Two of his men had been to the festival and had seen Eladrim guards on the castle walls. The arrest of the smith, the singing of the taralang, the sword poetry, Patira's fortuitous meetings with the daughter of his enemy—the thoughts swam in circles in his head. He knew that they were related, but there were pieces missing. No amount of thinking offered a satisfactory conclusion.

The most troubling of all were the hilt guard for Patira's sword and the sataliin. His friend the smith was at the center of all of it. What did he know and how did he know it? Verclan thought it peculiar that throughout all of this, the smith had been inaccessibly locked in the king's fortress. He alone held the answers, if indeed there were any answers at all.

He sat forward and rested his chin in his hands, his elbows on his knees, the cherry red coals of the fire drawing him into its slow demise. Life had never been easy, but it was always easier when he trusted deliberately in the promise of psadeq: that if one always looked for the best in others and fearlessly pursued psadeq with them and with Mah'Eladra, the result, in the grand view of life, was always good. Implicit in the trust was the knowledge that sacrifices often had to be made, and that the outcome was always worth the sacrifice.

So far, little had been sacrificed in the recent spate of activity, and much was at stake. He knew this imbalance was at the core of his apprehension. Although Mordara knew these principles as well as he did, and trusted in the promise of psadeq, he did not want her to be part of, or witness to, the sacrifice that might be demanded before the peace of psadeq was gained. On the other hand, her peculiar intensity about it may be part of the grand plan, and who was he to deny her involve-ment? Was part of the sacrifice his willingness to let her be part of it?

In the end, he knew he would have to trust. Right now, he needed sleep. As he set the iron grill in front of the fire for the night, he pon-dered the nature of sleep. It had a way of purifying thoughts; distilling and refining them into tangible, cogent pieces.

He had always thought it peculiar that he had been created to *need* sleep. With all the things that seemed so urgent in one's short life, would it not be better if he did not have to waste so much of it sleep-ing? He had concluded that its purposeful, rhythmic intervention in the lives of every created being was simply a mechanism that forced the sep-aration of days into manageable slices of time. It gave each being a respite from the unending assault of life's challenges. When he lived each day within its natural confines, accepting what it offered without regret and giving back as much as he could within its limits, without worrying about tomorrow's challenges, or disabled by yesterday's fail-ures, he remained content.

Today was done. The fire was secure, as was his mind, and he went to bed without fear, unconcerned about what he needed to face tomor-row. When he slipped into bed beside Mordara, she rolled over and laid her hand gently on his chest. He lay quiet for a moment, listening to her steady, rhythmic breath of sleep....

57

The desire for control is the stepchild of fear.

Pratoraman
The Middle Way

S ANDIHAR LEANED ON THE WINDOW FRAME, STARING OUT AT THE SUNRISE. HE had not enjoyed his birthday festival nearly as much as he had hoped. It was not that anything had gone wrong. His subjects had enjoyed it immensely, which was good—but the whole affair with the smith and Verclan had cast its pall over his enjoyment of it.

He watched as the servants in the courtyard cleaned up the inevitable trash left by the crowds and roused those who had slept there overnight, sending them on their way back to their homes. Two old men busied themselves shoveling ashes from the bonfires into an oxcart, while several women swept the courtyard with large brooms. There was a warm spot in his heart for the willingness and thoroughness of his servants. There were so many good people in Immerland. "But," he mused, "I *am* glad that *I'm* the king."

A knock on the door shook him from his reverie by the window. "Come in," he boomed, to make sure it was heard on the other side of the thick door.

The door swung open, and his advisors and Dors Galar and Windarad strode in, followed by Rapahoogin. They must have met in the hall and come together.

"My good Dors, scout and advisors. What is the good word for the day?" He tried to speak as warmly as possible, but his words rang apprehensive, hollow and tentative. The looks on their faces warned him that it was not going to be good news as they took their places in the circle from the day before.

Dor Windarad spoke first. "Sire, we went to the smithy in Shiloh, but there was almost no one there because of the festival. We asked about and found the smith's home, but there was no one there either, and no one we asked had seen the young smith. After spending most of the morning there, we returned, and I posted a guard at the castle gate to watch people coming and going. Unfortunately, we could not find anyone who knew the smith, that is, knew what he looked like, so we never saw him, if he was here at all. We went back to Shiloh after dark, but he had not returned to his house."

The king frowned. Little as he liked it, there was nothing to be done. "Rapahoogin?"

The scout stepped forward and bowed. A devilish smirk played on his face. Sandihar didn't really like this crooked little man, but he was glad he was working for him instead of against him. He could not tell what the smile meant so he raised one eyebrow and waited.

"I went to the princess's chambers at dawn yesterday. The door was locked from the outside as you said it would be. I waited until noon, watching and listening, and there was no sound." Rapahoogin glanced around at the other men, seeking their approval for his thoroughness. "I finally decided to find out if she was there, so I knocked, planning that if she were to respond, I would not let on who I was, of course. There was no answer, Sire. I unbolted the door and let myself in. Everything was in order, but wouldn't you know it: No princess!" That twisted, ironic smile appeared again.

The king could feel his anger rising. "Fool, she left before dawn and threw the bolt from the outside herself!"

"How would she do that—I mean how would she get out, Sire?"

"Someone must have helped her—the smith, perhaps—but how would he know she would be locked in, and why?" He knew that leveling his anger at the little scout would be useless. "Dor Galar, did you speak with the smith about arrangements for the meeting with Verclan?"

"I did, Sire, but he was vague. He would not give me a direct answer. In fact, he said that emissaries from you and Verclan were making arrangements as we were speaking."

"And what time was that? I mean, when were you having this conversation with him?"

"A little after noon, Sire. I found it hard to believe, given that—"

"Hard to believe? Of course, it is hard to believe; I sent no emissary. You were all here yesterday. I gave no one else leave. I was waiting to hear from the smith about when and where such a meeting could take place." He was having trouble containing his anger, but the men standing before him had done their jobs, and they had all been thwarted. It all pointed back to the smith somehow. "Who else would I have sent, anyway?" he thundered.

"It was I, Father." Sandihar whirled around to see his daughter standing in the open door of the hall. How long she had been standing there he did not know. Apparently, no one else had seen her there either, because they all turned to the door in surprise. "I went to make arrangements for the meeting."

"And how did you know to make arrangements for me? Who sent you?" He knew he was trying to intimidate her. In the past, she would have backed down, but things had been changing recently, and he had seen a personal strength emerging in her that he both admired and resented at the same time. She stood before him completely undaunted by his thunder. His anger was raging inside, but he knew somehow that to unleash it now would be pointless.

She strode past him into the circle of men in the room and stood tall and straight in the middle. She turned to face him. "I was not sent by anyone, and when I left here I did not know that this was what I was going to do. I took Paca, the smith's son, with me to meet Haniah the herbalist." She looked directly at Dor Windarad. "Paca had never met her or been to her house and needed someone to show him where to find her. When we got there, we were met by Patira." Her eyes swept the assembly of men and came to rest on Rapahoogin. He shifted his weight and looked at the king. "That's Verclan's son," she continued. "I have no idea how he came to be there, but Haniah's table was set for five when we arrived. Haniah seemed to know that we were all coming and had lunch prepared."

"Five?" interrupted the king "Who was the fifth?"

She told them all about Meshabo and Haniah's dream of four visitors. "Somehow Haniah did not realize that the fourth visitor was the she donkey." She smiled. The king knew he was frowning. The advisors glanced at one another and shifted uneasily in their places.

"When dinner was over, Paca and Haniah left Patira and me to talk while they cleaned up. By that time it was clear that the purpose of the meeting was to arrange for our fathers to meet. So we did, and—"

Sandihar interrupted her. "Verclan's message to me was to allow the *smith* to determine the time and the place for such a meeting." He did not like being upstaged by his daughter, and he felt the same helplessness that he had in the presence of the smith. What was happening? "How is it that you took it upon yourself to do such a thing without my knowing?"

"It all fell into place, and I knew that it was the right path, but I do not know how I knew it. I used to think that this was impossible, and it would make me afraid to trust that type of knowledge. But I have stopped fearing. When one stops fearing, one finds that there is real knowledge beyond physical proof, but this does not make it any less knowing."

"You are speaking nonsense! Carnados, what do you make of this foolishness?"

Carnados had been looking at the floor, saying nothing. Sandihar needed his support.

"I think," Carnados looked steadily into his eyes and then at his daughter, "that we should summon the smith. While we are waiting for him to come, we should discuss your daughter's plan. If her knowing is true, the smith will confirm it when he arrives. Either way we need to hear from the smith, by Verclan's request."

The king eyed Carnados carefully. What he was saying made sense, but he felt the evasive caution in Carnados's voice. He recalled what the smith had said about "wanting an accomplice" when seeking advice, and felt chastened and annoyed at the same time. "Guards!" he thundered. Two guards appeared at the door. "Bring me the smith from the tower."

He turned to his daughter and strode up to face her in the circle. He swept his hand around, as if presenting the group of men in the ring to her for the first time. "Now, tell this group of men your plan."

The princess remained undaunted by his posturing. She looked straight into his eyes as she spoke. "It was proposed that you and Verclan should meet together at Haniah's table for a discussion centered on a resolution of longstanding conflicts between you. At the table with you will be Verclan's son, Patira, and the king's daughter, me. Haniah will serve as the mediator. You may each bring no more than six additional persons of your choice onto Haniah's property, and there will be no weapons."

"No weapons?" said the king in disbelief.

"None whatsoever," responded the princess firmly. "They will be left outside of Haniah's property."

"What if I do not agree to these terms?" said the king.

"Then you will not meet with Verclan."

"Is Verclan being told the same things by his son, and if he is, how do you know he will agree to them?"

"He will," said the princess. "I know it."

He was in the process of deciding to ask how she knew, when the smith, followed by the two guards, appeared at the door. He walked in as if he owned the room and had called the meeting himself. "You called for me, Sire?"

"Good smith, we were all wondering if you have decided a time and a place for the meeting between Verclan and me?"

The smith looked surprised. "Good King, hasn't your daughter told you by now?"

"Yes she has—" The king felt his victory slipping away. "But what do *you* say? Verclan explicitly wanted *you* to select the time and place."

"I did. Your daughter and my son—"

"You sent my daughter?" the king interrupted angrily.

"No, I sent my son. Your daughter was the only one I knew who knew the way to Haniah's hut. I asked that she lead him there."

"You told the good Dor Galar that you did not know the time or the place."

"I didn't."

"But you then told him that emissaries of mine were making the arrangements—"

"Good King, let me clear up some confusion. When I sent my son to Haniah's I had no clear idea what it was for. I just knew he had to go there on that day. When Galar visited me, I suddenly knew why he had gone, but I do not know how I knew. His journey, in hindsight, was to lead your daughter there. She was your emissary. No one else in the kingdom could have gained Patira's trust. Moreover, probably no one else in the mountain clans could have gained Vrengnia's trust. No one else in your kingdom would have your best interest at heart more than your own daughter. She is a fine young woman and loves you profoundly. Could there have been a better choice?"

The king was frowning. He could feel it. Why was it that this always got turned back on him? He knew the smith was right, but he was still not ready to concede defeat. "Perhaps you are right," he said quietly. "But since it was Verclan's request that *you* choose the time, place and terms of the meeting, please tell me plainly what they should be."

"You shall meet Verclan at Haniah's table at noon tomorrow. You may take seven other persons, one of them is your daughter, who will sit with you at Haniah's table. Haniah will mediate the discussions between you and Verclan. There will be no weapons of any kind allowed on Haniah's land—"

"No!" shouted the king.

"No what?" the smith asked bluntly.

The king was saying something he did not want to say. "That is what my daughter said," he blurted angrily.

"I agree with your daughter." The smith said evenly. "Your daughter has negotiated wisely. I would not have selected better." The king was sulking inside. He knew he was making a fool of himself and was seeking desperately to blame it on someone else. "Ah, I see," continued the smith, "because we are in agreement, you suspect that I actually told your daughter what to arrange. I assure you, I did not."

"Enough!" snapped the king. "Verclan will have his meeting with me as arranged—tomorrow at noon at Haniah's table." He looked at the smith. "You may leave, good smith. I have many arrangements to make."

The smith bowed slightly and turned to the door. The two guards followed him out. The king silently hoped he would never see him again. He was not sure what to do now.

The princess broke the silence. "Father, are you angry with me for making these arrangements?" The tone of her voice was steady and strong; she was not begging for his acceptance; she seemed simply to want to know.

The king sighed. "No, Vrengnia, I am not angry with you. You have done well. The arrangements are fair and the plan is good."

"Then what are you angry about?" The princess was staring straight at him.

He looked at the floor. "I am angry…I guess…I am angry because it was done without my knowledge." He looked up and met the princess's gaze with his own.

"Father, you must understand—when I left with Paca yesterday morning, I had no idea what the purpose of the trip was going to be. I thought that I was simply guiding Paca to Haniah's place as a favor to the smith. Paca did not know either." Her voice was steady and full of confidence. "I would have told you except that you tried to lock me in my room again. That insulted my trust in you and I left without letting you know. I am sorry."

The king knew she meant it. His daughter was becoming everything he hoped that she someday would be. Why was this so hard to accept?

During the whole interchange between the smith, himself and his daughter, the other men in the hall had stood patiently, silent witnesses to the drama before them. He turned to them again. "Come, there are many preparations to be made. Vrengnia, we will meet about an hour after sunrise tomorrow morning at the castle gate. If you will now excuse us, I need to speak with my advisors in private."

The king thought that this dismissal might reveal a chink in the princess's newfound strength. Instead, she smiled at him, threw her arms around him, and hugged him. "I will be there, Father. It will be a great day together. By the way, I have chosen a name."

"A name?"

"My elder-name. Tomorrow is my birthday, my eighteenth."

"Yes, yes…your eighteenth!" How could he have forgotten? There had been so much going on, but that was no excuse. "What name have you chosen?"

"I will tell you at the celebration."

"Celebration?"

"Sure. After the meeting tomorrow…you celebrated your fiftieth, should I not celebrate my eighteenth?"

Sandihar felt his defensiveness melting into her smile as she stood before him. "Of course. I will be looking forward to that celebration."

She stepped forward and hugged him again, then turned and left immediately, without so much as a look back over her shoulder.

The king turned to the six men remaining in the room. "As I said, we have much to do." He had his own plan forming in his mind. There were many details to be worked out. "Get me Omberon."

He saw Dor Galar shift and look up at him. "We were not able to find him, sir."

"What?!"

"Yesterday you asked me to find him for you. He does not seem to be anywhere. I have asked around, and no one has seen him since the night before last."

"Did you ask Vishtorath at the gate?"

"I did. As far has he knows, he did not leave through the portcullis."

"Are you saying he found another way out?"

"No, Sire, just that Vishtorath said he did not leave across the draw-bridge, and we are not able to find him in the castle. I am at a loss to explain it."

Sandihar stopped for a moment, trying to assimilate yet another strange event. He struggled to find how this piece fit into the changing landscape of a journey he did not want to be taking. He looked down and shuddered. "All right," he said, "we need to make appropriate preparations for tomorrow's meeting." He called to the attendants, "Chairs!" It was going to be a long session.

58

It is one thing to make a mistake, or to have an evil thought cross one's mind. It is quite another to make a life out of inventing evil.

Pratoraman
The Middle Way

PACA HAD TO WALK RAPIDLY TO KEEP UP WITH HIS FATHER. IT SEEMED THAT IT had always been that way, for though twenty-five years or more his elder, the smith was still strong, and there was no time to waste today. They had met at the Yendel Fork in the gray light of the predawn fog. His father hugged him. "We have little time to lose," he said as he gestured vaguely west into the fog. Paca knew the road well and knew there was nothing except fields where his father had indicated. "We need to get to Haniah's before the king. There are arrangements I need to make with her before he arrives," he explained.

They plunged into the fog across the fields. Paca was not sure how his father knew where he was going, but he was following vague trails through the fields. Occasionally they would pass a farmhouse and his father would stop as if remembering something very distant. "I haven't been to Haniah's in about two years," he whispered during one such pause, "and the fog doesn't help." Paca had opened his mouth to speak, but his father had held his index finger up in front of his lips and whispered, "Not now."

He walked in silence behind his father, as if the fields had ears. He had many questions, but the need of the hour seemed to be silence. It gave him time to think.

After he had left his father, two nights before, he had gone home and slept soundly. Early in the morning, he heard the hoof beats of approaching horses. Without waiting to find out who it was, he had left the house through the back door. Too many strange things had been happening to take a chance on being caught off guard.

It was a dor accompanied by four of the king's soldiers. Paca watched them from behind the low stone wall by the lane to the side of the house. They stopped at the gate, dismounted and came to the door. After knocking, the dor had entered the house and remained inside for about two minutes and then came back out, uttering something to the soldiers. Seemingly satisfied that no one was home, they had left and headed back toward the castle. Paca decided not to risk remaining at the house and had spent the rest of that day and that night at Vordar's house.

The fog lifted just before Paca and his father reached the road from the castle to Mordan near the bridge across Rindara. They paused in a small gully that ran beside the road, and his father held his finger to his lips as he stole up the side of the roadbed. He looked both ways along the empty road, then waved to Paca to follow him. "No sign of the king," he said in the first normal voice since they had started the journey. "We must be well ahead of him. Keep your eye out for scouts, but I think we can talk freely now."

"Why couldn't we talk in the fields? It seems there would be less chance of anyone hearing us there."

"I was not afraid of being heard, but we were traveling under the protection of Allimah Ki. It is simply a matter of respect for the people who live there and work the land." Paca knew about Allimah Ki, but had never used its privilege. It was an ancient Tessalindrian tradition that granted any being on foot free passage across any piece of land. Passage was allowed as long as the passer did not injure the land or its owners in any way. Though it had been made a law in Immerland by the king's mother, many landowners did not respect it, so there was a certain risk in invoking it.

"Well, I *do* have a lot of questions," Paca opened.

"Speak."

"I want to know more about Mankar."

"Something specific?" His father stared straight ahead as he spoke. They were alone on the road as far as they could see. Just above the eastern horizon, the sun was beginning to penetrate the clouds and the last patches of fog that lay in the small depressions in the carpet of fields surrounding them were yielding to its warmth.

Paca breathed deeply. "Was it really as bad as the legends say. I mean—"

"It was worse than *any* of the legends." His father interrupted him bluntly as he continued to stare at the horizon.

"Worse?!" It was hard for Paca to imagine. The legends told of unimaginable barbarism by Mankar and his generals; brutal acts that went far beyond the thirst for power and control. "How could it be worse?"

They walked for some distance before his father spoke. "The legends only tell of the heroics of brave men who stood up to Mankar. One might *expect* an evil man to respond to such threats with sadism and horrific injustice." As he spoke, his sentences were filled with emotion, rolling back and forth between deep pain and anger. "But the legends seldom speak of the torture and indiscriminate bloodletting levied at anyone and everyone in Mankar's path. The evil he carried in his heart was like a sport. Do you recall the legend of Thiadar?"

"Wasn't he the one who led a band of followers against Mankar with pitchforks? He was blinded, deafened and caged in the town square, as I recall, and kept alive in the cage until he froze that winter."

"Yes, but do you know *why* he rebelled?"

"Uh…no."

"Mankar and his generals paid a visit to the small town of Mindaquora on the border of Tessamandria. When he arrived the elders of the town were in a meeting in the central meeting hall. He blockaded the building and set it afire. He and his minions took turns beheading the elders as they tried to escape the flames through the front door of the hall. Later, they gathered all the heads and boiled them in a large pot in the center of the town. That night, they forced everyone in the town to drink from the unholy brew. Anyone who refused was killed on the spot.

"Thiadar was one who drank. Later, repulsed and infuriated by his cowardice, he led his rebellion. He almost succeeded." As his voice trailed off, Paca looked up and saw tears running down his father's cheeks. "There was so much more…ugly…evil…unbearable."

Paca did not know what to say, so he said nothing to let his father continue.

"His crowning insult to justice was the institution of Kli-marana Waru."

"I have heard of it, but I never understood what it was."

"Kli-marana Waru was devised to taunt those who would stand up against him. It was a fight to the death with swords, one man against another. Each was allowed to choose a second, to back him up. Mankar instituted it as the only legal method of challenging his authority. Many people challenged him, in the remote hope that they could end his reign of terror. They all died—the sword my father had made gave him too much of an advantage. It was a brutal and sadistic thing."

Paca looked at his father. His eyes looked beyond the horizon, reliving the horror of things he had never forgotten. "When Mankar disappeared, Kli-marana Waru was banished. Its memory was too vile to allow its practice by any nation on Tessalindria. The Moorimans practiced it for a while, but even they abandoned it."

"What *did* happen to Mankar?"

"We don't know exactly. There is much conjecture, but little evidence. Several of his generals had been killed by daring men who paid with their lives. At some point, his sword was stolen by the Twins of Huravag, along with the swords of his generals, and Mankar and the generals who remained disappeared. Many think that the Eladra were involved in his overthrow. If the swords you saw the other day are what I suspect, it is of great interest that there are only seven. It means that six others are still lost."

"Why didn't the Eladra get involved sooner?"

"That's a tough question, Pacahara. There are many things about the Eladra that we do not know. There is a lot about Mah'Eladra's plan that we don't know. Many think that the NarEladra were supporting Mankar, and if *that* is true, then it all makes a lot more sense. Their penchant for evil would explain much of what happened. It's possible that the rise and reign of Mankar was the extension of a much bigger conflict between Mah'Eladra and the NarEladra."

They fell silent. His father seemed to be deep in thought, and Paca was trying to assimilate the conflict between the bits of what he knew and what seemed so wrong about the dark events surrounding Mankar's history. So much did not fit; so many pieces had no place in the puzzle.

The sun had burned away all remnants of the fog, and the sky overhead was cloudless azure. Despite his father's brisk pace and the fresh exhilaration of the bright new morning, the conversation left him with an overriding sense of darkness. Paca shuddered and forced his thoughts elsewhere.

Vrengnia and her father were probably on the road somewhere behind them. Patira and his father were making their way down some mountain trail toward Haniah's. Paca busied his mind imagining what they were thinking as they all traveled toward the unique location and time that lay before them.

59

Loneliness is not measured by the absence of other beings, but by the absence of friends.

Hispattea
The Essences of Corritanean Wisdom

VRENGNIA WOKE EARLY. IT WAS STILL DARK, BUT SHE COULD TELL FROM THE air in her chambers that the morning was heavy with fog. In the courtyard, she could hear the stirrings of the castle help. It was earlier than she had expected because whenever her father left the castle, it was a big affair.

Horses stamped and snorted as they were led out onto the cobblestones, and she could hear the grooms trying to calm them down in the darkness. Carts and wagons were being pulled and pushed and various things dropped here and there. She peered down into the dark mist, but could see nothing, except the faint glow of lanterns that had been hung about the courtyard.

She was excited about the day. In her heart, she knew she had wanted this for a long time. Her father was a good man, but this cruel obsession with vengeance on Verclan was twisting much of his goodness. Perhaps today it could be mended, even if it was only in the slightest way.

It was peculiar, though, she thought, that amidst all the uncertainty of what might happen, she felt no fear whatsoever. She was beginning to understand the way the smith looked at his world, and as she tried to imitate it, she found herself becoming more and more confident, relaxed and at peace. Today she felt unusually strong.

It was also her birthday. Today she would be eighteen and she liked the sound of it. Eighteen: long ago she had chosen it as her favorite number. There was no particular reason; she just liked it and that was all that mattered.

Many things had begun to change from her association with the smith, Paca and Patira, and she had been thinking lately about shedding the image of the Pied Princess. She had no recollection of her mother, and many of the images she had of queens were based on legends and were those of weakness and overindulgence in the feminine mystique of excessive and impractical clothing and makeup. So she had resisted any such "queenly" thinking. The exception to this was her grandmother, about whom she knew relatively few details. Recently, she had developed a new image for what a queen could be, and her confidence in her ability to create this image was at the point where she was ready to try. *Perhaps today should be the day,* she thought as she stared into the wardrobe.

Her attendants had lit the lanterns in her chambers and were busy with other chores about the room. She dismissed them so she could work out the details alone.

She decided that she would wear her best for her father. He had ordered many clothes made for her, hoping that she would wear something more in line with his vision of a princess. He had tried everything, so she had every color, arrangement and style except the feminine extreme, which she loathed so absolutely he had never even bothered to offer it to her.

Her wardrobe was filled with the selection of clothes, many of which she had never worn. She began pulling them out and examining them. She did not have time to deal with all of it that morning, so she worked through the wardrobe until she had found a suitable outfit: light gray pantaloons, made from a sturdy light cloth that looked like satin, but wasn't. She also found a black blouse with long loose sleeves and a wide-open collar. It matched perfectly with her tunic. The gray and the black accented the yellow sunburst and the blue slashes and made them stand out marvelously.

She also decided not to wear her hat. She held it for a moment and smiled. Suddenly it seemed out of place and she wondered briefly at the years of silliness when the hat was her statement of who she was. Who she was would change today. She tossed it aside and turned to the large oval glass beside the wardrobe. If she wore no hat, what would she do with her hair? She pushed it to one side, then the other, then straight back. "This is the hard part," she thought. She had always worn it tucked up under her hat. It was not long enough to braid. She brushed it all straight back and held it behind her head. That seemed to fit, so she rummaged through the top drawer of her dresser until she found a single bright blue leather thong.

She pulled her hair back and tied it with the thong so that it hung loosely behind her neck. "That's it," she decided and then smiled. She was ready to go.

She grabbed a long blue riding cloak to stem the chill of the morning mist. It was full length and would fall over her horse in such a way as to capture the animal's body heat and keep her warm.

As she headed for the door, she saw her sword lying on the entrance table by the door. She paused and picked it up. *No*, she thought, *today is to be a day of peace.* There would be no need for any sword.

By the time she reached the courtyard, the darkness had given way to the slow gray light of morning, and the mist had risen slightly so that she could see almost to the other side. It was filled with people, horses and carts, and everything was moving. Her father was sitting on his horse in the middle of it all, calling out orders that sent men and women scurrying in all directions at his bidding. She headed straight for him, working her way through the busy-ness to reach him.

She caught his eye as she approached, and he stared at her for an instant. "Vrengnia! The hat—"

"It's gone, Father," she said firmly as she smiled. "Forever. What else needs to be done?" It was then that she noticed her father's attire. He was dressed for battle. Under his riding cloak, he wore chain mail and his new sword hung at his side in a new sheath. She could not see it very well because of the cloak. He wore his fighting boots, plated with bits of steel to protect against errant swordplay. The riding pack on the back of the horse looked as if it held his war helmet.

She wanted to express her dismay tactfully. "Father, I was thinking that this meeting today was to be one of peace. Surely you will not need your sword and armor!"

Her father frowned sternly. "I can take no chances. We will leave our weapons at the trailhead onto Haniah's land, as agreed."

"We?" The princess looked around and realized for the first time how many soldiers were in the courtyard. "Father, you may only take seven others," she said darkly.

"Onto the Haniah's land, you said. The others will wait outside." A faint gloating smile curled around the corners of his mouth.

She felt indignant anger rising inside her. She turned away, intending to find Mahala. Could her father really be so small-minded? He was up to something of his own design. She could not help feeling a sad disappointment that he would not let this happen the way it was meant to happen. He always had to keep his control and have his way in everything. What was it? Something was wrong, but she was having a hard time putting a name to the wrongness of it. Until she could name it, she did not feel adequate to confront her father.

She found Mahala being held by the old groom with whom she had spoken in the stables. He looked at her directly as she approached, and she felt him saying something. "What is it?" she asked him quietly. Somehow, she knew she could trust him and speak freely.

"It is fear," he said as he turned to settle the restless gelding. "Your father is afraid, with good reason. But it is not Verclan he fears."

She was puzzled. "What do you mean?"

"Your father is afraid, but not of Verclan. The fear he feels, he cannot name; so he will not admit it, even to himself."

"I...I think I felt the same thing just now, as I left him,"she responded.

"Yes you did. I could see it in your eyes as you approached. Good and fair Princess, do not give way to fear, even if you cannot name it."

"I know that, but how?"

"Fear is a strange enemy. We allow her in, and she feeds on herself, becoming larger, and more looming than she could possibly be. She weakens your sense of purpose, cuts off the El in you, and begins the slow task of eradicating your nephus. Sessasha once said, 'She robs you of yourself, then turns what's left into everything you hate.' You must not let fear get a foothold in your life."

She knew he was right. It made too much sense to be wrong, but she felt confused by the knowing. The old man was gently brushing Mahala's coat as he talked. "You must trust in what you know is right; trust in the El and act on it. To do otherwise is to give in to fear."

She stared at him. "I'll have to think about that—are you coming with us today?"

"No, good Princess, I will stay at the castle." He looked at her steadily for a moment. She thought he wanted to say more.

"Well, up you go," he said cheerfully. "It's a bit of a ride, I would say. We packed some food in the saddle packs in case you get hungry before you get there. Farewell, my good friend."

"Farewell, and thank you. You have been kind and helpful. I will see you this evening when we return." The princess sat in the saddle looking down at the old man. There was something special about him. She suddenly realized what it was. *He* had no fear.

She shook the reins and urged Mahala forward. The old man did not move, but raised one hand as the gelding carried her forward and out of his sight in the shuffling mass of the crowded courtyard.

It was much lighter now and up on her horse she could see more of the activity clearly. There were at least a dozen carts, filled with many things: tents, blankets, food baskets, tools and other miscellaneous provisions for an overnight journey. If there were not seventy soldiers, there must have been at least fifty: all on foot, all dressed for war. She counted twelve dors. She recognized seven or eight of them, including Galar and Windarad, but could not recall all their names. Several of them she had never seen before.

The advisors were on horseback, near the king, and as she approached, wending her way slowly through the crowd, she could see that they were not happy about it. Near the gate there was a clump of scouts, dressed in black, huddled close together, talking and trying to ignore the rest of the activity. It was a grand scene in some respects, but out of proportion for her expectations of a short day-trip to Haniah's farm. This was going to be a parade and she was embarrassed by it.

As she approached her father again, he stood up in his stirrups and raised a horn to his lips. The sound burst forth, clear and startling in the mist and rattled off all the walls of the castle. The crowd hushed as he shouted:

"Today, we travel to Mordan and south, to meet with Verclan and the mountain people, to seek resolution. May Mah'Eladra be with us. May we return in victory!"

The crowd cheered, and those between the king and the gate fell back to leave a path for his entourage. Dors Galar, Windarad, Luracon and Mondarta led the procession, followed by the king and the princess. The advisors fell in behind, with the rest of the dors following them. Foot soldiers filed forward rapidly to either side, forming a wall to the left and to the right of the party. The princess looked back. The carts followed behind the dors. The scouts had vanished. It was a strange procession, and she was not sure whether she was being escorted or held prisoner by the rows of men surrounding her. She was the only woman.

As they marched under the portcullis, she looked over to see Vishtorath. He was not there. A chilling loneliness swept over her. She could not remember a time that he had not been there. And where were Paca and his father? She hadn't seen Paca since yesterday, and there was no indication that they had been invited to join in the king's entourage.

"Is everything all right?" asked her father as they started across the drawbridge.

She looked at him thoughtfully. This was her father, the King of Immerland, perhaps the person she knew best in the whole land, but his words were distant and seemed far away, lifeless. "I was hoping that Paca or his father would be with us, but I don't see them anywhere," she said, injecting a hint of disappointment into her last words on purpose.

Her father looked straight ahead. "I invited the smith last night. He declined to join our party, though I have a sense that he will be there. We have not seen so much as a hint of his son. He seems to have vanished."

The princess did not want to look at her father anymore. On the surface, everything seemed right, as it always had in his presence, but increasingly she was getting in touch with a reality that went much deeper than the surface. In that reality, something was very wrong. She did not have enough experience to know how to define it. "Fear," was what the old groom had said. *Is it fear?* she thought to herself.

"You really like this Paca, don't you?" her father droned.

This Paca! The words stung her heart. *Is that the way you think of my friend? "This Paca"?* She held her tongue, marshalling self-control. "He is my friend, Father," she said at last. "I would have liked to have him with us. His father is quite a remarkable man, as you know. I would think that *you* would have wanted him to be here also."

"I did want him to be here!" he said emphatically. She thought she saw him looking at her out of the corner of her eye. "He refused to come with us!"

"He would have come if he sensed a genuine desire on your part, but something is wrong. Something is twisted. I don't know what, but I can tell. I can only hope that no one gets hurt."

Neither spoke. They entered the woods south of the castle gate in utter silence except for the steady tramp of the soldiers' boots, the horses' measure gait and the creaking of the wagons trundling along behind them.

60

*True leadership is earned before it is
assumed.*

Hispattea
The Essences of Corritanean Wisdom

PATIRA LISTENED TO HIS FATHER AS HE FACED THE SMALL GROUP OF HUNTERS and mountain warriors gathered in the clearing. He was struck once again by his mother's beauty as she stood resolutely behind his father. She was dressed for riding, with a long brown-gray mountain cape nearly down to her ankles and her hair pulled back behind her head so that it covered her ears, allowing only the small silver earrings to show, accentuating the stark simplicity of her visage. Even in the dusky light of the fog-bound morning air, she stood out in the party like a beacon.

"We do not know what will happen today," his father said firmly. "I, my son, and six others will meet the King of Immerland today at noon. It is my hope that we may make some progress toward peace, toward some mutual agreement that will benefit us all. We must all hope this, and we must set it in our hearts to do the best we can to achieve it.

"But we must also be wise. We have reports that the king is bringing at least fifty armed soldiers and that his scouts will be watching the area around Haniah's land. By agreement, there will be no weapons on her land. Outside these boundaries, there are no rules.

"We will travel as a group until we reach Morahura. There we will head north to the stream bounding Haniah's land. After the eight of us enter her field, the rest of you must retreat and remain hidden in the woods to the south. You are free then to make decisions concerning your own safety. Be careful. Be alert."

Patira could tell the men were restless. It was hard to know if it was eagerness to be off on the adventure, or uneasiness about the danger that lay before them. Each of them represented the best and most faithful of Verclan's warriors and trackers. Each was a skilled woodsman and easily a match for any three of the king's soldiers, particularly in the woods. It was hard to imagine that they were afraid.

It seemed to Patira that those going to Haniah's land had the most to fear. They would be more exposed if there was any treachery by the king or his men. They would have to have the greater trust in the plan he had worked out with Vrengnia.

His father seemed at ease as they climbed onto their horses and headed off down the trail toward Morahura. He rode behind his father's lead and his mother followed him. Three advisors rode behind them, and they were flanked by about twenty warriors and guards on foot, moving through the woods noiselessly, perhaps fifteen feet off the trail.

The woods were quiet. The thick carpet of fog rolling down from the mountains gave a sense of seclusion and safety, for any invader would be worse off in the fog than these men. They moved swiftly, talking and laughing in low voices and enjoying their camaraderie.

Patira wondered what his father was thinking. "Do you think it is a good plan, Father?" he asked at last.

Verclan looked back at him and smiled. "I could not have thought of a better one. I do not know for sure, but I believe the Eladra are watching over Haniah's land. If this is true, then we are safer there than anywhere else. I have much hope that today we will witness the dawn of change where the mountain people must no longer feel as outlanders to Immerland's wealth and glory."

"Why do you suppose the king is bringing soldiers?" he asked quietly.

"I do not know. That troubles me more than anything. I have to trust that he is just fearful. His fear of me has always been somewhat irrational."

They rode together for a while, each engaged in private thoughts. Patira knew his father had brought his sword and he had brought his own. He was hoping he would never have to use it. It still had the strange hilt guard that the smith had made. "Did you bring that thing the smith made for you? The...the..."

"The sataliin?"

"Yes, that's it. The sataliin. Did you bring it along?"

His father was grave. "I did. I thought that if the smith made it, it must have a purpose. My only fear is that today will be the time I need it. But it does not make sense."

"What doesn't make sense?"

"Well, today! Today seems to be a time for reconciliation and everything points that way: the way you and the princess worked out the details, your friendship with her, that we are meeting at Haniah's place, that the king agreed to meet on the terms specified. All of it is positive, what I have hoped for over many years. But then the smith sent me this sataliin. And your hilt guard, the curious way it attached itself to your sword—" Patira was watching his father as he spoke. There was a far-away tone in his voice, as if he were seeing a future on the horizon that Patira himself could not see: a sort of inevitability that their horses were carrying them to. There was no apprehension, only the nagging curiosity about the pieces the smith had given them. They were pieces that did not seem to fit, but somehow he knew they did.

"Father," said Patira, "do you suppose the smith knows the details of what will happen at Haniah's today?"

"No, he does not."

"How are you so sure? I mean, some of the things he has done are so specific—he must know something we don't."

Verclan turned and looked into Patira's eyes. "The smith listens to the Eladra, and he does what they ask him to do. *They* know what will happen. It is likely that the smith has done many things by their instruction, but even *he* does not know exactly why."

"The smith has seen the Eladra?" Patira had never heard of anyone who had actually met an Eladrim being. He knew little of them. They were a vague legend to him: stories, told as history, but lacking an anchor in reality, as they were to most people of his acquaintance.

"I don't know the details. He arrived in Immerland when he was about twenty. No one knew him and we never knew where he came from. He taught us things that we had never seen on the forge—things from somewhere else, but he never talked about it."

"He told me once that he had learned bladesmithing from the Eladra. I laughed. He didn't. I don't think I offended him exactly—he never took offense at other people's ignorance—but it was clear from his reaction, that look in his eyes, that he was sincere in what he had said." His father paused and was silent for a time.

Patira let his mind slip into his imagination on what the Eladra would be like. The legends were legion. Many of them had been read to him as a child. They were written and told in such a way as to never deny their truth outrightly, but never to affirm it either. It was as if it was understood that each person was honored with the right to believe or not to believe; that eventually one's belief or disbelief would be confirmed and that any position on the issue was accepted without contention. He found it curious that he did not know exactly what his father, who had read the stories to him, believed. Even this last statement about the smith carried no judgment whatsoever about the validity of the smith's claim.

His father's voice broke into his thoughts. "I saw one of the Eladra once."

Patira looked at his father questioningly, but said nothing, so Verclan continued.

"The smith often worked late on the forge, doing his own work after the stable work was complete. I had left one evening and he was still working. There was some piece of bladework he was doing. I don't remember what it was. I had eaten my dinner with the grooms and stable hands when I remembered something I had left at the smithy. As I approached, I heard the smith singing in the Kor-Alura. It was beautiful, but I could not understand a word of it.

"I did not want to interrupt so I crept up silently to see what he was doing. As I looked in one of the windows, I could see the smith at the forge. He held a long blade in his hand, examining it carefully. On the other side of the forge was another man, well, a being, tall like the smith, but almost an apparition. He, or she, I wasn't sure, was also examining the blade and speaking softly to the smith in the same original language.

"The smith would listen and then go back to the forge and anvil and do something else to the blade while he sang. The other looked on. They were like teacher and student. I watched for about fifteen minutes, but needing whatever it was I had come for, I finally went to the door and knocked. As I entered at the bidding of the smith, the teacher had vanished completely. I never asked the smith about it. The smith never offered."

His father stopped again. The fog was lifting and the warriors had become silent as they traveled swiftly along beside the horses. There was no sound except for the gentle rhythm of the horses' feet on the trail, the dripping of dew off the trees and an occasional bird. In the far distance, they could hear the faint roar of the Morahura.

Patira had always loved Morahura. The giant cascade plunged close to four hundred feet straight off the edge of a vast rock outcropping on the side of the mountain. At the top it was a sheet of glassy water that fell off the edge of the world. At the bottom, it was a thunderous chaos of foam and spray as it slowly carved its way into the rock. Thousands of years of such pounding had chiseled a bowl into the base of the mountain. No one knew how deep it was. No one wanted to try to find out. It was easy to sit for hours and marvel at its power and majesty.

Out of the bowl at the bottom of the falls, the water ran swiftly to the north, bringing its life-giving flow to the plains of Immerland as the river Rindara, where it nourished the land in its path. To the people of Immerland, it was much needed water. To the mountain people, it was a symbol of power and life.

The falls could be seen top to bottom from the fields of Immerland, but few of the Immerlanders made the effort to go there. Morahura belonged to the mountain people. It was their pride and their identity.

Today the small band heading to Haniah's hut for the meeting with the king would stop and rest at Morahura. Patira was eager to be there. His father had led them on the high trail to the falls, avoiding the lower road. The high trail would be much safer for the mountain men. It was narrow and winding, switching back and forth along the side of the mountain as it approached Morahura. With every step, the roar got louder and louder until one could hear nothing except the falls.

As they approached the opening from the trail onto the huge rock plateau at the base of Morahura, his father suddenly stopped his horse and listened. With a swift motion of his hand across his chest the warriors vanished into the woods. Patira knew how it happened, but he was always amazed at how quickly they were gone. All who were left on the trail were he, his father, his mother and the three advisors, all on horseback. Then, as though nothing at all had happened, they started on their way again, allowing the horses to amble easily along.

Coming out onto the stone plateau always took Patira's breath away. It was a single piece of rock, a hundred paces across in both directions, and wet with the fine mist of the falls. A column of white water, ten paces in diameter, fell from above straight down into the bowl carved in the black rock. It boiled like a cauldron before spilling over through a shallow gorge in the northern edge of the plateau.

The riders dismounted and led their horses to the edge of the cauldron to drink. Hand signals were the means of communication; one's voice would be useless. They stared at the falls, everyone had a drink, and they smiled exuberantly at each other, slapped each other on the back, and laughed silently in the din of the falls. Patira saw his father raise his hand and twist it slightly. In unison, they all turned in behind him as he led the way across the plateau to the gorge. They were approaching from the west. On that side of the gorge a staircase cut from living rock led down the face of the plateau to where the river started on its way north to Immerland. At the base of the stairs, sheltered somewhat from the direct fury of the cataract behind them, they stopped again and waited. They could talk here, but barely.

"What was it back there, Father?" Patira shouted.

Verclan held a finger to his lips then pointed to the trail coming out of the woods along the river. Three warriors were struggling along the path, carrying something among them that looked as though it did not want to be carried. It was not a difficult guess as to what it was.

"Scouts," shouted Verclan, smiling at Patira. He pointed again, this time to the right at the base of the cliff. Four other warriors were dragging another figure, clothed in black, by the arms. By the time all the warriors had returned, there were four scouts in all, and none was very happy about his plight. Patira knew them all by sight. They had been captured before, but let go by his father's order.

As the scouts stood before them surrounded by the woodland warriors, Patira tried not to smile, but it *was* a laughable sight. His father eyed each thoughtfully, and with a simple hand sign, had their hands bound by the warriors, who took great delight in the task. Verclan remained stern. Two more signs were delivered subtly to the entourage, and they all started down the trail away from the falls, each scout walking between two warriors along the broad trail. The horsemen walked this time.

Patira loved his father, but times like these made him admire him profoundly. There was such loyalty from his men, such command in a simple hand movement; so much authority based in his knowledge of the woods, of horses, of men. He wondered if he could ever be like that.

They traveled warily, each man fully focused on the woods around him, scanning and rescanning the details for the slightest disturbance. When they had traveled about halfway from the falls to the border of Immerland, the trail cut through a small meadow that was waist deep in brilliant wildflowers. In the center of the hundred foot diameter stood the Ebondar. The Ebondar was a huge stone, perhaps four feet in diameter at its irregular base and twenty feet tall. Its presence dominated the meadow, giving it a solemn reverence.

His father halted the group and circled it around him to one side of the stone. The scouts were pushed roughly into the middle with him, and he stood facing them quietly. He stared at them for a moment, as if he were trying to chart the best course of action.

He addressed the scouts: "Do any of you know what this is?" he asked pointing to the huge stone. The scouts looked down at their feet. "Answer me," he commanded. "Do you?"

The small men shook their heads. Patira loved to hear the story of the Ebondar. He hoped his father would tell it again.

"Then look at me and I will tell you, so you may never forget. Look at me!" he commanded. The scouts looked up.

"Fifteen years ago, not one hundred yards from this place the mountain clans fought their first unified battle against King Sandihar's army. It was not a pretty sight. Fourteen mountain men were killed by the king's arrows. Eighteen more were wounded. My three advisors, whom you see behind you, were there.

"After we drove the king's soldiers from the woods, back into Immerland, we buried the dead, bandaged the wounded and grieved on this spot. You are standing on the graves of men who were killed confining the greed of your king." The scouts looked down at their feet nervously, but said nothing.

"Look at me! It took us a day to finish the task, and at the end of the day, those who were left dragged this stone to the middle of the clearing. Our plan was to erect it the next morning. We slept in the woods so that we would not dishonor the noble deaths of our brothers. When we woke in the morning, the stone was standing, as it still is today, and each of the new graves were overgrown with wildflowers, the ancestors of those you see here today. No one in our party knew how the stone was raised. Out of honor for those beneath us, speculation about what happened is forbidden as is the picking of flowers growing here. Each mountain man who sees the stone ponders what he will, and cherishes the memory, but no one speaks of it save the facts of the story.

"The Ebondar stands as a testimony to the strength of the mountain people. Until it falls, we will resist any evil that tries to take our land."

Verclan paused. No one spoke or moved. The Ebondar seemed to cast its immense shadow in all directions as the party stood; the woodsmen with their heads high and the scouts staring at the ground. Patira believed the Eladra must have raised the stone, but he had never asked or heard anyone else say it.

His father changed the tone abruptly, speaking more gently to the scouts. "Each of you has been captured before, am I right?" The scouts nodded sullenly. "Some of you, several times, no?" Two of the scouts nodded again and shifted their weight. "Ordinarily, I would send you home in loincloths with some witty note for your king, but today is no ordinary day." He paused for effect and began pacing back and forth rubbing his chin. "No, today I meet the good King Sandihar face to face at Haniah's table for a discussion about peace between Immerland and the mountain clans, am I not mistaken?" This time he turned to his advisors.

Omisar smiled, "No, good Verclan, you make no mistake." Chronista and Phartang laughed as Verclan turned back to the scouts. He walked down the line looking closely at each one.

"But the good king sends his spies before him. Why?" At first, he seemed to be throwing out a simple rhetorical question as he paced down the row of frightened scouts. Suddenly his face turned dark. "I want to know why!" The scouts looked at the ground. Patira watched as his father turned away and suddenly, as fast as one could comprehend what was happening, he whirled, drew his sword and lunged, the tip of the sword stopping just as it grazed the throat of the first scout in the line. The little man was too scared to move. "Why?" shouted Verclan angrily. No one in the ring around the scouts was smiling any longer. Patira had never seen his father so angry. He knew the scouts could be clever, but they were not very brave. Verclan held the sword steady, looking straight into the scout's eyes.

"He...he is afraid, sir," stammered the scout.

"Afraid? Afraid of what?"

"Of you, sir—and your men."

"How many armed soldiers accompany the king?"

"Fifty, sir."

"Were they given orders to do anything else except wait for the king? Were they told to surround Haniah's land?

"I don't think so. I mean, I didn't hear it if they were."

Verclan slowly lowered the sword. Patira felt the relief flow over him like the first rays of sun after a cold night.

"This is what I am going to do. I will say it once." Verclan grabbed the youngest of the four scouts, and with a quick and sudden movement of his hands stripped off the little man's shirt. "You. Go intercept the king and tell him I have these other three. Any move by the soldiers other than waiting for the king, will result in their deaths before nightfall." He nodded, and one of the warriors stepped forward and unbound the little man.

The young scout, terrified as he was, did not hesitate to take his leave. The warriors parted as he scampered out of the circle and disappeared quickly down the path by the river, heading toward Immerland. "Bind them together." Verclan's order was terse and gentle at the same time.

Two warriors tied the three scouts together with leather thongs so the possibility of escaping was eliminated, but they could still walk. With a quick movement of Verclan's hand, the party started off again leaving the Ebondar behind them. This time, they separated. Several warriors followed the horsemen with the scouts, but the rest moved off in bands of three or four and disappeared into the woods.

61

There are eyes that see and understand,
and there are eyes that only see.

The Tessarandin, Book 6

T HEY WERE APPROACHING THE TRAILHEAD INTO HANIAH'S FIELDS WHEN HIS
father broke the long silence that had prevailed since the conversation about Mankar. "Paca, we were not invited to be here today by
either Verclan or King Sandihar, so I must go ahead and speak with
Haniah on several things before either of them arrives. You must wait at
the trailhead until I return. Keep yourself hidden so that the king and
his men will not be able to see you. Is this clear?" He was grave, and his
words were spoken softly but powerfully.

"Very clear, Father." Paca responded.

"What will happen today is unknown to me at this time, but I know
that today's meeting will determine the course of history for Immerland
and the mountain clans. We must be watchful and patient. We cannot
be hasty. We will both be tested." He looked at Paca and continued
evenly, "There will be a time to take action, and it will be very clear. You
must be prepared to act."

"How…how will I know?"

"You will know. If there is any doubt, then do not act!" His father's
emphatic assertion of his ability to know reassured him only slightly.

When they reached the trailhead, his father paused as he surveyed
the wooded area to the left of the trail. "Do not go onto Haniah's land.
Hide up in that chestnut tree. It is a curious thing about Immerland
people that they never think to look up into the trees. No one will see
you there, and you will be able to see the king's approach. If I am not
back when you see them come over that rise in the hill, whistle."

He laid his hand on Paca's shoulder. It was firm. Their eyes met.
"Do not fear. Do not fear anything." He turned and headed down the
path. Paca watched him until he disappeared around the stone wall on
his way into the second field.

Paca breathed deeply. There were so many riddles that he decided the only way to handle it was to take each event as it happened and try not to fear. It seemed like there were plenty of reasons for fear, but his father's words implied that there were even others he was not aware of.

He made his way over to the large chestnut tree that stood just to the left of the trailhead. It stood like a sentinel. It was, in fact, the first tree at the edge of the woods and the extensive expanse of Immerland fields that led up to it. As he climbed up the first branches, he pondered what his father had said about the Immerland people. It was true. He would never have thought to look up into the tree. The thought frightened him, but it comforted him to know that, up in the tree, he would be safe.

He climbed to a spot where he could see the road as it came over the rise his father had indicated. From there, he could also see the area immediately in front of the trailhead. A large limb afforded him a comfortable seat where he could rest against the trunk and he sat on it, waiting.

It was very still, almost as if everything was waiting in anticipation of the meeting at Haniah's table. An occasional insect flitted by on some busy errand, but no breath of wind stirred the leaves of the tree. No trace of the morning fog remained, and the cloudless sky extended in all directions. From his perch in the tree, Paca could see both Immerland and the mountains.

To the left was Haniah's land, quiet, serene and brilliant with sun and the early changes of autumn color that had started settling over the mountains. To the right was Immerland, its golden fields and rolling meadows sloping gently upward with its castle far in the distance on the hill. Except for small clusters of trees interrupting the view here and there, it was all field.

Paca watched and waited.

The first thing that interrupted the stillness was a hurried conversation coming from below and behind him. He turned carefully to see what it was. He could not make out the words but he caught sight of three of the king's scouts on the edge of the trees. They were in an animated conversation and seemed to be having some sort of disagreement. He wished he could get closer, but any movement could have caught their attention.

After several minutes, the group broke up. One scout headed up the trail to the east that skirted Haniah's land. The second went the opposite direction, coming almost directly under Paca's perch before moving along the stone wall that divided the Immerland field from Haniah's meadow. The third plunged into Haniah's woods and disappeared.

Paca waited again. About two minutes had passed when there was a sudden, frightened yelp and followed by a frantic thrashing about in the woods below him. A tall warrior, dressed like the one Paca had seen in Haniah's hut, was dragging the scout through the woods by his upper arm. When they got to the edge of the woods, the warrior hurled the scout out into the field, where he tumbled like a sack of grain. The scout was up in a flash. Not wanting to see what would happen next, he started running down the road that lead into the heart of Immerland.

Paca watched the warrior. As he turned to move back into the woods he looked up suddenly, straight into Paca's eyes. Paca froze. The warrior nodded. When Paca blinked, the warrior vanished.

The Eladrim guardians were obviously not very tolerant of intrusions into Haniah's domain, and it was comforting to know that they did not seem to be offended by his presence. He knew he would be no match for them.

Everything was quiet again, and Paca settled back against the tree to watch for the king. The presence of the scouts was disturbing, but he was not sure why. Perhaps the king was planning something devious under the cover of a peaceful meeting with Verclan. On the other hand, a little precaution on the part of the king could be expected, given his longstanding antipathy for the mountain leader.

Paca did not have to wait long. Judging from the elevation of the sun, he guessed it was about an hour before noon when the first movement appeared on the road as it crested where his father had indicated. He sat forward and with two fingers in his mouth, gave a long, shrill whistle. He knew his father would hear it.

He sat back to watch the little black knot of men and horses trudging down the road toward where he sat hidden. They were about a mile away, and he could not make out who was in the party. He guessed the princess would be there and wondered what she would be thinking. How different it must be from two days ago when they ambled together down the same road in the warm sunshine, at about the same time of the day. He thought about Meshabo, too. What had told her to come along with them and why? What had become of her? It was all very strange, but almost comforting compared to the approaching entourage of the king.

The group was no more than a fifth of a mile away when his father appeared at the end of the stone wall. Paca saw him briefly as he ducked back into the woods and vanished. All was silent again, except for the distant hoofbeats of the approaching horses. Suddenly his father was at the base of the tree. With a single swift leap he gained the first limbs and pulled himself up beside Paca. Paca felt his hand on his shoulder and turned. His father had his finger to his lips.

They could see the details now. There were four dors in front on horses, followed by the king and the princess, side by side. More dors followed and behind them the king's advisors along with a collection of carts pulled by donkeys. On either side was a row of battle-ready soldiers protecting the flanks of the procession.

They were about fifty paces from the trailhead when a peculiar thing happened. The two leading soldiers from each flank suddenly broke rank and started running toward the trailhead. One of the dors in the front began shouting at them and Dors Galar and Windarad spurred their horses into a gallop. Paca felt his father's breath near his ear. "Eladra! This should be interesting."

The two soldiers stopped at the trailhead and turned to face the approaching dors. As they turned, Paca caught a clear glimpse of the one on the left. It was Vishtorath, the gatekeeper. They drew their swords and crossed them across the trail, a symbol of denial of passage to anyone approaching. A piece fell into place in Paca's puzzle. The gatekeeper of the castle had been an Eladrim warrior, guarding the gate for all those years; watching out for the princess. Now he was guarding the gate to Haniah's land. He wondered if perhaps he had been the watcher in the tower.

Galar and Windarad reined in tight just before the two Eladrim guardians. "What is the meaning of this, Vishtorath?" said Galar angrily.

Vishtorath spoke. "This is the trail to Haniah's domain. No armed man or woman shall pass. Only the king and seven others will be allowed." The words were in the original language, but Paca understood them perfectly. He was sure that Galar and Windarad did also, maybe even the horses. Their faces fell and the horses started scrambling backward. The dors wheeled them around and cantered back to the king, who had halted the procession. A hurried conversation followed.

Paca had a moment to assess the group on the road. In addition to those he had seen before, there were several scouts. One of them was the one he had seen routed by the Eladrim guard not an hour before. A second one had no shirt, his skin comically white where he always wore black. He watched the princess. She was listening to the conversation between the dors and the king. They were about thirty paces away and he could see her face clearly. He was surprised that she was not wearing her hat and that her clothing was simple and uncluttered. *She looks more like a princess ought,* he thought to himself.

The king broke away from the group and approached the two guards. Vrengnia followed him, but the others remained behind. The guards still had their swords crossed and remained motionless as the king approached. At about five paces the king and princess dismounted. The guard on the right nodded to the princess.

The king stood facing Vishtorath with an odd expression on his face. Paca guessed it to be a mixture of fear, anger and confusion. "You would disobey me, Vishtorath?" he asked darkly.

"Only when there are a higher orders, Sandihar of Immerland."

The king paused. "I am the king!" he thundered.

"Only the King of *Immerland.*" Vishtorath countered calmly, his emphasis conveying clearly that Immerland was only a fragment of the greater order of the world.

The king stepped back uneasily, glancing briefly at Vrengnia. "You are my gatekeeper!" Paca sensed a hint of desperation in his voice.

"I am *a* gatekeeper. You ordered me here, O King."

"But not to bar my way!"

"I am not barring your way, Sandihar, I am keeping the gate. I am here to see you and your elect safely onto Haniah's land according to the agreement."

The king looked down and frowned. He seemed confused. His next words were those of yielding and resignation. "We have come for a meeting with Verclan of the mountain tribes. We ask passage into Haniah's domain."

"You may enter here," said Vishtorath. "You must lay down all weapons before entering. They will be safe here until you return. The princess may enter also, under the same conditions, and then six others."

The king paused for a moment and looked from Vishtorath to the other guard, as if assessing the reality of the situation in front of him. "It will be as you say," he remarked as he turned and walked back to the waiting dors. There was another quiet conversation, and he emerged, followed by Dors Galar and Windarad, his three advisors and Rapahoogin. All of them had dismounted, leaving their horses with soldiers. They approached the path on foot.

When they arrived in front of the guards again, the king bowed, and laid his sword on the ground in front of the guard on the right and stood up. What happened next was something Paca was sure he would never forget. The guards uncrossed their swords and the king stepped between them. Suddenly, the guard on the right leapt forward and in one quick motion, almost too fast to see, reached his hand into the king's tunic and pulled something out. A long thin dagger flashed in the sun as it came up under the king's throat. Paca was sure that the king had never been treated like this before. The terror in his eyes was masked by his surprise. The guard stared into his eyes, unmoving for several seconds, before he turned the blade over in his hand and with a single swift motion, sent the dagger spinning through the air. It hit the trunk of the tree where Paca and his father were hidden and buried itself to the hilt in the wood. He turned back to the king and shoved him roughly onto the path.

The princess stepped forward. She hesitated briefly as she looked directly at Vishtorath. Paca was sure that, in that instant, she understood who he really was, and had been. The giant stared back, as if speaking to her silently. In the next instant she looked up into the tree and met Paca's eyes and then, as quickly as she had looked up, she looked back. It was so brief that no one else saw what happened. The king was still nursing his wounded pride, and the dors behind the princess were busy removing their weapons. A smile lingered on her face as Vishtorath and his companion nodded. She stepped between them untouched.

Paca breathed out quietly as his father laid his hand on his shoulder. He had seen the exchange. Paca took comfort in the strength of his father's hand and the knowledge that Vrengnia knew he was there.

The dors obediently laid down their swords as well as the small knives they often carried in their boots, and stepped between the watchful eyes of the guards. The advisors and Rapahoogin passed though without even a glance from the guards. The king was silent. No one spoke to him. No one needed to. Paca watched him as he turned and headed down the trail with the others following. Vrengnia was directly behind him and she seemed unusually tall compared to her father for that brief time before they disappeared out of sight around the stone wall.

He looked back to the others whom the king had brought along. They were milling about. One of the other dors had assumed command and had ordered them to do something. It was hard to tell from their actions exactly what it was. They seemed to be just making themselves comfortable for a long wait.

His father leaned over and whispered again. "We must wait a little while longer, then we will go."

Go where? Paca wondered. Were they just going to clamber down out of the tree? If not, how would they sneak down? They were so close to the guards. So they waited. The guards never moved. The soldiers, dors, scouts and cart handlers milled about, chatting and laughing, and lying about in the warm noon sun. It was as if they had come all this way for something, but now they were not allowed to do it, and so they were trying to do nothing. Paca was uneasy. He wanted to know what was going on in the field in front of Haniah's hut. For now, he just had to wait.

The waiting seemed long, but Paca knew it wasn't. His father touched his shoulder and whispered, "Follow me." They began climbing down the tree. It was only two or three branches before they dropped out to the ground five paces from the guards. They didn't even flinch. Paca saw one of the scouts pointing excitedly, and two dors stood up, drawing their swords. His father headed straight for the guards, and Paca followed as the dors ran to meet them, yelling. As the smith stepped between the guards, they bowed to him and gestured to him to pass through. Paca followed quickly. Vishtorath looked him in the eye, but did not move to stop him.

He had only taken a couple steps past the guards when he heard the brilliant clash of two swords just behind him. He turned to look. One of the dors was running back to the shelter of the group sprawled on the grass. The other stood holding one hand in the other, his face contorted with pain and his sword lying on the grass in front of him. The Eladrim guards stood motionless, their swords crossed across the front of the path. Paca could only guess what had happened.

Paca turned back to follow his father who was now ten steps ahead. It looked like he had never even looked back. There were so many questions spinning in his head: How did his father know when to leave the tree? Why had the Eladrim guards bowed to his father? Why had the Eladra let *him* pass? It took a few running steps to catch up. They walked together down the path without saying anything.

62

Submission to the larger forces that define our path, is born in strength, and breeds a strength that is greater still.

Pratoraman
The Middle Way

VRENGNIA WAS STRUGGLING WITH TERROR ABOUT HER FATHER'S MOTIVES. THE dagger that he had hidden in his tunic was the most disturbing. Perhaps "why" was the wrong question, because it was clear enough that her father hated Verclan and intended to harm him if he had the opportunity. The discovery that Vishtorath and the other lead soldier in his caravan were actually not under his command had visibly shaken her father. In spite of all this, he had still tried to get past them with the dagger. How did they know he had it? She had never seen anything as quick or as powerful as the way it had been taken from him and thrown into the tree.

In their hurried conversation with her father, the dors had said these guardians were Eladra, but it was in that one moment, as she looked into Vishtorath's eyes before she stepped between him and the other guard, that she really understood who he was—who he had been—all these years. This Eladrim being, the gatekeeper, with his ever-watchful eye, had been guarding the castle gate. He had been guarding her. Now he stood guarding the gateway to Haniah's land, as solemnly as he had guarded the castle. What was he looking for? What was he really guarding? Perhaps the answer lay in Haniah's field.

She was not sure why she looked up. It was just one of those things that occurs so unexpectedly that it was over before she knew it was happening. Paca and his father were in plain sight, sitting in the tree and watching the entire strange affair. It was comforting to know they were there—she wanted them to be there—but why were they in the tree? How had they remained unseen by everyone else, especially the Eladrim guards?

All these events led her to a single undeniable conclusion: that something much bigger than the conflict between her father and Verclan was at work here. In the midst of it all, what amazed her most was the seemingly impervious mind of her father. He seemed blind to everything except his vendetta.

She walked behind him. His face was hidden and he had not spoken since they had passed the guards. Whatever he was thinking, it was not promising that she would find out. He led the tiny procession down the path, walking upright and dignified as a king ought. But she could not help be a little amused at how, having been stripped of everything he had brought along for protection and control, he was now just another man, walking a quiet path with seven others: almost naked, exposed, humiliated perhaps, and forced to face his sworn enemy and himself for the first time in eighteen years.

She looked around as they walked. The air was still and peaceful. The trees, the grass and the warm soil exuded a thick, rich smell that rolled up from beneath them as the noonday sun bathed the landscape. Vrengnia could feel its warmth on her shoulders and hair. It was comforting to feel its certainty, its enduring faithfulness in times when everything else seemed so uncertain.

It wasn't until they were entering into the last stand of trees that her father spoke. "Why do you suppose the smith selected this Haniah as the mediator?" he asked over his shoulder.

Vrengnia winced in surprise. "Have you never met her?"

"I have never had the occasion to do so," he said.

"Well, I'm not sure exactly why the smith selected Haniah. I might guess that it is because she owns the land and is somewhat neutral."

"But why *this* land? It seems a bit remote."

"Remote? Father, it is on the border of your kingdom—less than a day's march from the castle. You can't seriously consider it remote." It suddenly occurred to her how provincial her father really was. He had never been very adventurous. Perhaps anything outside of his immediate control would be considered "remote." Here, he was not the ruler, and the seven others that accompanied him offered little protection. He was out of his element. He needed reassurance, so she tried to offer it. "It's beautiful here, Father, and Haniah's land seems to be well protected."

"What do you mean?" he snarled.

"Well, if there are guards like the ones we met, protecting this property—and from what Rapahoogin said, it seems that there are—then we really have nothing to fear."

"I guess." His voice was sullen.

She wanted to change the direction of the conversation without being too obvious. "Besides, I think you will like Haniah."

The king turned suddenly. "Why?" He was looking directly at her. The procession stopped abruptly. She hated the question "why." She had never put her finger on it, but suddenly it became clear. It was seldom a sincere quest for understanding. As in this case, it was more often used as a defensive maneuver against the challenge of accepting something the person did not want to accept. Her father had decided that he was not going to like Haniah simply because he did not like this whole arrangement, and Haniah was part of it. Haniah had been given control, which made him uncomfortable, so she was someone to be disliked. The "why" was a defiant challenge to prove his prejudice wrong; a battle lost before it was begun.

Vrengnia could feel the rage rising in her throat. She wanted to say "Oh, Father, grow up!" but hesitated. There was counter-rage rising, a queen-like instinct...coming from where? She looked into her father's angry eyes and spoke evenly: "There are times, Father, when even the king must accept his place in the greater order of things. This is one of those times."

He stared at her but said nothing. There was more to be said. "Haniah is a woman worthy of your respect. She listens well and does not use words lightly. She is generous, she is thoughtful—and she is knowledgeable in many things. She has done you no harm and, by being the mediator today, she is doing the kindest thing she can do for her king: helping you to face your enemy in a place that is safe, without the need to fear. You must not bring your fear to the table."

Her father looked down at the ground. Vrengnia remained grave. She could tell that what she said had struck deep, and she watched his struggle without moving. He needed to face it himself. He looked up and there was a small tear in one eye. "You are right. Let's get on with it." He turned rapidly and started out of the trees into the brilliant light of Haniah's field. Vrengnia breathed deeply and quietly. There was a new-found strength welling up within her. She wondered at it, but decided to accept its almost imperceptible tide, as she fell in step behind her father as the others, quiet and reserved, followed obediently.

63

Come, eat. When the food is gone we will
concern ourselves with life again.

Mirradach
'The Tiger in the Tree'

THE APPROACH TO HANIAH'S TABLE LAY THROUGH ONE REMAINING ROW OF trees at the edge of her field. He wanted to be there, but Verclan was finding it difficult to imagine facing the king in person after so many years. Eighteen years it was. Eighteen years of exile for something he had never felt was wholly his fault.

If banishment from Immerland were not enough, he had also felt the continual antipathy of Sandihar through the endless stream of scouts who had invaded the mountains over the years, and through the armed confrontations with Immerland soldiers. It was true that some of these had been in response to food raids he had orchestrated on Immerland fields, but he knew that there was more behind the attacks than that. Now, he was going to face the king at a dinner table. Each would be without means of harming the other, and if his suspicions were true, they would be protected further by the Eladra.

He was quite sure that the two guards by the stream where they had entered Haniah's property must have been Eladrim warriors. Their dress and manner fit the descriptions he had heard, and they had spoken to him in the original language when he approached them. During the half-hour they had to wait until these guards let them pass, he had observed them carefully. They stood still as statues, with their swords crossed in front of them as if they were guarding the gate of the Infinite itself, and they were dressed in ancient warriors' armor.

Verclan had little personal knowledge of the Eladra. As did most people of his time, he knew the legends, but since they were just legends, he could not be sure what truth lay behind them. Even from what he did know, why would they be here *now*? In the legends, they showed up at significant times and places, usually when there was a great confluence of forces that punctuated a change in the course of Tessalindrian history. Perhaps it was just that such events were talked about and passed on, but still, in all his lifetime, except for the one occasion with the smith, he had never been aware of encountering an Eladrim being.

There was no turning back now, however. The small party behind him had passed through the last line of trees and had started up the gradual rise across the field. He could see Haniah's hut and now the table in front of it. It was a familiar scene. He and his family had often come here to visit Haniah and to get advice and medicinal remedies of various sorts for the mountain people. They often stayed and had a meal with Haniah. Her hospitality was contagious and hard to refuse. He knew today would be the same, and yet it would have to be different.

"No one else is here," remarked Mordara quietly. The words startled him. She was walking beside him, but he had been lost in his own thoughts.

"It seems curious, doesn't it?" Verclan's trained eye would have noticed any motion. In front of the hut, an old donkey grazed on the tufts of green grass interspersed between the sunburned late summer grass.

"There—on the other side of the field," said Patira, "just coming out of the trees..."

Verclan's eyes followed his son's finger. He could tell that they had also noticed him and his men. He had always found it curious that two people, at such great distances, could know that they were looking at each other. "I think that Sandihar is leading. That's the way he walks," he said. It was the same stride, with the slight hitch after each left step. The mild swaying at the shoulders and the long strides. How subtle it was, and yet how distinct.

"Are you ready for this?" Mordara squeezed his hand.

"I'm...I'm not sure there is any way to be ready, but I think I am." He looked at his wife as he spoke.

She smiled. "You have faced tougher men."

It would not be long before they would meet. What should he say? What should he do? They had been friends at one time, close friends, at least as close as a king and his best farrier could be, but Verclan felt the tug of a deeper kinship than even that would explain. There was so much to like about the king, and yet he had been forced all these years to regard him with a certain dislike. What was it? He also had many reasons to hate this man: his exile, the accusations of his killing Viarda, the distrust and attacks through the years, the hard life in the mountains, the near starvation every winter.

Yet he had received blessings that the king had never known: standing at the foot of Moruhura or watching the stars from the top of Mount Eliia in the Crown of Tessalindria...sitting around a fire with the mountain princes and hearing their songs and stories…tasting wild boar roasted on an open fire, served with the mangar roots, salt brush and mountain mead…and hearing the cacophonous migration of the orwilla in the spring.

Verclan probed feelings that he had hidden for years as he watched his…his…there was no word, no thought, no right impression that correctly categorized his relationship with the king. Soon they would meet, as men. Perhaps it was not necessary to name the relationship accurately. There was a task to be done, a discussion to be had, and a negotiation to be hammered out, perhaps like a horseshoe or a new wheel for a cart; a simple emotionless task finished by facts and reason. But perhaps it was a tortuous and slippery trail, full of emotion, missteps and pain. How could he tell? Mordara squeezed his hand again.

Both parties were twenty paces from the table when Haniah burst from her hut. Verclan was instantly distracted from the king by the explosion of energy. She ran to the table, grabbed something from it, and ran headlong toward Verclan. Without a word, she threw her arms around his neck and hugged him. Her weight nearly threw him off balance. She stepped back and slipped a wildflower garland around his neck and then just as quickly, turned and bolted toward the king, repeating the same ritual.

Verclan was not sure if this was some quirky strategy to break down the barriers, but it didn't matter. Haniah's energy, as she raced back to the table, drew the two parties toward one another like magnets. She stood at the table, beckoning both groups together. Verclan felt himself deciding to not hesitate, to not hold back, to make the most of this opportunity and he sensed the same in the king's eyes as they met.

Haniah grabbed his hand and the king's hand and put them together, holding both of their large hands cupped between her own. It was then that she spoke. "To the good Immerland King," she looked the king in the eye, "and the fair Mountain Prince." Verclan felt her eyes penetrating his soul. "Welcome to my table. May you sit in peace. May you eat in peace. May you leave in peace."

Verclan locked eyes with the king. "Greetings, good King Sandihar of Immerland."

The king stared back. "Greetings, fair Prince Verclan of the mountains," he said mechanically.

Haniah stepped between them and started seating the guests. Verclan counted the seats. She had set the table for nineteen: nine on each side and one at the end. "Master Verclan, shall sit in the middle on this side," she said, pointing to a specific chair, "and King Sandihar, there." The king was directly opposite him. "The fair Mordara, beside the king, on his left, Master Chronista on the other side—Master

Carnados, right here." She had her hands on the back of the chair to Verclan's right, "and Master Cordas, here." She stepped behind him, lightly touching the chair to his left. So it continued, until each person was seated beside two others who were sworn enemies. Haniah knew every name, even those whom Verclan was certain she had never met.

Verclan's single warrior and the king's dors were at the far end with a single, empty seat on each side at the end. When everyone was properly seated, she took her seat at the head of the table with Princess Vrengnia on her right and Patira on her left.

No one spoke, and Haniah made no effort to break the pall that seemed to be settling over the table. Verclan looked at the king. He stared back, and his eyes revealed how uncomfortable he was. It made Verclan want to laugh. He decided it would be inappropriate, but that decision was useless. It came up slowly, from somewhere down inside, like a volcano. The absurdity of the situation was overwhelming him from the inside out. He felt the smile come first, wriggling up the corners of his mouth until everything collapsed, and the laughter burst forth like water from a breached dam.

He saw the king turn red with anger as others began to snicker, cough and choke on their own laughter. They were all looking at their plates. The scene went from absurd to idiotic in seconds as everyone at the table gave up and joined in with him. Finally, the king himself, unable to contain it any longer, smiled, then laughed heartily.

Haniah stood up. "Drinks," she called above the din. Two young men and two young women came out of the hut with pitchers. "The finest wine for the mountain men—aged mountain cider for the Immerlanders—for the bold of heart, there is maclin." The conversation broke down into small chattering clusters as the flagons were filled, and they began to realize that those sitting to either side of them were just like them: insecure, prideful, resentful, but none with any reason behind the feelings save the feud between the kingdoms.

It was somewhere in the midst of all this that Verclan saw the smith and his son arrive, without fanfare or introductions, almost as if none were needed. They strode across the field and without hesitation seated themselves at the end of the table in the two empty seats. Verclan was relieved that they were there. He tried to guess what the king was thinking.

Verclan had once heard a wise man say that a party would last only as long as the food. If this were true, they were in for a long one. He wondered where Haniah had obtained the quantities and quality of food that poured out of the hut. There was every imaginable preparation of vegetables and herbed salads, subtle combinations of fruits and seeds, bowls of grain, flavored with ginger and thyme, and delicate meats, for those who chose them...prepared where? Haniah had a simple wood stove and very few of the utensils that would be necessary for such a preparation. Mountain men tasted the finest cuisine of the kingdom, while their neighbors tried the heartiest of mountain stew and bread.

Verclan, between mouthfuls of food and words with Carnados and Cordas, observed the servers. They were, tall, thin and quiet. They did their job with a peculiar efficiency without calling attention to themselves. Where had Haniah found them? How did she get them to come *here*?

He noticed that Patira and the princess were engaged in an animated discussion with Haniah most of the time. They looked very comfortable with each other. His advisors were relaxed, and he took note that his warrior made it a point to try everything on the table and made continual efforts to convince the king's dors to do the same.

The only one who looked unreasonably uncomfortable was the king's scout. He guessed that if a man's business was snooping around, looking for ways to get others in trouble, it must be miserable when those around him are enjoying themselves. The little man was seated between Patira and Omisar, dwarfed by their presence, and he fiddled with his food, glancing furtively around the table.

The king was affable, but preoccupied. Verclan felt it here and there in the words he chose and an occasional odd emphasis in his phrases, but it was not strong enough to be called resentful.

When dinner consumption began slowing down, the servers cleared the table for dessert. Verclan marveled again at their efficiency. When they arrived with dessert, it was altogether different than he expected. Pies! He had never seen pies served for dessert, and apparently, neither had the king or his party. They all glanced at each other and raised their eyebrows. Verclan looked at Haniah, and she smiled a knowing smile. The servers then cut the pies into pieces. To everyone's surprise, the pies had some sort of fruit in them! How strange. He had seen meat, egg and vegetable pies, but no one in their right mind would make a pie with fruit. The servers put the pie onto plates and distributed them around the table, a plate in front of each person.

Verclan could see that Haniah was amused. He looked at her. "What is it?"

Haniah laughed. "You all must try it. It may seem quite different, but I can assure you, it is rather good." She put her fork into it. As she lifted a bite to her mouth, her face lit into a smile of mock ecstasy as she tasted the dessert in front of eighteen pairs of curious eyes. "Ummmmmm," she intoned, closing her eyes to enjoy the first taste.

Everyone sat and stared. Verclan laughed again. With deliberate, exaggerated motion, he mimicked Haniah's tasting exhibition. The warm, spiced and sweetened fruit was a totally new and otherworldly taste that was hard to describe, but certainly pleasurable. He leaned back. "Ummmmmm." Then he charged his fork for another bite. He looked up. Everyone was staring. "Ho!" he laughed, "this is incredible," and he plunged his fork into the pie. "Everyone, you must try it!"

His warrior was next, followed by the king's dors, then the king himself. Everyone crowed with delight and marveled at the new idea of a *fruit* pie. The conversation resumed as they all finished their unusual dessert.

Then suddenly, there was a pause. Haniah rose. "And now good folks, we have come to the purpose of the meeting here." The servers whisked away the tableware and vanished into the hut while Haniah outlined the plan for the discussion between Verclan and the king.

fear cannot penetrate the armor of perfect love.

The Tessarandin, Book 6

VRENGNIA WATCHED THE TWO MEN CLOSELY AS HANIAH OUTLINED THE PLAN. There was a sparkle in Verclan's eyes and a flare of resentment in her father's. The two leaders were to remain where they were, and each was to select a single advisor to remain beside him. "The smith and I shall remain here to moderate the discussions. Everyone else must leave the table. You may go anywhere you would like, but you must not leave my property. I will blow a horn when we are ready to have you back."

Several men stood up, stretched, stared at one another, and tried to think of something to do. An uneasy silence settled over the group. They slowly gravitated into groups of two or three and wandered off.

Vrengnia looked across and down the table at her father. His eyes were empty and cold, and he was looking into nothingness. She got up and came around the table, approached him from behind and gave him a hug around the neck. She thought he might need it. He was tense and shrugged her away, gently, but coolly. It did not leave her with a good feeling about what was about to happen. She felt the fear rising from her belly, curling its way up into her chest. She had to stop it before it got to her head.

On the other side of the table, Patira and Paca had paired up and were heading south toward the stream. As she started around the table to head after them, she noticed Mordara sitting beside her husband, watching her. Vrengnia felt her eyes as she rose slowly and moved to intercept her. She glanced toward Paca and Patira, now twenty paces away and engaged in an intense conversation, then looked back to Mordara.

The beautiful Mordara, riding instructor to her mother and wife of the man her father had accused of murdering her mother, made her way around the end of the table. She moved with grace and purpose, never breaking eye contact until she stood directly in front of Vrengnia, where she dropped her eyes. With a brief bow, she spoke: "Fair Princess. May we speak?" It was said in a way that allowed no room for refusal and no time for hesitation.

"We may. Shall we walk?"

"Perhaps the herb garden would interest you?" Mordara's gentle statement folded into a question.

"Indeed, it would." As she turned to head toward the hut and the garden behind it, she glanced over her shoulder. Her father had chosen Dor Galar who was sitting beside him, but his eyes were following *her*. He gave her a questioning, angry look that implied that she was betraying him. She shrugged and turned away.

She also felt angry. It coiled up inside her like a snake and churned all through her. She was not sure what it was, or why it had to be this way or why her father could not see the opportunity that was before him.

"Are you all right?" Mordara's firm, confident voice broke the grip he had upon her.

"Yes—well, no, but thank you for asking."

Mordara raised her eyebrows.

"No, I'm really fine. It just my father—he—my father just doesn't get it." Her own voice surprised her with its vehemence.

"Get what?"

"It! The opportunity he has to get everything straightened out. He...he treats all this as...as a threat. I mean, what is he afraid of, really?"

Mordara remained silent. Vrengnia decided she had said enough. The snake was coiling and uncoiling in her belly. She had to trust that the smith knew what was going on. Of all the people in Tessalindria, Haniah and the smith would be her first choices to resolve this conflict, and both of them were there. She had to trust, had to wait. She turned to look back. Haniah was standing. Her father was leaning over the table, gesticulating at Verclan. It did not look good.

"I have wanted to meet you for a long time," said Mordara.

Vrengnia was thankful for the distraction. "I have wanted to meet you also, though I have only known about you for a short while."

"When Patira came home and told me that he had met you, my heart leapt for joy." Mordara's dark eyes sparkled. Her peculiar beauty was arresting to the eye. "I do not believe we were meant to be strangers. Now perhaps we do not have to be."

Vrengnia stared away to the mountains. "I hope so." She was puzzling her mind about why this near stranger seemed to be so easy to talk to. Mordara had gained her trust with the first words that she spoke. Perhaps it was because she was a woman in the company of so many men, but that could not possibly explain it all. Something about her manner and her unassuming openness drew Vrengnia in.

As they came around the corner of the hut to the edge of the extensive herb garden, Mordara asked, "Are you afraid, Vrengnia?"

Vrengnia was startled at the question. There it was again. It seemed that all the people who knew who they were in this world were concerned about fear in other people. The smith had told her not to fear several times. She thought she understood it in the context of their conversations, but it was completely unexpected from Mordara. "May I ask you a question about that?"

Mordara had knelt down to smell the orange-yellow blossoms of one of the herbaceous shrubs beside the path as they entered the garden. She looked up when Vrengnia spoke. "About what?"

"About fear. I mean…it seems that many people recently have been concerned about whether I was…or am, afraid. I don't *want* to be afraid. I'm often not sure if I am or not, but the way it is asked, it always seems to entail more than just being afraid. As if…as if there is some dimension of fear which I don't understand, that…oh, I don't know—"

Mordara was silent. She looked back at the blossoms and lowering her face into the bush, inhaled deeply, then standing, she faced Vrengnia. "Fear is a formidable enemy. Perhaps it is the greatest enemy of all, because when we fear, then the enemy is inside us. Everything else is outside, but fear eats us up on the inside and weakens us." Mordara's eyes sparkled as she spoke. "Fear destroys psadeq, with other beings and with Mah'Eladra."

"Why did you ask me if I was afraid just *now*?"

"There is much to be afraid of here," she said as she turned and stepped farther into the garden. "The king—your father—has much fear. It is in his eyes. It will interfere with his judgment and wisdom. If you are fearful, you face the same danger."

Vrengnia knew she was right but her rightness brought up another question: "Are *you* afraid?"

"I have chosen not to be."

"Just like that? You simply *choose*?"

"In essence, yes. One always makes a choice, but it is not simple. One has to learn how to choose and then it takes much strength."

"How did you learn?"

"From my husband, from Haniah, from the mountain people."

"And how did your husband learn?"

"The smith—when they were together in the…in your grandmother's stables."

It all came back to the smith. Vrengnia sensed that he was the focal point of all that was happening. "How would I learn?"

Mordara had knelt down beside a small clump of purple flowers growing close to the ground. "You are already learning. I can tell. Have you spoken much with the smith?"

"A couple times—"

"And Haniah?"

"Many times."

"*They* have been teaching you."

"But I don't remember them saying anything specific about fear—other than to not give in to it."

"Courage is not learned by teaching *about* fear. If you think back to conversations you have had with them, you will see common elements that, when grasped, teach us how to deal with fear."

Mordara stood up. She held a handful of the small purple flowers. "Smell this."

Vrengnia bent over and smelled the blossoms. It was a pungent, aromatic fragrance that made her nose tingle all the way back to where it met her throat. "What is it?"

"Faganwort. Its aroma heightens one's perceptions. The mountain warriors and trackers use it when they are on patrol to help stay focused on their surroundings."

As Vrengnia sniffed the small bouquet again, she felt the subtle effect of the smell. It engendered an awareness of detail that was stunning. She looked up at Mordara. New details of her facial features were suddenly visible: the glint of the mid-afternoon sun on her hair and the fine, faint lines of her face. She looked down. The garden sprang to life before her, and new scents and colors flooded over her as she stood still with wonder.

"Take these with you. They will help you not be afraid."

"How?"

"Awareness helps us control fear."

Mordara turned away and started down another row of herbs. Vrengnia remained where she was, clutching the small bouquet in her right hand. She thought she understood what Mordara had told her as she tried to think back over the conversations she had had with the smith and Haniah. They flooded together, indistinct and vague. She had never thought of them as teaching. Teaching was something that was done by "teachers."

It occurred to her quite suddenly that maybe real teaching was subtler, that all her life she had been taught indirectly by the people that surrounded her. Perhaps the teachers in her life, having lacked focus, plan and purpose, had left her as unpurposeful and unfocused as *they* were. Having now encountered several others who *did* have genuine depth and direction, the teaching, though still indirect, produced noticeable changes in her life. The thought was profound and new, and so different from the way she had always thought, that it was hard to place it and realize it.

She sighed heavily. Mordara turned to look at her and opened her mouth to speak. She was interrupted by the clear, resonant sound of a ram's horn, floating around the side of the hut from the direction of the meeting table. Mordara looked directly into her eyes. It was too soon. They could not have come to a resolution so quickly. The words sprang to Mordara's lips, "Something's wrong!"

Vrengnia felt Mordara slip her arm around her waist. "We ought to get back, Princess." Vrengnia thought she detected a slight tremor in her voice, but was not sure if it might be her own sudden distress. Mordara pulled her gently, and they started back to the table.

As they came around the corner of Haniah's hut, Vrengnia sensed what had happened. Haniah, the smith, Dor Galar and the king were all standing. Verclan remained seated at the table with Chronista, his fingertips pressed together and his mind deep in thought.

65

*Oh, the surprise, the wonder, when one
we consider to be but a beast, speaks to us
with wisdom beyond our own.*

*Mortag of Horrinaine
Of Beings*

PATIRA WAS RUNNING IN FRONT OF HIM AND WAS ALMOST TO THE TABLE, AS were several of the other men. He was approaching the table from his father's end so he could not see his expression, but Haniah's face was stern and tight. Verclan was still seated. The king's eyes were stormy and dark, and a deep anger loomed there. Paca did not know the king well, but one does not always need to know a man to recognize the distortion of hate in his face.

They were all waiting, but for what? They could have been statues. The king's advisors were the last to arrive around the table, sweating and breathing hard and looking as if they were cramping in their stomachs.

Haniah stood up a little straighter and motioned for silence. It seemed to Paca that the whole world held its breath in anticipation for what she was about to say. "Good men and women," she began. Paca could not say he knew this woman very well, but the tone and intensity carried a formality that was out of character for all he knew of her. "The King of Immerland has challenged the Mountain Prince to a contest of Kli-marana Waru." The king's advisors gasped and shook their heads, but no word was spoken. "The Mountain Prince has accepted the challenge." There was a stunned silence. Paca looked at his father who looked back at him. There was a grim darkness in his face that Paca had never seen. How did this happen? He turned to Vrengnia. She was terrified, but seemed to have no inkling of the significance of the statement.

Haniah continued, "The Immerland King has chosen his daughter, Vrengnia, as his second. The Mountain Prince has chosen his son, Patira."

The various pockets of men began to stir and look at one another. Whether they were just stunned or ignorant of what was happening, Paca could not tell, but no one spoke aloud.

"Stupid, foolish king!" The voice was nasal and rolling, possessing a kind of staccato tremor as it rolled over the crowd. It was the original language, but everyone around the table understood it. Paca could tell by the looks on their faces.

The king's face flashed crimson as he slammed his fist to the table. "Who said that?"

"It is I," the voice continued as the old gray donkey nosed her way into the circle of bewildered onlookers. Paca gasped. Vrengnia threw her hands to her mouth. "Meshabo!" she whispered. Paca looked at his father again, and thought he saw the hint of a smile. He looked back to the king. The redness of his face had been replaced by an ashen white, and his jaw hung loosely. It was obvious that he did not want to believe what was happening.

"What you are doing...is one of the stupider things...that I have *ever*...seen a being do," continued the donkey. Everyone stared.

The king was being insulted. It was his responsibility to defend himself, no matter how surreal the situation. "I will not be told by a dumb animal that I am stupid!" he thundered, some color returning to face. By this time, Meshabo was standing nearly beside Verclan facing the king across the table. Verclan was studying the king.

"I am obviously not dumb," said Meshabo. There were snickers in the circle somewhere, but it was hard to tell where. "If you meant a 'stupid' animal...then I should ask you...a question: Who is stupider...the man who lays down a challenge...that leads to his own death...or the animal who tells him...that what he is doing is stupid?" Meshabo had to pause and breathe frequently. The nasal voice fluctuated up and down as she spoke. Between the original language and the strange intonations of a donkey's voice, it should have been hard to understand, but it wasn't. Meshabo waited patiently for the king to respond, flicking a fly off her back with her tail, and twitching her ears slightly. She was looking straight at the king.

"How would you know the details of this situation—to pass judgment on my actions?" the king snarled.

Meshabo remained impassive and aggressive. It was hard to tell what she was thinking. All the usual body language that accompanied human discussions was foreign; there were few facial expressions. "I passed judgment on you...the day you pushed your wife...causing her death."

The king looked around the circle hastily. Paca guessed he was assessing the damage done by that statement. No one moved. Each person was watching Meshabo. The donkey continued: "I was there...a young foal...you blamed Verclan...you have continued to do so..."

"Stop!" snarled the king.

Meshabo was undaunted. "Your self-deceit has…fed on itself for years…now it destroys you…it is arrogant…as well as stupid…Klimarana Waru?" She spat on the ground, stamped on it with her left front hoof and turned away from the king, making her way casually out of the circle, suddenly just a donkey again.

Everyone stared at the king. Paca felt his predicament. Probably everyone else did also. It was one of those moments when history hangs in the balance, history that would be defined by the next decision, the next words proceeding from one man's mouth.

"The challenge remains!" declared the king.

A murmur rippled through the circle, Verclan shook his head and looked at the king in disbelief. Haniah sat down suddenly. It was then that the smith spoke: "The challengers will retire with their seconds to prepare for the contest. We will meet here again in one hour."

It was then that Paca noticed Mordara. She was standing behind her husband, with both hands resting on his shoulders. As Verclan rose, he turned to face her, and she followed his eyes as their level rose above hers, until she was looking up into them. He bent forward and kissed her, and she threw her arms around him putting her chin over one of his shoulders. She was looking at the sky as a single tear rolled down from the corner of her eye. Paca looked down. He knew that even in the midst of all the other people this was a private moment.

A deep anger rose inside him toward the king, whose selfish pride was the cornerstone of Mordara's sorrow and the source of such conflict that divided relationships and rent the fabric of psadeq in so many directions all at once.

Vrengnia stood not five feet from Paca. Her eyes were full of tears and questions. It was obvious she had no idea what was about to happen. He stepped toward her and hugged her around the shoulders, leaning over to whisper in her ear. "You must not fear. Listen to the El in you." He was not sure why he said it. The sound of it wasn't even right. It was hollow and weak, pathetically inadequate to the situation.

She turned to look at him, wiping the tears back, with her fingers. "Thank you," she said genuinely. She broke away from him and headed off to join the entourage of her father's men heading back to where they had entered Haniah's land.

Verclan's men were filing off in the opposite direction. Paca watched, hoping to catch Patira's eye, even for a moment. They were about twenty paces away when Patira looked back. Their eyes met before he turned away. Paca kept watching, but Patira did not look back again.

66

History's threads are spun by those who value the greater needs of civilization over their own.

Mindar Colloden
The Great Fathers

THE SMALL PROCESSION WAS SILENT AS THEY TRAVERSED THE GROUND BACK TO the stream where they had left their weapons with the guards. Each seemed preoccupied with his own thoughts, fears, guilt and perhaps anger. Patira was simply wondering what was happening. He knew there had to be a time to ask, but this was not the time. He also wondered what his mother was thinking. Surely, she had not prepared for what was developing around her.

When they arrived at the stream, the guards were standing under a large tree. None of the rest of the party was around, having scattered into the woods when his father and those accompanying him had left for Haniah's field earlier. His father whistled and two warriors leapt out of the woods. "Set the scouts free. Strip them and send them back to the castle." His words were short and without feeling. All his emotional energy was concentrated somewhere else.

Now was the time. "What is Kli-marana Waru? And what does it mean—that I am your second?"

His mother was helping his father as he adjusted his war belt about his waist. "Kli-marana Waru was Mankar's cunning method of enticing his enemies to challenge his leadership. He invented it during The Grayness. His enemies were so terrified of his army and his power, that he established it as a way to engage his enemies in one-on-one combat with him."

Patira felt his skin crawl across his arms and up onto his shoulders.

"It's very simple, really," his father continued. "A man challenges another. Whoever wins the contest is heir to all the other's dominion and authority."

"What happens to the loser?"

Verclan looked him straight in the eyes and stopped adjusting his belt. "It's a fight to death." He looked away and continued his adjustments. Patira looked over his father's shoulder at his mother. She looked back at him, her eyes full of life and determination.

"And the seconds?"

Verclan laughed angrily. "No one dared challenge Mankar alone. He established seconds to make it seem a more fair fight." His eyes glittered cruelly as he spoke. Patira had never seen this side of his father.

"How does it work, then—these seconds?"

"You stand to the side. If I get in trouble and call for seconds, you come and join the fight."

"I fight to the death also?!"

"Yes." His father was grim and matter of fact. "But only if you are needed."

"And I could end up fighting against *Vrengnia*?"

"If it goes that far...you could."

Patira felt the anger rising within him. "Why did you agree to this? Could you not have just left? The king has no authority over you." Was his father, after all, as stubborn and stupid as the king?

Verclan looked up into his eyes. There was a new softness. "Patira," he said slowly, "for nearly eighteen years I have been exiled from my homeland by an irrational man who has no intention of seeking peace, at any price. You saw what happened with the donkey, did you not?"

Patira nodded and looked down. "It is time to put an end to this tyranny. It became clear that, even given the opportunity to change, the king will not rest until he has killed me, and he will continue to drag others into his misery until it is settled. If I kill him, then I inherit Immerland as the new king."

Something was not making sense to Patira. "You are a much better fighter than the king. He must know that. Why would he challenge you to a one-on-one contest? And choosing the princess as his second...it doesn't make sense."

His father continued his adjustments and took his time with his answer. "The princess is well trained, but I have the same questions," he said at length. "Either the king is so consumed with fear and jealousy that he is lacking sound judgment, or there is some treachery involved. I think this is the key." His hand moved quickly and the sataliin suddenly appeared between them.

"What...how?"

"I don't know, but now is not the time to fear."

"What if the king kills you *and* me?"

"Then the king will inherit the mountain kingdoms and they will become part of Immerland." His father read his fear and spoke before he had time. "Isn't this what we wanted anyway, to be accepted into Immerland, to be able to trade freely, to travel freely, to share in the crops?"

Patira, though not wanting to fear, could feel it inside him.

"Put on your weapons, Patira. Inevitability stalks us. We must be ready."

"But won't there be further vengeance by the king on the mountain clans and princes?"

"I don't intend to lose. But if I do—and you do—then I think that the king will be satisfied. He hates me, not the mountain clans, nor the princes. If he wins, a peaceful accord will follow quickly."

The picture was clearing now. His father was willing to sacrifice himself if necessary, realizing that the king's antipathy was leveled only at him, but he was not willing to do it without a fight. The king's invitation for the one-on-one contest afforded his father the arena to finish the antagonism, one way or the other.

"How is it that I have never heard of Kli-marana Waru before?"

"It was forbidden as a practice when Mankar was finally defeated. It was seen as shameless arrogance."

"So how can the king invoke it now?"

"He is the *king*. The fact that he invokes this barbaric practice is testimony to his arrogance. It was believed that Mankar's sword gave him much of his power. When his sword was stolen, he was so arrogant, that he believed he could still conquer without it. Some believe that he was finally defeated in his own contest, though no one is sure." His voice trailed off. He lifted the sataliin again and examined it closely. Patira saw his eyes narrow.

"What is it, Father?"

"Get dressed. You have to be ready. There is more to this than we can see. Come, we have very little time."

Patira adjusted his belt and checked his armor as his father explained the consequences of this contest to the mountain princes. His mother stood behind him, unmoving, looking up at the sky through the trees. The princes were angry, but understanding of the situation. They wanted to help, to be part of the fight, part of the resolution, but his father made it clear that they were forbidden. They would have to stand and watch. They wept and hugged Verclan and Patira. Patira knew their love and respect. He wished he had their strength of character. He was not sure he did. Everything was uncertain, except his father: determined, bold and unwavering, he held them all together. With great spirit and resolve, he led the small procession across the stream back toward—what?

The Eladrim guards watched keenly, but made no move to interfere.

67

He who strikes by the sword, seeks his own death by the sword strike of another.

Hispattea
The Essences of Corritanean Wisdom

A LARGE CIRCLE, PERHAPS FIFTEEN PACES IN DIAMETER, HAD BEEN DRAWN IN the soft soil of the field. Paca had helped his father draw it. They had talked briefly while they worked with two hoes that Haniah had brought to create the slight break in the sod that formed the perimeter. His father had explained the rules. They were simple, and it only took a few sentences. Paca perceived that he did not want to talk very much. He was preoccupied with something other than the upcoming contest. Paca sensed that he accepted the turn of events with little fear, but there was something else. Haniah had disappeared into her hut while they were outlining the contest field. Paca assumed she was continuing to clean up after the dinner. When they were almost finished, she came running out and ran up to his father. After a hurried and carefully guarded conversation, she disappeared into the hut again.

His father strode up to him. "No matter what happens, do not interfere."

"Why would I?"

His father laid his left hand on his shoulder and spoke gently. "A trial like this is not just a test for the contestants; it is a test for every observer as well. The penalty of interference by a non-contestant is death. There is no second chance. Now, take your place on the circle."

"I understand." Paca guessed that his father knew something else, but it was not time to ask about it.

The two parties were nearly to the circle by this time. Paca made his way to the side where the sun was at his back so he would be able to see everything more clearly. His father stood in the middle, impassive and waiting. Two Eladrim guards, quiet and austere, followed each of the small bands.

It was then that Paca first noticed the dark clouds moving in from the east. They hung low and towered in huge billows, rolling over one another as they made their way toward them. In the distance, they seemed to be moving slowly, but Paca knew they were coming fast. It would be a matter of only half an hour before they would be overhead. He looked anxiously back toward the makeshift arena before him.

The thin circle of turned soil posed a clear barrier that no one crossed as they filed quietly around its perimeter. The Eladra took stations equally spaced to the north, south, east and west around the circle. Vishtorath fell in beside Paca. They stood attentively, feet spread apart to the width of their shoulders and the tips of their swords resting casually on the ground between them. Paca noticed that they were all left-handed.

Haniah had returned. She stood on the opposite side of the circle beside Mordara. Aside from the princess, they were the only other women, but that was not the thing that caught Paca's attention. Haniah's eyes sparkled with a bright eagerness. In anyone else, he would have assumed it to be bloodlust in anticipation of the carnage that would soon happen in the circle, but with Haniah, there was something different. Perhaps she knew the outcome. Perhaps either way, there would be a settling of accounts. Paca found himself staring at her, not wanting to look away.

His father moved, waving to the king and to Verclan, ushering them into the circle. He gestured to Vrengnia and Patira, inviting them in also. Paca glanced at Vrengnia and waited until she looked back at him. Her expression was blank. He was not sure whether it was terror or bewilderment. She did not acknowledge his eyes as she looked quickly back into the circle.

She was dressed for fighting. A light helmet covered the top of her head and ears from glancing blows, but a direct hit would probably be lethal. She had put on a light chain mail shirt, covering both arms and her torso almost down to her thighs, which were protected by leggings with small steel disks on the sides and front, and with plated foot guards. Fine mail gauntlets covered the outside of her hands and wrists, leaving her palms free to grasp her sword, which she held in her right hand.

The sword! Paca could see every detail and it burned into his memory. The matte finish glowed in the low afternoon sun as she stood rigidly watching her father. How did she have her sword? Paca was sure that she would not have brought it herself. He guessed that her father, in his schemes against Verclan, must have brought it without her knowledge.

Her father was dressed similarly, but his armor was heavier, designed to take a more substantial impact, and he carried a small shield on his left arm. He seemed large, standing in front of her. His sword, held tightly in his right hand, gleamed dully.

Verclan and Patira were clad more lightly. Their armor was dark plates of steel strategically sown onto snug leather clothing, designed for flexibility and silence. They were the color of the soil from head to foot. Their swords were shorter but had both edges sharpened until they gleamed. As they hung in their hands, their tips came only midway between their ankles and their knees. Each wore a leather helmet, with steel straps over the top and ears, with a fine weave of leather and steel rings hanging down behind their necks. Their feet were unprotected except for the dark leather moccasins laced up over their ankles. Their grim faces focused on the challenge ahead of them.

Without a word, Paca's father stepped back from the center of the circle until he was standing outside with the rest of the onlookers. Verclan and the king advanced until they were about three paces apart and stopped, eyeing each other carefully. Paca could tell the king was tense; Verclan was relaxed, but aware; each was ready to move—to respond to the slightest hint of an attack from the other. The gray boiling clouds moving fast from the east and the brilliance of the scene before him, fully illuminated by the sun behind him, created a surreal image he would never forget.

They circled slowly—carefully. Paca looked again at Haniah; her light hair shone and the same peculiar sparkle still read in her eyes. They were fixed on Verclan. Vrengnia was as still as stone. She was rigid and vertical, like the statue of a queen, captured forever by a gracious sculptor. Patira stood like a cat ready to spring, his sword was ready. Everyone was silent and still, waiting…waiting.

The king lunged forward. His sword swept the air. Verclan dropped like a stone and the sword sang over his head. Paca was startled by the sound. A gasp followed the otherworldly whistle-singing of the blade. Vishtorath raised his sword suddenly and then stopped. Verclan had rolled to his left and was up on his feet almost instantly. Paca saw the king sneer. The secret was out. The sound of the sword had had its effect, and Verclan's eyes narrowed as he stepped back.

As the king lunged forward again, Verclan slid to the left. The king slashed the air with the sword, three times, back and forth; it was not a strike at his enemy, but merely for the effect of the sound. Verclan stepped back again. He seemed to know that the danger was greater than he had anticipated.

The king thrust forward again, but where he should have struck Verclan's body, there was only air. Verclan's sword swept in, and the king barely had time to raise his shield to meet the blow. They separated and circled. The king's sword sang again. Verclan raised his weapon to challenge it and the two swords collided. There was a bright flash and a gasp from the observers as Verclan's sword was severed, a third of its length remaining with the hilt. He wasted no time and dropped the useless piece as he stood facing the king.

Paca stood horrified. The weapon he had crafted, that he had shaped and hardened, moved at the whim of a determined killer. His hands went to his face. The horror of the moment sank into his heart like a stone. He looked again as the king pressed his advantage with a smile full of malice. "Ha!" he shouted. Paca felt the impact of the evil intent like an arrow through his liver. He wanted to cover his face again but could not. Verclan backed up empty handed. *Call for seconds. Call for your seconds,* Paca's mind yelled, but the words never came. Patira waited. Paca wondered what he must be thinking, feeling.

The king lunged and swung. Verclan ducked and rolled toward the king and came up just in front of him. His hand flashed and a fist full of dirt flew in the king's face. The sword sang, but Verclan was not where the king thought he should be. The king could not see. He cursed and struck blindly. Verclan ducked and rolled away. As he stood up again to face the king, he held a strange piece in his right hand. Where had it come from? Paca's mind was racing. He had never seen anything like it. It was short and broad, like a fan. The king had wiped the dirt from his eyes, and the two stood facing one another again.

Both were breathing heavily, the king worse than Verclan, and there was a fury in his eyes. He stepped forward and swung his sword with both hands. What happened next was so unexpected that Paca was never sure exactly what he saw. Instead of ducking, Verclan seemed to step into the path of the sword; there was a clash, a bright flash, and Verclan's left fist smashed into the nose plate on the king's helmet. The sword flew from the king's hand and did a strange dance in the air. He staggered backwards. "Seconds!" he roared as Verclan stepped toward the king, the sword swinging from the device in his hand. With a quick thrust and a strange twist of his wrist, Verclan sent the tip of the sword slicing through the chain mail of the king's right shoulder with a flash and a puff of yellow smoke.

It was then that Paca saw the princess. The king's sword had fallen to the ground, and the king was on his back. Verclan was reaching for the sword when the princess arrived. She swung mightily and Verclan rolled. The sword's song was fiercer than that of the king's. The blade hit the ground where Verclan had been. It flashed yellow, and smoke burst forth from the explosion. Verclan leapt to his feet, the strange tool still in his right hand, waiting for the princess's attack. She was undaunted. Stepping over her father, she swung her sword down. Verclan raised his weapon, and the princess's sword met it on the way down. There was a flash and a yelp of pain as the blade swept through, severing the steel like celery and slicing off half of Verclan's hand. Verclan dropped and rolled back. Somewhere in the middle of the roll there was a muffled yell. "Seconds!"

Patira lunged into the battle. He came in from the side, moving fast. The princess turned and Paca could see her eyes. They flashed and danced, strangely drunk with the passion of battle. Patira brought his sword down with all his might. The princess stepped nimbly to the side and swung her sword in horizontally to meet Patira's chop. Her sword caught the tip of his. With an ear splitting squeal, her blade ran the length of his, splitting it in half on its journey toward Patira's belly. There was another bright flash as her sword stopped against Patira's hilt guard.

Paca held his breath. Everything had stopped except the clouds that boiled high above them, defying the sun, their dark shadow crawling across the mountains. The king lay on the ground on his back unmoving. Verclan was sprawled face down and bleeding from his right wrist. Patira stood beside the princess, both of them frozen for that instant as the reality of what was happening struck them. It seemed like an hour. It was probably less than a second.

The princess looked into Patira's eyes and he into hers. A tear ran down her cheek. "No!" she said with a firm tenderness. "No, no, no!" she sobbed. She yanked the sword out of the cleft in Patira's blade and turned toward her father on the ground. He was two steps away. She took one step, and in a sudden mighty effort plunged the blade into the ground. There was another flash, a shower of sparks and smoke, and she leapt to her father's side. When the smoke cleared, only the hilt of the sword remained above the ground.

Patira stepped back. He looked bewildered and not sure what he should do. He dropped his useless sword and ran to his father. "Father—Father!" he shouted, rolling the fallen prince onto his back. It must have been in about the same instant that the king and Verclan both opened their eyes. Vrengnia and Patira both shouted. "Help, somebody help." Paca stepped forward involuntarily. A huge fist crashed into his stomach, knocking the wind out of him. He remembered little else, other than being dragged out of the circle by Vishtorath and left to recover on his own outside the circle, flat on his back, as the clouds occluded the blue sky above him.

The sword of malice makes a deep wound.
Old Tessamandrian Saying

S HE SAW HIM OPEN HIS EYES. SHE SAW THE PAIN. "HELP, SOMEBODY HELP!"
Her father's words were distant and hollow. She thought she heard
someone else saying the same thing. He tried to speak again, but there
was no sound. Vrengnia leaned forward to hear him better.

He could barely manage a hoarse whisper. "It's cold…so cold," he
gasped. The wound seemed to be superficial where the sword had sliced
the mail and cut a swath perhaps an inch deep across the front of his
left shoulder, but the pain was overwhelming him. "It's cold," he gasped
again and shuddered.

A large hand took her hand. She looked up. It was the smith. She
looked into his eyes through her tears. *"You must be brave. Do not fear,"*
he said; his lips never moved. He reached down gently. Everything was
in slow motion. He removed the king's helmet carefully. The king
gasped again. When he saw the smith, he tried to lift his head, but it fell
back, exhausted. "You!" he whispered, "…cold."

Vrengnia heard but did not understand, "Why is he cold?" she
sobbed. "What is wrong?" She looked hopefully at the smith.

"He has tasted the blade forged for his own death." He spoke again with
his eyes. "There is nothing else that can be done," he said aloud. "Stay
with him. He needs you now." The smith rose. The sword—why had her
father brought his sword? Why had he brought *her* sword? She had left
it behind on purpose. The irony of the scene before her wrapped its
arms tightly around her chest, making it hard to breathe.

Vrengnia grabbed the smith's right hand. "Get Haniah, she can
help—" He looked into her eyes again and stroked her head with his left
hand. "No, Haniah cannot help. You must be brave. You must let him
know you love him." He pulled his hand free. Vrengnia watched him
stand; then she collapsed onto her father's chest. "Father…Father…"
Everything else was just a blur as a grave darkness settled in around them.

The darkness of death brings many things to light.

Oratanga
Passages

VERCLAN COULD FEEL THE COLD CREEPING UP HIS ARM. HE HAD NEVER FELT anything like it before. It was not just the cold; it was a strange brightness that was creating the shadows all around him. He could hear Patira. "Help, somebody help!" But no one came. Somehow, he knew no one would. They couldn't. There was no help. It must have been that sword. It sliced right through the sataliin; right through his hand, he thought, but now it was all cold and an intense light shone so brightly it nearly blinded him. "Don't shake me, Patira," he tried to whisper, but he was not sure the words made it out.

Another shadow. The smith? My friend? My enemy, perhaps? Who are you anyway? Why did you do this to me?

"Tell Mother I love her. Your sisters…tell them to be strong." *Did Patira hear me? Did I even say it?* "Please let me know that all this has been worth it." *Where are you carrying me? What is happening?*

Verclan was alone with his thoughts, when suddenly the cold receded slightly. The brightness abated, and he felt someone holding his left hand. It was a firm strong grip. He tried to move his head—had to move his head. Who was it? He screamed inside and with everything he had, swung his head to the left to look. He saw the king. "No!" Panic surged through him.

"I am…sorry…I am sorry…my friend." The voice of the king came out of the brightness. He struggled to open his eyes. He could barely see in the brilliance. The king was looking at him. "I am sorry…so sorry."

Verclan knew that it was genuine. He moved his mouth to speak. Nothing happened. He must speak now. Everything he had, everything. "I am sorry…too."

There was a sudden clatter of hoofbeats. A shadow darkened what was left of the sun for a brief moment, and his sight faded into the all-encompassing light. He heard Patira calling and weeping. He felt Patira's hand, but it was far away.

70

The specter of an evil past continually haunts the future.

Mindar Colloden
The Great Fathers

H E WOULD HAVE CONSIDERED HIMSELF A SKEPTIC IF ANYONE HAD EVER cared to ask. No one had, so Carnados had never had to explain where he stood on all the questions that suddenly confronted him. The king sought his advice, but seldom listened and never, ever asked his personal opinion. It was only about facts, and it always was centered on the king's immediate situation.

The line between the facts, as he knew them, and these new realities was suddenly blurred. He had seen things today that he had only heard of in ancient legends, hardly a reliable source of truth. Starting with the guards at the trailhead, the donkey who had confronted the king, the terrible power of the king's and princess's swords—the "facts" stood on shaky ground.

Both the king and Verclan were close to death. The four soldiers, who had appeared to be guardians of the contest ring, had carried them to the edge of the ring. The princess was weeping over her father, and Verclan's son held his father's head, gently stroking his hair. Haniah stood behind both of them, her face buried in her left hand. She too, was weeping. She held Mordara's hand, whose face was turned toward the sky as tears streamed down her cheeks.

Dark clouds were sweeping over them, heading west on a collision course with the sun, but there was still no breath of wind on the ground. Carnados looked up anxiously when the first thunder cascaded down from the mountains across the fields of Immerland. Was all this significant? He was not sure.

The smith was in charge. He had attended to both injured warriors and seemed to command the guardians. He stood in the ring, having picked up the king's sword. As he stooped to pull the princess's sword out of the ground, there was a commotion outside the circle, and the donkey that had confronted the king burst through the outer ring, galloping toward the smith. She stopped abruptly. There was a hurried exchange in the original language that Carnados did not understand. The smith's face turned dark as the donkey galloped out of the ring on the opposite side from where she had entered.

For all the strange events of the day that Carnados was grappling with, the next sequence of events was stranger and more unreal.

The smith bent down suddenly and grabbed the handle of the princess's sword. He pulled it from the ground with his left hand, and the blade sizzled and smoked as it yielded to his hand. He stood up and took several strides in the direction of Haniah's hut and stopped, still in the circle. The onlookers, sensing that something else was about to happen, parted, leaving the path open between the smith and the hut.

The smith looked up and raised both swords to the dark sky, his back to the brilliant sun that still flooded the contest field.

"*Hirath ala rama din kala*
Pira holl om kirath dalu
Pissha, dala, omrath mala or
Mahan Kli-marana Waru!"

It rolled off his tongue and a clap of thunder from somewhere behind Haniah's hut punctuated the last words. The smith lowered the swords, crossing them in front of him as he spread his feet apart. Carnados had no clue what he had said except for the final phrase. There was a stir in the hut in response to them; then everything was silent for perhaps ten seconds as the smith and the onlookers surrounding him stood motionless. The brief stillness was interrupted by the first gust of wind from the clouds overhead as it rippled over the field, approaching from the east as the clouds had.

As it passed over Haniah's hut, the front wall of the hut vanished. Carnados was not sure that was the proper description of what happened. It appeared to melt; perhaps it exploded into dust or smoke, but suddenly it was not there. The cloud of dust, carried by the wind, swept across the circle. Seven men strode out of the hut into the sunlight, each dressed as an ancient warrior, and each brandishing a sword. One man was larger than the others, and he walked in front of the advancing line. The four guardians stepped into the ring behind the smith as the others approached.

The six warriors from the hut stopped suddenly as the leader continued to advance. His countenance was fearsome and his face was grim. He stopped two paces from the smith and smiled. Carnados watched; he was not sure it was a smile; one might rightly call it a sneer—a fierce, mocking sneer. "Ahhhh…the young son of Valraddica, the smith! We meet at last. Surely it was not you who challenged me just now in Kli-marana Waru?" His eyes flickered. The warriors behind him laughed.

"It was I," declared the smith grimly.

"Look here...what is your name, by the way?"

"My name does not matter. You will learn it at the proper time."

A suspicious look flitted across the warrior's face and then was gone. "No," he laughed, "I suppose it really doesn't matter, *does* it?" He chuckled and the others laughed again. "But look here, little man, do you see this sword? Do you recognize it?"

The smith did not move. "I do. My father made it."

The leader looked back over his shoulder with a cruel smile and laughed. "His *father* made it." The six warriors laughed again. He turned back to the smith. "How nice," he said sarcastically as he examined the sword's edge up close.

Carnados looked around. The onlookers around the circle had drawn back. They remained silent as the smith stood steadfast in the face of the leering warrior. The four guardians stood behind the smith, impassive and ready.

The big warrior continued his taunting. "Do you realize how long I have been looking for this? I mean, it was the best sword I ever had. Whoever stole it, well—never mind. But listen little man, you must know that you cannot stand against it. Yet you challenge me in Waru?"

"I do," said the smith.

The warrior's face darkened. Apparently, his taunting was not having the desired effect on the smith. "And these little swords you hold, did you make them?"

"No, my son made them."

"Your son?" The warrior leaned back in mock laughter. "How cute." The other warriors laughed. He looked back at the smith and smiled cruelly. "You will need them both if you intend—"

"NarEladra Mankar," interrupted the smith, "do you accept my challenge?"

Mankar? Carnados stepped back involuntarily. How could this be? A ripple of whispers ran through the onlookers around the circle.

Mankar studied the smith, still sneering. "And what are the stakes?"

"If I am victorious, I will have your sword, and the swords of your generals. If you conquer me, you will have the throne—and Immerland."

Out of the corner of his eye, Carnados saw a sudden movement as Vrengnia stood up. "Immerland is not yours to wager," she said angrily.

The smith continued, his eyes fastened on Mankar, "Vrengnia, Queen of Immerland, is my second."

Mankar turned and looked at Vrengnia. "The Queen of Immerland, you say?—I would rather have her." He laughed and took a step in the direction of Vrengnia.

The smith's blade flashed in front of him as a warning to stop. "You will have nothing unless you kill me first. Do you accept my challenge?"

Mankar turned to his men and made an obscene mocking gesture. They laughed uproariously and he turned back to the smith. "Look, little man, if you consider your life to be of so little value..."

"I consider my life to be of great value," interrupted the smith evenly. "Do you accept my challenge?"

"With pleasure. I'll even let you keep both your swords." Mankar bowed mockingly to the smith. "When do we start?"

"We start when your generals lay down their swords, you select a second, and step into this circle." The smith never took his eyes off the warrior. Carnados looked at the princess. She stood about five paces behind the smith, straight and tall. The anger had left her eyes, and a deep calm seemed to have settled across her entire being. She looked like a queen.

"Omberon!" Mankar barked over his shoulder. Looking back at the smith but still speaking to his general, he said, "You will be my second. We must hand this impudent little man over to his oblivion."

Omberon stepped up behind him; that crooked smile curled across his lips. Another ripple of voices cascaded over the edge of the crowd.

Carnados squinted to see better. He felt a choking anger rising in him. His emotions raged, *Traitor!*...but self-discipline arrested his tongue.

The smith stepped back into the center of the circle. "Have the swords thrown into the circle. Vishtorath!" he called over his shoulder. "Give the queen a sword."

Vishtorath walked over to Vrengnia and bowed, handing her his sword. Vrengnia bowed back and accepted the sword with grace and appreciation, spoken without words.

71

Transcendent strength is found in perseverance in the unfinished task.

Karendo Marha
Journey to the Infinite

S HE TOOK THE SWORD WITHOUT A WORD. WORDS SEEMED USELESS TO HER right now. Her father lay dying and deep within her, she knew that whatever was happening in front of her was connected to his death; that somehow, the smith's challenge was still key to whatever remained of her father's life. She lifted the sword. Despite its size, it was light and well balanced. She felt it holding her hand.

The smith had backed up beside her, while Mankar conferred quietly with Omberon. The smith turned to her. She knew he would have put his hand on her shoulder, but both hands held swords. He looked her in the eye. "You know, don't you?"

She nodded. Omberon's betrayal weighed heavily, casting a pall of anger on top of a weight that she was already not sure she could bear.

"Do not fear and do not hate. There is a time and a place for both, but this is neither that time nor that place. You will not have to fight, but you must be brave for my sake."

She looked into his eyes and nodded again. A strange strength flowed out of their depths and flooded her. The smith looked back toward his adversaries and she followed his eyes. Mankar and Omberon were both in the circle now. The generals had thrown their swords to the ground inside the circle as the smith had requested, and they stood in a line along its perimeter with their backs to the hut. Everyone else had withdrawn from them. Vrengnia studied these strange warriors. Wherever there was power, evil men could be found trying to take it and use it. She had seen evil men, but she had never seen the evil so concentrated. She wasn't truly "seeing" it, but she could sense it; a sort of sixth sense she had never been aware of was suddenly awake, and the presence of these warriors made it as real as her sense of touch and smell. It was so new there were no words to describe the sensation:

acrid, bitter, lonely, empty, black—all came to mind, but none of them fit exactly. They were standing in full sunlight, but even the brightness of the sun was dimmed as it reflected off their faces and armor. They looked more like the clouds behind them than the sun.

Now she waited, watching Mankar and the smith. They were circling slowly, just as her father and Verclan had circled. Mankar struck first. His sword shrieked as it cleft the air toward the smith. The smith feinted slightly, and the sword swept over his head and shoulder without contact. The sword in the smith's right hand flashed, with a lightning quick flick of his wrist, catching a corner of Mankar's gantlet and severing it from his arm.

The smith stood still. Mankar snarled. He wasn't hurt, except perhaps his pride, but it made him angry. The smith waited.

Mankar lunged again, a straight thrust. The smith moved so that the thrust passed his right side, deftly glancing it away with the sword in his right hand. There was a shower of sparks as the blades screeched by one another. The sword in his left hand flashed, and a piece of Mankar's shoulder epaulette fell to the ground smoking. Bare skin showed itself.

Someone laughed; it was distant and hollow, and the princess could not tell who it was. She dared not look; she knew she had to concentrate. Mankar's eyes narrowed as he and the smith continued to circle. "Well, little man...you have been taught well...." He lunged again, slicing downward with his sword. It sang on the way down, and there was an explosion as the sword in the smith's right hand came up and met the full force of the descending blow. The smith's sword shattered in his hand and pieces flew in several directions. Her father's new sword was no more, and the smith dropped the smoldering, useless stump to the ground. Mankar laughed cruelly. His generals cheered.

She never saw how the smith got the strange tool, which he now held in his right hand. It must have been hidden in his tunic somewhere, but it gleamed brightly, reflecting the rays of the late afternoon sun like a rainbow. It was similar to the one Verclan had used against her father, but there was a small flat surface on it that had been polished like a mirror, and the smith was deftly reflecting the sun directly into Mankar's eyes, taunting him.

Mankar was having a hard time seeing what it was that the smith was holding. He cursed and swore at the smith obscenely. The new queen had never heard such profanity. It was in the original language, but she understood it perfectly. It was meant to offend the smith and possibly her. She remained passive—waiting.

The smith had stopped circling now. As Mankar moved, he moved with him, keeping *him* from circling, playing his advantage with the sun's location relative to the battle. The wind was at his back and he scuffed with his feet to send puffs of dust scurrying toward his enemy. One of Mankar's generals called, "Unfair!"

The smith remained unconcerned and calm. "Paca MahMoralda," he uttered suddenly. It was said softly, almost, but it rang like a bell as it left his mouth.

Mankar stiffened and swore again. He switched sword hands and struck boldly at the reflector the smith held in his right hand. It happened fast, but the smith was faster. His hand rose to meet the descending blow and caught Mankar's sword deftly between the tines of the strange tool. The force of the blow would have crumpled another man's arm, but the smith withstood the impact.

"No!" It was a desperate, helpless cry, issued from Mankar's mouth as the sword in the smith's left hand flashed between them. There was another explosion, and Mankar was left with only four inches of his sword. "Seconds!" he yelled, leaping back. The smith stepped forward and his sword sang again, slashing across Mankar's right shoulder.

Omberon launched himself toward the fight. "Seconds," said the smith firmly. Vrengnia leapt forward to the smith's aid. His sword flashed again as he lunged into Mankar. Straight into the heart it went. What followed was the strangest thing she had ever seen. There was a sort of un-explosion, as if all the light reflecting off Mankar was suddenly absorbed. Utter blackness appeared where the sword had entered Mankar's chest. The darkness crawled out and swallowed Mankar and then closed in on itself, disappearing as it flickered out along the length of the sword. The blade of the sword was now pitch black. No reflection whatsoever could be seen on it. At almost the same instant, a ribbon of lightning darted across the sky overhead and spiked downward into the woods to the south of the field, exploding in blinding flash of light behind the smith. The thunder struck instantly, and the onlookers gasped.

Omberon was approaching fast from behind the smith. Vrengnia could not get there in time. He swung his blade horizontally, aiming at the smith's upper body. The smith dropped and the blade swept over his shoulders. As the momentum and surprise of the missed impact threw Omberon off balance, the smith rolled, coming up beside the general before he could recover. His sword, finding its mark by piercing the NarEladra's torso from under his right arm, went directly through the heart. The same anti-explosion absorbed Omberon into the blackness of the sword's blade as another bolt of lightning zigzagged down into a tree on the north side of the field, shattering the wind with its impact.

The smith turned toward the other generals, who had started running toward the hut. "Stop them!" he ordered pointing his sword after them. The four guardians were already running in pursuit. Vrengnia watched as the five remaining generals vanished in flight, fading into dark smoky shapes before disappearing with a hiss. The guardians followed, with a withering luminescence. Vrengnia was transfixed. "They won't get far," said the smith quietly, as he knelt down to the ground and picked up a small gold and black object that had fallen from Omberon when he vanished.

She looked back toward him; he stood still, holding her sword in his left hand, looking straight at her as the clouds swallowed the sun behind him.

72

The path to peace is not peace itself.
Pratoraman
The Middle Way

PACA FELT BADLY BRUISED WHERE VISHTORATH HAD HIT HIM, BUT HE WAS standing and he could breathe. The battle was over and Verclan and the king, holding hands as friends, lay dying beside each other on one side of the circle, with Vrengnia and Patira comforting them in their final moments. Haniah stood behind Patira with her arm around Mordara and her hand resting gently on his shoulder.

Paca watched his father, still standing in the center of the circle. He had not moved since he had ordered the Eladrim guardians to follow Mankar's generals into who-knew-where. He seemed to be waiting, Vrengnia's sword hanging loosely in his left hand.

No one else moved. No one else knew what to say. Paca did not know what to say. Life as he had known it seemed to have taken a left turn, and the path of history now lay in an uncertain direction. He was guessing that everyone else felt the same thing when his father interrupted him.

"Paca, Carnados, Chronista! Gather the generals' swords. Find all the pieces of Mankar's sword and Sandihar's, and bring them to me. Then come, let us be with our friends." He started walking toward where Verclan and the king lay. Like iron filings to a magnet, the circle of men began to draw together toward the two fallen leaders.

Paca gathered the general's swords while Carnados and Chronista searched for pieces of the other two. They were heavier than he expected. He had to take off his tunic and roll them up in it to carry them all. It was still dark from the cloud-cover. As he looked up, it seemed as if the sky were boiling, and the wind tumbled across the field in rolls, creating shadowy ripples in the grass of Haniah's field.

When he joined the circle around the two men, it was obvious that they were very close to death. Paca had seen dead people before, but he had never seen a man *die*. He had often wondered about that fine line between life and death; the infinitesimal change that happens when the vorn leaves behind the inanimate body. Everything of real value would be gone, and all that the man may have valued—his strength, his appearance, his wealth, his intellect or position—would suddenly be reduced to nothing, and the empty body of the man, devoid of this thing called life, would become an object of dread. What exactly was it that left? And where did it go? Things had to go somewhere, it seemed, but perhaps not. The Eladra had vanished, but they seemed to be going somewhere—another time, another place?

He watched closely. Vrengnia was pleading softly with her father not to leave. Patira was quiet. Tears were streaming down his face as he held his father's head gently, rocking slowly back and forth. The two lives evaporated at almost the same time. Paca saw it happen but was not sure what it was that he saw. Patira simply said "No!" and Vrengnia gasped and sobbed. Mordara fell to her knees and buried her face into the fabric of Verclan's tunic. Haniah moved quickly to the ground beside Patira and placed herself so that Patira could hug her. He held her tightly, and she whispered something in his ear. Paca never knew what it was.

A flicker on the horizon caught his attention, and he looked up to see a bright crack tearing the clouds apart from the northern horizon. It looked like lightning, but moved slowly, winding its way overhead. Paca pointed and gasped, and everyone had time to look up. They watched, mouths hanging open as several other streaks joined with it. It passed overhead and hesitated over the mountain to the south for an instant before plunging downward into the forest with a force that shook the ground under his feet. Several seconds later, the thunder smashed across the field with an impact that left Paca's ears ringing. The gusting wind stopped abruptly, and the small gathering of beings stood speechless in the still air. No one even breathed until Mordara fell to her knees beside her dead husband and gasped in a hushed cry, "The Ebondar—Oh my husband, the Ebondar is no more."

No one else knew what to do except his father, who knelt down beside Vrengnia and gently lifted her chin so that she looked into his eyes. He said nothing. He didn't have to. They stood up and she threw her arms around him, sobbing.

Verclan's warrior knelt down beside the fallen leader, removed his own cloak, and spread it over him to hide the now empty body. Carnados did the same for the king. No one else moved for several minutes as each man waited respectfully for someone else to take the lead. The smith spoke first. Gently breaking away from Vrengnia, he said softly, "Come, everyone. There is so much to be done."

Vishtorath and one of the other Eladrim guardians appeared suddenly, materializing with a bright hiss as they strode up to the group. They saluted the smith and took up stations beside the bodies of Verclan and the king.

His father led the somber procession back to the table. He was carrying Vrengnia, and Haniah walked between Patira and Mordara, supporting them with her singular strength. Paca felt left behind, and found himself angry for not having been more in touch with Vrengnia's trial. Perhaps it was not anger, but jealousy that rose from his belly as he walked behind the others, carrying the swords rolled up in his tunic.

His father set Vrengnia in her father's place at the table, and Haniah led Patira to the place where Verclan had sat. Mordara seated herself beside her son as Haniah returned to her seat at the head of the table. "Everyone sit down," she said quietly. It was clear that she meant that they should return to their previous seating arrangement. "We gathered here today for the purpose of seeking peace between the Immerland kingdom and the mountain clans." Paca watched Haniah's face. The clouds had lifted slightly, and the sun shone obliquely across the table, its yellow warmth flooding over her. She was beautiful, he thought, so poised and purposeful, gentle and firm.

She continued speaking: "The path to peace is not peace itself. Sometimes that path is troubled and elusive, fraught with malice and mischief beyond our planning, and beyond our expectations. Today much pain and loss mar the path to peace, but we have come to the end of the path and seek peace itself. I ask the new Queen of Immerland— she smiled at Vrengnia—"and the son of the Mountain Prince to finish what their fathers came here to do."

Dor Windarad started the applause as Haniah sat down, but the whole table burst forth and stood up, smiling alternately between Patira and Vrengnia. Vrengnia stood up and motioned for silence. "If the Mountain Prince would be so good as to give ear, I propose that we end the enmity between Immerland and the mountain clans—" She looked down, struggling to restrain tears that wanted to flow. "—that we find a way to unify our peoples, so that we all may live in peace—" She looked up, wiping a tear back with her hand and sniffing gently before continuing, "—trade in peace, intermarry in peace and share our resources with the other. It is time that we find strength rather than strife in our differences and in the end, realize how much more the same we are than different." Vrengnia sat down to renewed applause.

Patira stood. "In my respect for the new Queen of Immerland, I heartily accept this proposal, and propose myself that we start immediately, and not leave this place until we have a plan for our doing as the queen suggests." He sat down. This time there was no one to interrupt the applause. Paca thought it would last forever.

When it finally died down, the smith stood. "Let us leave the queen, the prince and their advisors to confer with one another. Everyone else, come with me."

Paca rose with the others and followed his father. Haniah took Mordara by the hand and headed off toward where the bodies of the king and Verclan lay, guarded by the Eladrim warriors. When they had gone a short distance away, his father dispersed the various men on errands in preparation for the customary cremation fires that would be required that night. It was getting on toward sunset; wood had to be gathered, and much of it.

Paca was finally alone with his father. The smith had reserved the task of preparing the bodies for the funeral pyre for himself and Paca. There was not a lot to do, but it was important.

Mankar and his generals had nearly destroyed Haniah's hut, but they entered it and found several empty bowls. As they set off to the stream to get water, Paca looked up. The clouds were rising and turning salmon and green as they thinned out against the azure sky above them.

Paca breathed deeply. There were so many things he wanted to ask. He started timidly. "Did you know that the king was going to die?"

"No, we can never know when one will die."

"Did you know that Mankar would come after his swords?"

"No—not for sure. But there were so many things coming together that I guessed something beyond the meeting between the king and Verclan would take place. You told me the swords were here."

"Yes."

"Well, all I knew about these swords was that it was my job to destroy them. I was not given an explanation of how. I think this is true of many things in our lives. We have a purpose. How we fulfill that purpose is often up to us."

"But the swords—Mankar's sword destroyed the king's sword, but then Vrengnia's destroyed Mankar's. How is that?"

"I do not know all the details. They have become clearer in hindsight, which is usually the case. It seems that this meeting and its outcome were determined to some extent. When I was prevented from making the swords that would be needed, you did. I made the sataliin for Verclan and the hilt guard for Patira. Each had its perfect purpose. Meshabo publicly confronted the king. It was part of the greater plan, but we may never understand what may have happened if she had not done so. I did not know all these years that Mankar and his generals were NarEladra. It makes sense now, but I doubt if anyone ever knew it. I am sure my father did not."

"He was disgusting."

"He is no more," continued his father. "The sword you forged was apparently destined for his destruction. I knew there was something special about it, but had no inkling…"

"What happened to Mankar? I mean that blackness…?"

"It was the onset of oblivion."

"Oblivion?"

"I believe so."

"What about Verclan and the king?" Paca saw his father's eyebrows go up. "I mean, when they died. What happened? Where did their vorns go?"

The smith was filling the bowls from the stream. "You know there is much debate about what happens when one dies."

"I know. I guess I meant, where do *you* think their vorns went?"

"I am not in the position to know the state of psadeq between each of them and Mah'Eladra." His father paused. It was not a hesitant pause, but a thoughtful one. "Any attempt to do so would be only conjecture." Paca waited patiently. They carried the bowls full of water back to the area where the bodies of the king and Verclan lay on the ground beside each other. This would be the first trip of many that evening. His father was silent until they had set down their burdens and were headed back to the stream with more empty bowls.

"Have you ever looked up at the night sky," his father continued suddenly, "and looked at the stars and thought how incredibly many there are?"

"Yes," said Paca hesitantly. He was not sure whether his father was continuing the discussion or going somewhere completely different.

"Have you ever wondered what is between all the places where there are no stars?"

"No—not that I can remember."

"Suppose one of those countless stars suddenly stopped shining, would you be able to tell it was not there by studying the stars that are there?"

"Unhh…No…I don't get it."

His father looked at him intently. In the gathering dusk, his gray eyes were dark, but they gleamed with energy. "Paca, the decisions we make in our lives, the path we choose that leaves us where we are when we escape our bodies, determines forever whether we shine like a star in the eternal fabric of time or are dark like the space between the stars. This is how Mah'Eladra see us and have always seen us."

"What do you mean?"

"Mah'Eladra see all time as the eternal present. They see the ocean of lives as we see the stars that are either shining brightly or they are dark in oblivion. If a life is shining, it has always been shining, if it is dark, it has always, and will always, be so."

"Then how do we have a choice? How could we change one way or the other?" Paca was struggling to see what his father seemed to see so clearly.

"We choose by the way we live. Each of us has the responsibility, the privilege, and the freedom to do so. But as our decision unfolds, if one lives in the psadeq of Mah'Eladra, though we move through time in only one direction, to Mah'Eladra, that state of psadeq just *is, has been* and always *will be*, in all directions of time at once. You appear as a star, eternally shining before Mah'Eladra. If you turn away and do not live in that psadeq, then that state *is, has been* and always *will be*."

His father paused and looked at him thoughtfully as though he could see his confusion. "Suppose you are walking through a field and find a large stone. The stone *is*. From every direction it *is*. If you lived only in the present, and had no sense of the past or the future, all you could say about it is that it *is*. You would not speak of when it became, because that would be in the past. You are unconcerned as to whether it will disappear because that is the future." He stopped, his inquiring eyes probing into Paca's. "If you came to the same field and did not find a stone, then no sense that there ever was a stone would be comprehensible."

"I think I see," said Paca tentatively.

"Our vorns live in this infinite present. However, our bodies anchor our vorns to a single thread of time, and they are separated temporarily from the rest of the vorn when they have served this purpose. We are limited—confined—so that we are forced to make timewise decisions that define our nature, our character and our destiny. No such decisions are made in the infinite present."

"I seem to remember you saying one time that we keep our bodies."

"I believe they are restored to us in the infinite present, when we enter the deep sky, but they are different."

"Different?"

"Yes, different. But I am not *at all* clear about the details. I think that is left for us to find out then." His father smiled and breathed deeply.

"I am going to have to hear more," Paca sighed. He had the vague feeling that this would actually make sense if he had a chance to reflect on it some more. "I will sleep on it tonight and let it settle. Can we speak again tomorrow?"

"Yes, there will be plenty of time tomorrow. I think we are settling into a long period of peace between Immerland and the mountain clans. By the way, did you see this?" His father opened his hand, and in his palm lay the gold plated signature star that had been stolen from his night table. "Omberon dropped this as he died." He handed it to Paca. "Keep it as a remembrance of all the things that happened here tonight."

His father dropped another piece of the puzzle into Paca's hand.

73

The fires of the dead burn brightest in the hearts of those left behind.

Old Tessamandrian Saying

PATIRA STOOD IN FRONT OF THE TWO PYRES BUILT FOR THE CREMATION OF HIS father and the king. In his left hand, he held a burning torch, and in his right was Vrengnia's left hand. The assembly of beings on Haniah's land had grown as all those accompanying the king and his father's scouts and warriors had been asked to join in the farewell to the fallen leaders.

The smith and Paca had overseen the preparation of the bodies and the building of the two pyres while he and Vrengnia had talked at the table. They had reached a tentative agreement to cease all hostilities and to open trade between Immerland and the mountain clans. It was a small step, but a first and good one. Anyone violating the peace would be punished severely by his own people. Time would be given for easing of tensions, and progress would be watched. He planned to meet with Vrengnia again in one month to talk further. He needed the time to establish his leadership in the mountains, and she needed it to establish her sovereignty.

The smith's voice silenced the muttering and shuffling of the circle that surrounded the pyres. "The time has come. We will honor our fallen leaders. Let no one speak. Let the fire consume what is left behind and deliver it into the Infinite." His voice rang with strength; a voice that would not be defied.

Patira knew the custom. He waited. Vrengnia waited beside him. Aside from his torch and the one in her right hand, there were no lights except Tal and Meekar rising over the mountains behind him. He would wait in silence until he knew it was time to light the fire. Together, he and the new queen would set fire to the wood that would engulf their fathers' bodies. No one would move until they moved, and no one would speak until one of them spoke. It was up to them how long they would pay this tribute to the dead before them.

Patira waited a long time as the still night engulfed the circle, then he turned slowly and looked at Vrengnia. She looked back and squeezed his hand. He felt her strength. She was so different than the first time they had met. She stood straight and tall beside him, with the stature of a queen, her straight hair pulled back behind her formed a halo around her head, illuminated by the torch she carried. He wanted to lean over and hug her, but this was not the time for that.

He nodded and she turned away, dropping his hand and moving deliberately toward her father's pyre. Patira turned and walked to his mother. He hugged her with his free arm. Her hug was full of passion and warmth, the pathos of a woman who has lost her husband, and though keenly feeling the loss, knowing that life is much bigger than her husband. She let him go and he stepped back, turning to the carefully laid pile of wood.

The flames leapt upward as the fine boughs at the base of the pyre caught the fire of the torch. Vrengnia had set her fire in several places already and he did the same. By the time he had walked around its base with his torch, the heat of the fire was driving him back. He tossed the torch onto the top of the pyre. Vrengnia met him where they had started and, holding hands, they backed up until they were standing in the circle, his mother on his left and the smith to Vrengnia's right.

Both fires roared and crackled, and with each explosion from within, showers of sparks scattered and leapt skyward. The circle of onlookers stood transfixed, mesmerized by the fire and the somber intensity of the moment. Patira looked over at Paca, standing beside his father. He was staring up at the sky, his mouth open in wonder. Patira followed his gaze upward into the expanse above them.

It took a second for his eyes to adjust and he saw what Paca was seeing. "The stars," Patira shouted, "the stars of the deep sky come to visit us." Even as he said it, he knew it was a strange way to break the reverent silence of the circle. Moreover, the words he chose puzzled him. He had only heard about the deep sky from the legends, but knew little about it. An invisible realm beyond the stars, the deep sky defied the capabilities of the imagination of those who lived in the confinement of Tessalindria. He continued staring up at the sky.

All around the field, tiny lights that looked like stars fell slowly toward the field. They drifted downward, growing larger and descending faster, like snow, but out of the cloudless crystal of the night sky. He looked around. From all directions the stars fell, faster and brighter with each passing moment. They landed on the edges of the field. As they touched the ground, each flashed brightly. When the brilliance of the flash faded, a luminous being could be seen making its way toward the fires.

They were clothed in white tunics that sparkled like a thousand diamonds in the sun, and their skin shimmered with a faint yellow cast. They sang as they walked, faintly at first, but with increasing vigor and clarity as they approached. The circle of beings around the fire shifted nervously. Patira saw that in a matter of minutes, the gathering ring of beings from the deep sky would dwarf them. "To the King!" he shouted, "To the Mountain Prince!" The circle of men cheered, and the singing rose in pitch and fervor.

"The song, the song of the ages
Bringing light to the beings of this world.
Bringing vision for the days to come.
That death has culminated in victory.
The bonds, the chains, the enmity.
Fallen, fallen and falling away.
New strength is found.
A new purpose in psadeq.
A beginning, a fresh beginning..."

It was the original language, thin and high in quality, an intense resonant whisper that filled the air and seemed to come from everywhere at once.

"Sing O Tessalindria,
Sing with one voice out of the darkness of this night..."

Suddenly, the thin, nasal singing was underpinned by sonorous bass tones that did not sound like voices at all, but almost as if Tessalindria itself were resonating in harmony with the voices of the approaching circle of light.

"...For the swords are found
Found to be destroyed in the fire,
Found that they might trouble Tessalindria no more,
And Mankar is revealed and trapped in oblivion.
His minions captured and thrust
into that singular timelessness.
That their evil might no longer
Terrify this world and
Occlude the vision of deep sky...."

More stars fell and their brilliance outshone the light of the funeral fires themselves.

...that I might catch even a brief glimpse of the deep sky, behind the curtain of stars; beyond Tal and Meekar, in the infinity of Mah'Eladra.

Mirradach
'The Tiger in the Tree'

Vrengnia felt the tears rolling down her cheeks. The beauty of the voices and the brilliance of the strange beings closing in around the fires caused the tears to flow from deep within. She was unsure whether it was fear of the unknown surrounding her or joy evoked by the song, but she shook uncontrollably.

The smith's arm swept around her and squeezed her as the first row of enlightened beings converged on the circle. Tall and thin, they moved with an effortless grace, as if weightless. They passed through the circle noiselessly. "What's happening?" she whispered.

The smith looked at her and raised his index finger to his lips. He leaned over. "Just watch," he said softly in her ear.

Several of the Immerlanders and mountain people fell to their knees as the bright travelers passed them. One of them stepped between her and Patira like a tongue of fire that licked her left arm and leg, then passed without injury. Deep sobs welled up within her and a new flood of tears poured forth.

"*A new queen is found,*
A queen who will prevail in justice.
One who will know Psadeq among her people,
Who will bring peace to her land.
We lift up the queen.
We hold her hand,
That unity, harmony and peace might prevail...."

Once inside the circle, they headed straight toward the fire where Verclan's body was being consumed in the flames. They stepped into it and disappeared without hesitation. It seemed to get brighter with the entrance of each one until the white heat blinded her. Vrengnia looked around. The circle retreated slowly under the pressure of the increasing brilliance. Haniah and Mordara had covered their eyes, and others squinted, trying desperately to see what was happening.

Vrengnia looked up at the smith. He stood transfixed with his eyes closed, breathing deeply with a faint smile on his lips. She watched him. His strength seemed indomitable, and the sharp contrast of the white light on his face and the deep blackness behind him heightened her awareness of his presence beside her.

A sudden gasp from the circle made her look back toward the fires. The beings still streamed into it, singing, but she could no longer recognize the words. A white column of pure light rose slowly from the middle of Verclan's fire. She looked at her father's fire. Where there should have been orange flames, all she could see was charred wood, collapsed in a heap of coals that were completely eclipsed by the brilliance of the other fire so that it seemed to not be burning at all.

The white column rose faster now and when it reached about a hundred feet, it shot skyward like an arrow from a bow. As it did, the white beings still left on the ground seemed to be sucked into the fire. The column splashed against the night sky, almost as if it were burning a hole into it. The hole widened, and the edges rolled back until half the sky was missing. Behind the black curtain of night was the naked illumination of the deep sky itself, opened for a brief moment for this small group of beings to see.

Vrengnia felt that she could see to infinity and perhaps beyond. There was no sensation of depth. Creatures defying her imagination swarmed around structures whose expanse and design could not be comprehended. The web of pathways leading everywhere at once, but seeming to go nowhere in particular, obscured all sense of proportion. She felt helpless to grasp even a fragment of its complexity and scope as the column of the fire poured into it.

As the column of light shot forth into the vastness, it exploded into a dazzling fountain of sparks that wound their way down the tangled pathways, shouting with joy. The words echoed and rolled down to Tessalindria in waves, a euphony that defied description. Somewhere in the center of it all, if one could describe it as a center, the brilliance of the light absorbed everything, as if everything were flowing there and flowing from there at the same time. This core writhed with frenetic motion and activity, but Vrengnia found herself unable to look directly into it for its brightness and overwhelming intricacy.

She watched as the rising column of fire pulled itself into this vastness. As the last of it vanished into the infinite brilliance, the night sky rolled back, until, quite suddenly, with a singular last flicker, everything was gone, leaving the speechless circle of awestruck beings staring at the familiar, dark canopy of the silent Tessalindrian sky.

75

For all that's good; against all that's bad; stand I must and stand I will, that my name shall be lifted above the nameless hoards that, on the path to the Infinite, sat down to rest, and in that resting, died.

Erengnira
'The Tiger in the Tree'

PATIRA WATCHED THE SMITH AS HE STARED INTO THE COALS OF THE FIRE. A small group had gathered there to garner the last vestiges of its warmth against the breeze settling down from the mountains to the south. The others had left for their encampments after the cremation fires had died down. He poked a stick into its heart and a shower of orange sparks leapt upward on their journey to the sky.

"I heard that you have chosen your adult name," the smith said to Vrengnia without taking his eyes from the fire. "Perhaps now would be a good time to share it, before Meekar and Tal pass overhead."

"Is today your name day?" Haniah seemed genuinely surprised. "I wish I had known."

"Me too." Patira felt a twinge of guilt, although he knew that not knowing was clearly not his fault. It must have come from his desire to know more about Vrengnia than he did. He wondered why that made him feel guilty.

Paca and Phartang, sitting to his right, nodded, and Carnados, to the left of the smith, on the other side of the fire sighed and shook his head in frustration, murmuring something to himself. Mordara smiled faintly and continued staring into the fire. Patira guessed she was reminiscing about her own name day.

The smith broke the embarrassed silence. "Well, since we all missed it—and with all the events of the day, it is completely understandable—let us let it go no longer. Come Vrengnia, what is your chosen name? It will now become your queen name as well—" Patira knew this was important. The smith was trying to say it with a gentle encouragement, leaving his last sentence hanging to give Vrengnia the space to share it in her own time and her own way.

Vrengnia stared into the coals for several moments, before rising slowly in acknowledgment of the request. She smiled and opened her hands with a shrug. "I will be Queen Erengnira of Immerland."

Patira jumped to his feet. "'For all that's good; against all that's bad...'" he cried as he started the applause, "Queen Erengnira of Immerland!" The others stood and joined in the applause. He looked around. By the looks on their faces, he could tell that, apart from the smith and Haniah, no one else knew what the name meant.

Haniah stepped forward and hugged her warmly, then stepping back and looking into her eyes with her hands on Erengnira's shoulders, said, "It is a fine name and a fitting name for our queen. Perhaps, you should tell us all why you chose this name," she said, as she motioned for everyone to sit down. "It is a fine name, and a worthy name, but we want to know more."

When everyone was seated, Erengnira began: "It is from the ancient play, 'The Tiger in the Tree.'" Carnados snapped his finger and his lips curled into an understanding smile. "Mirradach, the hero of the story, has been enlisted by the Eladra for the task of rescuing three foolish young men from a perilous situation of their own making. They had been unwittingly beguiled by the NarEladra to carry out a sinister murder of a foreign prince. Mirradach is sent after them to prevent them from carrying out the task and to bring them back to their senses before they are destroyed by the evil that they are perpetrating. At one point in his journey, Erengnira, the daughter of a woodcutter, rescues Mirradach from certain death at the hands of several NarEladra who trap him in a pit in the woods.

"Erengnira's bravery and wisdom inspire Mirradach and guide him through the final hours and trials he faces until he is able to finish his assignment. At the end of his quest, Erengnira dies in a heroic final confrontation with the NarEladra and saves Mirradach again, along with the other young men. The three young men are all saved to live out their lives, altering the destiny of both countries forever. I thought it was a fitting name for a queen—and it almost rhymes with Vrengnia!"

Paca stood up and started clapping again. The smith smiled as he and the rest of the group stood for the applause. Patira thought back to the first time he had ever heard of 'The Tiger in the Tree.' It was around a fire, just like this—

"Good smith—" Carnados's words cut into his thoughts. The smith looked up. "Have you ever read 'Tiger in the Tree'?"

"It was read to me once, but I remember it as if it were yesterday. It was part of my education under Sessasha."

"Sessasha read it to you!?"

"No, after I had become acquainted with Sessasha's friends—I was just about the age of our new queen—one of the women in the group could read, and Sessasha had appointed her to read whatever we could get our hands on, out loud, whenever there was time. Her name was Erinshava. In the evenings, she would read legends, stories, plays and poetry…and from the Tessarandin. Everyone who was available would sit and listen. When she was done reading, Sessasha would teach on the reading until late into the night—that was a long time ago." He stared into the fire and poked it with his stick.

"What kinds of things did he teach?" Mordara asked. Patira looked up to see his mother staring at the smith intently.

"Many things—about many things. He seemed to know everything—everything about life anyway. He never taught about science, or mathematics, or—his emphasis was on beings, what they were about, and what they were like. He taught us about the Eladra and Mah'Eladra. It was from him that I first heard about the deep sky. He said that he—"

"Is that what we saw tonight?" asked Mordara suddenly. Her eyes shone in the light of the dying fire.

"I believe so. I have wanted to see it all my life. Tonight was the fulfillment of a hundred dreams, yet it was so brief. But just to get that glimpse…" Everyone was quiet as the smith drifted back to his memories of Sessasha. "His descriptions of the deep sky were always difficult, because there were no words that could describe it. That's what he always said, anyway. Having seen it now, from a distance, I am inclined to agree. Sessasha said he had been there. It was always difficult to believe when he talked about it because no one in the company had ever seen it, but he made it seem so real."

"I guess I don't understand," interjected Carnados. "What was it you saw?"

"When the stars fell and shot up into the sky from Verclan's fire. The sky opened—" Paca stopped in mid-sentence.

Carnados wore a worried frown. "I'm not sure what you are talking about. When we were all standing around the fire?"

"Yes. When that column of fire shot up—didn't you see it?"

"I guess I didn't. I mean, I saw the fire—and the tall beings…were they Eladra?"

"They were," said the smith.

"I didn't see anything like that either," interjected Phartang.

A silence fell over the small group. Paca shifted uneasily in the awkward stillness and said, "Perhaps only certain ones of us could see it. It was clear as crystal to me."

"What did you see?" asked Phartang.

The smith jumped in. He explained what the others had seen to a stunned Carnados and Phartang, the only two of the group who had seen nothing. "Sessasha often said that Mah'Eladra reveal things to some without showing them to others. It is somewhat like the original language—some beings understand certain parts and not others. We don't know how—or why—Mah'Eladra choose to do this, but they also teach us not to fear, or be envious when it happens. There is a purpose in all of it, that is sure, but we may never know what that purpose is. Sometimes we know in hindsight. I think we are beginning to see the details of the last few weeks more clearly, even now."

A long pause followed. The fire drew everyone's eyes in like a magnet as each pondered the recent events that had drawn them there. "Sessasha taught us to be thankful," said the smith, his voice gently guiding their thoughts. "Not about thankfulness, but to be thankful...for the smallest things...and not to dwell on things we don't or can't have, but on what we do have.

"When we are grateful, we are able to recognize gratitude in others. It compels us. It is the root of compassion. It is the foundation of contentment and peace, the 'birthplace of genuine love and psadeq' as he often said. He taught us that when we are thankful for what we have, we are able to realize its value; and when we know its true value, we become less likely to hoard it, but to share it freely, especially with other thankful people."

More silence followed. Patira would never have put it that way but thought he understood the simplicity of it. There was so much to be thankful for, even amidst the hardships, and it had always been his experience that, when he was grateful, he was more alive, more alert and more aware of who he was. His mother had taught him this through years of patient counseling. He looked up from the fire at her as she opened her mouth to break the silence.

"I am thankful for my husband," she said quietly without lifting her eyes. It was the first word she had spoken of him since his death. "I am thankful that his death was honored by Mah'Eladra." Patira felt the choking in his throat as he watched his mother's tears stream down her cheeks, her eyes glued to the heart of the fire. "My husband was a grateful man...he spoke often of how thankful he was for so many things. He loved the mountains...he loved Immerland."

Haniah put her arm around his mother, but other than this, no one moved. Patira knew she had to grieve and it seemed that everyone around the fire knew it also. They waited patiently as she continued in the slow, tender expression of her pain.

"He said that this might happen—but he felt he needed to make every effort to settle this matter with the king, for the sake of the mountain people—for the sake of Immerland—for us. But it is so much bigger than just us." She buried her face in her hands and sobbed. Patira moved to put his hand on her back, and the smith caught his eye and waved him off with his index finger on his lips. Somehow, he knew the smith was right and he stopped, sitting quietly while his mother wept openly for the death of his father. He knew it would be his turn sometime; for right now, the moment belonged to his mother.

She wept a long time. The others in the circle stared into the flames, searching their own hearts and feelings without moving. When she finally stopped, and took her hands from her face, she sat up, turned to Patira, and hugged him. "I am all right for now," she whispered. "I love you." Patira hugged her back. As he laid his chin over her shoulder, he saw Erengnira, tears streaming down her cheeks with her arms crossed forcefully in front of her, rocking back and forth slightly.

He saw the smith put his arm around her. "It was a noble death. One that will long be remembered by Immerland and the mountain clans. It is a great price to pay, but the value for which he fought is without measure."

Mordara sniffed. The tears were done for now. "I know—I knew that when we came here—it was just hard to watch." She stood up and stepped toward Erengnira, motioning for her to stand and holding out her arms for an embrace. As the young queen unfolded her arms to embrace his mother, the dams in her eyes broke, and she fell on his mother's shoulders and wept. His mother held her firmly. "It's all right, my young queen. It was the providence of Mah'Eladra that brought you here—that brought us here. Our lives are now safer—and richer. You will see this in time. For now, your tears will purge your fear and anger."

They stood for a long time as Erengnira wept, sobbing deeply. Patira knew that his mother's arms were a healing refuge. He knew that when she was done, Erengnira would make her peace with the horror of this day. So they waited.

When they finally sat down, the smith broke the silence again. "It is very late. We have many days of resolution ahead of us. Tal and Meekar have flown overhead, and we are all due for some sleep. Tomorrow is nearly upon us. It will be a new day. Go now and sleep. We shall gather again when we are refreshed."

Everyone stood at once. Each hugged the others, and Patira put his arm around his mother as they headed off into the darkness toward the black line of trees to the south of the field. He looked back once to see Erengnira walking slowly back the other way, flanked by Haniah and Carnados. He knew he would see her again, and that was enough for now.

The smith stares into his fire, and there
he sees his past, his present and his
future.

Timmanaeus

H E WAS FINALLY ALONE, SITTING IN FRONT OF THE FIRE. HOW MANY HOURS, days, years had he stared into the fire? Fire was his life, and he never tired of watching it. In its heart, he could see the thousands of blades he had made and unmade. It was the soul of his art, the origin of his trade, the ever-changing and infinite source of power that guided much of his life. Fire had consumed the bodies of the king and his friend Verclan. It had allowed his father to fashion the unholy instruments of destruction for which he had searched all his life, and it had claimed the life of his father in the inferno of his own smithy.

The smith leaned close to the fire, and with his stick, raked a piece of metal from deep in the bed of coals. It glowed bright orange as he propped it up on a rock and watched it cool. When he could see no more color in it, he turned back to the fire and raked another piece from it. This one was as black as the night sky, like a shadow with nothing to cast it. He spat on it. The spittle should have danced and hissed on the hot metal, but it did not. Reaching down, he tapped the piece with his the back of his fingernail. It was not even warm.

He leaned back and looked up at the night sky. There were many questions he wanted to ask, but most of all, he wanted to know what he had to do to destroy Mankar's sword. He stroked his beard and stared back into the fire. He had recovered seven of them. Six were still hidden somewhere in the fabric of space and time. If he had Lonama's map, he would be able to locate them, but he had no idea whether the map existed in Immerland or the mountains or where it might be. His thoughts drifted back to his first encounter with the map.

He remembered it well. It was made of some dark fabric, woven so finely that it was more like leather. It was perhaps three feet wide and two high, and the detailed calligraphy defied description in its intricacy and depth. He was not sure whether there was only one map or several, though he believed that there had to be more than one copy.

Somewhere in the middle of a thought about the Lonama's map, he was interrupted by the faint hiss of an Eladra engaging his timespace. The characteristic sound was unmistakable, and he turned to see Vishtorath and his old friend Vishtava approaching from behind.

As his eyes met theirs, Vishtorath spoke. "May we join you at your fire, MahMoralda?"

The smith stood. It was not often that he was called by his adult name. "You are welcome guests. Have you brought a gift?"

"We have many gifts for our friend, if you will have them," said Vishtava, smiling as he embraced the smith. It was a powerful hug. Long ago he had gotten used to contact with the Eladra. For some reason, in spite of their ability to imitate Tessalindrian beings, they were always cold to the touch.

He pulled free and hugged Vishtorath the same way. "Sit down, please," he said motioning to the large log benches beside the fire. The three sat down, and the smith waited until the Eladra were ready to speak. It did not take long.

"Mah'Eladra send their favor for finding the swords and revealing Mankar and his generals," said Vishtava. "It has been a long task, but well noticed. You must now destroy the swords, utterly."

"I am aware of this, though I must admit, I may not know the poetry for their destruction."

"There are six others, as you know," said Vishtava. "We believe we can find them now.

"How will you find them?"

"We have located Lonama's map—here in Immerland."

"In *Immerland*? Where?"

"There is an old groom in the stables at the castle. He has been there for years. He served under the grandmother of the new queen. We believe that the Great Queen gave him her piece of the map when she died."

"A *piece* of the map?"

The Eladra ignored his query and continued their story. "He kept it secret—as he should. Tonight, he saw the deep sky when it opened, just as you did, and he pulled the map from its box. When he opened it, we were summoned to investigate. He has been told to help you use the map to find the other swords."

"This is a gift beyond asking," said the smith, breathing deeply.

Vishtava continued, "You must take all the swords to the Crown of Tessalindria. Queen Erengnira will provide you a suitable escort. In the Verrilain Dale, at the trailhead to the Jualar springs, you will find the Eladrim smith Vishortan—"

"The smith who taught Timmanaeus?"

"The same," said Vishtava. "You, your son and Vishortan must take the swords deep into the heart of the desolation of the Great Margah in the bowl of the Crown. There, on the slopes of Mount Eliia, you shall build a forge. Fire it with wood from the desolation, and feed it with the mountain wind from the caves of Eliia. Burn the swords in this fire until nothing remains. They contain great evil, and only in the Crown can this evil be dealt with. You will be given the poetry you need when it is necessary."

MahMoralda sat and stared into the fire, envisioning the task laid out before him.

"There is more," said Vishtorath. The smith looked up in astonishment. "The new queen, Erengnira, will ask you to serve in her court."

"Me?"

"She will request you to be her advisor," said Vishtava, "to train her other advisors and to be her personal counselor. You must not refuse."

"It would be an honor."

"Your task will be to unify Immerland and the mountain people. There is still much fear and resentment. Like the destruction of the Ebondar, the enmity between Immerland and the mountains will be destroyed. At times, it may be violent and discouraging. Erengnira and Patira do not yet have the maturity to resolve these difficulties."

Vishtorath continued when Vishtava paused: "Patira and Erengnira will wed one-and-a-half years from now, but you must not reveal this to them. There will be many difficulties. They will find their course, but Mah'Eladra want you to know so that you would not despair."

"Your son will take over your shop. His cymbic relationship with Erengnira will continue to grow and it will be strong. She will appoint him as master smith for Immerland, to train the other smiths. He will wed Haniah in time and—"

"But Haniah is—"

"We know, but this is the way. She will bring him much happiness and will keep him strong to the task in front of him. The land on which we stand belongs to the Eladra, and we will guard the portal, but Haniah's assignment here is complete. Paca will help her rebuild her hut, but it will not be permanent."

There was a long pause. The smith, in spite of his long association with the Eladra, was not used to such open revelation. It occurred to him that all this activity might have been preparing him for a deeper trust with Mah'Eladra, a more direct conduit into the affairs of this tiny world. It pleased him at some deep level and overwhelmed him at the same time. He had nothing to say.

He looked from one Eladra to the other. They were watching him carefully. As he looked into Vishtava's eyes, the giant smiled. "There is one more gift."

Vishtorath opened his huge hand, and lying in the middle of if was a small blue stone. It was shaped like an almond and glowed faintly. The smith looked at it wonderingly.

"Stand up, MahMoralda." Vishtorath spoke with words that could not be disobeyed. Vishtava reached across the smith's chest as he stood up, and pulled his tunic back from his left shoulder, tearing it down the middle as he exposed the smith's shoulder. Vishtorath took the small stone between his fingers and pressed it into his flesh. It burned slightly, and the smith winced under the pressure as the stone sank into his skin. When the giant withdrew his hand, the stone was embedded in his shoulder.

"The Stone of Marhana," he gasped.

"You thought it to be legend only?"

"Yes, that's right." He reached up and touched the stone. It sparkled as his finger made contact. Both Eladra stood up straight in an attentive stance.

"We are your guardians. You shall not fear. Mah'Eladra present this gift to you. When you touch it, we will come to your service. You must wear a covering at all times, that no one may know you have this sign. Is this clear?"

He nodded, looking from one to the other. "Vishtorath, will you no longer guard the castle gate?"

"I will, unless you need me more."

"I will need you to guard our young queen. She needs your strength. She needs your watchfulness." He looked at both of the guards. Each had served him well and protected him. Vishtava had saved his life. He knew they were only doing what they were assigned to do, but he had grown to love them. "You both have my undying affection. I thank Mah'Eladra for these gifts." They both nodded.

"We must leave now," said Vishtava. "Be wise, be careful." With a faint hiss, they both disengaged and left the smith alone in his own spacetime by his dying fire.

He smiled to himself. There was much to be thankful for. There was much to be hopeful about. He stared into the fire, and there, deep in its heart, he saw his past, his present and his future.

About the Author

Frederick W. Faller was born on Cape Cod in 1955 and lived there for five years before spending a year in Sweden with his family. There, his mother came in contact with Christian missionaries, thus beginning the spiritual journey that has shaped most of his life. On returning to the United States, the family stayed for two more years on Cape Cod and then moved to suburban Washington D.C. where he lived until completing high school.

He graduated from MIT in Cambridge, Massachusetts, with a degree in earth and planetary sciences (with a focus on meteorology and oceanography). It was during this time that a spiritual awakening moved him through a series of jobs that brought him to the point of being a minister for two and a half years. He remains active and productive in the local church ministry, leading small group Bible studies, teaching, counseling and writing.

Through the years, he has written a number articles and essays on various issues related to Christian faith and life. *A Sword for the Immerland King* is his first foray into fiction. The work is a reflection of his devotion to finding basic truths through his study of the Bible and applying them to the reality of our lives in this complex spiritual world. It is part of a larger picture: a series of books about the small planet of Tessalindria, deliberately removed from the religious milieu of our own planet.

A man who thrives on the creative process—when time allows between the demands of his family, his job and the work of the ministry—Frederick enjoys the hobbies of blacksmithing and bladesmithing, which spawned the theme for his first book. He has been a sculptor and woodcarver for as long as he can remember. He works as a mechanical engineer for a firm that makes medical devices and has a number of patents, attesting to a broad range of technical inventiveness. For a number of years, he has enjoyed listening to and playing folk music. He plays the banjo, hammered dulcimer and single string bass for the occasional evening gatherings he hosts at his home.

Frederick lives in a Boston suburb with his wife, Ellen, and three teenage children, Rachel, Jesse and Samuel.

DOXA Press is the fiction imprint of
Discipleship Publications International.
More information can be found on the
World Wide Web at www.dpibooks.org.